PREFACE

I HOPE that this book will be accorded the indulgence due to pioneering work. I know of only three books in which my subject-matter is discussed, and it implies no disrespect to the authors to say that their treatment of it is superficial, since in each case my topic is only marginally relevant to their themes. J. J. Hogan's short book *The English Language in Ireland* (Dublin, 1927) is concerned on the one hand with the Middle Ages and on the other hand with the present day: the early modern period is discussed only in passing, as a transitional stage between the two. J. O. Bartley's *Teague, Shenkin and Sawney* (Cork, 1954) is, as its sub-title tells us, "an historical study of the earliest Irish, Welsh and Scottish Characters in English plays"; the language of the Irish characters is only a minor element in the study, and non-dramatic evidence is not considered. J. P. Sullivan's unpublished doctoral thesis *The Genesis of Hiberno-English: a Socio-historical Account* (Yeshiva University, New York, 1976) is primarily, as its title implies, a sociological study; it deals with only a small number of linguistic features, most of which do not become prominent until after the end of my period.

Because so little work has been done on my subject, I have thought it desirable to print in full the sources on which I mainly rely, and to provide a very full apparatus. The evidence on which I base my conclusions is cited at some length, and the glossarial index gives numerous references for every form, so that those who do not accept my conclusions should have no difficulty in finding evi-

5

dence with which to controvert them. I have also given ample references to secondary sources. Where I have been unable to reach a firm conclusion I have said so; no one will be better pleased than I if others can solve problems which I have found too difficult.

In 1947 the spelling of Irish was officially simplified, and since that time the new spelling of the *Caighdeán Oifigiúil* ('Official Standard') has been generally used. Two of my texts are in Irish, and in accordance with my editorial practice I have left the spelling of the originals unchanged; quotations from Irish writers, like quotations from English writers, have been given in the original spelling: to avoid confusion I have therefore cited all Irish words and names in their "Classical" forms. For typographical reasons no accents are printed on capital letters; the number of instances is small, and I believe that none will give rise to any difficulty.

In the preparation of this book I have inevitably incurred many debts. I wish to thank those friends and colleagues who have helped me in various ways, and I list them in alphabetical order: Derek Britton, Andrew Carpenter, Eric Dobson, Terry Dolan, Chris Jeffery, Hermann Moisl, and Nicholas Williams. I owe a special debt to Alan Harrison, with whom I discussed every stage of my work: he read the whole book in typescript, made many suggestions which I gratefully adopted, and saved me from more errors than I care to remember. It would be a poor recompense for the help I have received if I did not make it clear that the deficiencies of my book are my responsibility alone.

I also wish to thank the compositor Jim Hughes, who single-handed set the whole of this difficult book in type with great skill and accuracy: I need say no more, since his work is here for all to see.

A.B.

SPOKEN ENGLISH IN IRELAND

DOLMEN TEXTS 5

The Civill Irish Woman

The Civill Irish man

The Wilde Irish man

The Wilde Irish Woman

From John Speede's map *The Kingdome of Irland*, 1610.

Spoken English
IN IRELAND
1600-1740

Twenty-seven Representative Texts
Assembled & Analysed by

ALAN BLISS

THE DOLMEN PRESS
North America : Humanities Press Inc.

*Set in Baskerville type
and printed and published in the Republic of Ireland
at the Dolmen Press
North Richmond Street, Dublin 1
in association with the Cadenus Press*

*Published in North America by
Humanities Press Inc.
Atlantic Highlands, New Jersey 07716, U.S.A.*

Designed by Liam Miller

First published in limited edition by the Cadenus Press, 1979
First trade edition (Dolmen Texts 5) 1979

BRITISH LIBRARY CATALOGUING IN PUBLICATION DATA

Spoken English in Ireland, 1600–1740.—
    (Dolmen texts; 5).
    1. English language — Dialects — Ireland —
    Texts   2. Irish — Literary collections
    3. English literature
    I. Bliss, Alan Joseph
    820'.8'027   PE2408
    ISBN 0-85105-351-3

ISBN 0 85105 351 3 THE DOLMEN PRESS
ISBN 0 391 01119 7 HUMANITIES PRESS INC.

© 1979, Alan Bliss

ACKNOWLEDGMENTS

My thanks are due to the authorities of the National Library of Ireland, the Bodleian Library, and the British Library, for permission to print extracts from manuscripts in their keeping. I also wish to thank the staffs of the National Library of Ireland and the libraries of the Royal Irish Academy, University College, Dublin, and Trinity College, Dublin, who gave me indispensable help in the preparation of this book. Andrew Carpenter of the Cadenus Press has been patient and understanding at every stage of the book's development, and I should like to express my gratitude to him.

CONTENTS

8

ABBREVIATIONS AND SYMBOLS

CG	Common Gaelic
HE	Hiberno-English
Ir.	Irish
Lat.	Latin
ME	Middle English
MHE	Mediæval Hiberno-English
MIr.	Middle Irish
OE	Old English
OF	Old French
OIr.	Old Irish
ON	Old Norse
ScG	Scottish Gaelic
StE	Standard English
WS	West Saxon

Abbreviated titles of books will be found in their alphabetical places in the Bibliography, pp. 341–8.

In general the symbols used are those of the International Phonetic Association. The symbols T and D are used to distinguish true dental stops from the alveolar stops t and d; the symbol L is used to denote Irish unlenited *l*. The acute accent ′ following the appropriate symbol is used to distinguish Irish palatal phonemes from the corresponding neutral phonemes.

THE HISTORICAL BACKGROUND

IT WAS the Earl of Pembroke, Richard de Clare (nick-named "Strongbow"), who planned the Norman invasion of Ireland in May 1169, but the first landing on the coast of Co. Wexford was carried out by one of his supporters, Robert Fitzstephen. Strongbow himself did not arrive until August 1170, and it was not until October 1172 that Henry II crossed over to Ireland. The conquest proceeded slowly, and Henry seems to have planned no systematic settlement of the country; he was content to receive the allegiance of the Irish chieftains, which they gave readily enough—perhaps without any realization of what allegiance implied under the feudal system. However, the Norman barons had different ideas, and within a hundred years of the invasion they had taken over most of Leinster and parts of Munster and Ulster: the coastal strip extending northwards from Dublin as far as Dundalk, the district which later became known as the "English Pale", was particularly heavily settled. The towns, Scandinavian rather than Irish foundations, were also firmly secured by the invaders. The invading forces consisted of Normans, Englishmen from the counties adjacent to Bristol (the port from which the invading fleet set sail), Welshmen from Pembrokeshire, and Flemings from the Flemish settlements in the Gower peninsula. The Welsh and Flemish languages seem to have left no trace in Ireland, but both Norman French and English became established as vernacular languages in rivalry with Irish. Norman French was the language of the great lords, of

11

the more important churchmen, and of the growing class of merchants; English was the language of most of the tenants of the great lords; Irish remained the language of the vast majority of the population.

Norman French soon began to decline in significance, in spite of its value as a kind of lingua franca current in all parts of the Norman realm, in Normandy, in England, and in Ireland. The loss of Normandy by King John in 1204 cut the language off from its cultural roots, and it began to be replaced by local vernaculars: in England, by English,[1] but in Ireland, by Irish. The Normans had always been linguistically very adaptable: the original "Northmen" had spoken a Scandinavian language, which they soon gave up when they settled in northern France. In Ireland the gaelicization of the Norman lords proceeded apace: most of them began to follow Irish customs and to speak the Irish language; a few became competent and even accomplished poets in Irish.[2] The English language, too, was under pressure. Many English settlers, irked by the high-handed methods of their Norman overlords, returned to England; those who remained tended, like their masters, to adopt Irish ways. The notorious Statutes passed by a Parliament held in Kilkenny in 1366 attempted to halt the progress of gaelicization by the imposition of drastic penalties. The Statute which concerns us most closely reads as follows (in translation, since ironically the original Statutes were drawn up in Norman French):[3]

1. See §121. (From p. 186 onwards the paragraphs are numbered for convenience of reference and cross-reference.)
2. Curtis (1919) 251. (All references to sources and authorities are given in this form; for details of the books referred to see the Bibliography, pp. 341–8).
3. Curtis & MacDowell (1943) 53.

Also it is ordained and established that every Englishman shall use the English language and be named by an English name, leaving off entirely the manner of naming used by the Irish . . . and if any English or Irish living amongst the English use the Irish language amongst themselves contrary to this ordinance and thereof be attaint, that his lands and tenements, if he have any, be seized into the hands of his immediate lord.

Needless to say, these Statutes proved unenforceable, and the English language continued to give way to the Irish.

From the late fifteenth century onwards, documentation of the linguistic situation becomes plentiful. Though the evidence is sometimes conflicting, the picture presented is one of a steady decline of the English language, not only in rural districts but also in the towns, those bastions of English civilization, and even in Dublin. In 1492-3 the municipal archives of Waterford record that

it was enacted that no manere man, freman nor foraine, of the citie or suburbes duellers, shall en-pleade nor defende in Yrish tong ayenste ony man in the court, but that all they that ony maters shall have in courte to be mynstred shall have a man that can spek English to declare his matier, excepte one party be of the countre; then every such dueller shalbe at liberte to speke Yrish.[4]

This interesting enactment seems to envisage the existence of Englishmen who were monoglot Irish-speakers. It provides that, if either party to the suit is a native Irishman, the use of Irish is permissible; anyone, therefore, who has to have "a man that can spek English to declare his matier" must be an Englishman who speaks no English—

4. *Historical Manuscripts Commission* (1885) 323.

or at least speaks it so badly that he would be disadvantaged if he attempted to conduct his own case in that language. Equally, however, there must have been Englishmen who could speak no Irish, since otherwise no party would be inconvenienced by the use of Irish. The population of Waterford must have been linguistically very mixed.

In 1541 a Bill proclaiming Henry VIII as King of Ireland was presented to a parliament in Dublin attended by all the chief "Old English" magnates.[5] The Bill was proposed by the Speaker of the House, and answered by the King's Chancellor. Then, it appears,

> bothe the effecte of the preposicion and answer was briefly and prudentlie declared in the Irysshe tong, to the said Lordes, by the mouthe of the Erle of Ormonde, greately to their contentation.[6]

Of all the great lords who attended the parliament, only the Earl of Ormonde was well enough versed in English to understand the speeches in comfort. In 1578 Lord Chancellor Gerrarde reported that

> all English, and the most part with delight, even in Dublin, speak Irish, and greatly are spotted in manners, habit and conditions with Irish stains.[7]

In a letter of 9th August 1630 a Welshman named James Howell drew a comparison between the Irish and the Welsh languages:[8]

5. The term "Old English" was and is used to distinguish the English whose ancestors had settled in Ireland during the Middle Ages from the "New English" who came under the Tudors and Stuarts.
6. *State Papers* (1834) iii 304.
7. Hamilton (1867) 130.
8. Jacobs (1892) 461.

When first I walk'd up and down *Dublin* Markets [he wrote], methought verily I was in *Wales*; then I listened unto their speech; but I found that the *Irish* Tone is a little more querulous and whining than the *British*.

The decline of the English language did not pass without protest. In 1537 the great lords were criticized because, in their search for maximum profit, they preferred Irish to English tenants: [9]

They bring into the hart of the English pale Irishe tenants, whiche neither can speke the Englishe tonge, ne were capp or bonet, and expulseth ofte the auncient good Englishe tenantes, that therfor the same be likewise provided for; in effecte, by that meanes, the pore Englishe tenantes are dryvin hither into Englande and Wales, and the Irishe tenantes in their roulmes [i.e. 'places'] and fermes.

In the same year Justice Luttrell tells us of Co. Kildare that

in the said countye, whiche was more parte Englyshe, as the countye of Dublyne now is, ther is not one husbondman, in effect, that spekeith Englyshe, ne useith any English sort ne maner, and ther gentyllmen be after the same sort. [10]

The fullest and most detailed accounts of the linguistic situation in Ireland are to be found in Stanihurst's *Description of Ireland* (1577), but unfortunately his evidence is not self-consistent. On the one hand he tells us that

all the ciuities and townes in Ireland, wyth Fingall, the king his lande, Meeth[,] the Countey of Kildare,

9. *State Papers* (1834) ii 449.
10. Ibid. ii 503.

Louth, Weisford, speake to this day Englishe (whereby the simplicitie of some is to be derided, that iudge
the inhabitantes of the English pale, vpon their first
repayre to England, to learne their English in three
or foure dayes, as though they had bought at Chester
a groates woorth of Englishe, and so packt vp the
reast to be caryed after them to London), euen so in
all other places their natiue language is Irishe.[11]

In another place, however, he tells a different story:[12]

The inhabitantes of the english pale haue bene in
olde tyme so much addicted to all ciuilitie, and so
farre sequestred from barbarous sauagenesse, as their
only mother tongue was English . . . but when their
posteritie became not all togither so wary in keeping,
as their auncestors were valiant in conquering, and
the Irish language was free dennized in the English
pale: this canker tooke such déepe roote, as the body
that before was whole and sounde, was by little and
little festered, and in maner wholy putrified.

"It is not expedient," he says,[13] "that the Irish tongue
should be so vniuersally gagled in the English pale," and
he asks somewhat plaintively "why the English pale is
more giuen to learne the Irishe, then the Irishman is
willing to learne Englishe? we must embrace their language, and they detest oures."[14] This seems to have been
a very sore point, since he tells an anecdote to much the
same effect about the great O'Neill:[15]

One demaunded meryly, why O Neale, that last was,
would not frame himselfe to speake English? what:

11. Holinshed (1577) f. 3*v* col. 2.
12. Ibid. f. 2*v* col. 2.
13. Ibid. f. 3*r* col. 2; for *in* the original reads *in in*.
14. Ibid. f. 3*v* col. 2.
15. Ibid.

16

quoth the other, in a rage, thinkest thou, that it standeth with *O Neale* his honor, to wryeth [i.e. 'distort'] his mouth in clattering Englishe? and yet forsooth we must gagge our iawes in gybbrishing Irish.

One political development in the first half of the sixteenth century had an effect which was no doubt unexpected by those who planned it, and led to a further decline in the use of English. A Parliament held in Dublin in 1536–7 enacted for Ireland the Reformation legislation already passed in England: the Dissolution of the Monasteries, and the Act of Supremacy which required the acknow-ledgement of Henry VIII as supreme head of the Church. This legislation served merely to drive the "Old English" into the arms of the native Irish: the two parties were now united by their religion against the Protestant "New English", and the symbol of the Catholic religion was the Irish language. As we have already seen, some of the "Old English" probably spoke Irish only; henceforward those who were bilingual refused to speak English to the "New English" and took refuge in Irish. The situation is vividly described by Fynes Moryson, one of the "New English": [16]

The meere Irish disdayned to learne or speake the English tounge, yea the English Irish and the very Cittizens (excepting those of Dublin where the lord Deputy resides) though they could speake English as well as wee, yet Commonly speake Irish among themselues, and were hardly induced by our familiar Conversation to speake English with vs, yea Common experience shewed, and my selfe and others often obserued, the Cittizens of Watterford and Corcke hauing wyues that could speake English as well as

16. Hughes (1903) 213.

17

wee, bitterly to chyde them when they speake English with vs.

Meanwhile newer forms of English were being introduced by fresh settlements in Ireland. Under Mary the territories of Leix and Offaly had been settled and given the names of "Queen's County" and "King's County". A rebellion in Munster in 1579, unsuccessful in spite of help from Spain, resulted in the plantation of that province. Successive rebellions in Ulster culminated in 1607 in the so-called "Flight of the Earls", when the Earls of Tyrone and Tyrconnel, the leaders of the revolt, took ship for the Continent: James I seized his opportunity, and large parts of the province were colonized by English and Scottish settlers. The most significant plantation from the point of view of the English language, however, was the one which took place in the 1650's, the Cromwellian Settlement. After the execution of Charles I in 1649 the royalist forces in England were in total disarray, but in Ireland they were still strong, and in August of that year Cromwell found it necessary to sail to Dublin at the head of a force of 3,000 Ironsides. His sacking of Drogheda soon after he had landed earned him lasting obloquy, but this was only the first of a series of victories; by the time he returned to England in May 1650, large parts of the country had been subdued; the work of re-conquest was completed by his generals, and in 1652 the English victory was complete.

By the terms of the Adventurers' Act of 1642, those who had advanced money towards the support of the Parliamentary Army were to be repaid with land in Ireland; in spite of these advances, money had often been lacking for the wages of the soldiers, who were paid instead with debentures also exchangeable for land in Ireland. Cromwell was therefore faced with two problems, the problem of "pacifying" Ireland once for all, and the problem of finding enough land to satisfy the legitimate claims of the Adventurers and the soldiers. With remarkable breadth of imagination he found a single solution for both problems: according to his plan, all the native Irish and "Old English" landowners were to be removed from Leinster and Munster into the inhospitable wastes of Connacht, where they were to receive grants of infertile land proportionate to the estates they had forfeited. This grandiose scheme sounds like one which might work well on paper but could never be put into effect; in fact it was put into effect, and by the end of the 1650's the massive transfer of population across the Shannon was complete.[17]

The Cromwellian Settlement marks a crucial turning-point in the history of the English language in Ireland. It completed the work begun by the Ulster Plantations under James I: in three of the four provinces the landowners were now Protestant and English-speaking, owing allegiance to the English Crown, different in culture, religion and language from their tenants and servants. It seems unlikely that the diffusion of the English language formed any part of Cromwell's conscious purpose, but no more efficacious means of achieving this end could have been devised. Everywhere except in Connacht the great houses formed centres where the English language was spoken: tenants and servants alike had to learn some English in order to communicate with their masters. The masters themselves, isolated as they were from frequent converse with their own kind, were soon affected by the gaelicized English of the native Irish with whom they

17. The standard authority on the Cromwellian Settlement is still Prendergast (1865).

19

spoke every day, as Swift's evidence shows.[18] The English spoken in most parts of Ireland today is descended from the English of Cromwell's planters, and since the early part of the eighteenth century no other type of English has been spoken in any part of Ireland except in Ulster.[19]

At this point we must look back to the fate of the older English spoken in Ireland, the English of the Middle Ages. Though there is no clear documentary evidence, we are perhaps entitled to assume that English had a continuous history, however attenuated, in the towns, since municipal records continued to be kept in English. There is ample documentary evidence for the survival of an unusual variety of English in two rural areas, the adjacent baronies of Forth and Bargy in Co. Wexford, and the district north of Dublin known as Fingall. There is no early record of the Wexford dialect, and we can dismiss it fairly briefly; several of our texts reproduce the dialect of Fingall,[20] and in due course this will need to be discussed at greater length.

The earliest evidence comes from the indefatigable Stanihurst:[21]

> Of all other places, Weisforde with the territorye bayed, and perclosed within the riuer called the Pill, was so quite estranged from Irishry, as if a trauailer of the Irish (which was rare in those dayes) had picht his foote within the pile [i.e. 'pale'] and spoken Irishe, the Weisefordians would commaunde hym forthwith to turne the other ende of his tongue, and

18. See §§ 153, 157, 161, 164–5, 213.
19. Ulster dialects differ from those of the rest of the country mainly because they are based, not wholly on English, but partly on Lowland Scots.
20. See §§ 227–8.
21. Holinshed (1577) f. 2*v* col. 2 – f. 3*r* col. 1.

speake Englishe, or else bring his trouchman [i.e. 'interpreter'] with him. But in our dayes they haue so aquainted themselues with the Irishe, as they haue made a mingle mangle, or gallamaulfrey of both the languages, and haue in such medley or checkerwyse so crabbedly iumbled them both togyther, as commonly the inhabitants of the meaner sort speake neyther good English nor good Irishe.

This statement is illustrated by a vivid and amusing anecdote: [22]

There was of late dayes one of the Péeres of England sent to Weiseford as Commissioner, to decide the controuersies of that countrey, and hearing in affable wise the rude complaintes of the countrey clownes, he conceyued [i.e. 'understood'] here and there, sometyme a worde, other whyles a sentence. The noble man beyng very glad that vpon his first commyng to Ireland, he vnderstood so many wordes, told one of hys familiar frends, that he stoode in very great hope, to become shortly a well spoken man in the Irishe, supposing that the blunte people had pratled Irishe, all the while they iangled Englishe.

"Howbeit to this day," Stanihurst concludes, "the dregs of the old auncient Chaucer English, are kept as well there as in Fingall." He proceeds to give examples of some of the archaic words used, and describes a peculiarity in the accentuation of disyllabic words.[23]

Stanihurst's evidence is in fact not self-consistent. At one point he says that the people of Wexford have made a "mingle mangle or gallamaulfrey" of English and Irish, and in this he is supported more than a hundred years

22. Ibid. f. 3r col. 1.
23. This passage is quoted in §16.

later by Eachard, who says that "in some places (particularly in the County of *Wexford*) they make use of a
mungrel sort of speech between English and Irish." [24]
A little later, however, Stanihurst tells us that they use
"the dregs of the olde auncient Chaucer English", and
the comparison with Chaucer was repeated by Colonel
Solomon Richards when he reported to Sir William Petty
in 1682: [25]

> Shilburne, Bargye, and Forth are the English baron-
> ies, but Forth chiefly retains the name, and justlie.
> Its idiom of speech, tho its not Irish, nor seems
> English as English is now refined, yett is it more
> easy to be understood by an Englishman that never
> heard Irish spoken than by any Irishman that lives
> remote. Itt's notorious that itt's the very language
> brought over by Fitzstephen, and retained by them
> to this day. Whoever hath read old Chaucer, and is
> at all acquainted therewith, will better understand
> the barony of Forth dialect than either an English
> or Irishman, that never read him, though otherwise
> a good linguist.

In the late 1770's Arthur Young visited the barony of
Forth, and reported that "they all speak a broken saxon
language, and not one in an hundred knows any thing
of irish." [26] The conflicting evidence might perhaps be
reconciled by the assumption that, having passed through
a period of bilingualism, the people of Forth and Bargy
reverted wholly to English: though they might now be
ignorant of Irish, many Irish words might have been
adopted into their English, so that their dialect could

24. Eachard (1691) 16–17.
25. Hore (1862–3) 86.
26. Young (1780) 81.

properly be called a "mingle mangle or gallamaulfrey".[27] However, even this hypothesis is not without its difficulties: Arthur Young, in a passage cited below (p. 27), seems to imply that the dialect of Forth was distinguished from that of Fingall by the fewness of the Irish words in it; and the glossary of the dialect of Forth compiled in the early nineteenth century by Jacob Poole certainly lists very few words of Irish origin.[28]

Properly the name *Fingall* denotes the part of Co. Dublin lying north of the river Liffey, but it seems sometimes to have been applied loosely to the larger area enclosed between the rivers Boyne and Liffey, including not only the northern half of Co. Dublin but also the south-eastern half of Co. Meath. In its description of Fingall *The Irish Hudibras* (1689) tells us that "it extends from the County of *Dublin,* and part of *Westmeath,* by the Sea-Coast; and is called the *English Pale*";[29] *Westmeath* must surely be an error for *Eastmeath,* the name formerly given to what is now called Co. Meath. Fingall has a long history of conquest and settlement. As the name *Fine Gall* 'kindred of foreigners' implies, this was the seat of the earliest Scandinavian settlements, and its population quickly developed distinctive characteristics:

> As early as 856, within a generation of the first settlements, we begin to hear of a mixed population of Norse Irish, the Gall-Ghoídhil, who were evidently recognized as distinct from both the Irish and from the Scandinavians proper.[30]

27. For a conjecture about this process see p. 26, footnote 37.
28. Barnes (1867).
29. For *The Irish Hudibras* see below, pp. 56–8. The quotation is on sig. [A3*r*]; for *English* the original reads *Englist.*
30. Jackson (1962) 4.

Fingall seems to have developed what can only be called a tradition of bilingualism:

> To begin with there must have existed a certain kind of pidgin in use between Norsemen and Celts, especially in the first generation, but as soon as the first conquerors and settlers got offspring—and they got offspring very quickly, fond of women as they were—bilingual groups arose, people who must have spoken the two languages fluently though they must have carried idioms and constructions over from the one to the other as bilingual people do.[31]

After the Norman Conquest Fingall occupied a special position. Whatever the fluctuations in the size of the Pale, Fingall was always within it; the rivers Boyne and Liffey protected it from attack by the native Irish; the great fertility of the soil ensured its prosperity. Fynes Moryson describes Fingall as

> a little Territory, as it were the Garner of the King-dome, which is enuironed by the Sea and great Riuers, and this situation hath defended it from the incursion of Rebels in former ciuill warres.[32]

Camden, writing at about the same time, gives a very similar account. He describes Fingall as

> a little country, but very good and passing well husbanded; even the garner and barn of this king-dome, so great store of corne it yeeldeth every yeere. And heere the soile striveth after a sort with the painfull labour of the husbandman, which in other places throughout this Iland lying neglected, without tillage, and manuring, seemeth to make a very

31. Sommerfelt (1962) 74.
32. Moryson (1617) 158.

grievous complaint of the inhabitants sloth, and laziness.[33]

We have already examined complaints about the spread of the Irish language into the English Pale: that it spread even into Fingall, at the heart of the Pale, is proved by the evidence of the so-called "Census of 1659".[34] This interesting document provides a description of Ireland (except for a few counties for which the returns are missing) barony by barony, parish by parish, and townland by townland. What makes it particularly important for our purpose is the fact that the inhabitants of each district are divided into two categories, which for most of the country are designated "English" and "Irish". In themselves these terms are not very enlightening, since the basis of the discrimination is nowhere explained; but there is reason to suppose that the distinction is linguistic rather than ethnic. For six of the nine counties of Ulster (Antrim, Armagh, Donegal, Down, Fermanagh, Londonderry) the two categories are differently designated, one being called "English and Scottish", the other "Irish"; for the barony of Bargy (though not, curiously enough, for the barony of Forth) the two categories are called "English" and "Irish and Old English". It seems clear that, in the Ulster counties, speakers of any language which is not Irish are lumped together, and in the barony of Bargy, speakers of any language which is not standard English are lumped together. In the light of these facts the figures given for the three baronies (Nethercross, Balrothery and Coolock) which together constitute Fingall are of special interest: altogether there are 1,255 "English" and 4,888 "Irish",[35] so that apparently four-

33. Camden (1610) 94.
34. Pender (1939).
35. Ibid. 382–390.

fifths of the inhabitants of Fingall were Irish-speaking. The "Census" also lists for each barony the "Principal Irish Names"—presumably the names of those who spoke Irish. Among the "Irish Names" listed for the three baronies are White, Browne, English, Fulham, Russell, Archbould, and Smyth; one of these names, Russell, is among the names of the "right worshipfull families nobly descended of English bloud" listed by Camden as resident in Fingall.[36] It would appear that the huge majority of English settlers in Fingall had adopted the Irish language by the middle of the seventeenth century.[37]

Other evidence, however, seems to tell a different story. In 1691 Sir William Petty published an interesting but tantalizingly vague account of the languages of Ireland:[38]

> The Language of *Ireland* is like that of the *North* of *Scotland*, in many things like the *Welch* and *Manques*; but in *Ireland* the *Fingallians* speak neither *English*, *Irish* nor *Welch*; and the People about *Wexford*, tho they agree in a Language differing from *English*, *Welch*, and *Irish,* yet 'tis not the same with that of the *Fingalians* near *Dublin*.

This statement needs to be interpreted in the light of what Arthur Young wrote nearly ninety years later. Writing of the village of Hampton, near Balbriggan, Young tells us that

36. Camden (1610) 94.
37. Curtis [(1919) 245] gives a vivid if conjectural picture of what this process must have entailed: "In the sixteenth century there were old people in Fingall and Wexford who still spoke a Chaucerian English which was crumbling away, and stammered in an imperfect Irish which was rapidly coming in." *The Fingallian Travesty* (see below, p. 47) refers to "A sort of English-Irish Clamour that/Hotch-potch Fingallian[s] us[e] to hammer at" (f. 5r).
38. Petty (1691) 106.

this place is in Fingal, which is a territory from near Dublin, extending along the coast, inhabited by a people they call Fingalians; an english colony planted here many years ago, speaking nearly the same language as the Barony of Forth, but more inter-mixed with irish in language, &c., from vicinity to the capital.[39]

Petty tells us that the Fingallian dialect is "not the same", Young that it is "nearly the same" as the dialect of the Wexford baronies: the two statements can be reconciled if we assume that by "not the same" Petty meant "not identical", since Young also points out that, despite a basic similarity, there was an important difference.

Neither Petty nor Young gives us any information about the characteristics of the dialect of Fingall. Some of the texts printed below purport to represent Fingallian, and others seem to do so even though they make no such claim;[40] but these are literary texts, and their authenticity needs to be proved. Fortunately there are two short specimens of Fingallian which can fairly be called documentary rather than literary. In the course of his journeyings through Ireland in 1698 John Dunton heard Fingallian spoken, and gives the following account of it:[41]

In a small territorry called Fingaal neare Dublin . . . they have a sort of Jargon speech peculiar to them-selves, and understand not one word of Irish, and are as little understood by the English. I'le give a sample of it in a lamentation which a mother made over her sons grave, who had been a greate fisher and huntsman: Ribbeen a Roon, Ribbeen Moor-neeng, thoo ware good for loand stroand and moun-

39. Young (1780) 95.
40. See §§ 227-8.
41. Dunton (1698) p. 15.

teen, for rig a tool and roast a whiteen, reddy tha
taakle, gather tha Baarnacks, drink a grote at Nauny
Hapennys.[42]

In a later passage he gives another small specimen of the
dialect:[43]

I was told that at the Tryall of a Fingallian for
stealing a cow, the Mayor told the prisoner, he was
sure he was a rascall for he saw a rogue in his face;
which the Irish man answer'd, My soul me Lord
Meier, ee never knew me faace was a Looking glass
before.

Once again we have an apparent conflict between the
assertion that the people were ignorant of Irish and the
presence in Dunton's first brief specimen of a number of
words of Irish origin: *Ribbeen* is the Irish name *Roibín*
'Robin', *a Roon* and *moorneeng* are the Irish endearments
a rú(i)n and (*a*) *mhúirnín*,[44] and *Baarnack* is Ir. *báirneach*
'limpet'.

If we piece together all the evidence about Fingall and
its dialect, we arrive at the following picture. Originally
Fingall, at the heart of the English Pale, had been more
completely English in language and customs than any
other part of Ireland. Gradually it was penetrated by
the Irish language, to such an extent that Stanihurst
could be worried about the possible extinction of English.
Subsequently, however, the English language underwent
some revival; yet it remained so distinguished by the
archaic character found also in Forth and Bargy, and by
the survival of extensive Irish influence, that it could

42. *Nauny Hapennys* is no doubt the name of a tavern, "Nanny
Halfpenny's".
43. Dunton (1698) p. 24.
44. See §139.

reasonably be described as a distinct language. What none of the writers specifically mentions is the existence of bilingualism; yet, as we have seen, there was a tradition of bilingualism in this area, and the ebb and flow of English and Irish is best explained in terms of a bilingual population preferring now one of their languages and now the other, as external influences made each of them more useful or acceptable.

Documentary evidence about the linguistic situation in Ireland is surprisingly plentiful, but it is nevertheless very incomplete. We know that two varieties of a non-standard type of English were in use in Fingall and in two Wexford baronies, but our information about the nature of this type of English is scanty indeed, and nearly all of it comes from Stanihurst. We know that it was archaic; we know a few of the words used in it; we know that it had an unusual stress-pattern; and we have some conflicting evidence about the influence on it of the Irish language. We are entitled to assume that some English continued to be used in the towns, but we have no information about the extent of its use, or about its nature: the surviving municipal records are mainly in English, and contain a few non-standard forms, but in default of any information about the men who compiled the records, this does not get us very far. Some English must have been used in parts of the country other than those for which we have direct evidence. Systematic plantation began in the 1550's and continued steadily though slowly thereafter, and the planters were English-speaking; the administrators acting on behalf of the Tudor and Stuart monarchs, and those who organized the Cromwellian Settlement, were certainly ignorant of Irish, so that they must have communicated in English with the people whose lives they organized; in all parts of the country there must have been *some* Irishmen who knew *some* English. It is the purpose of this book to try to establish as far as possible what that English was like.

To fulfil this purpose I have assembled a series of texts covering the period 1600–1740 as evenly as possible. The initial date, 1600, is dictated by the almost complete absence of any earlier evidence.[45] By 1740 the new English introduced by Cromwell had displaced the earlier forms of English, and indeed there are clear traces of it in the later texts. I have had to be selective in my choice of texts, since the total number available is large, and the evidence is often duplicated. The most plentiful source of texts is to be found in the drama: throughout the period, except during the closure of the theatres under the Commonwealth, there is a steady flow of plays depicting Irish characters; for the period up to 1640 there are in fact no texts at all outside the drama. After 1640 there is a wider choice, and from this date onwards only about a third of the texts I have printed are drawn from plays. I have tried to make my choice as representative as possible of what is available; subject to that prime consideration I have chosen the pieces which seemed to me most interesting and entertaining. The difficulties involved in the interpretation of the pieces chosen are discussed at length in the analysis which follows the texts; but the first need is to describe the texts and to give what information is available about the authors and their knowledge of Ireland.

45. One scrap of evidence is printed on p. 178.

DESCRIPTION OF THE TEXTS

In this section I have tried to supply for each of the texts printed below, pp. 76–171, the minimum of information necessary for the proper evaluation of the evidence. Where further information is readily accessible I have written little; my account of the less well-known pieces is more exhaustive.[1]

I. *Captain Thomas Stukeley*

The play of *Captain Thomas Stukeley* was entered in the Stationers' Registers on 11th August 1600[2] and printed in 1605. The title-page of the sole edition runs as follows: THE/Famous Historye of/the life and death of Captaine/*Thomas Stukeley.*/With his marriage to Alderman/Curteis Daughter, and valiant ending/of his life at the Battaile of/ALCAZAR./*As it hath beene Acted.*/ [Device]/Printed for Thomas Panyer, and are to be sold at/this shop at the entrance into the/Exchange, 1605. In Philip Henslowe's diary[3] there is a reference to a play called *Stewtley*, a new play acted by the Admiral's Men on 11th December 1596; in view of the notorious vagaries of Henslowe's spelling, there can be little doubt that this was *Stukeley*. In the Bodleian copy of the play there is a manuscript note by E[dward] M[alone] which runs as follows:

---

1. Much of the information in these pages is drawn from standard works of reference, especially the *Dictionary of National Biography*.
2. Arber (1875–94) iii 169.
3. Folio 25*v*; Greg (1904–8) 50.

> This play was popular before 1588 when TAM-
> BURLAINE and other noisy tragedies [of the same
> kind *deleted*] were in vogue. It is mentioned by
> G. Peele in 1589, who, I suspect, was the author;
> and perhaps also the author of the *Battle of Alcazar*.

Malone's authority for this statement does not appear.
The reference in Peele's *Farewell* (line 22) to "Tom
Stukeley" as one of the dramatic heroes of the time is
very vague, and may have nothing to do with our play.
Peele's authorship of *The Battle of Alcazar* is now gener-
ally accepted.

Captain Thomas Stukeley was a typical Elizabethan
adventurer who engaged in military exploits in many
parts of the world, and became involved in a number of
highly dramatic episodes; it is not at all surprising that
he appeared in at least two Elizabethan plays. He was
reputed to be a natural son of Henry VIII, but this is
unconfirmed. In the 1560's he was much concerned with
activities in Ireland, and took part in the defence of
Dundalk when it was besieged by Shane O'Neill in May
1566; this siege is the subject of the short scene printed
below, pp. 77–8. By some curious chance this, the
seventh scene of the play, has survived in two different
versions, printed consecutively in the sole edition of 1605:
the first, like the rest of the play, is in blank verse, and in
standard English; the second is in prose, and in broad
Hiberno-English dialect. The relative priority of the two
versions, their relationship to each other, and the reason
for the inclusion of both versions in the printed text, have
been much discussed,[4] but these problems are not directly
relevant to our purpose. One attractive speculation is that
the Hiberno-English version of the scene formed part of

4. Adams (1916); Duggan (1937) 51–7; Bartley (1954) 14–16.

a different play dealing exclusively with Stukeley's activities in Ireland; that it was used by the author of the surviving play as a basis for his treatment of the siege of Dundalk; and that a manuscript copy of the scene was accidently included among the papers sent to the printer.

This is only one of a number of hypotheses which would allow us to assume that the author of the Hiberno-English scene was not the same as the author of the rest of the play. Whoever he was, he writes with some authority: he has a good knowledge of the geography of the neighbourhood of Dundalk, and he uses a large number of Irish phrases with considerable correctitude (below, §§ 135, 137); we are therefore entitled to assume that his representation of Hiberno-English is likely to be reasonably trustworthy.

II. *Sir John Oldcastle*

On 16th October 1599 Philip Henslowe recorded in his diary[5] the payment of £10 to Anthony Munday, Michael Drayton, Robert Wilson and Thomas Hathway for "the first parte of the lyfe of Sir Iohn Ouldcasstell & in earnest of the Second parte"; early in November "Mr Mundaye & the Reste of the poets" received a gift of ten shillings "at the playnge of Sir Iohn oldcastell the ferste tyme"; in December[6] Henslowe paid a further £4 "for the second parte of Sir Ihon ould Casell." It does not appear that the second part of the play was ever printed, and no text of it is known, but the first part was printed in quarto in 1600; no author's name is given. A second

---

5. Folio 65r; Greg (1904–8) 115.
6. Folio 65v; ibid. 116.

quarto, printed by William and Isaac Jaggard in 1619 with the original date 1600, attributes the authorship to Shakespeare, and the play was included in the second impression of the Shakespeare Third Folio (1664) and in the Fourth Folio (1685). The attribution to Shakespeare may be related to the fact that, when *Henry IV* Part II was first performed, the character known to us as Sir John Falstaff was named Sir John Oldcastle; the change was made at the request of the Lord Cobham of the time, one of whose forbears had married Oldcastle.

Sir John Oldcastle, known as Lord Cobham in the right of his wife, was a leader of the Lollard movement at the end of the fourteenth century. He was declared a heretic in 1414 and was imprisoned in the Tower; he escaped, but was eventually recaptured and hanged and burned in 1417. The first part of the play deals with the protracted proceedings against him in the reign of Henry V, who tried to protect him; in face of his obduracy, however, the king had to allow action to be taken against him; the play ends with his escape from the Tower. The lost second part dealt with his recapture and execution. The episode of the Irish servant who murders and robs his master, printed below on pp. 79–80, is ingeniously linked with the main action, and is the occasion of Oldcastle's escape into the country. The scenes printed here include all but five lines of the Irishman's speech.

III. William Shakespeare, *Henry V*

Not all of Shakespeare's plays are easy to date, but the date of *Henry V* can be deduced from the text. The Chorus at the beginning of Act V includes the following lines:

34

Were now the Generall of our gracious Empresse,
As in good time he may, from Ireland comming,
Bringing Rebellion broached on his Sword;
How many would the peacefull Citie quit
To welcome him?

The reference here is to the Earl of Essex's campaign in Ireland, which was plainly not yet completed; since the campaign lasted from 27th March to 28th September 1599, there can be no doubt that the play was written in the summer of that year.

Henry V was first printed, in quarto, in 1600. This is one of the "Bad Quartos", and differs in a number of respects from the text printed in the First Folio of 1623. A number of passages in the Folio do not appear in the Quarto: these include all the chorus material, and the whole of the "Four Nations" scene printed below, pp. 82–4. The origin of the "Bad Quartos" is still a matter of controversy; it seems likely that most of them were based on memorial reconstruction of versions of the plays cut for the theatre. If this is the origin of the quarto *Henry V*, the omission of the "Four Nations" scene might be explained in a number of ways: the memorial reconstruction might have been incomplete; the scene might have been cut in performance as not essential to the action; or the scene, including as it does a not very flattering portrait of a Scotsman, might have been deliberately omitted from the quarto out of respect for James VI of Scotland, soon to become James I of England. If any of these explanations is valid we are clearly justified in treating the scene as original. It remains possible, however, that the scene might have been added at some unknown date between the performance of the play and Shakespeare's death in 1616: the occurrence of just such another "Four Nations" scene in Thomas Randolph's *Hey for Honesty* (VIII) suggests that there might have been a fashion for such scenes, a fashion which might have provoked the writing of an additional scene. The balance of probability seems in favour of an early date.

IV and V. Thomas Dekker, *Old Fortunatus* and *The Honest Whore*, Part II

Thomas Dekker was born about 1570 in London where, so far as is known, he passed the whole of his life. From about 1598 onwards he was employed by Philip Henslowe to supply plays, mostly in collaboration with other writers; in a period of twelve months from 1599 to 1600 he was at work on twelve different plays (most of which have not survived), and of three of these he was the sole author. In spite of this frenetic activity he was afflicted by continuous poverty, and spent some time in debtors' prisons; yet he was known for his sunny temperament, which makes itself felt in his plays. He died in 1632.

Dekker is the only writer represented in the texts printed here by more than one work. Though he is not known to have had any Irish connections of any kind, he was plainly much interested in the Irish, and took pains in the representation of their speech; possibly his Irish interest was merely one aspect of an interest in non-standard speech in general, since Welsh characters appear in his *Patient Grissil* (1600/1603),[7] *Satiromastix* (1601/1602) and *Northward Ho* (1605/1607). Though only six years separate the two plays in which he recorded Hiberno-English speech,[8] there are marked differences

7. Where two dates are given for a play, the first is the date of composition or performance, the second the date of publication.
8. I leave aside for the time being the possibility that Dekker might also have written *The Welsh Embassador* (VII); see further below, pp. 39–40.

36

between the two representations: in *The Honest Whore*, for instance, there are a number of Irish words and phrases, but none appears in *Old Fortunatus*. It is true, of course, that in *Old Fortunatus* we have only pretended Irishmen, whereas in *The Honest Whore* we have a real Irish footman, and that a real Irishman would be more likely to use Irish phrases; yet one may wonder whether Dekker's writing would really have been quite as sophisticated as this. Possibly between the writing of the two plays he had further and better opportunity of observing Irishmen, and therefore took the opportunity of improving his technique.

Old Fortunatus was written in 1599 and printed in 1600. It is based on a German story first printed in 1509, and dramatized by Hans Sachs in 1553. The Hiberno-English episode is not integral to the story: it represents a practical joke played by Fortunatus' son Andelocia and his servant Shadow. *The Honest Whore* is in two parts, both probably written at the very beginning of the century, though Part II was not published until 1630; the first part was written in collaboration with Middleton, but Dekker seems to have been the sole author of the second. It is a powerful play, though melodramatic by modern standards. Part II is somewhat enlivened by a comic sub-plot involving Candido the linen-draper. The Hiberno-English element is supplied by Brian, Hippolito's Irish footman, who is marginally involved both in the main plot and in the sub-plot. The passages printed below, pp. 88–91, include all the Hiberno-English material in the play.

VI. Ben Jonson, *The Irish Masque*

Ben Jonson was born in 1573. He was a posthumous child, and his widowed mother married a master bricklayer in Westminster; his stepfather sent him to Westminster School, where he received an excellent Classical education. After leaving school he served for a time as a soldier in the Netherlands; by 1597 he was back in London, an actor in Henslowe's company. From acting he progressed to writing plays, and became one of the most prolific of the later Elizabethan and Jacobean dramatists; in his later years he gathered round him a "tribe" of aspiring young writers, in whom he inspired extreme devotion; one of these was Thomas Randolph—below, p. 41. He died in 1637 and was buried in Westminster Abbey.

From 1605 onwards Jonson devoted part of his time to the devising of "masques", dramatic entertainments usually performed at Court by amateur actors, and depending for their effect as much on elaborate scenic and musical effects as on plot and character: he was responsible for the development of the genre, and invented the "antimasque", a comic foil to the main masque. *The Irish Masque*, performed at Court on 29th December 1613 and 3rd January 1614, was one of these antimasques; it formed part of the celebrations in honour of the wedding between the Earl of Somerset and the daughter of the Earl of Suffolk. There was some feeling at the time that the representation of Irish characters was ill-advised, since it might serve "to exasperat the nation by making yt ridiculous." [9]

The Irish Masque was the first and most elaborate of Jonson's attempts to represent Irish character and speech on the stage. In *Bartholomew Fair* (1614/1631) the disreputable Irish procurer Captain Whit speaks a dialect very similar to the one in *The Irish Masque*; in *The New*

9. Herford & Simpson (1925–52) x 541.

Inn (1629/1631) one of the characters, Lady Frampul, disguises herself as an old Irish nurse, and uses a number of Irish phrases, such as *Tower een Cuppan d'usquebagh doone*, i.e. *Tabhair aon chupán d'uisce beathadh dúinn* 'Give us a cup of whiskey.' Jonson also took an interest in the Welsh language. Whereas the Irish in *The New Inn* is given in an anglicized spelling remote from Irish orthography, the Welsh phrases used by Jonson's Welsh characters are given in Welsh orthography, which Jonson drew from Rhys's *Welsh Grammar* published in 1592. *For the Honour of Wales* (1618/1640) is another anti-masque like *The Irish Masque*. Jonson's interest in non-standard varieties of English, and the care he took over the Welsh phrases, obliges us to treat his representation of Hiberno-English with respect, in spite of the unexpected features it contains (below, §§ 88, 109, 221).

The text of *The Irish Masque* printed below, pp. 92–6, is complete except for the omission of some 45 lines in Standard English at the end.

VII. *The Welsh Embassador*

The manuscript of *The Welsh Embassador* is in Cardiff Public Library; it was not printed until 1920.[10] It is in the hand of the same scribe who copied the manuscript of Massinger's *Parliament of Love*,[11] which was licensed on 3rd November 1624; this fact, together with a mention in the play itself of "the yeares 1621: 22 & 23" has led to a general acceptance of 1623 for the most probable date of composition.

No author's name is given in the manuscript, but the play was attributed by Lloyd[12] to Dekker on the basis of

10. Littledale & Greg (1920).
11. Greg (1931) 279.
12. Lloyd (1945).

numerous linguistic and stylistic similarities to the known works of that playwright. This attribution is supported by an entry (which apparently Lloyd had not seen) in a list of manuscript plays compiled by a certain Abraham Hill at some time after 1677:[13] *the Welch Embassador or a Comedy in disguises—Tho Dekker*. That this entry refers to the same play is confirmed by the fact that the phrase *comedy of (Welsh) disguises* occurs twice in the dialogue.[14] It has been suggested with some plausibility that *The Welsh Embassador* is a reworking of Dekker's play *The Noble Soldier*,[15] first printed in 1634 but probably written in 1622.[16] Some features of the use of Hiberno-English in *The Welsh Embassador* and in the two plays by Dekker represented in our texts lend support to the hypothesis of common authorship (below, §232); one very striking parallel is the similarity between a passage in *The Welsh Embassador* (vii 83–6) and the passage in *The Honest Whore* printed below, p. 177.[17]

The plot of *The Welsh Embassador* is exceedingly complex, and it is unnecessary to enter into it in detail. The scene is set in the reign of the Saxon king Athelstane: his brothers Eldred and Edmund, together with Penda the son of the Duke of Cornwall, are thought to have been murdered at Athelstane's instigation by a certain Captain Voltimar. In fact the young men are not dead, and they return to the court to claim their rights: Penda is disguised as a Welsh ambassador, Eldred as his Welsh servant, and Edmund as an Irish footman.

13. Adams (1939) 73–4; Bentley (1941–68) iv 865–6.
14. Adams (1939) 86; Bentley (1941–68) iii 268.
15. Lloyd (1927).
16. Bentley (1941–68) iii 268.
17. Adams (1939) 87.

VIII. Thomas Randolph, *Hey for Honesty*

Thomas Randolph was born in 1605 near Daventry in Northamptonshire; like his hero Jonson, he was educated at Westminster School. In his youth he was extremely precocious, and it is said that he was already writing plays before he left school. In 1624 he was admitted to a scholarship at Trinity College, Cambridge, where he received his B.A. in 1628 and his M.A. in 1631; he was, it seems, a distinguished scholar, and he was elected a Minor Fellow of his College in 1629 and a Major Fellow in 1632. He was a prolific writer, and some of his poetry was published while he was still an undergraduate. The duties of his Fellowship cannot have been very onerous, since in 1630 he was acting as the regular playwright for the Salisbury Court theatre in London. It was probably at this period that he was "adopted" by Ben Jonson. In 1632 he was back in Cambridge, where at the request of the Master of Trinity he wrote a play, *Jealous Lovers*, to be performed by members of the college in the presence of the King and Queen. Subsequently he became tutor to the son and heir of a certain Captain William Stafford. However, he had undermined his health by immoderate indulgence in the dissipations of a London literary life, and he died of smallpox in 1635, when he was not yet thirty years old. Despite his youth his reputation among his contemporaries was great, and he was spoken of as Jonson's rival and heir.

His play *Hey for Honesty, Down with Knavery* was probably written before 1630: it is a very free adaptation and expansion of Aristophanes' *Plutus*, so that in a sense it combined his academic and dramatic interests. It was later "augmented" by a certain "F.J." (possibly Francis Jaques)[18] and first published in 1651, long after Ran-

18. Bentley (1941–68) v 981–2.

41

dolph's death. The scene printed below, pp. 103–5, is not integral to the plot but a "Four Nations" scene comparable with the one in Shakespeare's *Henry V* (above pp. 35–6).

IX. Maurice Cuffe, *The Siege of Ballyally Castle*

The ruins of Ballyally Castle are some two miles north of Ennis in Co. Clare; they stand on a small peninsula on the north side of Ballyallia Lough, not so much a lake as an enlargement of the River Fergus. In 1641 the castle was held on lease from Sir Valentine Blake, of Galway, by the widow of Maurice Cuffe, an Irish merchant of English extraction. At the first sign of rebellion by the native Irish against the Protestant landowners of the district, Mrs Cuffe retired to the castle with her seven sons and two daughters; Maurice Cuffe the younger was the third son, and in circumstances not now recoverable he drew up an account of the siege of the castle, which lasted from 4th February to 12th March 1642.

On 27th December 1641 Sir Barnabas O'Brien, sixth Earl of Thomond and Lord Lieutenant of Clare, sent his kinsman Dermot O'Brien to require the surrender of the arms held in Ballyally, so that they could be used for the defence of the county; this lawful demand was refused by Mrs Cuffe, and the occupants of thirty-one other castles in Clare followed suit. A further message was sent from the owner of Ballyally, as Maurice Cuffe described:[19]

> Heere uppon Sir Valenton Blake, who was the proprietor of the castell and land, sent a letter from Galewaie to my brother Thomas in my absents, dated 24th of January [1642], advising us that if wee thought oure selves not abell to withstand the

19. Croker (1841) 12.

force of the cuntrey whoe were preparing to com against us, that then wee should betake oure selves to som place of greator strength, and deliver the possesion of the said castell to Captaine Durmot O'Brien, whome he had by lettar intreated to take the possesion of the castell and keepe it for his use; the above lettar was not delivard tell the 28th of January, to which anshwer was returned that, by God's help, the castell should bee to the hasard of life keepet posseshon of for the King's Majesty's use against any that should oppose or beseidge it, and desired the said Sir Valenton to asist us with some powthar for the better defenc thereof, which hee nevar did.

On 4th February Dermot O'Brien began the siege of the castle, in order to enforce Sir Valentine's demand—though, as the Cuffe brothers pointed out, they had a 31-year lease on the castle of which more than thirty years had still to run. The main episodes of the siege are described in the passage printed below, pp. 106–8. The siege-engine known as a "sow" was captured on 27th February, but the siege continued until 12th March, when the besiegers left to lay siege to the castle of Inishcronane.

Nothing is known about the education of Maurice Cuffe. He wrote with considerable fluency and displays a natural talent for narrative; but his spelling reflects the non-standard features of his pronunciation.

X. *Páirlement Chloinne Tomáis*

Páirlement Chloinne Tomáis 'The Parliament of Clan Thomas' consists of two parts. The first part, with which we are primarily concerned, is roughly twice as long as the second: it is a cruel and sometimes bawdy satire on the rustics of south-west Munster in the early years of the seventeenth century. The most noteworthy episodes are two imaginary parliaments that take place in north Kerry in 1632 and 1645. It has generally been assumed that the work must be later than the date of the second parliament, 1645; certainly it did not become widely known until about 1650. It is possible, however, that the imaginary parliaments were deliberately set in the future, and in fact internal evidence suggests that it was written in the early part of the century.[20]

The name of the author is unknown, but it seems clear that he was a Gaelic man of letters. His chief concern is to satirize the churls of Gaelic society; there is no hint of hostility between the native Irish and the foreign administration, and indeed the English are rarely mentioned. He tells how Clan Thomas trace their origins to Tomás Mór, 'Thomas the Great', the great-great-grandson of Beelzebub; when Beelzebub was driven out of Hell he settled on the earth, and his descendants married human wives. The author's chief satirical technique is burlesque, and in describing the boorish behaviour of the churls he parodies the high-flown and ornate style of the romances: in Clan Thomas brawls are a frequent occurrence, and he treats them as if they were the encounters of the noblest heroes of Irish story-telling.

The influence of the *Páirlement* was widespread, and the second part of the text as handed down, which seems to be by a different author, was only the first of numerous imitations. The second part describes an imaginary parliament of agricultural labourers and minor tradespeople, held near Mullingar at some time during the Common-

20. This hypothesis will be strongly argued in a forthcoming edition by N. J. A. Williams.

wealth. The members of the parliament display un-
bounded love and respect for Oliver Cromwell, but it is
plain that the author did not share their opinion; unlike
the first part of the work, the second part displays an
unmistakeably anti-English sentiment. The author was
probably a minor landowner who had lost land under
Cromwell and hoped to regain it under the Restoration
settlement. Internal evidence shows that he was writing
after 1662, though the boors speak as if Cromwell had
still been alive.

The passage printed below, pp. 109–10, represents a
minor incident in the first part of the work, designed to
illustrate the ignorance and naïveté of the peasants: the
ignorance of Tomás with his pathetic travesty of English,
and the naïveté of the others in their admiration of his
performance.

XI. *The Fingallian Dance*

The Fingallian Dance is one of two short poems found
in MS Sloane 900, the manuscript which also contains
The Fingallian Travesty (below, p. 47). The other poem,
The Fingallian Hunting of the Hare, was printed by Ball
in a modernized text which unfortunately removes the
few features of dialectal interest.[21] Ball performed the
useful service of identifying some of the persons mentioned
in this latter poem: Michael St Lawrence of Howth, a
long-lived man who was already adult in 1638 and still
alive in 1712; John Radmore, whose will was proved in
1687–8; and Robert Hilliard, whose will was proved in
1677. Since the poem implies that these three gentlemen
were still young and active, it seems unlikely that it can
have been written any later than 1660. There is no

21. Ball (1917) 119–20.

evidence that *The Fingallian Dance* was written at the same time as *The Hunting of the Hare*, but the best guess seems to be that it dates from 1650–60.

XII. Richard Head, *Hic et Ubique*

Little is known about the life of Richard Head: even the dates of his birth and death are uncertain. His father, an English clergyman, took service as a nobleman's chaplain and went with him to Ireland, where he lived in Carrickfergus; it was here that Richard was born about 1637. In the rebellion of 1641 Richard's father was murdered, and after terrible sufferings he and his mother escaped to Belfast, where they took ship back to England. Nothing is known of his early education, but he is said to have studied in Oxford before being apprenticed to a bookseller. In due course he married and opened a bookshop in Little Britain; but he gambled his profits away and (apparently without his wife) retired to Dublin in straitened circumstances. In Dublin he wrote *Hic et Ubique*, which had some success; the version performed was considerably more indecent than the published version. On his return to London he opened another bookshop, this time in Paternoster Row, but all the profits again went in gambling and other forms of dissipation. He was drowned while crossing to the Isle of Wight, probably in 1686.

The title-page of the sole edition of *Hic et Ubique* runs as follows: Hic et Ubique;/OR, THE/HUMORS/OF/DUBLIN./A/COMEDY/Acted privately, with general Applause./Written by *Richard Head*, Gent./*Facilius est Carpere quam Imitare.*/LONDON,/Printed by *R.D.* for the Author. 1663. As the title implies, this is a play of "humours", and the plot serves only as a thread to link together the fortunes of the various characters whose "humours" are observed. We are interested in the affairs of Colonel Kiltory and his Irish servant Patrick. When we first meet Kiltory he is courting Cassandra, the daughter of Alderman Thrivewell; before long, however, he has transferred his affections to a certain Mrs Hopewell. Mrs Hopewell is thought to be a widow; at her instigation Kiltory makes over all his property to her as a proof of his love; but her husband is still alive, and together they go off to enjoy the benefit of Kiltory's property, while Kiltory and his servant are left destitute. The scenes printed below, pp. 112–6, include all the speeches of the servant Patrick.

XIII. *Purgatorium Hibernicum*

The full title of the poem from which this extract is taken is *Purgatorium Hibernicum: or, the Sixt Booke of Virgills Æneis; Travestie Burlesque a la mode de Fingaule.* It is one of three extant versions of a work to which we can give the general title *Fingallian Burlesque,* and it has never been printed: it is to be found in MS 470 in the National Library of Ireland. There is another manuscript version in MS Sloane 900 in the British Museum, under the title *The Fingallian Travesty: or the Sixt Book of Virgills Ænœids A la mode de Fingaule,* and a third version was printed in 1689 under the title *The Irish Hudibras* (below, p. 56). The *Fingallian Burlesque* consists of a humorous retelling of the events of Book VI of Virgil's *Æneid,* transferred to an Irish locale and ingeniously adapted to fit the circumstances of Stuart Ireland: the extract printed here (below, pp. 117–20) describes the encounter of Nees (Æneas) with his former mistress Dydy (Dido), and corresponds closely to *Æneid* vi 450–76.

The author of the work is not known. At the end of the manuscript the scribe has written *By Francis Taub-*

man, but gives no authority for the attribution; though the name Taubman was known in Ireland, no suitable Francis seems to be recorded. Possibly he was related to Matthew Taubman, who wrote several London pageants in the Jacobite and (after the Glorious Revolution) in the Williamite cause. Whoever the author was, he had an extensive knowledge of Irish history and legend, and more than a smattering of the Irish language.

The date of the work is difficult to determine. There is a suggestive phrase in the Preface to *The Fingallian Travesty*, part of which is printed below, pp. 54–5, where the work is said to have been "writ in an age when Burlesque was more in fashion." The fashion for "travesties" was inaugurated in 1648 by Paul Scarron's *Le Virgile Travesty en Vers Burlesques*. After a considerable lapse of time Scarron was imitated in English by Charles Cotton in his *Scarronides: or, Virgile Travestie; Being the First Book of Virgils Æneis in English, Burlésque* (1664). In 1665 Cotton produced a travesty of Book IV, and R. Monsey one of Books II and VII. After another lapse of time two further travesties appeared in 1672, one of Book V by John Phillips, and one by Maurice Atkins of Book VI; in 1673 Phillips published another travesty of Book VI. Thereafter, though burlesque remained popular, there were no more travesties of Virgil until 1692 (after the date of *The Irish Hudibras*), when James Smyth published one of Book II. Ireland may have been a year or two behind the English fashion, but even allowing for this it seems unlikely that the original *Fingallian Burlesque* could have been written later than 1675.

It seems clear that *Purgatorium Hibernicum* is the earliest of the three versions of the *Fingallian Burlesque*, and there is no evidence that it differs materially from the original. Its precise date is difficult to establish, since

48

by an unfortunate chance the most "political" section of the poem, which would have been the most revealing, is missing from this version, apparently because of the loss of a bifolium in an earlier manuscript. No surviving reference seems to belong to a later reign than that of Charles II; the general tone is such as might be expected in the early 1670's, and the handwriting and orthography can hardly be much later than this. A common ancestor of the other two versions was subjected to substantial revision: see below, p. 56.

XIV. Thomas Shadwell, *The Lancashire Witches*

Thomas Shadwell was born in Norfolk about 1642. After the Restoration his father, John Shadwell of the Middle Temple, was appointed Recorder of Galway, but there seems to be no likelihood that Thomas ever visited him in Ireland: he was already grown up when his father took up the appointment, and had studied for some years at Caius College, Cambridge, though he left without taking a degree. Like his father he became a member of the Middle Temple, and then spent some time travelling abroad. When he returned to England he embarked on a literary career, and for many years produced an annual comedy: his first play *The Sullen Lovers*, based on Molière's *Les Fâcheux*, was produced in 1668. He was an avowed disciple of Ben Jonson, and Dryden's lukewarm praise of his hero led to the feud which is perhaps Shadwell's chief claim to fame. In 1682 Shadwell attacked Dryden in a work entitled *The Medal of John Bayes*; Dryden in return satirized Shadwell as *Mac Flecknoe*, and as Og in the second part of *Absalom and Achitophel*. Richard Flecknoe was an Irish poet (some said, an Irish priest) who had been lampooned by Andrew Marvell in 1645; Dryden wrote of Shadwell as the son of Flecknoe and an Irishman (perhaps because of his father's appointment in Galway)—a charge which Shadwell indignantly and naïvely denied. When after the Glorious Revolution the Catholic Dryden resigned his Poet Laureateship, Shadwell was appointed to succeed him; he died in 1692, probably as the result of an overdose of opium.

Though Shadwell was an admirer and imitator of Jonson, he drew his material from the foibles of contemporary society; in his play *The Lancashire Witches, and Tegue o Divelly the Irish Priest*, produced in 1681, he was one of the first to cash in on the anti-Catholic fervour generated by Titus Oates's "Popish Plot" (below, p. 180). In the early seventeenth century there had been two trials for witchcraft in Lancashire, one in 1612, the other in 1633. The second of these was the subject of a play by Thomas Heywood and Richard Broome, *The Late Lancashire Witches* (1634); Shadwell was certainly familiar with this play, and borrows several incidents from it. However, the characters in Shadwell's play are drawn from the two real-life trials, Mother Demdike from 1612, the other witches from 1633. The new element introduced by Shadwell is the character of Tegue O Divelly "the Irish Priest, an equal mixture of Fool and Knave",[22] who volunteers to exorcise the witches and spirits who are plaguing Sir Edward Hartfort. There is a direct link with the Popish Plot: Tegue O Divelly says that "they do put the name of Kelly upon me", and Kelly was the name of an Irish priest supposed to be one of the murderers of Sir Edmondbury Godfrey, before whom Oates had sworn an affivadit about the plot. The Master of the Revels, after first agreeing to license the play, had

22. From the list of *Dramatis Personæ*.

second thoughts and ordered that a number of scenes should be left out; when the play was published in 1682 the omitted scenes were restored, distinguished by being printed in italics. The scene printed below, pp. 121–3, is one of those which were left out by order of the Master of the Revels.

XV. *Bog-Witticisms*

The full title-page of this curious work is reproduced on the next page. It is printed in foolscap duodecimo, and before the pages were trimmed by the binder they must have measured $5\frac{2}{3}'' \times 3\frac{3}{8}''$. It is sewn in sixes, and plainly consists of two separate parts: the collation is §⁶, B–F⁶, A–K⁶. As well as separate signatures there are separate paginations, the first running from 1 to [60], the second from 1 to [120] (the preliminaries are not paginated); the last page of the first part and the last two pages of the second part are blank. There is a difference in type-size between the two parts: Part I is printed in "pica", Part II in "english" (the preliminaries are printed in "great primer"); a change of type-face, but not of size, occurs between gatherings D and E in the first part. It seems certain that the two parts were separately conceived; if Part I had originally existed on its own, with its preliminaries in the missing gathering A, it might have been inserted between the preliminaries and the text of an independent Part II; however, no edition of either part by itself is known to exist. Two other editions of what is plainly the same work concern us here.[23] One is undated, and bears the title *Teague-land Jests, or Dear Joy's Bogg Witticisms*; this is known only

23. See also Bartley (1947) 59.

Bogg-VVitticiſms :

OR,

Dear Joy's

Common - Places.

BEING

A Compleat Collection of the moſt Profound *Punns*, Learned *Bulls*, Elaborate *Quibbles*, and Wiſe *Sayings* of ſome of the Natives of *Teague-Land.*

Shet fourd vor Generaul Nouddiſicau-ſhion: And Coullected bee de grete Caare and Paniſh-Tauking of oour Laurned Countree-maun.

Mac O Bonniclabbero of *Drogheda* Knight of the *Mendicant* Order.

PRINTED

For Evidanſh *Swear-all* in *Lack-Plauſh* Lane,

Price Bound Two Shilling Sixpence.

from Lowndes' *Bibliographer's Manual*,[24] and no copy has been located. The other is dated 1690, and bears the title *Teague-Land Jests, or Bogg Witticisms*; the only copy known is in Harvard University Library.[25] The Term Catalogues list the publication in November 1689 of a work entitled "The Quaker's Art of Courtship . . . By the author of '*Teague*-land Jests' ";[26] this plainly cannot refer to the 1690 edition, which had not yet been published, nor to *Bogg-Witticisms*, the title of which does not include the phrase *Teague-land Jests*; it must refer to the undated edition, which therefore cannot have been published later than in 1689. The wording of the titles suggests the following sequence:

(1) *Bogg-Witticisms, or Dear Joy's Common-places* [undated]
(2) *Teague-land Jests, or Dear Joy's Bogg Witticisms* [undated: before November 1689]
(3) *Teague-land Jests, or Bogg Witticisms* [1690]

Other editions of the same work continued to be printed until as late as 1750,[27] but these need not concern us.

It is difficult to date *Bogg-Witticisms* by internal evidence. The only clue in Part I is a reference on p. 45 to *the P. of O.*, the Prince of Orange; since the Prince was crowned as William III in February 1689, this gives us the latest possible date for the composition (though not necessarily, of course, for the printing) of Part I. On p. 35 of Part II there is a reference to Charles II as "his late majesty", a term which would hardly be used of the last king but one, and which therefore puts composition in

24. Lowndes (1871) iv 2600.
25. Wing (1972) T 605.
26. Arber (1903–6) ii 290.
27. Bartley (1947) 59–61.

the reign of James II, 1685–88—a conclusion confirmed by the whole tenor of the anecdote. In another anecdote on p. 24 the date 1686 on a sign outside a livery stable is taken by an ignorant Irishman to refer to the number of horses inside. The most probable date of composition seems to be 1687, and the first printing no doubt followed this with little delay. The name of the author or compiler is not given, but the preface "To the Reader", written informally in the first person, is followed by the word *Farewell* in the position appropriate to a signature. The word may, of course, be no more than a greeting, but it might possibly be the signature of, or at least a punning reference to, James Farewell the supposed editor of *The Irish Hudibras* (below, p. 57).

Bog-Witticisms was certainly known to the editor of *The Irish Hudibras* (XVI). In the preface "To the Reader" already referred to, he says of his hero Nees (Æneas) that "wherever it fell, he bit so hard, there was no Armour against the Artillery of his Wit; as you will find him all along, in his *Bogland-Witticisms*, and sharp *Repartees*, alias, *Bulls* and *Blunders*." *The Fingallian Travesty* in MS Sloane 900, which also contains *The Fingallian Dance* (XI), has a longer version of the same preface, in which the reference is still more explicit:

> Here it may be Objected this way of Writing in Burlesque is obsolete and out of fashion, besides 'tis but a Transversing Dear Joys Bulls into meeter, and converting the late dull Irish Witticisms into duller Rime.
>
> To this I answer. This Travestie was not only begun but writ in an age when Burlesque was more in fashion, and has been so long out that it may now come into mode againe.
>
> Nor can you upbraid us of Teigelands Jests, or

Dear Joys Witticisms as borrowing of either, for tho'
that had the Birthright, this was the Elderborn[,]
the originall coppy being for some yeares in the
hands of a Gentleman who kept it for his privat
diversion.

The reference to "either" seems, curiously enough, to
imply that two works were here in question, and there is
a further implication that one was called *Teigelands
Jests* and the other *Dear Joy's Witticisms*. Though *Bog-
Witticisms* contains two parts, there is no suggestion that
the parts have different names; the general title merely
gives an alternative name, and each of the two parts is
headed *Bog Witticisms*. However, if the two titles in the
passage quoted above are read as one, the result is very
close to the title of the undated *Teague-land Jests*, and
this is probably the edition referred to.

The preface is highly disingenuous, since even though
the original composition of the *Fingallian Burlesque* certainly antedated *Bog-Witticisms*, equally certainly the
revised text from which both *The Fingallian Travesty*
and *The Irish Hudibras* were copied made extensive use
of *Bog-Witticisms*: there are eight clear parallels, and
several more probable ones; for an example see the note
on xv 63–4. *Bog-Witticisms* seems also to have been known
to the writers of some of the plays: see, for instance, the
notes on xxiii 70–74 and xxvii 143–55. It is, of course,
perfectly possible that the playwrights drew on some
source also used by the compiler of *Bog-Witticisms*, but
it seems scarcely possible that the reviser of the *Fingallian
Burlesque* could have hit on so many close parallels by
chance. Lawrence attributes to *Bog-Witticisms* the linking
of bulls and blunders with the name of Irishman,[28] but
in the nature of things such a claim is difficult to prove.

28. Lawrence (1937) 156.

XVI. *The Irish Hudibras*

The full title of *The Irish Hudibras* runs as follows: THE / Irish Hudibras, / OR Fingallian Prince, / Taken from the / Sixth Book of *VIRGIL's Æneids*, / AND / Adapted to the Present Times, / *Nimium Vobis Romana Propago.* Virg./*LONDON*,/Printed, and are to be Sold by *Richard Baldwin*, near the / *Black Bull* in the *Old Baily*, MDCLXXXIX. This is the latest version of the *Fingallian Burlesque* (above, p. 47). The common ancestor of the *Travesty* and the *Hudibras* was marked by extensive revision and alteration of the original text, partly to bring it up to date, and partly to make it more suitable to the English taste. The Irish characters were now depicted, not as they really were, but as Englishmen expected them to be; they are referred to as *Dear-Joys*, an expression of very recent origin which became so popular in the late 1680's that in 1691 Eachard could say that the Irish "are vulgarly called by the names of *Teague* and *Dear-Joy*" [29] (see also below, §141). A large number of not very creditable anecdotes are borrowed from *Bog-Witticisms* (above, p. 55). Of the 200-odd Irish words and phrases which occur in *Purgatorium Hibernicum*, only about a third survive in the *Hudibras,* and these (together with some dialectal English words) are glossed either in marginal notes or in the alphabetical "Table" at the end. The final editing of the *Hudibras* must have been very hasty, and the Table must have been taken without revision from some earlier text, since half a dozen words glossed in it do not appear in the *Hudibras*, though all of them appear in one or other of the earlier versions.

No author's name is given, but Anthony à Wood

29. Eachard (1691) 17.

attributes it to a certain James Farewell, about whom he gives the following information: [30]

> James Farewell, son of Thomas Farewell of Hor-
> sington in Somersetshire, gent. became com. of Wadh.
> coll. in Easter term, an. 1684, aged 18 years, left it
> without a degree, and went to Lincoln's-Inn to study
> the common law. . . . He died of the small-pox in or
> near Lincoln's-Inn, in sixteen hundred eighty and
> nine, leaving then behind him the character among
> his acquaintance of a witty young man and a toler-
> able poet.

Farewell cannot possibly have been the author of the *Fingallian Burlesque*, since he would have been less than ten years old when it must have been written, but it is perfectly possible that he might have edited it for the English market; as we have seen (above, p. 54), it is possible that he also edited *Bog-Witticisms* (XV), and perhaps also *The Quaker's Art of Courtship*. This kind of work would have been a suitable occupation for a "witty young man" who wished to turn an honest penny by topical journalism. The name Farewell was known in Ireland, and he may have had Irish relatives.

The date of the final re-writing of the *Hudibras* can be determined with great precision. James II entered Dublin on 24th March 1689, and according to a pamphlet called *Apology for the Protestants* a banner flew over the Castle bearing the inscription *Now or never, Now and forever.*[31] The following four lines are found in the *Hudibras* (p. 40):

30. Wood (1721) col. 837.
31. Simms (1969) 64.

Draw, draw thy *Madog*, says the Elf,
And now or never shew thyself:
Now is the word, *Nees*, Now or Never;
And do it Now, 'tis done for Ever.

Only the first two of these lines appear in the other versions, the last two having been added by the *Hudibras* with plain reference to the banner; the *Hudibras* cannot, therefore, have taken its present form earlier than 24th March. On the other hand, the book was licensed on 29th May 1689,[32] and the Term Catalogues show that it was in fact on sale in June,[33] so that it must have been cast into its final form in April and May of 1689.

The two passages printed below, pp. 126–9, are taken from the early part of the book. Nees (Æneas) and Shela (Sibylla) have approached the bounds of St Patrick's Purgatory (the Other World), and the first passage gives us Nees's prayer to St Patrick, corresponding to Æneas' prayer to Phoebus in *Æneid* vi 56–76. Shela warns him of the dangers that lie ahead, and he replies in the second passage, which corresponds closely to *Æneid* vi 103–18.

XVII. *The Irishmen's Prayers*

This piece is taken from a broadsheet in the collection made by Samuel Pepys and bequeathed by him to the Library of Magdalene College, Cambridge. The full title runs as follows: THE Irish-mens prayers to St. Patrick, To make their PEACE with K. William, and Q. Mary: Being a Dialogue between two *Teagues*, concerning the Army sent over to *Ireland*, Commanded by *Mareshal d' SCOMBERG*. In the year 1689 Schomberg, offspring of a German father and an English mother, was seventy-

32. The licence is printed in some copies of the book.
33. Arber (1903–6) ii 276.

four years old, but still active; such was his reputation that when, after long delays, he eventually anchored off Bangor on 13th August, it was expected by both sides that Jacobite resistance in Ireland could not be prolonged. The Jacobites were already depressed by the loss of Derry (below, p. 63), and the army was below strength; there was panic in Dublin, and the Protestants entered into secret correspondence with Schomberg.[34] However, the extreme caution of Schomberg (for which he was frequently reproved by William III) gave the Jacobites time to re-organize, and in the end it was not until nearly a year after he had landed that Schomberg won a decisive victory at the Battle of the Boyne in July 1690.

The Irishman's Prayers plainly belongs to the period immediately after Schomberg's landing, before expectations of a rapid victory had been disappointed; it can hardly have been written later than September 1689.

XVIII. John Dunton, *Report of a Sermon*

John Dunton was born at Graffham in Huntingdonshire in 1659. His father, grandfather, and great-grandfather were all clergymen; his father was a Fellow of Trinity College, Cambridge, and subsequently chaplain to Sir Henry Ingoldsby, whom he accompanied to Ireland. Dunton did not accompany his father, who eventually returned to England and became rector of Aston Clinton in Buckinghamshire. Dunton had been intended for the Church, like all his forebears, but he proved a wild and intractable lad, and at the age of fourteen he was apprenticed to the bookseller Thomas Parkhurst of Cheapside. In 1685 he set up shop as a bookseller and publisher at the sign of the Raven, near the Royal Exchange. In 1682

34. Simms (1969) 124.

he had married Elizabeth, a daughter of the well-known preacher Samuel Annesley; another daughter, Ann, married Samuel Wesley, and became the mother of John Wesley the founder of Methodism; a third daughter married Daniel Defoe. Dunton's wife was a tower of strength to him, managing the business while he indulged in his favourite occupations of travelling and writing. In 1686 he spent eight months in New England and then visited Holland and Germany. He returned to London towards the end of 1688, and opened a new shop in the Poultry. From 1690 to 1696 he published a weekly philosophical journal called at first *The Athenian Gazette*, later *The Athenian Mercury*. His wife died in 1697, and in the spring of 1698 he set out for Ireland—ostensibly to auction a parcel of books, but in fact no doubt for the sake of what he called a "ramble". After spending some time in Dublin, and recording his experiences in a book called *The Dublin Scuffle* which he published in the following year, he set out for a tour of Ireland, penetrating as far as the wilder parts of Connemara, where he visited Roderic O'Flaherty, author of the *Description of Iar-Connacht*;[35] on his return journey he attended the funeral at which he recorded the text of the funeral sermon printed below, pp. 133–7. Later in his life Dunton's eccentricity verged on madness, and he died in poverty in 1733.

Dunton's *Report of a Sermon* is an extraordinary *tour de force*. He claims to have taken it down in shorthand:[36]

It was because I would not interrupt the description of the funeral preparation and pomp that I did not take notice of the sermon which Father Laurence

35. Hardiman (1846).
36. MS Rawlinson D.71, p. 13.

was pleased to give us on this occasion. Have you seene the oration that Anthony made at Cæsar's obsequies, or any other the most celebrated among the Romans? If you have, prepare yourself then to heare one not in the least like anything that is like 'em, and beleive it was more to satisfye your curiosity than my one that I was at the trouble to take it in shorthand.

Of the numerous systems of shorthand current at this period, none would have been adequate for the noting of details of Father Laurence's pronunciation; if, therefore, he did take down the sermon in shorthand, it can only have been Father Laurence's words that he recorded— he must have added the pronunciation later at his leisure. If so, he certainly had a remarkably good ear: as we shall see later in detail (§§ 79, 80, 97), he records features of pronunciation not noticed in any of our other texts.

XIX. George Farquhar, *The Twin Rivals*

George Farquhar was born in Derry in 1677: he came of a clerical family long established in Ireland, and his father was Prebendary of Raphoe. Little is known about his childhood and adolescence. He was educated at the Derry Grammar School; while this was closed during the siege of Derry he presumably lived with his parents in Raphoe, and must have seen much of the fighting of the time. According to tradition he was present at the Battle of the Boyne in 1690, but since he was then only thirteen years old this seems improbable. In 1694 he was elected to a sizarship at Trinity College, Dublin: his father was already dead, and it seems that his studies were now being subsidized by Capel Wiseman, Bishop of Dromore, apparently a relative of Farquhar's mother; at all events, the death of the Bishop led to his withdrawal from Trinity in 1696 without taking a degree. Like Thomas Sheridan nearly fifty years later, Farquhar now turned to the stage, and became an actor at the Theatre in Smock Alley; his most distinguished part was Othello. During a performance of Dryden's *Conquest of Mexico* he accidentally stabbed a fellow-actor; though the wound was not fatal and the wounded man eventually recovered, the shock was so great that Farquhar abandoned the stage and went to London to earn his living as a dramatist. Though his plays were successful he lived in continual poverty, and his circumstances were not improved by his marriage to a widow ten years older than himself, with two children by her previous marriage and no resources of her own. The Duke of Ormonde promised to help him but failed to live up to his promise. Oppressed and weakened by constant hardship he fell sick and died in April 1707, not yet thirty years old; he lived just long enough to see the spectacular success of his last play, *The Beaux' Stratagem.*

In 1698 a great sensation was caused by the publication of a work entitled *A Short View of the Immorality and Profaneness of the English Stage*, by a Cambridge clergyman named Jeremy Collier; this was a virulent attack on the Restoration Theatre, and the works of Congreve and Vanbrugh were especially singled out for condemnation. Farquhar's *Twin Rivals*, performed in 1702 and printed in 1703, was a response to Collier's attack, and represents an attempt to write a "moral" play, in which the innocent are rewarded and the guilty punished. The "Twin Rivals" of the title are the twin brothers Hermes and Ben Woudbee, and the mainspring of the plot is the attempt of the younger brother Ben to secure his elder brother's inheritance and to seduce his affianced bride Constance. On the death of their father during Hermes' absence in Germany, Ben first of all puts about a report that his brother had been killed in a duel, and then produces a will in his own favour forged by the lawyer Subtleman. When Hermes and his Irish servant Teague return from abroad they are faced by a *fait accompli*. By chance the lawyer Subtleman picks on Teague as a supposed witness to the forged will, and the conspiracy is revealed; Hermes is not yet out of the wood, however, since at Ben's instigation he is arrested and imprisoned as a madman. There are many further complications, but in the end all is unravelled through the efforts of Constance and Teague, and the play ends happily with Hermes restored to his inheritance and united to Constance.

XX. John Michelburne, *Ireland Preserved*

John Michelburne was born in 1648 at Horsted Keynes in Sussex. Nothing is known about his education or his early life, but it is clear that he spent some time soldiering on the Continent before he went to Ireland. In February 1689 he received a Major's Commission from the Prince of Orange, and in June of the same year he was promoted to the rank of Colonel and appointed Military Governor of Derry, which had already been under siege for six months and was in desperate straits. Though the siege was abandoned on 31st July, by then Michelburne's wife and seven children were all dead, and (according to his own account) he had spent most of his private fortune in attempting to relieve distress. Much of the rest of his life was spent in trying to secure repayment of this money. He made his home in Derry, where he was elected alderman, but he made a number of trips to London to try and promote his claims; it appears that he was more than once committed to the Fleet Prison for debt. He married again and died in Derry in October 1721.

Ireland Preserved is an extraordinary work. It consists, in effect, of Michelburne's memoirs, cast into the form of two plays, the first dealing with the raising of a Jacobite army and the preparations for the siege of Derry, the second with the siege itself. No doubt this record of the stirring events in which he had played a leading part was useful in Michelburne's campaign to recover the money he had spent—the book was privately printed in 1705, when he was deeply immersed in that campaign; what is not at all clear is the reason why he should have chosen to publish his memoirs in dramatic form. The plays could never have been performed—there are long speeches and theological controversies, and battalion orders of the day are given in full; it is true that a very vivid picture of events emerges in the end, but one would have thought that a straightforward narrative would have served Michelburne's purpose better. Still, we may be grateful for the lively picture that he has given us of the speech and customs of the native Irish.

The first edition of *Ireland Preserved* is a rare book; the second edition of 1708 with a new dedication is equally rare. The first of the two plays was never subsequently reprinted, but the second play about the Siege of Derry was frequently reprinted by itself, and indeed retained its popularity in Ulster until recent times. In 1841 a revised and bowdlerized version was published by the Reverend John Graham, Rector of Tamlaght and Magilligan in Co. Derry, and this was also popular, thought it never replaced the original.

Of the three scenes printed below, pp. 144–8, the first two are from Part I, and the third from Part II. The first shows the impact of the military preparations on the peasants of Ireland, and the second describes the efforts of Catholics to secure commissions in the army commanded by Richard Talbot, Duke of Tyrconnel; neither is very clearly localized, though the introductory stage-direction of the first scene suggests that it takes place in Fingall. The third scene is clearly localized in Derry, and shows the activities of the irregular troops known as *rapparees* (below, §145) during the siege. As we shall see below (§§ 47, 69) Michelburne seems to have attempted, without complete success, to distinguish between two different types of Hiberno-English.

XXI. *A Dialogue between Teague and Dermot*

This highly topical broadsheet, preserved in the Thorpe Collection in the National Library of Ireland, is a commentary on the riot which occurred in Dublin during the general election of 1713. The two speakers are given the names of Teague and Dermot, traditional names for the ordinary native Irishman. The poet David O Bruadair uses the Irish forms Tadhg and Diarmaid in just the same way:[37]

Is iomdha Diarmaid ciallmhar ceannasach,
Is iomdha Tadhg go meidhreach meanmnach.

'There is many a Diarmaid prudent in government, and many a Tadhg courageously jubilant.' (See also below, §143.) Teague and Dermot are seen as Tories and Jacobites, and the Whigs are seen as supporters of the Williamite settlement.

The Whig candidates in 1713 were John Forster, the Recorder of Dublin (in the following year promoted to the post of Chief Justice of the Common Pleas), and a banker named Benjamin Burton. The Tory candidates were Sir William Fownes and Martin Tucker. At this

37. MacErlean (1910–17) 102–3.

time there was, of course, no secret ballot, and the voting took place outside the Tholsel or courthouse. The two city sheriffs, both Whigs, were in charge of the proceedings, and when a high-spirited mob (most of whom had not the franchise) gathered and rushed the stage, they sent for a troop of dragoon guards who fired into the mob, killing one rioter and seriously wounding another. The election was postponed for a week, and eventually the two Whig candidates were elected. The rioting was the subject of a parliamentary inquiry, and gave rise to a very large number of controversial pamphlets.

XXII. Susanna Centlivre, *A Wife Well Managed*

Susanna Freeman was the daughter of a landowner at Holbeach in Lincolnshire. During the Civil War he had made no secret of his Parliamentary sympathies, and at the Restoration in 1660 his estates were confiscated. In circumstances which are not entirely clear he made his way to Ireland, and it was probably in Ireland that Susanna was born about 1667. The death of her father and mother when she was about eleven years old left her an unprotected orphan, and she made her way to London where she lived by her wits and became notorious for various exploits and escapades. At the age of sixteen she married a nephew of Sir Stephen Fox, who died twelve months later. She then married an officer named Carroll, who eighteen months later was killed in a duel. Abandoning matrimony as a means of livelihood she now turned to the theatre and made a living by acting and by writing plays. In 1706 she married Joseph Centlivre, chief cook to Queen Anne and later to George I, but continued to write for the stage. She died in 1723. Despite her harum-scarum early life, she was highly esteemed by her contemporaries, and counted Rowe, Farquhar and Steele among her friends.

A Wife Well Managed is not among Mrs Centlivre's better known plays, and is of no special interest. The scene printed below, pp. 151–3, includes all but a few lines of the Hiberno-English material in the play.

XXIII. John Durant Breval, *The Play is the Plot*

The father of John Durant Breval was a French Protestant refugee who became a Prebendary of Westminster. John was born in London about 1680, and, like Jonson and Randolph, was educated at Westminster School. Like Randolph he went to Trinity College, Cambridge, where he took his B.A. in 1700 and his M.A. in 1704. Like Randolph he became a Fellow of his College in 1702, but unlike Randolph he did not retain his Fellowship: in 1708 he was expelled because of an affray with the husband of his mistress. He then enlisted in the army in Flanders, and was gazetted successively ensign and captain; he was, it seems, employed on a number of diplomatic missions. When the war ended in 1713, Breval became a journalist, and published poems, plays and travel books. He is not known to have visited Ireland, but an interest in Ireland is suggested by his poem *MacDermot, or the Irish Fortune Hunter* (1719). He died in Paris in 1738.

The Play is the Plot is an undistinguished piece of work. The Irishman Machone plays an important part, and appears at intervals throughout the play. The scene printed below, pp. 154–8, is representative of his speech, and has the added interest of the successful masquerade by an Englishman as an Irishman (below, pp. 180–81).

XXIV. *The Pretender's Exercise*

The full title of this extraordinary piece is THE PRE-TENDERS / EXERCISE / To his / Irish *DRAGOONS*, and his Wild Geese. It is printed on both sides of a single sheet of paper, and the only known copy is bound up with other early eighteenth-century pieces in the Library of Trinity College, Dublin, under the pressmark A. 7. 4. The sheet is undated; it is bound up between pieces dated 1727, and some clues to the binder's reasoning are to be found in other pieces in the same volume, referred to below by the number of the folio. The son of James II did not become generally known as the Pretender until the reign of Queen Anne,[38] so the piece can hardly be earlier than that; after the general collapse of Jacobite hopes in 1746 public interest in him rapidly declined; but the range of dates is still very wide. Recruitment for the Pretender's forces was certainly widespread in the 1720's; a certain Captain Moses Nowland, for instance, was convicted of "Listing Men for the Pretender's Service" on 28th June 1726, and hanged at St Stephen's Green on 6th July (ff. 67, 68).

The location of the imaginary events depicted is not stated, but it must have been abroad, probably in France but possibly in Spain; Jacobite troops could not possibly have drilled in public in Ireland or England. Under the terms of the Treaty of Limerick (1691) Irish soldiers were allowed to leave the country to take service abroad, and the flow of emigration continued until well into the eighteenth century. The term familiarly given to such voluntary emigrants was "Wild Geese"; the occurrence of the term in the title of this piece antedates the earliest record in *NED* by more than a hundred years. The

38. Burnet (1723–34) ii 503.

humour of the piece depends on the fact that, although the native language of both sergeant and recruits is obviously Irish, they are constrained to conduct their drilling in English, a language with which they have only the most rudimentary acquaintance; a precisely opposite situation exists in the Irish army of the present day, where the language of command is Irish, though the vast majority of officers and men are English-speaking.

No printer's name is given. The word EXERCISE in the title is composed of large capitals cut in wood, and the X has the thick stroke running in the wrong direction, as if it had been cut by an amateur. The first E and the S closely resemble capitals in the word SPEECH in the titles of leaflets printed by a certain C. Hicks at the Rein Deer in Montrath Street in 1725–6 and 1726–7 (ff. 13, 101). Near the top of the second column of the verso the typeface changes from roman to italic, perhaps because of the abnormal run on the ligature *sh* used so frequently in the non-standard spellings; both roman and italic faces seem to be identical with those used by C. Hicks in the leaflets referred to. At a later date the students of Trinity College used to have their lucubrations printed in Montrath Street, and it is not unreasonable to suppose that *The Pretender's Exercise* was itself a Trinity production.

XXV. Peadar O Doirnín, *Muiris O Gormáin*

Peadar O Doirnín, the son of a small farmer of the same name, was born about 1704 in the townland of Rathsgiathach, one and a quarter miles north of Dundalk. He showed early promise in the composition of bardic poetry, and as a young man he travelled through Munster and Connacht, according to the custom of the time, seeking education wherever he could find it. Having obtained the best education that could then be had, he spent the rest of his life as a schoolmaster in Louth and Armagh. The education of Catholics was forbidden under the Penal Laws, and O Doirnín was subjected to considerable harassment by the notorious "tory-hunter" John Johnston of the Fews, and his henchman Cormac na gCeann 'Cormac of the Heads'. He had, however, a powerful protector in the person of Mr Colman of Ballybarrack near Dundalk, whose sister-in-law Rose he married, and in the latter part of his life he lived and taught unmolested in Forkhill, Co. Armagh. He died on 3rd April 1769.[39]

Muiris O Gormáin, the central character of the poem printed below, pp. 162–3, was also a schoolmaster, and apparently considerably younger than O Doirnín, since he did not die till 1794. There are conflicting accounts of the relationship between the two men. According to one story O Gormáin was the master of a school in Forkhill; when O Doirnín arrived there and set up his own establishment, most of O Gormáin's pupils transferred their allegiance to the new school and left him without employment. According to another story, the two men were rivals for the affections of Rose, the sister-in-law of Mr Colman, and O Doirnín wrote the satire to discredit his rival. At all events, it seems clear that the *shantleman brave* of line 47 is O Doirnín himself, who is presented as triumphing over his rival. It is difficult to date the poem: it reads like a young man's work, yet it cannot have been written until O Gormáin was at least fully grown; perhaps 1730–40 is the best guess.

39. The best account of the life of O Doirnín is in Flower (1926) 123–5; the account in the *Dictionary of National Biography* is unreliable.

XXVI. Jonathan Swift, *A Dialogue in Hybernian Stile*

A favourite relaxation of Swift's active mind was playing with words. He and his friend Thomas Sheridan used a number of "game-languages",[40] of which the general principle was the writing of one language under the guise of another: thus, an incomprehensible sequence of Latin words turns out, when read aloud, to make sense of a kind as English. His interest in words extended to the observation of the speech of others, and it is not surprising that he disapproved of the speech of all those whose usage was not the same as his own. The main published product of this interest in language was *Polite Conversation* (1738), in which Swift ridiculed the cliché-ridden conversation of the leisured classes. It has been demonstrated that, despite the statement in the "Introduction" to *Polite Conversation* that the material in it had been collected by personal observation, the vast majority of the proverbial sayings used by the speakers were taken by Swift from written sources.[41] This, however, was merely a time-saving expedient: the intention was to display the nature of the speech satirized by bringing together a large number of its imbecilities in a small compass.

The same device—the concentration of the features to be satirized—is used in the two short pieces in which Swift ridiculed the language of the Irish planters, *A Dialogue in Hybernian Stile between A. and B.*, and *Irish Eloquence*. It is difficult to date these two pieces with any accuracy: the paper on which the manuscripts are written corresponds to paper known to have been used by Swift in the 1730's, and the most probable date seems to be about 1735, when he was occupied with the final revision

40. Mayhew (1967) 131–48.
41. Jarrell (1956).

of *Polite Conversation* for the press.[42] The two pieces are not independent of each other: they are made up of the same material arranged in different ways. The *Dialogue* follows the same pattern as *Polite Conversation*, though the speakers are not named but are denoted merely by the initials A. and B.; in *Irish Eloquence* the material is improved, expanded, and arranged in the form of a letter. There can be little doubt that the *Dialogue* came first and *Irish Eloquence* second.[43] The *Dialogue* has been chosen for inclusion here because it is the more finished of the two pieces; *Irish Eloquence* seems never to have been properly revised, and the last two lines have been roughly crossed out as if an alteration was intended but never made.

The two speakers A. and B. in the *Dialogue* are members of the Protestant, English-speaking upper classes. B. is a planter (line 17); A. is plainly not a planter, since he knows nothing of country matters, and asks some rather naïve questions about life in the country. A. seems to be a townsman, since B. expects him to know the address of "Tom" who lives opposite the "Red Lyon" (line 9), and therefore presumably in a town. Possibly A. is a lawyer, and B. the planter may be in town for a visit to the Sessions (line 10). There is no noticeable difference of language between the two speakers. Apart from the evidence of Swift's two pieces, nothing is known of the language of the planters and their ilk at this period; Swift shows that their speech had sub-standard and dialectal features (§225), and that it had already been strongly influenced by the Irish language (§§ 153, 157, 161, 164–5, 213).[44]

42. Bliss (1977) 14–20.
43. Ibid. 20–25.
44. Ibid. 59–60.

XXVII. Thomas Sheridan, *The Brave Irishman*

Thomas Sheridan came of a distinguished Anglo-Irish family. The family was originally Catholic and Irish-speaking, but Thomas's great-grandfather Dennis Sheridan was converted by Bishop William Bedell, received Anglican ordination, and assisted his patron to translate the Bible into Irish. The family seat, Quilca House in Co. Cavan, was forfeited by the Sheridans for adherence to James II, and acquired by one Charles MacFadden; but Dr Thomas Sheridan (the father of our Thomas) recovered it by marrying the new owner's daughter Elizabeth. Dr Sheridan was a schoolmaster, and a close friend of Jonathan Swift, who stood godfather to the third son Thomas, born in 1719. Thomas was educated at first by his father, but he showed such promise that in 1733 he was sent, like so many of our other authors, to Westminster School, where he was immediately elected to a King's Scholarship. In 1735, however, his father could no longer afford the expense of maintaining him in England, and he returned to Ireland where he entered Trinity College; in 1738 he was elected to a Scholarship, and in 1739 he obtained his B.A. He had originally intended to become a schoolmaster like his father, but his inclinations turned more and more to the stage, and in 1743 he first appeared as an actor in Dublin. He then obtained an engagement at the Drury Lane theatre in London, but returned to Dublin to become manager of the Theatre Royal in Smock Alley. Eventually he settled in England, and became a writer and lecturer on elocution.[45] His son Richard Brinsley Sheridan acquired much greater fame than his father as both actor and playwright.

45. For Dr Johnson's opinion of Sheridan's qualifications for this profession see below, §44.

Thomas Sheridan's play *The Brave Irishman* can be dated with some accuracy. In a passage not included in the printed versions, the autograph manuscript contains a mention of Richardson's *Pamela*, so worded as to imply that no second part had yet appeared; since the first part was published in 1740 and the second in 1741, the earliest version of the play must have been written in one or other of these years, and more probably in 1740 when the réclame of *Pamela* was still fresh.[46] The first performance took place in February 1743, a week after Sheridan's own début: the leading part of Captain O'Blunder was taken by John Morris. The play proved exceedingly popular and was often revived, the actor Isaac Sparks particularly striking the public imagination in the part of the honest Captain. The first known edition appeared in 1754, and there were numerous reprints. There are two different printed versions, each of which differs substantially from the autograph manuscript. According to Baker[47] "the original copy being lost, it was supplied from the memory of the actors, who added and altered in such a manner, that hardly any part of the original composition now remains." This statement is hardly credible: apart from the fact that Sheridan's manuscript is still in the possession of his descendants, the differences between the manuscript and the printed text, though substantial, are not such as to justify the statement that "hardly any part of the original composition now remains." Probably the printed texts were taken from acting versions, to which the actors had made their own additions, but the basic shape of Sheridan's work still remains.

The ultimate source of *The Brave Irishman* was

46. Sheldon (1967) 26.
47. Baker (1782) ii 43, C 26.

Molière's *Monsieur de Pourceaugnac*. The more immediate source (disarmingly acknowledged in the dialogue
of the manuscript play) was a translation of Molière, of
doubtful authorship, which was called *Squire Trelooby*
and was published in 1704. *Squire Trelooby* had already
been imitated by Charles Shadwell in his *Plotting Lovers*
(1734), and Sheridan may have known this version too.[48]
The passage printed below, pp. 166–71, gives us Captain
O'Blunder's first arrival in London: it is taken from the
earliest printed edition of 1754.

48. Sheldon (1967) 21.

TEXTS

Since the interest of these texts is primarily linguistic, it is of the first importance that the originals should be reproduced exactly, letter by letter, and this I have done; but bibliographical minutiæ have been sacrificed in an attempt to make these difficult pieces as readable as possible. Non-standard spellings are more liable than standard spellings to be miswritten or misprinted, but I have altered the readings of the originals only in the relatively few cases where error seems quite certain; all alterations are recorded in the textual footnotes.

Nineteen of the twenty-seven texts are taken from contemporary or near-contemporary printed editions, and in reproducing these I have preserved not only the spelling but also the punctuation and in general the capitalization. However, I have silently normalized the capitalization in two ways: whenever names of countries or nationalities have been printed with a lower-case letter I have substituted a capital; and when (in I and VIII) the printer has wrongly printed prose as verse I have removed the capital letter with which he begins each spurious line of verse. The majority of the texts are scenes from plays, and for the sake of clarity I have partially normalized the layout of speeches and stage directions.

The manuscripts from which the remaining eight texts are taken vary greatly in character, and my treatment of them has been dictated by these variations. Wherever an accurate printed text is available I have followed it; when I have had to use the manuscript itself I have tried to present a conservative but readable text. Details of the treatment of each piece are given at the head of the notes on it.

I. *Captain Thomas Stukeley* (1596/1605)

Enter Shane Oneale, O Hanlon, Neale Mackener
softly as by night.

Onele. O Hanlon.

Hanlon. Owe.

Oneale. Fate is the token? fate siegne that *Brian Mack Phelem* said he would hang oot?

5 *Han.* I feate I kno not ask the Shecretary.

On. Neale Mackener.

Mack. Hest, *Oneale* hest, pease too art at the vater seed.

On. Fate is the token bodeaugh breene? That I sall

10 see ovare the valles of this Toone of Dundalke.

Mack. I feat *Oneale* thoo art Saint *Patrick* his cushin and a great Lord, but thou are not weeze. The siegne is a paire of feete trouzes, or a feete shurt, or some feete blankead, to be hang oote over the

15 valles, fan we sall be let in at the lettle Booygh dore by the abbay.

Oneale. Esta clamper, thoo talkest to much the English vpon the vall will heare the, loke, feagh bodeaugh dost thou see any thing feete.

20 *Mack.* No by this hand, *shan Oneal*, we see no feat thing.

One coughs within.

Han. Cresh blesh vs, fo ish tat ishe coughes.

Mack. Saint *Patrick* blesh vs we be not betraid.

2 *Hanlon*] *Humlon*   14 over] ober   18 loke] lake

Oneale. Mackener, Mack Deawle, marafastot art thou
25   a feete liuerd kana: Tish some English churle in
the toone that coughes, that is dree, some prood
English souldior hees a dree cough, can drinke no
vater. The English churle dees if he get not bread
and porrage and a ho[o]se to lee in: but looke is
30   the sieegne oote, zeele cut his troate and help him
of his cough fan I get into Dundalk.
Mack. Bee this hand *Oneale* der is no siegne, zee am
af[r]aid *Brian Mack Phelemy* is wyd his streepo,
and forgeats to hang a siegne or let vs in.
35   *Oneale.* No matter come, no noyse tis almost day,
softly let vs creepe aboote by the valles seed ane
awaie sone. At night euen at shuttene of the gates
fan *Ocane and Magennis* come from Carlingford,
we will Enter lustily the town. *Mackener O Hanlon*,
40   zee will giue you tree captaines to ransome.
Han. Zee wil take tree prishoners and giue thee too
and take de turd my self.
One. Speake softly *O Hanlon* and gow make ready
oore kerne and Gallinglasse against night, and bid
45   my bagpiper be ready to peep Ball[r]ootherie soon,
for I will sleepe in Dundalke at night. Come go
back into the Fewes again.
Han. Slane haggat *Bryan Mac Phelemy.*
Mack. Slane lets Rorie beg.   [*Exit.*

30 sieegne] sieegne,   37 awaie sone. At] awan sone at
39 town.] town   42 self.] self   46 Come] come
48, 49 Slane] Slaue

[Mack Chane the Irish servant has murdered and robbed his master, Sir Richard Lee the younger. He is observed by the priest Sir John of Wrotham and his wench Doll, who deprive him of his spoils.]

Enter the Irish man with his master slaine.

[*sir Iohn*] Stay, who comes here? some Irish villaine
me thinkes that has slaine a man, and drawes him
out of the way to rifle him: stand close Doll, weele
see the end.

The Irish man falls to rifle his master.

5 [*Irishman*] Alas po[r]e mester, S. Rishard Lee, be
saint Patricke is rob and cut thy trote, for dee
shaine, and dy money, and dee gold ring, be me
truly is loue thee wel, but now dow be kil thee, bee
shitten kanaue.
10 *sir Iohn.* Stand sirra, what art thou?
Irishman. Be saint Patricke mester is pore Irisman,
is a leufter.
sir Iohn. Sirra, sirra, you are a damned rogue, you
haue killed a man here, and rifled him of all that
15 he has, sbloud you rogue deliuer, or ile not leaue
you so much as an Irish haire aboue your shoulders,
you whorson Irish dogge, sirra vntrusse presently,
come off and dispatch, or by this crosse ile fetch
your head off as cleane as a barke.
20 *Irishman.* Wees me saint Patricke, Ise kill me mester
for chaine and his ring, and nows be rob of all,
mees vndoo.

Priest robs him.

sir Iohn. Auant you rascal, go sirra, be walking, come
    Doll the diuel laughes, when one theefe robs an-
25   other, come madde wench, weele to saint Albons,
    and reuel in our bower, hey my braue girle.
Doll. O thou art old sir Iohn, when all's done yfaith.

[Mack Chane seeks and find lodgings in an inn.]

Enter the hoste of the Bell, with the Irish man.

Irishman. Be me tro mester is pore Irisman, is want
    ludging, is haue no mony, is starue and cold, good
30   mester giue her some meate, is famise and tie.
Host. Yfaith my fellow I haue no lodging, but what
    I keep for my guesse, that I may not disapoint, as
    for meate thou shalt haue such as there is, & if thou
    wilt lie in the barne, theres faire straw, and roome
35   enough.
Irishman. Is thanke my mester hartily, de straw is
    good bed for me.
Host. Ho Robin?
Robin. Who calls?
40 *Host.* Shew this poore Irishman into the barne, go
    sirra.   [*Exeunt.*

[Sir John Oldcastle, his wife, and his steward Harpoole have
taken lodgings at the same inn. When the constable arrives,
Mack Chane changes clothes with the sleeping Harpoole, and
is arrested not as a murderer but as the servant of a heretic.]

Const[able]. First beset the house, before you begin
    the search.
Officer. Content, euery man take a seuerall place.

Heere is heard a great noyse within.

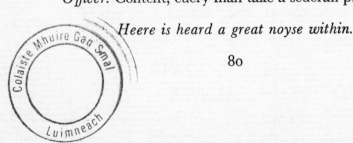

80

45 Keepe, keepe, strike him downe there, downe with him.

Enter Constable with the Irish man
in Harpooles apparell.

Con. Come you villainous heretique, confesse where your maister is.
Irish man. Vat mester?
50 *Maior.* Vat mester, you counterfeit rebell, this shall not serue your turne.
Irish man. Be sent Patrike I ha no mester.
Con. Wheres the lord Cobham sir Iohn Old-castle that lately is escaped out of the Tower.
55 *Irish man.* Vat lort Cobham?
Maior. You counterfeit, this shal not serue you, weele torture you, weele make you to confesse where that arch-heretique Lord Cobham is: come binde him fast.
60 *Irish man.* Ahone, ahone, ahone, a Cree.
Con. Ahone, you crafty rascall? *[Exeunt.*

[Harpoole is subsequently arrested as the Irish murderer, while Sir John Oldcastle and his wife escape.]

 Gower. The Duke of Gloucester, to whom the Order
 of the Siege is giuen, is altogether directed by an
 Irish man, a very valiant Gentleman yfaith.
 Welch. It is Captaine *Makmorrice*, is it not?
5 *Gower.* I thinke it be.
 Welch. By *Cheshu* he is an Asse, as in the World, I
 will verifie as much in his Beard: he ha's no more
 directions in the true disciplines of the Warres,
 looke you, of the Roman disciplines, then is a
10 Puppy-dog.

   Enter Makmorrice, *and Captaine* Iamy.

 Gower. Here a comes, and the Scots Captaine, Captaine *Iamy*, with him.
 Welch. Captaine *Iamy* is a maruellous falorous
 Gentleman, that is certain, and of great expedition
15 and knowledge in th'aunchiant Warres, vpon my
 particular knowledge of his directions: by *Cheshu*
 he will maintaine his Argument as well as any
 Militarie man in the World, in the disciplines of
 the Pristine Warres of the Romans.
20 *Scot.* I say gudday, Captaine *Fluellen*.
 Welch. Godden to your Worship, good Captaine
 Iames.
 Gower. How now Captaine *Mackmorrice*, haue you
 quit the Mynes? haue the Pioners giuen o're?
25 *Irish.* By Chrish Law tish ill done: the Worke ish
 giue ouer, the Trompet sound the Retreat. By my
 Hand I sweare, and my fathers Soule, the Worke
 ish ill done: it ish giue ouer: I would haue blowed

vp the Towne, so Chrish saue me law, in an houre.
30   O tish ill done, tish ill done: by my Hand tish ill done.
    Welch. Captaine *Mackmorrice*, I beseech you now,
    will you voutsafe me, looke you, a few disputations
    with you, as partly touching or concerning the
    disciplines of the Warre, the Roman Warres, in the
35   way of Argument, looke you, and friendly com-
    munication: partly to satisfie my Opinion, and
    partly for the satisfaction, looke you, of my Mind:
    as touching the direction of the Militarie discipline,
    that is the Point.
40   *Scot.* It sall be vary gud, gud feith, gud Captens bath,
    and I sall quit you with gud leue, as I may pick
    occasion: that sall I mary.
    Irish. It is no time to discourse, so Chrish saue me:
    the day is hot, and the Weather, and the Warres,
45   and the King, and the Dukes: it is no time to
    discourse, the Town is beseech'd: and the Trumpet
    call vs to the breech, and we talke, and be Chrish
    do nothing, tis shame for vs all: so God sa'me tis
    shame to stand still, it is shame by my hand: and
50   there is Throats to be cut, and Workes to be done,
    and there ish nothing done, so Christ sa'me law.
    Scot. By the Mes, ere theise eyes of mine take them-
    selues to slomber, ayle de gud seruice, or Ile ligge
    i'th'grund for it: ay, or goe to death: and Ile pay't
55   as valorously as I may, that sal I suerly do, that is
    the breff and the long: mary, I wad full faine heard
    some question tween you tway.
    Welch. Captaine *Mackmorrice*, I thinke, looke you,
    vnder your correction, there is not many of your
60   Nation—
    Irish. Of my Nation? What ish my Nation? Ish a
    Villaine, and a Basterd, and a Knaue, and a Rascall.
    What ish my Nation? Who talkes of my Nation?

60 Nation—] Nation.

Welch. Looke you, if you take the matter otherwise
65   then is meant, Captaine *Mackmorrice*, peraduen-
ture I shall thinke you doe not vse me with that
affabilitie, as in discretion you ought to vse me looke
you, being as good a man as your selfe, both in the
disciplines of Warre, and in the deriuation of my
70   Birth, and in other particularities.
Irish. I doe not know you so good a man as my selfe:
so Chrish saue me, I will cut off your Head.
Gower. Gentlemen both, you will mistake each other.
Scot. A, that's a foule fault.   [*A Parley.*
75   *Gower.* The Towne sounds a Parley.
Welch. Captaine *Mackmorrice*, when there is more
better opportunitie to be required, looke you, I will
be so bold as to tell you, I know the disciplines of
Warre: and there is an end.
                                                    [*Exit.*

IV. Thomas Dekker, *Old Fortunatus* (1599/1600)

Enter Andelocia *and* Shaddowe, *like Irish Coster-mongers,* Agripyna, Longauyle, *and* Montrosse *stay listening to them, the rest Exeunt.*

Both. Buy any Apples, feene Apples of Tamasco, feene Tamasco peepins: peeps feene, buy Tamasco peepins.

Agrip. Damasco apples? good my Lord *Montrosse,*
5   Call yonder fellowes.

Montr.   Sirra Coster-monger.

Shad. Who cals? peeps of Tamasco, feene peeps: I fat tis de sweetest apple in de world, tis better den de Pome water, or apple Iohn.

Andel. By my trat Madam, tis reet Tamasco peepins,
10   looke here els.

Shad. I dare not say, as de Irishman my countrieman say, tast de goodnesse of de fruit: No fayt tis farie teere mistris, by Saint *Patrickes* hand tis teere Ta-masco apple.

15 *Agrip.* The fairest fruit that euer I beheld,
    Damasco apples, wherefore are they good?

Longa. What is your price of halfe a score of these?

Both. Halfe a score, halfe a score? dat is doos many mester.

20 *Longa.* I, I, ten, half a score, thats fiue and fiue.

Andel. Feeue and feeue? By my trat and as Creeze saue me la, I cannot tell, wat be de price of feeue and feeue, but tis tree crowne for one Peepin, dat is de preez if you take em.

2 Tamasco[1]] Tamasio

25 *Shad.* I fat, tis no lesse for Tamasco.
Agrip. Three crownes for one? what wondrous vertues
haue they?
Shad. O, tis feene Tamasco apple, and shall make
you a great teale wise, and make you no foole, and
make feene memorie.
30 *Andel.* And make dis fash be more faire and amiable,
and make dis eyes looke alwaies louely, and make
all de court and countrie burne in desire to kisse di
none sweete countenance
Montr. Apples to make a Lady beautifull?
35 Madam thats excellent.
Agrip. These Irishmen,
Some say, are great dissemblers, and I feare
These two the badge of their own countrie weare.
Andel. By my trat, and by Saint *Patrickes* hand, and
as Creez saue me la, tis no dissembler: de Irish
40 man now and den cut di countrie-mans throate,
but yet in fayt hee loue di countrie-man, tis no dissembler: dis feene Tamasco apple can make di
sweete countenance, but I can take no lesse but
three crownes for one, I weare out my naked legs
45 and my footes, and my toes, and run hidder and
didder to Tamasco for dem.
Shad. As Creez saue me la, hee speakes true: Peeps
feene.
Agrip. Ile trie what power lies in Damasco fruit.
50 Here are ten crownes for three, So fare you well.
Montr. Lord *Longauyle*, buy some.
Longa. I buy? not I:
Hang them, they are toyes, come Madam, let vs goe.
[*Exeunt.*
Both. Saint *Patricke* and Saint *Peter*, and all de holy
Angels looke vpon dat fash and make it faire.

Enter Montrosse *softly.*

45 toes] tods

86

Shad. Ha, ha, ha, shees sped, I warrant.

Andel. Peace, *Shaddow*, buy any peepins, buy.

Both. Peeps feene, feene Tamasco apples.

Montr. Came not Lord *Longauyle* to buy some fruit?

Andel. No fat, master, here came no Lords nor Ladies,
but di none sweete selfe.

Montr. Tis well, say nothing, heres six crownes for
two:
You say the vertues are to make one strong.

Both. Yes fat and make sweet countenance and strong
too.

Montr. Tis excellent, here: farwell, if these proue,
Ile conquer men by strength, women by loue.

[*Exit.*

Enter Longauyle.

Both. Ha, ha, ha, why this is rare.

Shad. Peace, master, here comes another foole.

Both. Peeps feene, buy any peeps of Tamasco?

Longa. Did not the Lord *Montrosse* returne to you?

Both. No fat, sweete master, no Lord did turne to vs:
Peepes feene.

Longa. I am glad of it: here are nine crownes for
three:
What are the vertues besides making faire?

Andel. O, twill make thee wondrous wise.

Shad. And dow shall bee no more a foole, but sweete
face and wise.

Longa. Tis rare, farwell, I neuer yet durst wooe.
None loues me: now Ile trie what these can doe.

[*Exit.*

Andel. Ha, ha, ha, So, this is admirable, *Shaddow*,
here end my torments in Saint *Patrickes* Purgatorie,
but thine shall continue longer.

Shad. Did I not clap on a good false Irish face?

Andel. It became thee rarely.

V. Thomas Dekker, *The Honest Whore* Part II
(1605/1630)

[Bryan tells the courtiers why his master Hipollito is not yet ready to go out.]

Enter Bryan *the Footeman.*

Lod[ouico]. How now, is thy Lord ready?

Bryan. No so crees sa mee, my Lady will haue some little Tyng in her pelly first.

Caro[lo]. Oh, then they'le to breakefast.

5 *Lod.* Footman, does my Lord ride y'th Coach with my Lady, or on horsebacke?

Bryan. No faat la, my Lady will haue me Lord sheet wid her, my Lord will sheet in de one side, and my Lady sheet in de toder side.   [*Exit.*

[Hipollito has been delayed by the scholar Antonio, and has to ride after his wife Infælice.]

Enter Bryan.

10 *Bryan.* I faat di Lady is runne away from dee, a mighty deale of ground, she sent me backe for dine owne sweet face, I pray dee come my Lord away, wut tow goe now?

Hip[ollito]. Is the Coach gone? Saddle my Horse the
15 sorrell.

Bryan. A pox a de Horses nose, he is a lowsy rascally fellow, when I came to gird his belly, his scuruy guts rumbled, di Horse farted in my face, and dow knowest, an Irishman cannot abide a fart, but I

7 faat] foot   9 *Exit*] *Exeunt*   10 faat] fart

20 haue saddled de Hobby-horse, di fine Hobby is
ready, I pray dee my good sweet Lord, wut tow
goe now, and I will runne to de Deuill before dee?
Hip. Well, sir, I pray lets see you Master Scholler.
Bryan. Come I pray dee, wut come sweet face? Goe.
[*Exeunt.*

[Bryan has been falsely accused to Infælice of furthering an
intrigue between Hipollito and Bellafront, the Honest Whore.]

Enter Bryan.

25 *Infæ*[*lice*]. Come hither sirra, how much cost those
Satins,
And cloth of Siluer, which my husband sent
By you to a low Gentlewoman yonder?
Bryan. Faat Sattins? faat Siluers, faat low Gentle-
folkes? dow pratest dow knowest not what, yfaat la.
30 *Infæ.* She there, to whom you carried letters.
Bryan. By dis hand and bod[y] dow saist true, if I did
so, oh how? I know not a letter a de Booke yfaat la.
Infæ. Did your Lord neuer send you with a Ring, sir,
Set with a Diamond?
35 *Bryan.* Neuer, so crees sa me, neuer; he may runne at
a towsand rings yfaat, and I neuer hold his stirrop,
till he leape into de saddle. By Saint *Patricke*,
Madam, I neuer touch my Lords Diamond, nor
euer had to doe, yfaat la, with any of his precious
40 stones.

Enter Hipollito.

Infæ. Are you so close, you Bawd, you pandring slaue?
Hip. How now? why *Infælice*? what's your quarrell?
Infæ. Out of my sight, base varlet, get thee gone.

21 wut] wit   35 so] sa

89

Hip. Away you rogue.

45 *Bryan. Slawne laat,* fare de well, fare de well. *Ah
    marragh frofat boddah breen.*   [*Exit.*

[To avenge herself on her husband, Infælice has falsely claimed
that Bryan has seduced her.]

Enter Bryan.

Hip. It can be no man else, that Irish Iudas,
    Bred in a Country where no venom prospers
    But in the Nations blood, hath thus betraid me.
50   Slaue, get you from your seruice.
Bryan. Faat meanest thou by this now?
Hip. Question me not, nor tempt my fury, villaine,
    Couldst thou turne all the Mountaines in the land,
    To hills of gold, and giue me; here thou stayest not.
55 *Bryan.* I faat, I care not.
Hip. Prate not, but get thee gone, I shall send else.
Bryan. I, doe predy, I had rather haue thee make a
    scabbard of my guts, and let out all de Irish pud-
    dings in my poore belly, den to be a false knaue to
60   de I faat, I will neuer see dyne own sweet face more.
    A mawhisdeer a gra, fare de well, fare de well, I
    wil goe steale Cowes agen in *Ireland.*   [*Exit.*

[Before he returns to Ireland Bryan is persuaded to detain
Candido the linen-draper while one of the courtiers seduces
his wife.]

Enter Astolpho, Beraldo, Fontinell,
and the Irish Footman.

Asto. I thought thou hadst beene gone into thine owne
    Country.

45 *Slawne laat*] Slawne loot   48 prospers] prospers,
49 blood,] blood   54 giue] to giue   61 *mawhisdeer*] *mawhid deer*

65 *Bryan.* No faat la, I cannot goe dis foure or tree dayes.
   Ber. Looke thee, yonders the shop, and that's the man
      himselfe.
   Font. Thou shalt but cheapen, and doe as we told
      thee, to put a iest vpon him, to abuse his patience.
70 *Bryan.* I faat, I doubt my pate shall be knocked: but
      so crees sa me, for your shakes, I will runne to any
      Linnen Draper in hell, come preddy.

                    *   *   *

   Cand[ido]. Ha, ha, ha: you Gentlemen are full of Iest.
      If she be vp, she's gone some wares to show,
75   I haue aboue as good wares as below.
   Lod. Haue you so? nay then —
   Cand. Now Gentlemen, is't Cambricks?
   Bryan. I predee now let me haue de best wares.
   Cand. What's that he saies, pray' Gentlemen?
80 *Lod.* Mary he saies we are like to haue the best wars.
   Cand. The best wars? all are bad, yet wars doe good,
      And like to Surgeons, let sicke Kingdomes blood.
   Bry. Faat a Deuill pratest tow so, a pox on dee, I
      preddee let me see some Hollen, to make Linnen
85   shirts, for feare my body be lowsie.
   Cand. Indeed I vnderstand no word he speakes.
   Caro. Mary, he saies, that at the siege in *Holland*
      there was much bawdry vsed among the Souldiers,
      tho they were lowsie.
90 *Cand.* It may be so, that's likely, true indeed,
      In euery garden, sir, does grow that weed.
   Bryan. Pox on de gardens, and de weedes, and de
      fooles cap dere, and de cloutes; heare? doest make
      a Hobby-horse of me.
95 *Omn.* Oh fie, he has torne the Cambricke.
   Cand. 'Tis no matter.

   71 so] sa   80, 81 *(twice)* wars] wares   95 the] de

                         91

VI. Ben Jonson, *The Irish Masque* (1613/1616)

The King being set in expectation, out ranne a fellow attir'd like a cittizen : after him, three or foure foote-men.

Dennish. Donnell. Dermock. Patrick.

For chreeshes sayk, phair ish te king? Phich ish hee, an't be? show me te shweet faish, quickly. By got, o' my conshence, tish ish he! Ant tou bee king *Yamish*, me name is *Dennish*, I sherue ti mayesties
5   owne cashter-monger, bee mee trote: and cry peep'sh, and pomwater'sh i' ty mayesties sheruice, tis fiue yeere now. Ant tou vilt not trush me now, cal vp ti clarke o' ti kitchin, be ant be, shall giue hish wort, vpon hish booke, ish true.

10 *Don.* Ish it te fashion, to beate te Imbasheters, here? ant knoke 'hem o' te heads, phit te phoit stick?

     Der. Ant make ter meshage runne out at ter mouthsh, before tey shpeake vit te King?

     Den. Peash *Dermock*, here ish te king.

15 *Der.* Phair ish te King?

     Don. Phich ish te king?

     Den. Tat ish te king.

     Der. Ish tat te king? got blesh him.

     Den. Peash, ant take heet, vat tou shaysht, man.

20 *Der.* Creesh blesh him I shay. Phat reason I tayk heet, for tat?

     Don. Cresh blesh ti shweet faish, king *Yamish*; and my mistresh faish too: Pre tee, heare me now. I am

S.D. Dennish] Dennise   15 King? King.   19 *Den.*] *Don.*

come a great vay of miles to shee tee now, by my
25 fayt and trote, and graish o' got.

Den. Phat ish ti meaning o' tish, *Donnell?* Didsh tou
not shay a gotsh name, I should tell ti tayle for tee?
ant entrayt me com to te court, ant leaue me vare
at shixe, ant seuen? By got, ish true now.

30 *Don.* Yesh. But I tanke got I can tell my tayle my
shelfe, now I be here, I varrant tee: Pre dee heare
me king *Yamish.*

Den. Pre dee heare me king *Yamish.* I can tell tee
better ten he.

35 *Pat.* Pre dee heare neder noder on 'hem: Here'sh
Dermock vill shpeake better ten eder oder on 'hem.

Der. No fayt shweet hart tow lyesht. *Phatrick* here
ish te besht man of hish tongue, of all de foure;
pre tee now hear him.

40 *Pat.* By chreesh shaue me tow lyesht. I haue te vorsht
tongue in te company at thy sheruish. Vill shome
body shpeake?

Don. By my fayt I vill not.

Der. By my goships hand I vill not.

45 *Pat.* Speake *Dennish* ten.

Den. If I speake, te diuell tayke me. I vill giue tee
leaue to cram my mout phit shamrokes and butter,
and vayter creshes in stead of pearsh and peepsh.

Pat. If no body vill shpeake, I vill shpeake. Pleash ty
50 shweet faish wee come from Ireland.

Der. Wee be Irish men and't pleash tee.

Don. Ty good shubshects of Ireland, and pleash ty
mayesty.

Den. Of Connough, Leynster, Vlster, Munster. I mine
55 one shelfe vash borne in te English payle and pleash
ty Mayesty.

Pat. Sacrament o' chreesh, tell ty tale, ty shelfe, and
be all tree.

38 besht] vesht   54 Leynster] Leymster

Den. And pleash ty graish I vill tell tee, Tere vash a
60   great newesh in Ireland of a great Brideall of one
o' ty lords here ant be.

Pat. Ty man Robyne, tey shay.

Don. Mary ty man Toumaish, hish daughter, tey shay.

Der. I, ty good man, Toumaish, o' shuffolke.

65   *Don.* He knoke vsh o' te payt here ash we come by,
by a good token.

Der. I fayt tere ish very mush phoyt stick here stirring
to night. Hee takes vsh for no shquires I tinke.

Pat. No, he tinksh not ve be Imbasheters.

70   *Don.* No fayt I tinke sho too. But tish Marriage bring
ouer a doshen of our besht Mayshters, to be merry
pre tee shweet faish, andt be; and daunsh a fading
at te vedding.

Den. But tey vere leeke to daunsh naked, ant pleash
75   ty mayesty; for te villanous vild Irish sheas haue
casht away all ter fine cloysh, as many ash cosht a
towsand cowes, and garranes, I varrant tee.

Der. And te prishe of a Cashtell or two vpon teyr
backs.

80   *Don.* And tey tel ty mayesty, tey haue ner a great fish
now, nor a sheamoynshter to shaue teyr cloysh
aliue now.

Pat. Nor a deuoish vit a clowd to fesh 'hem out o' te
bottome o' te vayter.

85   *Der.* But tey musht eene come and daunch i' teyr
mantels now; and show tee how tey can foot te
fading and te fadow, and te phip a dunboyne, I
trow.

Don. I pre dee now, let not ty sweet faysht ladies
90   make a mocke on 'hem, and scorne to daunsh vit
'hem now becash tey be poore.

Pat. Tey drinke no bonny clabbe, i' fayt, now.

Don. It ish better ten vsquebagh to daunsh vit,
Phatrick.

72 pre] perht 77 garranes] garraues 87 a dunboyne] adunboyne

95 *Pat.* By my faters hand tey vill daunsh very well.

Der. I by St. *Patrick* vill tey; for tey be nimble men.

Den. And will leape ash light, be creesh saue me, ash he tat veares te biggesht fether in ty court, king *Yamish.*

00 *Der.* For all tey haue no good vindsh to blow tem heter, nor elementsh to presherue 'hem.

Don. Nor all te foure cornersh o' te world, to creepe out on.

Pat. But tine owne Kingdomes.

05 *Don.* Tey be honesht men.

Pat. And goot men: tine owne shubshects.

Der. Tou hasht very good shubshects in Ireland.

Den. A great good many, o' great goot shubshects.

Don. Tat loue ty mayesty heartily.

10 *Den.* And vil runne t'rough fire, and vater for tee, ouer te bog, and te Bannoke, be te graish o' got, and graish o' king.

Der. By got, tey vil fight for tee, king *Yamish,* ant for my mistresh tere.

15 *Den.* And my little mayshter.

Pat. And te vfrow, ty daughter, that is in Tuchland.

Don. Tey vill spend ter heart, in ter belly for tee, as vell as ter legs, in ter heelsh.

Der. By creesh, tey vill shpend all teyr cowesh for tee.

20 *Den.* Pretee make mush on 'hem.

Pat. Pretee, sweet faysh doe.

Don. Be not angry vit te honesh men, for te few rebelsh, & knauesh.

Pat. Nor beleeue no tayles, king *Yamish.*

25 *Der.* For, by got, tey loue tee in Ireland.

Don. Pray tee, bid 'hem velcome, and got make 'hem rish for tee.

Der. Tey vil make tem shelues honesht.

Den. Tou hasht not a hundret tousand sush men by
30 my trote.

108 *Den.*] *Der.*   117 ter[2]] rer   120 'hem.] 'tem,

Pat. No, nor forty, by my hand.

Don. By iustish Delounes hant, not twenty.

Der. By my Lo. deputish hant, not ten, in all ti great
Britayne. Shall I call hem to tee?

135 *Don.* Tey shit like poore men i' the porsh yonder.

Pat. Shtay te peepe ish come! harke, harke.

Der. Let vsh daunsh ten. Daunsh *Dennish.*

Den. By creesh sa' me I ha' forgot.

Don. A little till our mayshtersh be ready.

*Here the Foot-men had a daunce, being sixe men,
and sixe boyes, to the bag-pipe, and other rude
musique, after which they had a song, and then
they cry'd,*

140 Peash. Peash. Now roome for our mayshters. Roome
for our mayshters.

*Then the Gentlemen dance forth a dance in their
Irish mantles, to a solemne musique of harpes:
which done, the foot-men fell to speake againe, till
they were interrupted by a ciuill gentleman of the
nation, who brings in a Bard.*

Der. How like tow tish, *Yamish?* Ant tey had fine
cloyshs now, and liueries, like tine owne men and
bee.

145 *Don.* But te rugs make t'em shrug a little.

Der. Tey haue shit a great phoyle i' te cold, ant bee.

Don. Isht not pitty te cloysh be drown'd now?

Pat. Pre tee shee anoter dau[n]sh and be not veary.

136 ish] i'sh   137 *Dennish*] *Dennise*

[Edmond in the guise of an Irish footman is presented to King Athelstane.]

Enter Voltimar *and* Edmond *like an Irish man.*

Vol. Looke, sirra, thats the kinge.
K[*inge*]. Whats hee?
Vol. The embassadors Irish footman, full of desire to
see how much you and an Irish kinge differ in
5   state. Which of the Irish kings know you, sirrah?
Edm. I once serve and runne alonge by *Morrogh mac
Breean*, kinge of *Leinster*, and I know all de oder
Irish princes.
K. How does the kinge of *Leinster*?
10 *Edm.* Yfaatla, passinge merry. Hee loues dee deerely;
Dœardœry his queene too speake well of dee, and
O Shahanassah de kings broder, wid *Dermott Lave-
yarach*, tell mee and I come into England to giue
dee a towsand Comendacions.
15 *K.* Whats thie name?
Edm. Teage mac Breean.
K. How farr canst runne in a daie?
Edm. Yfaat, I shalbee loate to haue dine owne horse
runne so farr in a daie as I can. Euer since I Came
20 awaie from de salt water into *Wales*, and out of
Wales hidder, my toes and my feete never stawnd
still; for bee my gossips hawnd, I had a greate desire
to see dee, and dat sweete face a dine.
K. The kinge of *Leinster* is a noble soldier.

12 *O Shahanassah*] osha Hanassah

25   *Edm.* Crees sa me, hee does not care for de divill.
     Vol. Wiser man hee!
     K. The Queene is wonderous faire, sirrah, is shee not?
     Edm. Queene *Dæardæry*, yfaatla now, as white as de
         inside of a pome water, and as vppright as anie dart
30   in *Ireland*.
     Col[chester]. Goes your kinge in such Clothes?
     Edm. [In] trooses, a pox a die face. I priddy, what
         should h[e g]o in besides?

[Eldred and Edmond spend a merry evening with Voltimar
and a clown.]

     Vol. I muse they come not.
35   *Clo[wne].* Whoe, Captaine?
     Vol. The embassadors man, and the Irish footman
         new come ouer. Wee promist to bee merry heere in
         my Chamber for a spurt or so; they are a Cupple
         of honest-harted mad rascalls.

               Enter Edmond *and* Eldred.

40   *Clo.* See, Capten.
     Vol. Welcome.
     Edm. By dis hawnd, Capten *Voltimar*, de kinge bid
         mee seeke for dee, and to come away apace to him.
     Vol. Tyme enough. Since wee are mett, Ile steale out
45   of the kinges glasse one quarter of an hower to bee
         Iouiall.
     Eld. But where is wine and good seere to bee Iawfull?
         and pipes and fiddles to shake our heele at?
     Vol. Your good seere, looke you, is in bottles. Heeres
50   my Armory: theis are head peices will fitt you.
     Clo. With a murren.
     Vol. And now you talke of fidlinge, a musition dwells
         at very next wall. I'le step to him; entertaine thou
         theis gentlemen the whilst. As wee drinck, they
55   shall sound.

    42 dis] did

Edm. Crees sa mee, if I heare de pipes goe I cannot
forbeare to daunce an Irish hay.

Eld. As good hay in *Wales. Reese ap Meredith* was
daunce too.

60 *Clo.* Hey then for *England.* If my leggs stand still,
hange mee.

Vol. Good sport. I'le goe stringe the musique for
you.   [*Exit.*

Clo. Ith meane tyme, because tis scurvie to bee Idle:
65 pray, Mr *Reese ap Shon*, what is the reason that
wee English men, when the Cuckoe is vppon entrance, saie the Welsh embassador is Cominge?

Eld. Lett anie rascall sonne of whores Come into
Cardigan, Flint, Merioneth, Clamorgan or *Breck-*
70 *nock*, and dare prade so, was such a mighty wonder
to see an embassador of *Wales.* Whie, has her not
had kings, and Queens, and praue princes of *Wales*?

Edm. Yfaat hast tow.

Eld. But I now can tell you, for manie summers agoe
75 our valliant Comragues and feirce Prittons about
Cuckoe-tymes Come, and with Welse hooke hack
and hoff and mawle your English porderers, and so
fright the ymen that they, to still theire wrawlinge
bastards, cry out husht, the Welsh embassador comes.

80 *Clo.* I am satisfied. Now Mr *Crammo*, one question
to you. What is the reason all the Chimny-sweepers
in *England* are for the most parte Irish men?

Edm. I shall tell dee whie. St *Patrick*, dow knowst,
keepes purgator[y. If St] *Patrick* bee content to
85 make de fyers, tis noe shame fo[r Irish men] to
sweepe de Chimneys.

Eld. Tis prave answer.

Clo. And I hugg thee, sweete Tor[y], for it.

Enter Voltimar.

Vol. I give but the *Q*: and the musique speakes.

99

90   I cannot staie. Come, on your knees, a health to
     kinge *Athelstane*.
     Eld. Was pledge her in noe liquors but her owne
     Cuntries, whay or metheglin.
     Vol. Theres metheglin for you.
95   *Edm.* And Ifaatla, I shall pledge kinge *Aplestanes* in
     vsque bah or notinge.
     Vol. Theres vsqua for you.
     Clo. Ile pledge it in Ale, in Aligant, Cider, Perry
     metheglin, vsquebagh minglum, manglum, purr, in
100 hum, mum, Aquam, quaquam, Clarrett or sacum, for
     an English man is a horse that drincks of all waters.
     Vol. To'ot then — when.   [*Florish.*
     Clo. Off.

                        Daunce.

     Eld. Super naglums.
105 *Edm.* Hey for St *Patricks* honour.
     Eld. St *Tavy* for *Wales*.
     Clo. St *George* for *England*.
     Vol. Enough. Drinck what you will: I must hence.
                                                 [*Exit.*
     Edm. Kara ma gus.
110 *Clo.* This dauncinge ioggs all my dynner out of my
         belly. I am as hungry as a huntsman; and now I
         talke of meate, whie does a Welsh man loue tosted
         Cheese so well?
     Eld. Whie Does Cockny pobell loue toast and putter
115   so well?
     Clo. And whie onions and leekes you?
     Eld. And whie a whores plind seekes you awle Cuntries
         loue, one tevices or others?
     Clo. True, you love freeze, and goates, and Welsh
120   hookes, and whay, and flanell, and fighting.

     109 ma gus] magus

                        100

Eld. And you loue vdcocks, and praueries, and kanaveries, and fidlings, and fistings, and praue enches
with rotten trenches, and a greate teale of prablings
but little fightings.

125 *Clo.* One for one. And what loues my Irish man here?

Edm. Yfaatla, I loue shamrocks, bonny clabbo, soft
boggs, a great many cowes, a garron, an Irish-
harpe, cleene trooses and a dart.

Clo. But not a fart.

130 *Edm.* In dy nose, in dy teet. All de farts lett in *Ireland*
are putt into bottles for English men to drinck off.
A pox vppon dy nyes. By dis hawnd, I shall trust
my skeene into dy rotten gutts when agen tow
anger me.   [*Exit.*

[Edmond seeks the clown's support in a patriotic argument
with Eldred.]

Knock within. Enter Edmond.

135 *Clo.* Come in. Oh, Mr *mac Teage*, this may be
cronicled to see you heere.

Edm. Sawst thou *Reece*, datt coggin rascalls?

Clo. Not I.

Edm. I priddy tell mee, for *Reece* and I quarrell

140 vppon it, whedder is *Ireland* ore *Wales* more antient
or finer Cuntry.

Clo. Oh, *Ireland, Ireland.* Anie question of that?

Edm. Yfaat, I tinck so too. Dow and I iump into one hole.

Clo. Looke how much difference is betwene *Myle end*

145 and *Grauesend*, or betwene *Dover* peere and one of
the peeres of *Fraunce*: so short comes *Wales* of
Ireland.

Edm. Dow knowst our Cuntry, too, has noe virmine
int.

150 *Clo.* Oh noe; yett more cattell by far then *Wales.*

Edm. And dat der is not a toade or spider in *Ireland.*

Clo. Nay, thats certen: there are fewer spider-catchers in your cuntry then in anie else.

Edm. Reece saies to that a Welshman runns faster den an Irish.

Clo. Fye, fie, *Rice* is an asse. Your Cuntry-men are foote-men to lords and ladies, and so runne after honour.

Edm. Yfaat, after a greate teale of honour; and if kinge *Atelstanes* himself weare heere, I should tell him I my self was as well borne in my moders belly as the prowdest comrague in *Wales*.

Clo. My head vppon that, *Brian*.

Edm. And priddy now, tell mee, whoe is more terrible in battailes, de Irish or de Welsh?

Clo. Oh, Irish, Irish. Euery Irishman with a dart lookes like death, only death has not so much haire ons head.

Edm. Yett *ap Morris* saies, in warrs his *Brittaine* is more feirce.

Clo. Ap Morris lyes.

Enter Eldred.

Eld. Which *ap Morris*? Lugg you, you Mr *Hobbadery Coscombe*. The same *ap Morris* can mage your learned cronologicall nose lye heere n[ow.]

Edm. Crees sa mee, one Irish man and one Welsh man is abl[e to make] fooles of ten bushells such as dow art.

Eld. You cutt out thred-bare questions . . . .

Edm. Sholl de crow, tow horson teefe . . . .

VIII. Thomas Randolph, *Hey for Honesty*
(c. 1630/1651)

[*Enter* Penia *Poverty*, Higgen, Termock, Brun,
Caradock, *and an Army of Rogues.*]

Pen. So, so, well spoke, my noble English Tatter,
Lead up the Vant-guard, muster up an army,
An army royal of Imperial Lice.
Hig. And J will be the *Scanderbeg* of the Company,
5   The very Tamberlane of this ragged rout;
Come follow me my Souldiers ——
Brun. Yaws grand Captain, sir, suft and fair; gar
away, there be gewd men in the Company. Aies
Captain, for aies have more Scutch Lice, then thou
10   hast English creepers, or He Brittish Goats about
him.
Hig. What then? my Lice are of the noble breed,
Sprung from the *Danes, Saxons* and *Normans* blood;
True English born, all plump and all well favour'd:
15   Take warning then good sir, be not so proud
As to compare your Vermine sir, with ours.
Ter. Pleash ty shit grash, let nedder nodder of them
my shit Empresse have te plash of ty Captain, J am
te besht of edder odder. J have seen te fash of te
20   vild *Irish. Termock* knows vat it is to fight in the
Bogs like a valiant Costermonger, up to the Nosh
in ploud. Not to make much prittle and prattle to
none purposh, *Termock* has fight under *Oneale*,
for her King and Queen in te wars. Vat, J speak
25   tish by te Shoes of *Patrick*, if that *Termock* be the
Captain, thou shalt beat ty foes to peeces and
pashes.

Carad. Is *Caradock* no respected amongst her; Her
Lice are petter a pedecree as the gooddst of them
30 all. Her Lice come *ap Shinkin, ap Shon, ap Owen,
ap Richard, ap Morgan, ap Hugh, ap Brutus, ap
Sylvius, ap Eneas,* and so up my shoulder. An't her
Lice will not deshenerate from her petticree pretious
Coles. Her ancestors fought in the Wars of *Troy,*
35 by this Leek, as lustily as the Lice of *Troilus.* Nay,
by St. *Taffie,* the Lice of *Hector,* were but Nits in
comparison of her magnanimous Lice. Do not dis-
parage her nor her Lice, if her love her guts in her
pelly.
40 *Ter.* But if *Termock* have no Lish, sall he derefore
not be te Captain? Posh on her Lish. *Termock* hash
none grash a *Patrick*; no such venemous tings vill
preed in hish Country.
Hig. I will be Captain, for my Robes are martiall:
45 True martiall Robes, full of uncureable wounds.
My Doublet is adorned with thousand fears,
My Breeches have endured more storms and tempests
Then any man's that lyes perdue for Puddings.
I have kept Sentinel every night this twelve moneth;
50 Beheaded Ducks and Geese, spitted the Pigs,
And all to Victual this camp of Rogues.
Carad. 'Faith, and her clothes are as ancient a petti-
cree as thine, her fery Dublet is coshen sherman to
Utter Pendragons Sherken, or else *Caradock* is a
55 fery rogue by Saint *Taffie.*
Pen. You shall not thus contend, who shall be Captain;
I'le do't my self, Come follow me brave Souldiers.
Brun. I faith! she is a brave Virago mon.
Carad. By St. *Taffie,* she is an *Amashon,* a *Debora,*
60 a *Brunduca,* a *Joan* of *Oleance, Pucelle de Dieu,*
a *Mall Cutpurse,* a *Long-meg* of *Westminster.*
Ter. She sall be te Captain, for all tee, or any odder
in English lond.

54 *Utter*] utter

Hig. Whips on you all! follow the Fem[in]ine gender?
65   Fight under th' Ensigne of a Petticoat?
An act unworthy such brave spirits as we:
Remember our old Vertues, shall we forget
Our ancient Valours? Shall we in this one action
Stain all our honour, blur our reputations:
70   Can men of such high fortunes daign to stoop
To such dishonourable terms? How can our thoughts
Give entertainment to such low designes?
My spirits yet are not dissolv'd to whey,
J have no soule, so poor as to obey,
75   To suffer a smock rampant to conduct me.
Brun. Aife thou's keep a mundring mandring, mon,
i'se gang to *Edinborow.* The Deill lead your army
for *Brun,* aies no medle, Adieu, adieu.
Carad. Ah *Brun!* Blerawhee, blerawhee.
80 *Ter.* Ah *Brun, Brun!* Shulecrogh, fether vilt thou,
fether vilt thou?
Brun. What yaw doing mon to call *Brun* back; and
you be fules, I'le stay no lenger.
Carad. Ah *Brun, Brun!* shall be Captain, by all te
85   green Sheese in the Moon. *Brun* shall be Captain
for *Caradock,* if her would not give place to *Brun,*
her heart were as hard as *Flint-shire.*
Ter. Brun sall be te besht in te company, if tere were
a tousand tousand of 'um.
90 *Hig.* I'le not resigne my right, J will be Captain.
'Tis fit I should: Hath not my valour oft
Been try'd, at *Bridewell* and the *Whipping-post?*
Pen. Let *Higgen* then be Captain, his sweet tongue
And powerfull rhetorick may perswade the Rout.

105

IX. Maurice Cuffe, *The Siege of Ballyally Castle* (1642)

Aftar this the enemy would daily in our sight drae
forth there skenes and swordes, flurishing them, shwering many daingeroes othes that ear long thaye would
drae us forth and hack us to peeces, terming us
5 pewritan rogges, and all the base names that might
bee invented, vowing that shortly Sir Philem O'Neale,
and at lest 40,000 souldars, would com in to Thomond
and not leve a Protestant living, praing hartely for
hem, pretending that thaie then fought for hem, but
10 within a short time aftar thaye pretended that thaye
were wholy the Queenes armey, and that shee and
har mothar was in the north aiding them, but noe
Protestant admited to luck uppon har. This nott
suddenly altard, and then thaie were all for the King,
15 vowing depely that thaie had his Majesty's comishon
for what thaye did, and that thaye were his Majesty's
Cathelick foreces. To expres there base and wicked
termes were soe tedious and base that it were abell to
shame the readar to heere there wicked inventions and
20 damnable curses.

Now the enemi having finished there two sowes and
there letheren great peece, thaie brings them within
oure sight of the castell, and then sendes Captaine
Henry O'Gradey, of Cnockany, of the county of Lim-
25 rick, to sumen the castell; and being demanded by
som that were upon the battellment warding, what
athorety hee had to demand it, or right or claime he
could laie two it? Whereupon hee anshwerd that hee
had commission from his Majesty to banesh all the
30 Protestants of the Kingdom of Irland. Heere upon,

without furthar excamenation, there was a bullet sent
from the castell by one of the wardars to exsamen his
cumishon, which went through his thigh, but he made
shift to rumbel to the bushes and there fell doune,
35 but only laye by it sixteene wickes, in which time
unhapely it was cured.

This evening a poore maid that foremarly came
stript to the castell, being desiroes to venture to an
aunte she had at Balecare Castell, living with Mr.
40 Coalpes, had noe sonar began this har jurny, and got
without musket shot, but was by the enemie taken
and caried before there comandars, whome did putt
har to much torture to make har revell what secresey
she knew of the castell, and lickwaies whome it was
45 shot at the foresaid Gradey in the morning; the which
she was farced to confes, the partey being Andrew
Chapling minstar. This daie thaie advanst there sowes
and recovard har with in the outtar trench of the
castell iland, the forme and biggnes of the said sow
50 being as followeth:

The great sow was 35 foote long and 9 foote
broade; it was made upon 4 wheeles mad of whole
timbar, bound aboutt with hoopes of iron, there axell
trees where one she run was great round bars of iron,
55 the beames she was bult upon being of timbar. Thaie
had cros beames within to worck with there levars,
to forse har along as thaie plesed to gide har. The
hindar part of the sow was left open for there men
to goe in and outt at. The fore parte of the sow had
60 4 dowres, 2 in the ruffe and 2 one the lowar parte,
which did hang upon great iron huckes, but were not
to open tell thaye came close to the wale of the castell,
where thaie intended to worck through the castell
with there tooles thaie had provided. The ruffe of the
65 sow was bult lick the ruffe of a howse, with a very
sharp ridge; the lowar part as the wales of a howse.
She was dubell plancked with manie thik oken

planckes, and driven very thick with 5 stroke nailes, which nailes cost 5^{li} being intended for a howse of
70 corection which should have bin bult at Inish. This sow was lickwaies covard ovar with 2 rowes of hides and 2 rowes of sheepe skinnes, soe that noe musket bullet or steele arow could pearse it, of which triell was often made.

75 The lesar sow was mad only to goe before to cleere the waie, being but 6 foote long and 3 foote brod, bult strong, as above, only run but upon one whele lick a wheele barow, and cheefely inployd to goe for vittell for the great sow to the camp, and for any to
80 com to the bigg sow when thaie desired.

The said peece was aboutt 5 foote in length, not bult upon caredge, but fastened in a stocke of timber. This goon thaie planted in the great trench, neere the castell, to be redy when thaie found accation to
85 discharge har, the dimetrie being aboutt 5 inches; the lethar thaie made har withall was leetell bettar then halfe tand. Now having fineshed these inventions,

Sir Danell O'Brien gives advies this night, being dark, to make divars firres about oure sight, where by
90 wee might gase upon them and neglect oure charge, and in the mene for forty or more musketteeres to steele beyand the castell, and to get into the hadgard, and there to make sheltars of the corne and stone, both to defend shottes and sheltar themselves, by
95 which menes thaie might bar us from wattar and liberty of goeing outt, which plot, in regard of the dark night, tuck effect. This night thaye lickwaies intrenched themselves one the north sid of the castell within peternell shott of the castell, where thaye
100 planted thee fore said peece, so that now wee were soe compast in that wee were not abell to step forth of dore nor recovar any watar. The next morning thaie made triell of there lethern gun at us, but shee only gaue a great report, having 3^{li} of powthar in har, but
105 lett fly backwarde the bullet remaining within.

108

Níor chian dóibh annsin an tan do-chunncadar óglaoch gallda chuca.

"*Cia an fear gallda úd chuguinn?*" *ar fear díobh.*

"*As aithnid damhsa é,*" *ar fear eile, "is é Roibín*
5 *an Tobaca é siúd, agas is maith an tobaca bhíos aige do ghnáth.*"

"*Ceannócham cuid de,*" *ar Bernard O Bruic, "agas cia aguinn laibheórus Béarla ris?*"

"*Mise féin,*" *ar Tomás.*

10 *Táinig an t-óglaoch gallda, agas beannuigheas go ceannsa, agas adubhairt:* "God bless you, Thomas, and all your company."

Do fhreagair Tomás dó go neamhthuaisceartach, agas as eadh adubhairt: "Pleshy for you, pleshy, good
15 man Robin."

"*Dar anmuin mo mháthar,*" *ar Bernard O Bruic, "do dhubhshloigis rogha an Bhéarla!*"

Do thionólsad cách 'na thimpchioll, ag machtnughadh uim Bhéarla Thomáis.

20 "*Fiafruigh cunnradh an tobaca,*" *ar Bernard.*

Do labhair Tomás, agas as eadh adubhairt: "What the bigg greate *órdlach* for the what so penny, for is the la yourselfe for me?"

Adubhairt Roibín: "I know, Thomas, you aske
25 how many enches is worth the penny," *agas do thóguibh a dhá mhéar mar chomhartha, agas adubhairt* "two penny an ench."

"*Dar láimh mo chairdios Críost, maith an cunnradh,*" *ar Tomás.*

30 "*Créad é?*" *ar Diarmuid Dúr.*

"*Ordlach ar an dá phinginn,*" *ar Tomás.*

"*Déana tacuigheacht oruinn,*" *ar cách.*

"*Do-dhéan,*" *ar Tomás, agas adubhairt*: "Is ta for meselfe the mony for fart you all my brothers here."

Adubhairt Roibín, "I thanke you, honest Thomas, you shall command all my tobaco."

"Begog, I thanke you," *ar Tomás.*

Fuair Tomás an tobaco ar a fhocal, agas tug do chách é.

XI. *The Fingallian Dance* (1650–60)

On a Day in the Spring,
As I went to Bolring
   To view the jolly Daunceirs,
They did trip it so high
5 (Be me shole!), I did spee
   Six C—— abateing Seav'n hairs.

But wondering on 'ame,
Fat make 'em so tame
   Fen de catch at their Plack-keet,
10 The Maids of y-yore
Wou'd y-cree, and y-rore,
   And y-make a foul Rac-keet.

But fire take 'ame,
They made me ashame,
15   And when I went home to me weef
And told her the Chaunce
Of the Maids in the Daunce,
   "Peace thy prateing," sayd shee, "for dee Leef!"

9 Plack-keet] Plack-keel   12 a] o

XII. Richard Head, *Hic et Ubique* (1663)

[Patrick announces a visitor to Kiltory, who is totally absorbed in his love for Cassandra.]

Patr[ick]. Moistere, here is one beating de dore, wou'd make speak for dy shelf.

Kilto[ry]. Yet I cannot but love her, her sweet Idea is too deeply rooted in my heart, so easily to be
5   pul'd out; never did any eies behold a fairer object, shee's now the sole and continual subject of my cogitations.

Patr. O yea, between me and God achree, my Moistare will make mad for my shelf. Upjack and sup-
10   jack; rhoo fuate de Deole ale thee.

Kilto. No I must smother the ripe sallies of my inflam'd desires, and study what it is to be man again, and how much these admired pieces of imperfection fall short of his merit. . . . Great *Mars*
15   assist me, and conjure this Devil love out of me.

Patr. By my Gossops hand, and my Faders shaddle, *Kilphatrick* will be mush fear by and preshently, to see my Moistare make conjuration. *Arra Moistare* by St. Sonday, 'tis ill kind for dy Faders shild,
20   to be making speech wit dy shelf, and no body. Be me fet, and be, I do hate de De-vil, as I do *Olivers* soujer, and if he come presently, my shelf will run away. *Arraball*.

Kilto. *Patrick*.
25   *Patr*. Sha, sha, *ta tuggemi Moistare*.

20 body.] body,   21 fet,] fet

Patr. Dere is one wu'd fain be speaking for dee.

[*Exeunt.*

Kilto. What's the matter?

[Patrick describes the seduction of his wife by a pikeman.]

Enter Patrick *crying.*

Patr. Fuillilaloo!

Kiltor. How now Sirrah?

30 *Patrick.* The donny fellow make buse for my Moister.

Kilt. What Fellow?

Patrick. He was no Sougare nor Musketteer, but a
greyshy guddy hang of a Peek-man.

Kilt. And what of him?

35 *Patr.* Fuy by St. *Patrick* agra, he put de fuckation
upon my weef. I will tell dee tale if thou wilt Glun
ta mee. I came in wid my pishfork upon my back,
thou know'st, and I see a greyshy guddy hang upon
my weef, and I did creep in like a michear, to the

40 wattles upon de loft abow thou know'st, and there
I did see putting the great fuck upon my weef, as
if thy own shelf was there Moister; and because
I wu'd make haste, I fell down upon 'em, and leek
to have more than half break my neck; then wid

45 my pishfork I clap him upon de Narsum, and I did
make sharge for him in the Kings name, thou
know'st, to stay dere til I fetch the Cunt——stable;
but before I came, this chureeh crave Ruagh make
run away for himshelf: and looky there Moister.

50 *Kilt.* Why what wudst have me doo?

Patr. Feat can take my weef to thine own shelf, for
Patrick will not lie with his weef *Shuane* again.

Kilt. Why wudst a have me lie with her?

Patr. Yea feat if thou wilt.

55 *Kilt.* Oh Sir, 'tis so great a favour, I shall never be

36–7 Glun ta mee] Glunt amee.   48 chureeh crave Ruagh]
chvereeh craveRauge

113

able to make your brogues a requital. However take this [*kicks him*] in part of satisfaction; nay, this [*kicks him again*] too, that I may come out of your debt the sooner.

[Kiltory intervenes to stop a fight between two of Mrs Hopewell's suitors.]

60 *Kilt.* Madam, I'le quickly do you that courtesie, and by so doing, I may pleasure my self; her beauty hath already captivated me [*aside*]; *Villians*, Expect not the honour to fall by my hands. *Patrick* go cut their throats.

65 *Patr.* For *fuat* joy, to put the *Kill* upon my shelf.
Kilt. Go sirrah, or I'le cut your's
[*turns to Mrs.* Hopewel]
Patr. O yea, for Christis shake, make help for my shelf moyster, or else poor *Kilpatrick* will be made Kil upon.

70 *Kilt.* To provoke cowards too much, is the way to make 'em desperate. [*Beats 'em of*] sirrah, did not you tell me you cud fight, upon that account I entertain'd you.
Patr. Yes feat, at cuff, or skean.

75 *Kilt.* None serves me but those that durst blow in a charged pistol, and valew a sword no more than a cudgel.
Patr. See for this, by got a chree he wu'd put some lead in my belly but there was no sharge powder
80 upon the pishtol, he did make intention to cut off my head, feat.
Kilt. Be gone, I shall talk with you some other time, . . .

[Kiltory resolves to make over his estate to Mrs Hopewell as an earnest of his affection.]

Kilt. . . . Every minute of Delay seems to me an Age,

62 [*aside*];] ; (*aside*)

till I have fulfilled your request. *Pathrick* fetch me
85   a Scrivener presently.

Path. Scriboner, arra fuat de Devel; Scribner — my
shelf make no meyning for Dat at all.

Kilt. A Fellow that writes Bills and Bonds.

Path. Bills and Ponds! feir De vaiter is.

90   *Kilt.* Why a Clark then, thou Blockhead.

Path. Arra fuat de Tevil wilt dou do vid de Cleark?

Kilt. That, Goodman Raskal.   [*Kicks him.*

Path. If I make tell so for him before, he will not
come for me afterward.

95   *Kilt.* Why thou Bog-trotting Beetle-head, tell him,
I have business for him then.

Path. Arrah fuat de Devil must my shelf go make
fetch for de Clark, to put sheat upon my moyster,
and *Pathrick* himself.

                       [*Exit* Pathrick.

[Kiltory surrenders his estate, only to discover that Mrs Hopewell has a husband waiting to take her away.]

Enter Thrivewell.

100 *Thrive.* Save ye All: come Widow, are the Writings
      drawn?

Kilt. Here they are: and take notice that in these I
make a free surrender of my whole Estate to the
use of Mrs. *Anne Hopewell.*

105 *Thrive.* Goods and Chattels?

Kilt. All, all.

Path. Ub, ub, ub, boo! arrow moyster, wilt tow give
away all dine own tings, and leave noting upon me
poor *Kilpathrick*: fuate shall my wife *Juane* do for
110 de Cow dat make de buttermilk, and de bony clabber for dy child and my shelf, and de mulaghane,
and de garraane baane, and de garrane dough, thou

95 Bog-trotting] Bog-trotting,   98 fetch] fecth   110 buttermilk]
buutermilk

didst make promise for me.

Kilt. Sirrah leave thy howling.

115 *Path.* My shelf no howle, me make speak for you: By St. *Pathrick* and St. *Shone Batty*, my shelf will make no servant for de.

Thrive. Come, come, Sign, sign:

Kiltory *delivers the writings to Mrs.* Hopewell

So, so.

*   *   *

120 *Path.* Shoole a crogh, manam a dioule, thou greisie micheer, by my soulwation joy a chree, y told dee, de English vil put de sheat pon efry podyes.

Kilt. Woman was the first that ever took the Devils counsil, and first communicated it to man, to the
125 ruine of both their terrestrial happinesse; . . . 'twas well she had not cheated me out of my soul too.

[*Exit.*

Path. May starfing come to her sheeks, strepoh gran-ach, and may her fader's shild make dye in de prishon.   [*Exit.*

122 vil] vid

XIII. *Purgatorium Hibernicum* (1670–75)

Amongst this traine, who (thinke you) espied he
But his old mistres, Madam Dydy? —
That pin'd to death, the fawneing strapp!,
Some say for love, some of a clapp,
5   When Nees from Lusk turn'd helm alarbor
And tooke up quarters in his harbour.
Nees, glideing at her through the shade,
A sheep's eye cast from a calfe's head;
Who soon the Prince's courage dashes,
10 For she did looke as pail as ashes,
Did pull him out on's seaven sences.
"Sure, sure!" sayes Nees, "dis me old vench is!"
But when he drew more neare her qua[r]ters
And knew her by her *suggain* garters,
15 *"Ful Dea, ro,* dou unlucky jade,
Ill chance upon dee! Art thou dead?
Fat devill vas be in dee, vench?
Vas he soe hot is cou'd no quench
De flame?" "Indeed, oh no!, but Nees chief
20 Occasion is of all dis mischeif."
"But, be de hand of Gilarnoo,
By fader's sole, I tell de[e] true,
And be!, more sure [I] tell dee still,
I vent avay against me vill,
25 Comanded bee superior powers,
Is make me h[a]unt dese *donny* bowers;
And fate!, and be!, I never tought
Mee company had ever brought

14 *suggain*] Suggam   15 *Ful*] Fut   21 Gilarnoo] Galarna
24 I vent] avont   28 brought] trought

Such after-clapps! *Arra*, but stay!
30   Fat devill make it goe avay?
She cannot hold one touch, butt itching
She's after bee to run a-bit[c]hing!
Hold! Must she passe so vid her beares?
Nees is not see soe many yeares.
35   If it be soe dis good blad first
I'le [* * *] my Deedy for a maid first.
Shall ne're be said, me owne suit-heart,
Dat ve two shall with dry lips part.
Before dou goe, be me salvation!,
40   Nees vill imploy dee occupation,
Untill ve take a little pastime —
A parting kisse: dis is de last time!"
    The Prince's passion here was spent,
And rested in this complement;
45   But Dydy, like a sullen sow,
Fix't on the grownd her angry brow,
And noe more regards his babling
Than shee were a rocke of Mabline;
For, ever since the last *crangore*,
50   An inward grudge to th' Prince she boare,
For a small token he had lent her,
For ('twas without all peradventure
Belived by most) the active squire
Had set her lower roomes afire,
55   Which caused her to suspect the scullion
Had still a spice of the strangullion.
Have you seen porks in yoalk of Luske,
When they doe excer[c]ise theire tuske
Att trough? grunnt, foam, and seem to bee
60   Mov'd with impatience? — soe shee,
Chaffing and foaming att the mouth,

33 she] the   34 see] soe   37 said] laid   suit-heart] sait heart
47 babling] Balling   50 she] the   55 scullion] Sculline
56 strangullion] Strangillin

Did spite her venom at the youth.
　　"I, Nees," sayes she in mighty snuffe,
　　"And be! Is tink it varm enough,
65　If dou can shance but to find out
　　Dee old consort to have a bout —
　　And den, fen dou has play'd de vagge,
　　To give mee, as before, de bagge!
　　Butt I will vatch de vales, Nees,
70　And putt foile on dee, by dis chees!"
　　(Since which it to [a] proverbe grew,
　　When burne-breech hacknes will not doe.)
　　"And nowe in earnest let mee tell ho[w]
　　Dou art but an unvordy fellow,
75　A *tory* runagade and fo,
　　To use an honest voman so!"
　　　"Sure, sure!" sayes Nees, "she does but jeast!
　　It's not de nature of de beast!
　　Praie dee [come] here, mee joly rogue,
80　And gave [me] de one litle *poge*
　　For old acquaintance, for it's dee
　　Dat is mee only *gra-ma-cree*."
　　　"Kiss mee? Poo! Fart upon dee, Nees!
　　Is may as vel kisse my breesh!
85　I know de[e] vell enough, and bee!
　　'Is de old hawke have de old eye'—
　　Dou know de proverbe. Come noe neare!
　　De scald child, fate!, is feare de fire.
　　And now I know de[e] for a rogue,
90　I scorn de[e], as dirt of me *brogue*." —
　　Belching an oyster in her fist —
　　"I care not dis for all dee grist!"
　　Soe fledd as nimble as the wind
　　(And bid the Prince to kiss behind)

64 it] is　65 can] cam　66 consort] Co :sort　67 vagge] vugge
70 foile] faile　by] dy　76 use] u :　79 Praie] Praise　joly] Johy
84 breesh] breast　90 I scorn] Is : : :n　93 fledd] fleed

95 To Sichy, the old cuckold, nigh,
    Where shee had other fish to fry.
        "Swoop, swoop! *a callagh*, oh!" sayes Nees,
    "De Devill may dee coller spleece.
    'Twix me and Good and de hall door,
100 Dou art a rotten rosted whore!
    No vonder do' it be deare, in trote,
    Fen pole bushell is vort a groat!
    Fen beggars must be after chooseing!
    Marry, come up!, my dirty cousin.
105 I'le see her burne, and Devill have her!,
    'For I creep in her ———— for favour.
    Fat? creep to her? to her? a turd she!
    Since she is soe stout, I'le be soe sturdy!"

97 *callagh*] Cattagh   104 come] Comes

XIV. Thomas Shadwell, *The Lancashire Witches*
(1681/1682)

Enter Smerk *and* Tegue O Divelly.

Smerk. I am all on fire, what is it that Inspires me?
I thought her ugly once, but this morning thought
her ugly. And thus to burn in love already! Sure
I was blind, she is a beauty greater than my fancy
5   e'er could form; a minute's absence is death to me.
Priest. Phaat Joy, dou art in Meditaation and Consideraation upon something? if it be a Scruple upon
thy Conscience, I believe I vill maak it out unto dee.
Smerk. No Sir, I am only ruminating a while; I am
10   inflamed with her affection. O *Susan! Susan!* Ah
me! Ah me!
Priest. Phaat dost dou not mind me? nor put dy
thought upon me? I do desire to know of dy
Faather's Child, what he does differ from de Caa-
15   tholick Church in, by my fait it is a braave Church,
and a gaallant Church (de Devil taak mee) I vill
tell you now, phare is dere such a one? vill you
speak unto me now, Joy; hoh!
Smerk. 'Tis a fine Church, a Church of Splendour,
20   and riches, and power, but there are some things
in it —
Priest. Shome things! Phaat dosht dou taalk of shome
things? By my shoule I vill not see a better Church
in a Shommers day, indeed, dan de Caatholick
25   Church. I tell you there is braave Dignities, and
Promotions too; what vill I shay unto you? by St.
Phaatrick, but I do beleeve I vil be a Cardinal
before I vill have death. Dey have had not one
Eerish Cardinal a great while indeed.

30 *Smerk.* What power is this that urges me so fast? Oh, Love! Love!

Priest. Phaat dosht dou shay, dosht dou love promotions and dignities? den I predee now be a Caatholick. What vill I say unto you more? but

35 I vill tell you, You do shay dat de Caatholicks may be shaved; and de Caatholicks do shay, dat you vill be after being damn'd; and phare is de solidity now of daat, daat dou vill not turne a good Caatholick?

Smerk. I cannot believe there is a Purgatory.

40 *Priest.* No! Phy, I vill tell you what I vill shay unto you, I have sheen many Shoules of Purgatory dat did appear unto me: And by my trot, I do know a Shoule when I do shee it, and de Shoules did speak unto me, and did deshire of me dat I vould

45 pray dem out of that plaashe: And dere Parents, and Friends did give me shome money, and I did pray 'em out. Without money indeed, we cannot pray dem out; no fait.

Smerk. That may not be so hard; but for transub-

50 stantiation, I can never believe it.

Priest. Phaat dosht not beleeve de Cooncel of *Trent*, Joy? dou vilt be damn'd indeed, and de Devil take me, if dou dosht not beleeve it. I vill tell you phaat vill I say to you a Cooncel is infallible; and I tell

55 you, de Cardinals are infallible too, upon occasion, and dey are damn'd Heretick Dogs, by my shoulvaation, dat do not believe every oord dey vill speak indeed.

Smerk. I feel a flame within me; oh Love, Love!

60 whither wilt thou carry me?

Priest. Art thou in love Joy? by my shoule dou dosht Comitt fornicaation; I vill tell you it is a veniall Sinn, and I vill be after absolving you for it: but if dou dosht Comitt Marriage, it is mortall, and dou

65 vilt be damn'd, and bee, fait and trot. I predee now

65 damn'd, and bee,] damn'd and bee

vill dou fornicate and not Marry: for my shaak
now vilt dou fornicate.

Smerk. Sure I am bewitch'd.

Priest. Bewitch'd in love, Aboo! boo! I'll tell you
now, you must taak de Womands Shoe dat dou
dosht Love sho, and dou must maak a Jaakes of it,
dat is to shay, dou must lay a Sirreverence, and be,
in it, and it will maak cure upon dee.

70

72 be,] be

Bryan having been sent in an Errant to a Gentle-
mans house in the Country, fell deeply in Love with
a *Welch* Maid, who belonged to the Kitching there,
sometime after he met a Footman belonging to the
5   same Gentleman; *Bryan* desired him to *tauke* a pot
of *drenk vid him, for a quarter of an hour, vile he
did mauke request to shom Skrivishner to vrite* a
Letter for him to *Vrsula*; which being done, *be me
shoul Y did pray him to shend it upon* Ursula *by de
10   Waaterman indede.*

The Letter.

Shweet Mrs. Ursula,
    Be de ham of me Moddarsh Smock, aund be aul de
Usquebah daat vash drunk at mine Fadersh Vedding;
de Deevil take me indede, but Y be sho much in Lofe
15   vid dee, daat Y cannot go to Bed aul the long Night
for sleeping upon dee; aund Y cannot be upon vaaking
but the Deevil take me, Y do fall upon dreaming
consharning thy shweet shelfe indede, daan do Y tink,
vaat is the matre? vaat is the maatre vid mine awn
20   shelfe; Aund Y do feend it is aal for much Love
consharning dee, in fait: Be me shalwashion Y vill
tall dee vaat Y vill do indede, and Y vill put kish
upon dy faush indeede, and Y vill be for mauking
Child upon dy Body indeede, aund Y will mauke a
25   great del more consharning dee dan dyne own Moddar
in fait. Noow de Deevil tauke de fashion, daat van
two yong Cople of Man and Voman be for coming
togedder vid on anodder, daat dare musht be mauking

upon the great Sherimony of de Presht, aund aul de
30 People to mauke Witnesh upon it: Be me Shoul Y vill
not mauke staying sho long; but Y vill be dyne Husband vidout aal daat now, aund be Shaint *Pautrick*,
Y vill love dee like auny ting indede. Y vill shend to
Tredagh for mine Moddarsh tree Goats, four Sheep,
35 one Filly Mare, and the tauny Coow, and vee will
be for mauking a Daury in *Lincolns-Inn-Fields* be
Chreest, aund vee will mauke Butter and Chese, aund
Eggs, and shell our shelves into Plauce and Conferrmant every day indede. And we vill shing Curds
40 and Crame be Chreest, and Buttar and Eggs, Bony-
Clabber, and Tiff, untel de Coow shall have Cauf,
de Maure shall have Colt, de Goats shall have Kidd,
aund *Ursulah* shall hauve Child indede; Aund dan
vee vill shet up Housh-kepin and be for livein aul
45 togadder, be Chreest, as it is de fashion in mine awn
Country, in fait. Noow de Deevil tauke me, dear Joy,
dou shaut be for sending Aunswer to vaat Y hauve
sent dee by de Skriviwnar, aund if dee vilt mete me
to morrow morning at four of de Clock in de aufter
50 noons, aut de Hole in de Vaal, vee vill go to Bed aund
be Mawrry'd presantly indede, viddout de Charge of
de Vedding, aund de Priests fese be Chreest, aund
vee vill put de grate Chete upon our Parantsh, aund
be me Shoul vee vill be Mawrried, dear Joy; aund
55 none body shaul be vysher for it indede; Aund being
at such dishtansh daat Y cannot come to put Kish
upon dy shweet faush, Y vill put a hoondrad Kishes
upon dish Pauper, and shend me Sharvish, aund me
Affuction to dee indede, and me shalwashion Y vill
60 alwash be

Dine owne **Dear Joy,**

BRYAN.

Y have geeven de Vaaterman Shixpensh to breng it
to dee, to shave de charge of de Penny-Posht in fait.

125

The *Dear Joys* strait began to quake,
Stinking for fear, did Buttons make;
But *Nees* did pour out his Pray'rs
From the very bottom of his ——

5 "Dear Joy, St. *Patrick*, vil dou hear
Dee own Cheeld *Nees* make his Pray-ere,
Dat never did, or I'm a Teef,
So much before in all mee Leef.
Dear Joy, who sees our woful Case,

10 Will dou sit still upon dee Ars,
And see dese *Dutch* and *English* Rogues
Strip off our Trouses,[1] and our Brogues:[2]
Possess our Crates,[3] and dy poor Cheeld *Nees*,
And Culleens[4] flee, like flocks of Wild-gees.

15 De Devil take me, now I swear
(Dear Gossop) by mee own Mak-keer
Nees vill (if he no better speed)
Make hang upon himself indeed.
What though of Ready[5] nere a Plack

20 Yet many a plugg of good Toback
It cost me to come to dis Port;
And not a Turd de better for't:
Ycome like fool, ygo vidout
My skeal, vid finger in my mout;

25 Since I have seen dy own sweet Face,
I know doul't never be so base.
Derefore God bless it, Oh! Padeen.[6]

[1] Breeches.   [2] Shoes.   [3] Cabbin, or Irish Hut.   [4] Bore.
[5] Mony.   [6] *Patrick*.

2 for fear,] for, fear

126

Vill dou take a little for de *Queen*?
My Dear, my Joy, my Cram-ma-cree,[1]
30   I'll make much Prayer upon dee;
And all de rest ycoshere[2] here
It's now full teem to give Quar-teer.
And also dee, my prescious Nun,
Yknows what never is to come;
35   Grant dat I may but live at home,
And (fate) is *Nees* but ask his own;
To be my stay in my own Nation,
Without Exile or Transplantation:
To be restord without Reprisal,
40   Or Court of Clamper[3] to try Title;
Lest Innocence being question'd
Poor *Nees* shou'd chance to be postpond;
Or come in Rere of *Dutch* Debenturers,
Or be kickt out by *French* Adventurers.
45   If we ben't mortgag'd for a Summ,
And there's for *Nees* in *Ireland* room;
In peace to hold my few A-ceers,[4]
And Images of my Fa-deers:
And had I but one Cow, I tell dee,
50   In all the World, vidout my Belly,
I'de give it, fait, vid all my heart,
T'njoy my Land, or any part;
My Banniclabber[5] and Pottados,
Without these *French* and *Dutch* Granados.
55   And by my Gossops hand, I fate,
I vill an Abby Dedicate
To my Dear Joy, vidout no words,
As big as Monastery of Swords;
And to dy name make Holy-day,

[1] Dear Heart.   [2] Lodge.   [3] Court of *Claims.*   [4] Acres.
[5] Butter-milk.

51 it,] it

60   When all de Monaghans shall play:
     Ordain a Statute to be Drunk,
     And burn Tobacco free as Spunk;[1]
     And (fat shall never be forgot)
     In Vsquebah, St. *Patrick*'s Pot;
65   To last for never in our Nation,
     On pain of Excommunication:
     And unto dee, my precious Whore,
     A place to hang up dy Pic-ture.
     Much Grace upon dee ugly fash,
70   Where ev'ry one shall say a Mass;
     Where dy Mi-ra-cles shall be sung,
     By [e]very ting dat has no tongue.
     Only I pray dee now, my Dear,
     Let not dy Ars make a Clam-peer;[2]
75   Lest vid a Fart dou blow it from me,
     And put de great Moccage upon me.
     Nor let de Vind dy Notes profane,
     But sing dyselfe de sweet Cro-naan."[3]
     And so at length he brought about
80   An end of praying with his Mout.

           *   *   *

     "Pox on dy Tail"[4] (says *Nees*) "I tro;
     Vell vas dy vont for doing so;
     Spereen,[5] and an ill Chaunce upon it,
     I tought no better voud come on it;
85   Too vell I knew, by what's not past,
     'Twould come unto dis pass at last.
     But since no Balsom for this Wound
     Is left for *Nees* above de ground,
       "One Courtesie I must demand,
90   Since here's de Passage to dat Land;

[1] Tinder.   [2] Noise.   [3] Song.   [4] BRAULER A SKEAL.
[5] Despair.

And here is *Nees* beg dy Par-doon,
Dat I choos dee for my Gar-soon;
Dat I may pass de black Va-teer,
Once more to see my old Fa-deer;
95 Good[1] rest his Shoul, and Body too,
Is ly vidin de ground below.
O Hone! fait many a time, I swear,
Vas carry it on his Shoul-deer.
If dou believe me, fat I say,
100 My Bones yfeel it to dis day;
And fate, when he was after dee,
Vas give it charge to come to see:
And I meeself great Eye[2] have still,
To make performsh upon his Will.
105 Now for de Son, and de Fa-deer,
Conduct me to de black Va-teer.
For dou can do't, for fait dou wou'd not
Be a right Nun, if dou understood not
De next and ready way to Hell,
110 You Women know dat way too vell:
For I would try, if dat dere be
In Hell for *Nees* a Vacancy;
Since Soldering vill do no grace,
To try to get an Evidaunsh-Place:
115 And I deserve dat favour sure,
As vell as *Dermot o Con-noor*."

[1] God.   [2] DEULMORE IRICISM, Great Eye, great desire.

Teede

O broder *Teague*, and *Teague* my Roon,
Arra vat shall ve do full quickly and soon;
De brave *Ingalish* Army is coming ve hear,
And brave General *Scomberg* in de front vill appear:
5 O den ve must leave all our Citys Dear-Joys,
And yield them unto those *Ingalish* brave boyes;
    Because dat der Canons will make such a noise,
    Dey'l spoil all de *French*, and our *Ierish* Imploys.

Tho now new Devil in bot *Corke* and *Kingshail*,
10 Wid *Galloway*, *Limbrick*, and bony *Youghail*,
And all de Citys in de North but von,
And dats *London-derry*, dats quite lost and gone.
Dat plash our Army most sadly destroys,
Because all dats in it are Protestant boys;
15   Der Canons against us do make such a noise,
    Dat dey kill all de *French*, and our *Ierish* Dear-joys.

Den now broder *Teague*, vat more can I shay,
I fear dat King *Yeamus* he will soon run away,
Ven he hears dat Duke *Scomberg* and his Army is
                    come,
20 He'll sheek for *Fader Petre* to help him to *Rome*,
Vhile ve shall be left to Shaint *Patrick* to pray,
Dat he vud be pleas'd for to help us I shay;
    But der Canon against us so strongly will play,
    Dat unto de Bogs, we must all take our way.

25 Now *Tyrconel* lies shick of de old Cursed Plot,
Vhile ve for his knavery shall ne'er be forgot;
Now the Priests are all ready to bite off der nailesh,
To tink of de losh of de young Prince of *Wailesh*,
Vhile ve must be forsht for to stand the deveat,
30 For der putting on ush dat curshed great Sheat,
    For der Canons against us will make such a noise,
    Dey'll spoil all our shaying, Come on my brave Boys.

Teagues *Answer to* Teede.

Alas broder *Teede* dis thing it is hard,
And ve of our Lands now vill all be debarr'd,
35 Dey'll make all our Lords, and our Shentry bow,
And vat vill become of us, I do not vell know;
Dey'll make us surrender both City and Town,
And yield 'em to de honour of *Ingalands* great Crown;
    For der Canons against us so strongly will play,
40   Ve shall not have hearts to withstand 'em one fray.

And vhen de whole power the *Ingalish* hash got,
O den broder *Teede* vat vill fall to our lot,
I fear dat de sheif and de best of our fellows,
Dat are left, vill be forsht for to die on de Gallows,
45 Because in Rebellion so long we have stood,
Against all de *Ingalish* and Protestant good;
    Der Canons against us will tunder so loud,
    Ve shall not be able our selves for to shroud.

131

De boggs dey vill signify little to us,
50　For being so Loyal to Second *Yeamus*,
Altho dat our Priests and our Shesuits swore,
Dat ve should have Lands and Livings *Gillore*,
Not only in *Ireland*, but *Ingaland* too,
Dat makes us in shorrow look pityful blue;
55　　Because by der Canons dose Slats from us flew,
Voud the Tivel had had all dose Jesuite crew.

So to conclude, de best vay dat I know for to take,
Is to pray to Shaint *Patrick* our Peace for to make,
And quite leave off fighting for *Yeamus* late King,
60　And put Ropes round our Necks, and repent for our
sin.
So dus by repentance ve may be forgiven,
And find mercy bot from great King *Willam* and
Heaven.
Tho ve have Rebell'd at dish Curshed great rate,
Yet ve may find mercy of *Ingalands* great State.

56 Voud] Vuod

XVIII. John Dunton, *Report of a Sermon* (1698)

Ecclesiasticus de won-and-fortiet shapter and turd
vearse: *Nolito metuere judicium mortis; memento
quæ te ante fuerunt et quæ superventura sunt tibi;
hoc judicium a Deo omni carni.*

5   Deare Catolicks, you shee here de cause dat is after
bringing you to dis plaace: 'tis come bourying you
are de corp, de cadaver, of a verie good woman, God
knows!, fwom cruel deat hate devoure. And for because it would not be deshent nor handsom to put
10 underground like one of de vulgus or commonality de
sheild of her faader and mother (fwose souls God
rest in Heaven!), I am here as you shee to doe my
one function and occupaation at dis time; and dat
I may doe woordy of de holy caracter I beare, and
15 for the good of your souls, help me, deare Christians, to cal upon Holy Mary, Mooder of God. *Ave
Maria, &c.*

Nolito metuere judicium mortis, &c. Fwen de first
man and voman God did shend upon de vorld did
20 doe dat fwich deir Holly Maker did forbade 'em, and
eate a poore shilly bitt of apple dat vas not of woort
tree straws, dey dereby were lost Paradis, and all the
recreaations of dat sweet plaace. Shure enuff, deir
hearts were heavy and shad enuff, to be turned out
25 of it; for, Catolicks and Cristians, vould not none of
yourshelves be much grieve to be trust out of your one
houses or possessions? — aldough none of you have,
or ever shaw, such a garden as dat; beshides, deat was

1 *Ecclesiasticus*] Ecclesiasticis

anoder paine added to deir punishments. Well, fwat
30 voud you have of it? Deir hearts were full, full of
shadness and sorrow, and God de Faader, sheeing
deir contrition, told for deir comfort, de sheed of de
voman should break de sherpent's head—*quod semen
mulieris frangeret caput serpentis*, as it is wid de
35 original. Now, fwo tinke you was dat voman? Ochone,
deare Cristians, fwo voud it be but Blessed Mary
Virgo Shempiterna, Mooder of Savior Jesus Christ,
Queen of Heaven, to fwom, and befor fwom, all
angells, kings, and queens doe bow down and doe
40 vorship.

Now, after dis promise, de holy prophet Ecclesiasticus,
to keep up oure hearts from shinkeing, tells us: *Nolite
timere judicium mortis*, feare not the sentence of deat.
For fwy? Remember all dose who are gone before
45 you, and dose dat must come after you: dey died,
and soe must all dose fwo come after you. Was not
Darenus de greatest man upon eart, and Alexander
de Greate greater nor [h]e? And fwat became of
dem? Fwy, dey are gone — *abierunt in pulverem* —
50 meer dust and ashes! And fwere are deir crowns, and
all de gay tings made dem so proud? Fwy, I tell you
dey are dust and ashes, *pulvis et umbra fumus*, as
Bellarmine, dat great shampion of Holly Church, dot
well observe. Fwat avails Sampson's strengt? Had not
55 we great races of gyants in this country of our one?
And fwere now is Oscar, Nosheen, or Fan MacCool?
Fwy, dust and ashes! Did not Cræsus, fwo vas de
richest man upon eart, dye too? Ay, ay, Catolicks,
dey al died, and so did de famous saint and apostle
60 of our nation, Saint Patrick. Now, Christians, if great-
nes, or riches, or hollyness, or strent, could not keep
dose peoples now reshted from deat's all-dewoureing
mout, ohone, fwy vould he spare any of us? Deir is
no Patrick or Bridget among you (no, not won!) fwose
65 prayers or dewotions can prevaile against it; is none

of you strong enough, or stout enough, to owercome
him, or wise enough, or cunning enough, to sheate
him — no, no, 'tis a shad ting, not won! Well, den,
fwat's to be done? Fwy, noting at all!—only *memento*
70 *quæ te ante fuerunt.* Dey all are desheas, deat took
dem in his claws, and so it will sherve you but de
shame sauce it did all de vorld before you, for *hoc est
judicium Domini omni carni.*

Now, Christians, dere be two sorts of deat according
75 [to] de holly faders, won of de body (fwich is dat I
vas now telling you of), de oder of the spirit; and many
be de sorts of deat fwich happen to de body. As Saint
Augustin hate it, *una wia est witæ, moriendi mille
figuræ.* Aldough you have but won way of borning
80 into dis vorld, dere are a tousand ways and a tousand
tricks to sheat you out of it: you dye wid feaver or
long shickness, another maybe has a trust with a
meddoag or sword in his guts, a turd has long age to
kill him (as our deare shister here before you), and
85 many more tings *quæ nunc præscribere longum* —
fwich are now to long to rehears. Vwell, den, de deat
of de spirit is but won kind; but O Cristians, may
Mary and holly Saints and Confessors by deir prayers
deliver you from dat shad deat! 'Tis a deat you will
90 be ever, ever alive in, and yet you wil never dye,
dough you are always dyeing: dat is de deat of the
spirit, fwich de vwicked hypocrite, de heretick, and
sinners vwill fall into. And fwat is dat? Fwy, dat is
Hel, and de Divel, fwere you'l be trown into [a] greate
95 lake or lough of burning bremston. Did you never
shee how de fox, fwen he makes scape from de hounds
dat are barkeing after him, runs into de hole in de
eart? And how de huntsmen doe burn wet straw at
de moute of de hole, till he is almost shoak't, and
00 forced out to his destruction and deat? Fwy, soe it is
wid de shinners in Hell, dey are shoaked like so many
bees wid de smoke of de bremstone, for all dat dey

135

are still alive nor cannot get out, but are always
shoakeing and smuddering in dat darck place pre-
105 par'd *pro Satana et eius angelis* — for de Divel and
his angels.

Now, Cristians, sheeing *fashilis deshen[s]us Averni,
sed revocare gradus shuperasque evadere ad auras,
hic labor, hoc opus,* as a learned poiet hate it — dat is,
110 'tis easy ting to goe down hill into dat pit, but to come
out againe is not soe easye; I say, Cristians, seeing
dis, are you not mad fwen you will be giving yourshelves and sweet shouls to Divel, as you doe fwen you
are curseing and sweareing, "Divel taak me!", "Divel
115 break my neck!", "your gossip's hand", &c.? O conshider den of dis, for doe you tinke if Dives were out
of Hell he would ever goe dere againe? No, indeed,
vould he not! But maybe you doe not know fwo Dives
vas: fwy, listen wid me, and I'le tell you fwo he was.
120 He vas a man had greate estate of lands, many cows,
seeps, and horses, did never want any ting in his life,
nor never releave de poore shervants of God, the
priests dat sherve at de altar, but spent all his rents
upon meate and drink, among a company of fwores,
125 and rogues, and knaves, and sheats, and never vould
let poore Lazarus get won moutfull at his gate. Vwel,
dis man for all his riches did dye, and soe did poore
Lazarus too. And fwat becam of dem? Fwy, de man
dat used to vweare his brave scarlet coat wid shilver
130 lace, wid his coasht and hor[s]es, he vwent into dis
bottomless pitt; and Lazarus, dat had not a rag to
cover his quarters, he dye also, and was carryed by
holly angells into Heaven to de boosom of Abraham.

And now, Cristians, you dat have estaats, had you
135 not better give share to the poore shervants of God,
dat vwill pray you out of Purgatory, den to spend all
like Dives, and at last fall to de Divell's share your-

109 *labor*] labore   113 sweet] sweets

shelves? O, let your toughts be often upon doeing
sharity, for *teget multitudinem peccatorum*—it cowers
many, many shins. You shee how God and Mary
Queen of Heaven are angry at your shins: for fwat
greater shine can you have dat dey are angry wid you
den fwen dey widdraw the comforts of the clergye
from you? Are not all the regular clergy banish't out
of your country? And vwill not shome of you shee the
time dat a priest will not be found to doe holly offices
for you? Are your eyes open, and doe not you shee
dese tings comeing upon you, and more too? — as
de prophet Amos hate it (shapter de eight, vearse
eleavent), *Ecce dies veniunt, [dicit Dominus, et mittam
famem in terram: non famem panis, neque sitim
aquœ, sed audiendi verbum Domini.]*

150–2 *dicit . . . Domini*] *illegible in MS.*

XIX. George Farquhar, *The Twin Rivals*
(1702/1703)

[On his return from Germany with his Irish servant Hermes Woudbee discovers that his younger brother Ben has taken over their father's estate.]

Enter Teague *with a Port-Mantel.*
He throws it down and sits on it.

[*Elder Woudbee.*] Here comes my Fellow-Traveller. What makes you sit upon the Port-Mantel, *Teague*? You'll rumple the things.

Te. Be me Shoule, Maishter, I did carry the Port-
5   Mantel till it tir'd me; and now the Port-Mantel shall carry me till I tire him.

E.W. And how d'ye like *London*, *Teague*, after our Travels?

Te. Fet, dear Joy, 'tis the bravest Plaase I have sheen
10   in my Peregrinations, exshepting my nown brave Shitty of *Carick-Vergus.* — uf, uf, dere ish a very fragrant Shmell hereabouts.—Maishter, shall I run to that Paishtry-Cooks for shix penyworths of boil'd Beef?

15   *E.W.* Tho' this Fellow travell'd the World over he would never lose his Brogue nor his Stomach. — Why, you Cormorant, so hungry and so early!

Te. Early! Deel tauke me, Maishter, 'tish a great deal more than almost twelve a-clock.

20   *E.W.* Thou art never happy unless thy Guts be stuft up to thy Eyes.

Te. Oh Maishter, dere ish a dam way of distance, and the deel a bit between.

Enter young Woudbee *in a Chair, with four or five
Footmen before him, and passes over the Stage.*

E.W. Hey day — who comes here? with one, two,
three, four, five Footmen! Some young Fellow just
tasting the sweet Vanity of Fortune.—Run, *Teague*,
inquire who that is.
Te. Yes, Maishter. [*runs to one of the Footmen*] Sir,
will you give my humble Shervish to your Maishter,
and tell him to send me word fat Naam ish upon
him.
Footm. You wou'd know fat Naam ish upon him?
Te. Yesh, fet would I.
Footm. Why, what are you, Sir?
Te. Be me Shoul I am a Shentleman bred and born,
and dere ish my Maishter.
Footm. Then your Master would know it.
Te. Arah, you Fool, ish it not the saam ting?
Footm. Then tell your Master 'tis the young Lord
Woudbee just come to his Estate by the Death of
his Father and elder Brother.   [*Exit Footman.*
E.W. What do I hear?
Te. You hear that you are dead, Maishter; fere vil
you please to be buried?
E.W. But art thou sure it was my Brother?
Te. Be me Shoul it was him nown self; I know'd him
fery well, after his Man told me.
E.W. The Business requires that I be convinc'd with
my own eyes; I'll follow him, and know the Bottom
on't. — Stay here till I return.
Te. Dear Maishter, have a care upon your shelf: now
they know you are dead, by my Shoul they may
kill you.
E.W. Don't fear; none of his Servants know me; and
I'll take care to keep my Face from his sight. It
concerns me to conceal my self, till I know the
Engines of this Contrivance. —— Be sure you stay

139

till I come to you; and let no body know whom you belong to. [*Exit.*

60 *Te.* Oh, oh, hon, poor *Teague* is left all alone.

[*sits on the Port-Mantel.*

[The lawyer Subtleman recruits Teague as a perjured witness to a forged will.]

Sub[*tleman*]. There's a Fellow that has Hunger and the Gallows pictur'd in his Face, and looks like my Countryman. —— How now, honest Friend, what have you got under you there?

65 *Te.* Noting, dear Joy.

Sub. Nothing? Is it not a Port-mantel?

Te. That is noting to you.

Sub. The Fellow's a Wit.

Te. Fet am I: my Granfader was an *Irish* Poet. — He
70 did write a great Book of Verses concerning the Vars between St. *Patrick* and the Wolf-Dogs.

Sub. Then thou art poor, I'm afraid.

Te. Be me Shoul, my fole Generation ish so. —— I have noting but thish poor Portmantel, and dat it
75 shelf ish not my own.

Sub. Why, who does it belong to?

Te. To my Maishter, dear Joy.

Sub. Then you have a Master.

Te. Fet have I, but he's dead.

80 *Sub.* Right! —— And how do you intend to live.

Te. By eating, dear Joy, fen I can get it, and by sleep-ing fen I can get none. —— tish the fashion of *Ireland.*

Sub. What was your Master's Name, pray?

85 *Te.* [*Aside.*] I will tell a Lee now; but it shall be a true one. —— *Macfadin*, dear Joy, was his Naam. He vent over vith King *Jamish* into *France*. —— He was my Master once. —— Dere ish de true Lee, noo. [*aside.*

69 Fet] Fel   89 Lee, noo.] Lee : noo

Sub. What Employment had he?

Te. Je ne scay pas.

Sub. What! you can speak *French?*

Te. Ouy Monsieur; —— I did travel *France,* and
Spain, and *Italy;* — Dear Joy, I did kish the Pope's
Toe, and dat will excuse me all the Sins of my Life;
and fen I am dead, St. *Patrick* will excuse the rest.

Sub. A rare Fellow for my purpose. [*aside.*] Thou
look'st like an honest Fellow; and if you'll go with
me to the next Tavern, I'll give thee a Dinner, and
a Glass of Wine.

Te. Be me Shoul, 'tis dat I wanted, Dear Joy; come
along, I will follow you.

Runs out before Subtleman *with the Portmantel
on his Back. Exit* Subtleman.

[Teague reveals the plot.]

Enter Subtleman *with* Teague.

Sub. My Lord, here's another Evidence.

E.W. Teague!

Y[oung] W[oudbee]. My Brother's Servant!

Sub. His Servant!

    [*They all four stare upon one another.*

Tea. Maishter! see here Maishter, I did get all dish
[*chinks Money*] for being an Evidensh dear Joy,
an be me shoule I will give the half of it to you, if
you will give me your Permission to maake swear
against you.

E.W. My Wonder is divided between the Villany of
the Fact, and the Amazement of the Discovery.
Teague! my very Servant! sure I dream.

Tea. Fet, dere is no dreaming in the cashe, I'm sure
the Croon pieceish are awake, for I have been
taaking with dem dish half hour.

Y.W. Ignorant, unlucky Man, thou hast ruin'd me;

why had not I a sight of him before.

120 *Sub.* I thought the Fellow had been too ignorant to be a Knave.

Tea. Be me shoule, you lee, dear Joy —— I can be a Knave as well as you, fen I think it conveniency.

E.W. Now Brother! Speechless! Your Oracle too
125 silenc'd! Is all your boasted Fortune sunk to the guilty blushing for a Crime? but I scorn to insult —— let Disappointment be your Punishment: But for your Lawyer there——*Teague*, lay hold of him.

Sub. Let none dare to attach me without a legal
130 Warrant.

Tea. Attach! no dear Joy, I cannot attach you —— but I can catch you by the Troat, after the fashion of *Ireland.*   [*takes* Subtleman *by the Throat.*

Sub. An Assault! An Assault!

135 *Tea.* No, no, tish nothing but choaking, nothing but choaking.

[Hermes Woudbee has been incarcerated as a lunatic.]

Enter Teague.

Te. Deel tauke me but dish ish a most shweet Business indeed; Maishters play the fool, and Shervants must shuffer for it. I am Prishoner in the Con-
140 stable's House be me Shoule, and shent abrode to fetch some Bail for my Maishter; but foo shall bail poor *Teague* agra. [*Enter* Constance.] Oh, dere ish my Maishter's old Love. Indeed, I fear dish Bishness will spoil his Fortune.

145 *Con.* Who's here? *Teague!*   [*he turns from her.*

Te. Deel tauke her, I did tought she cou'd not know me agen.

141 bail] fail

142

Constance *goes about to look him in the Face.*
He turns from her.

Dish is not shivil, be me Shoul, to know a Shentleman fither he will or no.

50 *Con.* Why this, *Teague*? What's the matter? are you
asham'd of me or your self, *Teague*?

Te. Of bote, be me Shoule.

Con. How does your Master, Sir?

Te. Very well, dear Joy, and in prishon.

55 *Con.* In Prison! how, where?

Te. Why, in the little *Bashtile* yonder at the end of
the Street.

Con. Shew me the way immediately.

Te. Fet, I can shew you the Hoose yonder: Shee

60 yonder; be me Shoul I she[e] his Faace yonder,
peeping troo the Iron Glash Window.

Con. I'll see him tho' a Dungeon were his Con-
finement.   [*runs out.*

Te. Ah —— auld kindnesh, be me Shoul, cannot be

65 forgotten. Now if my Maishter had but Grash
enough to get her wit child, her word wou'd go for
two; and she wou'd bail him and I bote.

[*Exit.*

XX. John Michelburne, *Ireland Preserved* (1705)

Enter Teigue *Dancing and Wrigling his Body, leading in an* Irish *Woman with a Kerchief on her head, and a Mantle pin'd about her Shoulders.* Fingall *Dance.*

Teig. By my Gossips hand, Gossip *Nora*, de day is our owns, and fee fill maake de dance, and den Gossip *Nora*, dou and my shelf fill go home fid me, eat dy fill of Pease, Bread, and Ruscaan Butter.

They Dance, and at the end of the Dance, the Woman goes away. Dermot *comes Running in, setting up the* Irish *Cry*, Hub-bub-boo, Who-la-loo.

5   *Der.* By my Fait, *Teigue* Joy, the Micharr of a Trooparr, did maake Force my Fadders House, and did taake de Fafteen fair white Egg, and de dainty fine Yellow Bacoan; he did bate my Wife, and did trow her down stairs, and did call her a
10 Feisting, Farting, Stinking Shaad, and if dou did but see her A—— and her Shouldar, as blaake as de Brogue on dy foots; *Hub-bub-boo, Who-la-loo* [*clapping his hands*] *Hub-bub-boo, Who-la-loo*, I fill maake de spaake to hish Graash.

15 *Teigue.* Fait, de Trooparr fill not care.—— [*Makes a F—— with his Mouth.*] Fen he has eaten de Fafteen Egg, and de Bacoan, He will maake de Fornication upon dy Wife.

   Der. I fill run home, and fill put my Wife in de Priests
20 Shamber and she shall lye dare all de day and all de Night.

Offers to go out, Teigue *takes him by the Sleeve.*

Teigue. But pray Cozen *Dermot,* fy all dis Haste?
By my Fait, Deer Joy, I do let de Trooparr ly wid
my Wife in de bad, he does ly at de one side, and
25   my self ly at de toder side, and my wife do lye in
de middle side; for fen I do go out to work in de
cold Morning, to thraash my Corne, he doth cover
her, and keep my Wife fery faarme, and she does
get leave to get up, and look after de House, and
30   fen de Trooparr do get up, he does go and bring
home de Seep and de Muck, and de Shucking Pigg,
and we do Eat togeder, and do Sleep togeder, and
no body do taake any ting from me, de Trooparr
does taake care of every ting; you be de great Fool
35   to put your Wife in de Priest shamber, the Trooparr
be wort an hundred of the Priest.
Der. Arrah Joy, Cozen *Teigue,* fill you let de Trooparr
lye at my House, and keep my Wife faarme in de
Cold Morning.
40 *Teig.* No fait Dear Joy, dou salt not have my Trooparr, my Wife do like him fery fell, and I am fery
glad for it; get you anoder Trooparr, you shall not
have my Trooparr.   [*Exeunt.*

[Teigue, Dermot and a friend discuss the prospects of obtaining
commissions in Tyrconnel's army.]

Enter Teigue, Dermot, O Sulivan, *with a Snuff Horn
in his hand, giving them Snuff.*

Sul. Pox taake it, I have not de fortune to be wid his
45   Graash so soon as your shelfe; Ah, and a Pox taake
des Cows, and des Seep and five Mucke, to maake
de piece of Money to buy de *English* Cloaths, I
have been dis seven days to learn to wear de
English Brogue, for day tell me, his Graash *Tir-*
50 *connel* fill not let de Officer go in Brogue, or be in

49–50 *Tirconnel*] *Tirconnel,*

145

his Shamber, wearing de *Irish* Brogue, fait Joy, he
has been after wearing dem himself.

Teig. Cozen *O'Sulivan,* I'll bee after telling dee de
Raison, de *Irish* Brogue carry de ill smell wid dem;
55   you must not shit down on your two knuckle-bones,
and pull off your Brogue by de fire; never wash
your stockins till day be worne out; you must be as
shweet and neat, as you see others; especially when
you go into his Graashes Preshance Shamber: But
60   Cozen, Fy did not you maake Haast? First come,
first sherv'd, His Graash de Lord *Tirconnel* has
great kindness for dose dat be after first come.

Sul. No Body spaake, but day did ferry fell for demshelves, and I fill be after doing fell for my shelf.

65 *Teig.* But Cozen *Dermot,* dou hasht de good Relashon,
and I know dou wilt have de Plaash, fen oders shall
have no Plaash; dy Fadders Broder, *Shan-Duffe-
O'Neil,* and Captain *Manus Macmohon* be dy good
Relashon, day be de great Mans now.

70 *Der.* I have bin wid dem; dat which Plaagues me is,
day tell me, and by my Troate day do say, der fell
be no Waacancy, unless I be after buy de Plaash,
and I have a Shoul to be shaved, I fell be after
keeping my Cow and my Seep, and twenty Ewe
75   Lamb, but I fill be going home: How sall I be
getting de Money to maake de Waacancy?

Teig. I'll tell de, dou not maake de trouble, dou art de
Shentleman of good Family, a By blow of one of de
O'Neils, dy Fadder is a Priest, and dou wilt not
80   want Money, de main Ting is to get some of dy
Followers to be dy Soldiers, to serve de King and
de good Lord *Tirconnel.*

Der. Who-bub-boo, I can be after maaking twenty
thirty of my Fadders and my followers, dat fell go

85   wid me tro de World.

Teig. But however, de best way is to buy, dy Fadder
knows how fery fell to get de Money, and in one
or two year dy Fadder fill have de Money again,
I'll send de to One dat has de Waacancy, and ware
90   dou maake de spaake wid him.

[Outside the walls of Derry five rapparees discuss the plunder
that awaits them when the city is taken.]

Enter five Rapparees.

1 *Rap.* A false Alarm again,—Confound these Rebels,
we have no Throats to cut yet.

2 *Rap.* I tink by de Mash Book, dare fill be allway de
false Alarm.

95   3 *Rap.* We be dose, de Rebels call Rapparees, we be
de Kings gued Voluntiers.

4 *Rap.* Dere be none, dat be after coming in de Nort,
but get dat worth deir laubour axshept my own
shelf Joy.

00   5 *Rap.* Why Neighbour, you do be mauke de Rauvish
upon de young Womans, and when dere is a Purchas, you let others run away with it, my shelf and
my Comrade do get my part amongst de rest, as
mush *Holland* Sheets, Daamask Tauble Clot and
05   Napkin, with fine Linnen, as we can carry bot on
our back, but what do dee say to Chests full of
Plaat, Barrels of de Money, dat have been after
hid, dare is Treasure upon Treasure in *Darry.*

1 *Rap.* 'Tis plawgy hard to get at it.

10   2 *Rap.* How my Teet water! Dis is de thirteen time
I rid Whip and Spur twelve Miles; my Garran has
stood dis fifteen day bridle and sadle, expecting de

87 fell] fell,   88 year dy Fadder] year, dy Fadder,   98 worth]
worsh   110 water!] water?

147

good News.——One time *Derry* is taken, den whip
and spur; — Another time *Derry* is taken, den whip
115   and spur just as we did now, I think de Devil be
with *Derry*, it will never be taaken.
    3 *Rap.* My inclinaation is to Butcher des Heretic Dogs
des Rebels;——[*Pulls out a Skein out of his Pocket.*]
Dis be to Sacrifize de Womans and Shildrens.
120   [*Takes a crooked Knife out of his Pocket.*] Dis be
to rip open de great Bellyed Womans.
    4 *Rap.* Des are Weapons we never go widout de
Pocket full, de Priest fill not be after give us de
Absolushon widout dem, and must show dem every
125   time we go to de Mash.
    5 *Rap.* You vill see de fine Time in two or tree Mont,
it us'd to be five Pounds for a Pri[e]sts Head, but
now dou vill find it five Pounds for, vat do dey call
dem, de Minishteers Head. [*Scratches his Head.*]
130   And as de Priest tells us, dere is none to live in
Ireland, but de *French* Mans and de *Irish* Mans.
    1 *Rap.* Fat no Quaakers? Dey maintaine de Regiment
on deir own sharge for *James*.
    2 *Rap.* You be de Fool, de Quaakers be our own
135   Peoples, de Jesuite take care for dem.
    3 *Rap.* Come, de fray be over, I vill turn back. I have
de Cozen de Officer in de Army, dat vill send me
vord, 'tis tought de *French* Engineer falls to de work
in mining, in two or tree days dey vill not mind de
140   Valls, dey'll run deir Vork into de Towne, and
blow up de Market Plaash; dis is Trut, by de Hand
of my good Gossip.
    5 *Rap.* They be de braave *Franch-man*.   [*Exeunt.*

116 will] 'twill

148

D[ermo]t. I'le tell you fatt *Teigue*, by my Shoul,
F[orste]r and B[urto]n has most Poul,
    Oh! oh! hone.
T[ei]g[ue]. Yerrou but how came dat about?
5 De Taughts of't makes my Tears burst out,
    Oh! oh! &c.
D[ermo]t. Pox on you niff you'll hold your Pace,
I soon will tall you de whole Case,
    Oh! oh! &c.
10 I taught before deye did Begin,
T[ucke]r and F[owne]s voud shurely Vin;
For dey vent gedering up and down
All de *Tories* in de Town,
De very Shooe-Boys too, dey took
15 Out of de Street, I'le swear de Book —
Some Butchers say dey did not leave
One Fellow dat vou'd carry a Cleave,
And dese togeder made such Ball,
I taught dey'd do de Divil and all;
20 But ve de first Day had no Sport,
De Sheriffs did adjourn de Court:
Whin afterwards ve vent again,
Ve lost van Couple of our Min,
    Oh! oh! hone.
25 *T[ei]g[ue].* Fat were you by de Dogs forsaken?
O yei! Pray Gud de Divil take 'em,
    Oh! oh! &c.
D[ermo]t. Foh! now fat a noise you make,

16 leave] leave, 18 togeder] to geder 27 *Oh*] Dh

Pray let me go on vid my Spake,
30 Ve wint to the *Toulsill* in a Cluster,
Tinking to kill dat Day F[orste]r,
But first vee in a mighty Rage,
Pull'd down and trew about de Stage.
And thin some dam Whiggs call de G[uar]d,
35 Who Fir'd vid Balls; vas not dat hard?
And did shat van Man trew de Head,
And lift de Second a[l]most Dead,
                              Oh! oh! hone.

T[ei]g[ue]. Fatt did you do to de red Coats?
40 Leursuh, you shud have cut deir Troats,
                              Oh! oh! &c.

D[ermo]t. Fie, all of us did as vee shud,
Run away as fasht as vee cou'd,
                              Oh! oh! &c.

45 T[ei]g[ue]. Fete dat vas like breach of de *Boyn*,
Fere did again your Forces Joyn?
                              Oh! oh! &c.

D[ermo]t. 'Twas thin by his Grace Commanded
Dese had no Votes shud be Disbanded,
50 So whin dey lost de Tag-rag Crew,
Free Voters Numbers was but few:
So dat de Whiggs their Choice vill gitt,
And F[orste]r in de House vill Sit.
                              Oh! oh! hone.

55 T[ei]g[ue]. Ve must by my Shoul thin be very Civil,
Or ilse all dese Whiggs will drive ush to de Divil.
                              Pulilillew.

35 Who] who   37 a[l]most] a most   43 cou'd,] cou'd   44 oh] od
52 gitt,] gitt.   57 *Pulilillew.*] *Pulilillew* :

150

XXII. Susanna Centlivre, *A Wife Well Managed*
(1715)

Inis *goes to the Door and calls*, Teague.

Enter Teague.

Teague. Well Mrs *Inis*; What Commands have you
for Teague now?

Inis. Do you think you can do a Message cunningly,
Teague?

5 *Teague.* Cunningly! Yes Faith, we are all so cunning
now — What for a Message is it?

Inis. It is a Letter for Father *Bernardo* at the Convent
of St. *Francis*; if you do it handsomly, a Moidore
is your Reward; do you hear, but if you make any

10 Mistake —

Teague. Hub, bub, bub, bu, Mistake! No Faith won't
I, Arra! An will you be after giving me the Moidore indeed, and by my Shoul now?

Inis. Upon Honour. —

15 *Teague.* Arra, say no more now — I will be here agen
in a Quarter of an Hour. [*going.*

Inis. But you must stay for the Letter, *Teague.*

Teague. No, no, 'tis no Matter; I have a very clean
Letter in my Pocket which will do very well, upon

20 my Shoul, [*going*] and save Time, yes Faith will it.

Inis. Ha, ha; no, no, *Teague*, that won't do; come
along with me, and I'll give you the Letter; but if
you shou'd meet my Master *Don Pisalto*, not a word

19 Letter] Lettet   well,] well.   20 Shoul,] Shoul.

of the Letter for your Life —— And I charge you
25 to give it into no Hands but the Priest's, and bring
me an Answer, and then the Moidore is your own.
Teague. Faith will I. ——   [*Exeunt.*

Re-enter Teague *with the Letter.*

Teague. Arra, 'pon my Shoul, I have forgot this plaguy
Priest's Name —— Yes Faith have I —— Father
30 *Bom, Bom, Bom,* —— By St. *Patrick* I don't know
who to ask for now — Arra, What shall I do? ——
Who the Devil shall I get to read the Outside of
this Letter now?

Enter Don Pisalto *behind him, and looks
over his Shoulder on the Letter.*

Don Pis. For Father *Bernardo.*
35 *Tea.* Oh, 'pon my Shoulvation dat is the Name now.
                    [*turns quick upon* Don Pisalto.
Ha, my Maistre! What shall I say now?   [*Aside.*
Don Pis. Whither are you going with that Letter
Sirrah? It is my Wife's Hand.   [*Aside.*
Tea. Ha, ha, 'pon my Shoul, a very good Jest; first
40 reads the Direction, and then asks me whither it
goes.
Don Pis. It may not prove so good a Jest as you think,
Sirrah —— Who gave you that Letter?
Tea. Arra Maistre, you are very uncivil now to en-
45 quire into other Folks Business, so you are; yes
Faith are you.
Don Pis. I shall be so very uncivil to break your Head
Rascal, if you don't answer me to the Purpose; give
me the Letter you Dog you.
50 *Tea.* Faith won't I —— That's the Way to lose the
Moidore, which I am to have for carrying it.
Don Pis. A Moidore for carrying it! Sure the Business

152

must be very urgent, when the Postage is so dear. Give it me, I say, or, or,

[*Lays his Hand to his Sword.*

55 *Tea.* No pon my Shoul won't I.

Don Pis. Won't you Sirrah?   [*Draws and beats him.*

Tea. Arra, take the Letter. [*throws it down*] Pox upon me, if I don't wish the Devil had you both, yes Faith do I; for poor *Teague* loses his Moidore now,
60 and Mrs. *Inis* will never send me of no more Arrands, no Faith won't she.

Don Pis. Inis, Ho! Did she give it you —— [*Opens it.*

Tea. Yes indeed now, and I believe there is some very great Sin in the Letter now, that the Good Father
65 was to send his Pardon for, so I do.

Don Pis. Monstrous! What do I see? Yes here is a Sin with a Witness — [*Reads*] "Dear Father, you'll "forgive me when I tell you, that the more I see "you, the more I hate my Husband, (*very fine*) and
70 "the more I pray against Temptation, the more "powerfully my Inclinations plead in your Behalf, "(*Furies and Distraction,*) —— I implore your "charitable Assistance to conquer this unruly Sin — "(*Yes I'll help you with a Vengeance to you*) ——
75 "Nothing but your Company can prolong the Life "of *Flora.* (*Say you so Mistress?*) Very well. *Inis* gave you this Letter you say!

Tea. Yes Faith did she —— Arra dear honny Maistre; an you have don with the Letter give it me now,
80 that I may carry it to the Good Father, what de ye call him, or I shall lose the Moidore, yes Faith shall I.

57 Letter.] Letter

[Carbine *solus*]
Enter Servant *booted, with a Letter.*

Jer[*emy*]. I left the Colonel well Sir, three Hours ago,
he has dispatch'd me to your Honour, with his
Service, and this Letter, an't please you.
Car. Ha! it must be matter of Importance, if he sent
5   you express hither.   [*Opens the Letter and reads.*

Dear Ned, *I am inform'd that one* Machone *an*
Irishman, *who deserted from me with his Horse
and Accoutrements, before the Fight of* Dumblain,
has been some time entertain'd as a Domestick by
10   *your Neighbour Sir* Barnaby Bindover; *he is a red-
hair'd, well set, middlesiz'd Fellow, about thirty,
and has very much of the Brogue; if my Intelligence
be true, in securing him, you will oblige your sincere
Friend, and Servant,*   Charles Plume.

15   [*Aside.*] How! my Friend *Machone* a Deserter!
this is still better and better —— to have my Re-
venge of the Dog will be some Satisfaction, tho' I
get nothing else by it. —— But who knows? It may
turn to my Advantage another way; no Man has
20   so great an Influence over the Knight as that Rascal.
—— It must be so —— yes — Well *Jeremy*, I suppose you know partly the Contents of this Letter —
Jer. Something about a Deserter I heard the Colonel
say, who is now a Servant at yonder great House.

17 Satisfaction] Satisfation

Car. 'Tis even so *Jeremy*, and it may lye in thy Power
to do us a Piece of great Service. —— Wert thou
ever in *Ireland*?

Jer. Three Years, an't please your Honour.

Car. Thou hast the Brogue then a little sure.

Jer. As well as any *Teague* of 'em all Sir, if that can
do your Honour any Kindness.

Car. It may, *Jeremy*, the greatest imaginable; ——
we must go a cunning way to work with this Rascal;
his Master's a Man of Authority, has a Value for
the Rogue, and will never deliver him, that's certain, for he hates our Cloth heartily. — You must
therefore go to the House, do you mark me?
Enquire for the Knave under the plausible Colour
of being his Countryman, as you know how to be
sure, he's a true half-witted Bogtrotter, and 'twill
be a Matter of no Difficulty to decoy him in hither
to drink; ply him with Liquor, get out his whole
Story; I will hear all from a Corner, pop out un-
awares, and secure him. —— Run, fly him, lose no
time *Jeremy*, and depend on a Reward suitable to
your Service.

Jer. I am at your Honour's Devotion, and will give a
good Account of the Rogue, never fear Sir, let me
alone for playing my Part. [*Exit* Jeremy.

*   *   *

Enter Jeremy, Machone *and Boy.*

Mac. to *Boy.* And fen will you be a Paage again, Mr.
Boy? and how does my good Lady Countess?

Jer. Well, fat will you be after Drinking good Countryman?

Mac. Tree Noggans of Usquebaugh Joy, fat tink you?
all in one Jug —— go, run you little Tief you, we
shall be a great while drinking out this half Crown
in plain Drink. [*Ex. Boy.*

Jer. Yes, and I am upon a Peregrination, and have a graat way to go, Joy.

60 *Mac.* Ay, and the Days are very short too, Joy, and if you Travel in the Dark, be me fait you won't see a Step of your way —— and what Man's son be you pray?

Jer. I was *Maghloghan Moor*'s Joy.

65 *Mac.* Brave Man's Son! betters and betters; the *Maghloghans* are all my Relashons, and 'twas my Cushen *Macshaan* sent you with this Token you say? His Fathers were very graat People, Kings of the Nations and Princes.

70 *Jer.* And how far do you make it to *London* Shity from here Joy?

Mac. Be me Soul now, me Dear, if it were well maade, 'tis a good forty Mile; but from *London* to this Plaas again, it is not so far by a deal —

Enter Boy, fills a Glass, and goes out.

75 Are you brewing the Usquebaugh you little Rogue, that makes you be such a long while? ——

Jer. [*setting.*] Arrah fat, and here is a Health to all our Relashons in *Tiperary* dead or alive.

Mac. Fait, and I have many good Friends and Cor-
80 respondents there too, Joy.

Jer. And how often do they write to you, Master *Machone*?

Mac. [*taking a Glass.*] Be me Soul they never write to me at all, Joy —— [*Drinks*] I hate these fiddle
85 faddle Glasses, they don't hold half a Bumper.

Jer. [*drinking again.*] Come, here is your Inclinations now, Joy, and what was the first Prefarment that was upon you in *England*?

Mac. Be me Soul I was Gentleman of the Horse to a
90 great Inn at *Cofentry*, and they prest me for a Volunteer, to make me a brave Trooper-Man; and

just as we were going to put the fight upon the
Rebels, my Garon-reagh run away with me, and I
brought the first News of the Battel.

Jer. [*giving him a Glass.*] Don't stand preashing over
your Jug —— and how came you here, Joy?

Mac. [*after Drinking.*] Why after I had sould my
Garon-reagh, then did I meet upon the Road with
this very good Gentleman, for we were both upon
our Journies the very saam way Joy; and I took
a fancy to him Fait, and he to me, and so we bot
hired one another; and I discover'd a Plot to carry
off his nown Daughter by a deefil of a Captain
here, Joy; and am very much in his Urship's good
Graases upon 't; and have a design upon his old
Virgin Cheester, who has Five thousand good
Pounds, Joy.

Enter Carbine *with three Dragoons.*

Car. Mr. *Machone*, your Servant —— a pleasant
Gentleman truly! —— [*to his People*] come where
are the Handcuffs?

Mac. to *Jer.* Fat is de meaning of all this, Joy?

Jer. Bit, by St. *Patrick*; that's all, honest Countryman.

Car. This Intrusion's a little uncivil; but I only
came to introduce these Gentlemen to your better
Acquaintance ——

Mac. Ubbo bo-boo! I know no Business they have
with me at all? what is it I pray, Joy?

Car. To secure you for a Deserter, in order to be
remov'd as your Colonel shall direct, and try'd for
your Life, Sir; we have your own Confession I
think, and other good Evidence ——

Mac. Be St. *Patrick*; and I did confess nothing; and
you have no Evidensh here but this Gentleman, and
he will not be after hanging his Countryman.

Jer. By my Soul but he will, Joy —— what think you

157

now of an old Virgin with Five thousand Pound,
Mr. *Machone*?

Mac. Arrah, is not the Brogue upon [your] Tongue
Joy? —— but be me Soul it is upon your Face tho'
130 —— but I will not be put in Preeson Joy for all this,
for my Master has his Majesty's Commission of
Peash, and I am a priviledg'd Parson.

Car. And I have his Majesty's Commission of War,
and will secure you in spite of your Master's Teeth,
135 you shall see.

Mac. [*to Jer.*] And have you betray'd me then you
English Dog you, I will swear Treason against you
too Joy, and one Rope shall serve for us both.

Car. Faith Mr. *Machone*, you have plotted your self
140 to the Gallows at last; you have hinder'd me of a
Wife, and I will help you to a Halter.

Jer. Ah! you want it here, Mr. *Machone*.

126 of] of of   132 Parson] Parsoh

[A sergeant is enrolling cavalry recruits.]

Question. Fat Name upon you dere?
Answer. My Name *Byrn.*
Quest. Fer vash yo[u] Born?
Ans. County of *Killamountains.*
5   [*Quest.*] De Tivil take you, can't you call him Countys
    of *Wicklows?* I make English upon you, you make
    English upon me again, and be hang'd you Tief.
    Fere dere?
Ans. Glanmalora. It ish a good Plashe, a bad Name,
10   all von for dat.
Quest. Fat Relishion?
Ans. A Roman Catalick.
[*Sergeant.*] Very vell. To de Right, put in your Toe,
    put out your Heel, shit ub strait!

[Twelve more recruits are enrolled in similar terms.]

15   [*Sergeant.*] Now Major by my Shoul your own Troops
    is full.
    [*Major.*] Vell put dem in Order between de Vall and
    de Vaters, I am Excercise dem by and by.
    [*Sergeant.*] Silence dere Shentlemens, vas de firsht
20   vords of Command in de Englishes, for I make
    Speech pon you.
    I am Point in a Plash fere de Vaters vas pon [de lift
    Hand, and de Valls vas pon] de right Hand, ash
    you vere ash my shelf, and adva[n]sh ash my shelf,
25   dem four tings is all for the firsht time, if you not

no de lift Hand, you not no de Vaters, if you not no de Right Hand, you not no de Valls; you were ash my shelf, and advansh ash my shelf, dem four tings ish all for de firsht time.

30   Advanch; dat's come up here to my shelf, my shelf is my shelf, vith a grash come up here to my shelf, for you no my shelf is my shelf.

[*Recruit.*] Hub! hub! hub! hub!

[*Sergeant.*] Ha! who's dat crys hub hub upon his
35   Horsh? Fat Name pon you cry hub pon your Horsh?

[*Recruit.*] My name *Turlough.*

[*Sergeant.*] De Tivil take me, any Shentlemens be of dat Name you Tief, fat make you cry hub pon
40   your Horsh?

[*Recruit.*] My Horsh is no Horsh.

[*Sergeant.*] Fat ish your Horsh?

[*Recruit.*] My Horsh ish a Mare.

[*Sergeant.*] Ha! Pox take you, full of your Contradik
45   you Tief. Fat make your Mare go lame?

[*Recruit.*] She vas go lame since she loose her too fore Broge.

[*Sergeant.*] Call dem Shoos and be dam'd, call dem Shoos you Tief, you call your Horsh Mare, and
50   Mare Horsh, Broge Shooe and shooe Broge, make trouble pon my shelf, and disgrace pon de Preten-der and de fole Nashion, *viry Creecrator Scrashtee Vodee brane Gran[a]gh Clootough*, you vill never be good shall you vill be hang, no more Mens cry
55   hub pon ish Horsh, if I vil catch any more Mens cry hub pon ish Horsh, I vill shoot dem thro' de Heads long with de *Turloughs.*

To de lift, to de left. Tivil take you, you not no de lift hand you not no the Vaters, you not no de
60   Right Hand, you not no de Vals. Ash you vere, ash

34 who's] hows   52 fole] foule   59 you not] younot
60 you²] you you

you vere again. I am tell you my shelf ish my shelf, and ash you vere vas my shelf, look my shelf in de Fash you Tiefs, but like vild Gooses von look von vay, another look another vays, look my shelf, look my shelf in de Fash you Tiefs altogether like von Mans himshelf.

65

I am break my Hearts vid you, to de Right, to de Right, to de Right, to de Val, to de Val, to de Val, de Tivil take you all, I am ashame on you.

69 ashame] a shame

XXV. Peadar O Doirnín, *Muiris O Gormáin*
(1730–40)

Air ma[i]din Dé Máirt, is mé 'dul go Draeigheacht
Ath,

 Theagamh dhamh an stáid air a' Turnpike Road.
Sí is deise dar tharla oram de mhnáibh
O gineadh mo lá go b[h]faca mé an tseoid.
5 *Gobhamsa [a] láim[h] an uiread 's a rádh*
 "Shal Travel vith *bláth na finne,* sweet Joy!"
"Yes, *dar* be me [o]an trath," *air sise, 'thabhairt*
sásaidh,

 "Far vill se kal, or feadar shal go?"

Fhreagair mé an tráth sin lile na mbánchroth,
10 *[Ba] ghile nó bláth na n-ab[h]ull faoi dhó,*
Is tráth aithneas gur pháiste Saxsonnta gállta
Ainnir na bhfáinnidh, chas mé mo ghlóir:
"Me is go to *Draeidheacht Aath,* shal give you a *cárta,*
 And heartily *fáilte,* Madam, vith *póg!*"
15 *D'amhairc mo dháilse, is rine sí gáire:*
 "Shad is the kas, me Money has None!"

Tráth thainic mé an sméid[i]ugh 'teacht fó mo dhéin
On ccoinnioll mar ghréin na maidhne gan cheó,
'S go mb['fh]ear[r] liom nó saedhbhrios Mharcuis is
Séasar

20 *Ise is mé a bheith 'ccumann 's aig ól.*

1 mé] sme 3 de] a 5 an uiread 's a] a Nuiread so 8 Far] fat
9 mé] me me 10 n-ab[h]ull] Nábull 11 aithneas] hainis
17 mo] ma 20 ól] eól

Las mé sa mBéarla, is labhair mé léithe:
"If him had apron file [of] the *ór,*
The Devil a halfpenny me Let you pay —
Shal Drink the good ale Whil feather-Cock crow!"

25 *Thaitin mo Bhéarla blasda le spéir*
Na ndearca mar réalta glasa go mór,
'S do labhair de shéimhghuth [ba] bhinne nó téuda,
"Fath was you Name, or town was you home?"
Fhreagair mé scéimh na cruinne go léir,
30 "Me is Cristan Moresious Goraman *cóir,*
I is Very school-Measther; *dar* bi my soulvation
Shal Carry good favour for you *go deóigh.*"

Air ndul go táoidh an óil do s[h]ui[o]ghmar air bórd
Mar Pharis ón Tróigh, nó mar Helan ó' nGréig.
35 *Bhí mise dá pógadh, is ise (mar lóchrann*
Solais gan bhrón) aig molamh mo léighin:
"You is Very fine Cloaths, you is pretty bright proges,
You is Latin vell spoke, and fath me can['t] Name."
Ach bhí[o]mar aig ól gur thuit mise 'mo cheó —
40 *Don Deamhon sin órlach fuair Muiris dá féim!*

Air dteacht as mo Néull dhamh, dhearcus gach táoibh
Den halla a roibh an spéirbhean, is mise fón mbórd,
'S ní fhaca me áon a bhéaradh dhamh sgéala
Ach gasún gan chéill, nach ttuig[f]eadh mo ghlóir.
45 "Did you see fair, fine, hansome white Lady,
That was me Comrady Night Last *aig ól?*"
"She make run away Vith a shantleman brave —
Back horse with race, and Up the *ród mór!*"

27 de] do   30 Goraman] *Goraman*   31 bi] *bi*   36 aig] aige
mo] me   37 bright proges] vright prose   39 aig ól] aigeól
41 dteacht] ndeacht   dhearcus] dhearcuis   42 Den] Don
45 white] while   46 ól] eól

163

XXVI. Jonathan Swift, *A Dialogue in Hybernian Stile* (c. 1735)

A. Them apples is very good.

B. I am *again* you in that.

A. Lord, I was so bodderd t'other day with that prating fool Tom!

5 *B.* Pray, how does he *get* his health?

A. He's often very *unwell*.

B. [I] hear he was a great pet of yours. Where does he live?

A. Opposite the "Red Lyon".

10 *B.* I think he behaved very ill the last sessions.

A. That's true, but I cannot forbear loving his father's child. Will you tast a glass of my ale?

B. No, I thank you; I took a drink of small bear at home before I came here.

15 *A.* I always brew with my own bear. You have a country house, are you [a] planter?

B. Yes, I have planted a great many oak trees and ash trees, and some elm trees round a loough.

A. And a good warrant you have, it is kind father for
20 you. And what breakfast do you take in the country?

B. Why, sometimes sowins, and sometimes stirabout, and in summer we have the best frawhawns in all the county.

A. What kind of a man is your neighbor Squire Dolt?

25 *B.* Why, a meer buddogh. He sometimes coshers with me, and once a month I take a pipe with him, and we shoh it about for an hour together.

A. Well, I'd give a cow in connaugh to see you together! I hear he keeps good horses.

30   *B.* None but garrawns, and I have seen him often
     riding on a sougawn. In short, he is no better than
     a spawlpeen, a perfect Monaghan. When I was
     there last, we had nothing but a maddor to drink
     out of, and the devil a night-gown but a caddow.
35   Will you go see him when you come into our parts?
     A. Not *without* you go with me.
     B. Will you lend me your snuff-box *till* I take a pinch
     of snuff?
     A. Do you make good chese and butter?
40   *B.* Yes, when we can get milk; but our cows will never
     keep a drop of milk without a puckawn.

XXVII. Thomas Sheridan, *The Brave Irishman*
(1740/1754)

SCENE, *a Street.*

Enter Captain O'Blunder, *and* Sergeant.

Capt[ain]. Upon my shoul, this London is a pretty sort
of a plaash enough. And so you tells me, Chergeant,
that Terence M'Gloodtery keeps a goon.

Serg. Yes, Sir.

5 *Capt.* Monomundioul! but when I go back to Ireland,
if I catches any of these spalpeen brats keeping a
goon, to destroy the shentleman's creation, but I will
have 'em shot stone-dead first, and phipt thorrow
the regiment afterwards.

10 *Serg.* You mean that they shall be whipped first, and
then shot.

Capt. Well, ishn't it the same thing? Phat the devil
magnifies that? 'Tis but phipping and shooting all
the time; 'tis the same thing in the end sure, after
15 all your cunning; but still you'll be a wiseacre.
Monomundioul, there ishn't one of these spalpeens
that has a cabbin upon a mountain, with a bit of a
potatoe-garden at the back of it, but will be keeping
a goon; but that damn'd M'Gloodtery is an old
20 poacher, he shoots all the rabbits in the country
to stock his own Burrough with.—But Chergeant,
don't you think he'll have a fine time on't that
comes after me to Ballyshamus Duff.

Serg. Why, Sir?

23 Ballyshamus] Ballyshans

166

Capt. Why, don't you remember that I left an empty hogshead half full of oats there?

Serg. You mean, Sir, that you left it half full, and it is empty by this time.

Capt. Phat magnifies that, you fool? 'tis all the same thing, sure. But d'ye hear, Chergeant, stop and enquire for Mr Tradwell's the merchant,—at the sign of the—Oh! Cangrane, that's not it, but it was next door—Arrah, go ask phat sign my cousin Tradwell lives at next door to it.

Enter a Mob, who stare and laugh at him.

1 *Mob.* Twig his boots.

2 *Mob.* Smoke his sword, &c, &c.

Capt. Well, you scoundrels, you sons of whores, did you never see an Irish shentleman before?

Enter Sconce.

Sconce. O fie, gentlemen! are you not ashamed to mock a stranger after this rude manner?

Capt. This is a shivil short of a little fellow enough.
　　　　　　　　　　　　　　　　　　　　[*Aside.*

Sconce. If he is an Irishman, you may see by his dress and behaviour that he is a gentleman.

Capt. Yesh, you shons of whores, don't you see by my dress that I am a shentleman? And if I have not better cloaths on now, phat magnifies that? sure I can have them on to-morrow. By my shoul, if I take my shillela to you, I'll make you skip like a dead salmon.

Sconce. Oh, for shame, gentlemen, go about your business: The first man that offers an insult to him, I shall take it as an affront to myself. [*Mob exeunt.*

Capt. [*to* Sconce.] Shir, your humble servant; you seem to be a shivil, mannerly kind of a gentleman,

167

55   and I shall be glad to be gratified with your nearer
      acquaintance.   [*Salute.*
      Sconce. Pray, Sir, what part of England come you
      from?
      Capt. The devil a part of England am I from, my
60   dear; I am an Irishman.
      Sconce. An Irishman! Sir, I should not suspect that;
      you have not the least bit of the brogue about you.
      Capt. Brogue! No, my dear; I always wear shoes,
      only now and then when I have boots on.

                    Enter Cheatwell.

65   *Cheat.* Captain O'Blunder! Sir, you're extremely wel-
      come to London—Sir, I'm your most sincere friend,
      and devoted humble servant.
      Capt. Arra then! how well every body knows me in
      London—to be sure they have read of my name in
70   the newspapers, and they know my faash ever
      since—Shir, I'm your most engaging conversation.
                                                 [*Salute.*
      Cheat. And, Captain, tell us how long are you arrived!
      Capt. Upon my shoul, I'm just now come into London.
      Cheat. I hope you had a good passage.
75   *Capt.* Passage d'ye call it? Devil split it for a passage.
      By my shoul, my own bones are shore after it—
      We were on the devil's own turnpike for eight-and-
      forty hours; to be sure, we were all in a comical
      pickle.——I'll tell you, my dear: We were brought
80   down from Rings-end in the little young ship to the
      Pool-pheg, and then put into the great ship—the
      horse—ay, ay—the Race-horse they call'd it. But
      I believe, my dear, it was the devil's own post-horse;
      for I was no sooner got into the little room down
85   stairs, by the corner of the hill of Hoath, but I was
      taken with such a head-ach in my stomach, that I
      thought my guts would come out upon the floor;

so, my dear, I call'd out to the landlord, the captain
they call him, to stop the ship while I did die and
90   say my prayers: So, my dear, there was a great
noise above; I run up to see what was the matter.—
Oh hone, my dear, in one minute's time there wasn't
a sheet or blanket but phat was haul'd up to the top
of the house—Oh, kingrann, says I, turn her about
95   and let us go home again; but, my dear, he took no
more notice of me than if I was one of the spalpeens
below in the cellar going over to reap in harvest.

Cheat. No, Captain?—the unmannerly fellow! And
what brought you to London, Captain?

100   *Capt.* Fait, my dear jewel, the stage-coach; I sail'd in
it from Chester.

Cheat. I mean what business?

Capt. How damn'd inquisitive they are here! but I'll
be as cunning as no man alive. [*Aside.*] By my
105   shoul, my jewel, I am going over to Wirginny to
beat the French——they say they have driven our
countrymen out of their plantations: By my shoul,
my jewel, if our troops get vonse among them, we'll
cut them all in pieces, and then bring them over
110   prisoners of war besides.

Cheat. Indeed, Captain, you are come upon an hon-
ourable expedition—But pray, how is the old gentleman your father? I hope you left him in good
health?

115   *Capt.* Oh, by my shoul, he's very well, joy; for he's
dead and buried these ten years.

Cheat. And the old gentleman your uncle?

Capt. I don't believe you mean that uncle, for I never
had one.

120   *Cheat.* No! I'm sure—

Capt. O, I'll tell you who you mean; you mean my
chister's husband; you fool you, that's my brother
in law—

Cheat. Ay, a handsome man—as proper a man—

169

125 *Capt.* Ha, ha, a handsome man! Ay, for he's a damn'd
crooked fellow; he's bandy-shoulder'd, and has a
hump on his nose, and a pair of huckle-backs upon
his shins, if you call that handsome, ha, ha!

Cheat. And pray is that merry joking gentleman alive
130 still—he that us'd to make us laugh so— Mr———
Mr———A———

Capt. Phugh, I'll tell you who you mean; you mean
Scheela Shagnassy's husband, the parson.

Cheat. The very same.

135 *Capt.* Oh, my dear jewel, he's as merry as he never
was in his life. Phin I'm by, he's sometimes pretty
smart upon me with his humbuggs—But I told him
at last, before Captain Flaharty, Miss Mulfinin,
and Miss Owney Glasmogonogh—Hark ye, Mr par-
140 son, says I, by my shoul, you have no more wit than
a goose. Oh hone! he was struck at that, my dear,
and hadn't a word in his cheek. Arra, my jewel, I'll
tell you the whole story. We took a walk together;
it was a fine calm morning, considering the wind
145 was very high; so, my dear, the wind 'twas in our
backs going, but by my shoul, as we came back,
'twas in our faash coming home; and yet I could
never persuade him that the wind was turn'd—

Cheat. Oh the fool!

150 *Capt.* Arra, so I told him, my jewel. Pugh, you great
oaf, says I—if the wind blows in your back going,
and blows in your faash coming, sure the wind is
turn'd—No, if I was to preach, and to preach till
last Patrick's day in the morning, I could not dis-
155 suade him that the wind was turn'd.

Cheat. He had not common sense—Well, and does
the old church stand where it did?

Capt. The old church—the devil a church I remember
within ten miles of us—

137 humbuggs] bumbuggs

50   *Cheat.* I'm sure there was an old building like a
        church or castle.

     Capt. Phoo, my jewel, I know what you call a church
        —By my shoul, 'tis old lame Will Hurly's mill you
        mean—the devil a church—indeed they say mass in
65   it sometimes. Here, Terence, go to that son of a
        whore of a taylor, and see whether my cloaths be
        done or no.   [*Exit* Terence.

THE NATURE OF THE EVIDENCE

Hiberno-English was never a written language : the few Irishmen able to write English would aim to write standard English. It is true that we occasionally find such unbuttoned scraps as the inscription of ownership on p. 162 of MS 509 in the Library of Trinity College, Dublin (another inscription in the same hand gives the date 1709) :

> John dowling his Book and if it be lost preay
> Send it home and the Berer shall have for
> his peanes tree stroakes
> of a foxe teale

This, however, is not only an informal but perhaps an intentionally humorous note : probably John Dowling wrote his letters in excellent English. There are within our period, so far as I know, only two pieces of formal writing which betray any extensive traces of Hiberno-English usage : one is Maurice Cuffe's *Siege of Ballyally Castle*, from which an extract is printed as No. IX above, pp. 106–8; the other is the extraordinary work entitled *An Aphorismical Discovery of Treasonable Faction*. Nothing is known of the education of Maurice Cuffe, who was one of many sons of a prosperous merchant; his account of the siege is written with considerable fluency, but this may have been a natural gift, and his spelling is certainly very far removed from that of standard English. The anonymous author of the *Aphorismical Discovery*, who at some time in the 1650's wrote what his editor J. T. Gilbert described as "A Contemporary History of Affairs in Ireland from 1641 to 1652" [Gilbert (1870)], was plainly a man of considerable education, since he quotes from a number of languages, Classical and modern; he may perhaps have been educated abroad, since his distinctive style has continental rather than English affinities. His hibernicisms are too scattered to make it worth while printing an extract from his work, but the total number is considerable, and I have often cited them; Gilbert's edition concludes with an admirable *index verborum* which makes reference easy.

Only one of our extracts, then, represents the natural composition of an English-speaking Irishman : all the rest are more or less humorous and satirical in intention, and some were written by Englishmen who may have had little opportunity of familiarizing themselves with the features of Hiberno-English. The reliability of such pieces for purposes of linguistic analysis cannot be taken for granted and needs to be established. It will appear below (§§ 215–22) that the majority of the extracts, far from consisting of any kind of "Stage Irish", seem to represent original observation and ingenious notation within the limits imposed by the absence of a phonetic alphabet. This conclusion may at first seem somewhat surprising, but it must be remembered that an interest in spelling and pronunciation was very much part of the climate of opinion in seventeenth-century England. The problem of spelling reform had perplexed writers from the middle of the sixteenth century, and continued to do so until the middle of the seventeenth; a scientific interest in the study of phonetics appeared at the beginning of the seventeenth century and gained momentum until it attracted the attention of some of the most distinguished members of the newly-founded Royal Society.

Evidence that this concern with spelling and pronunciation was not limited to scientists but had achieved a more general popularity is to be found in the preface to John Crowne's play *City Politiques* (1688). One of the characters in the play, Bartoline "an old corrupt Lawyer", had been identified by some of those who saw the play with a real person, and Crowne disclaims the identification in the following interesting passage (the "Mr Lee" referred to is the actor Anthony Leigh) [Crowne (1874) 97] :

> Nor is any one old man more then another mimiqued by Mr Lee's way of speaking, which all the comedians can witness was my own invention, and Mr Lee was taught it by me. To prove this farther, I have printed Bartoline's part in that manner of spelling by which I taught it to Mr Lee. They who have no teeth cannot pronounce many letters plain, but perpetually lisp, and break their words, and some words they cannot bring out at all. As for instance, th is pronounc'd by thrusting the tongue hard to the teeth, therefore that sound they cannot make, but something like it. For that reason you will often find in Bartoline's part, instead of th, a y; as yat for that, yish for this, yosh for those; sometimes a t is left out,

as housand for thousand, hirchy for thirty; s they pronounce like sh, as sher for sir, musht for must; t they speak like ch, therefore you will find chrue for true, chreason for treason, cho for to, choo for two, chen for ten, chake for take. And this ch is not to be pronounc'd like k, as 'tis in Christian, but as in child, church, chest.

These non-Standard spellings are carried through with great consistency in the printing of the part, as the following short extract from a speech of Bartoline's will show :

> I wrong'd my shelf, cho entcher incho bondsh of marriage, and cou'd not perform covenantsh. I might well hinke you wou'd chake the forfeychure of the bond, and I never found equichy in a bedg in my life. But I'll trounce you boh! I have pav'd jailsh wi' the bonesh of honester people yen you are, yat neve' did me nor any man any wrong, but had law o' yeir shydsh, and right o' yeir shydsh.

Though a modern phonetician would use different terms, it would be difficult to improve on Crowne's description of the effect of the loss of one's teeth on the articulation of speech-sounds : in modern terms Crowne tells us that the dental sounds [ð] and [θ] are replaced by sounds resembling [j] and [h] respectively, and that the alveolar sounds [s] and [t] acquire more palatal articulations resembling [ʃ] and [tʃ] respectively. We can be sure that at least one English dramatist was an acute observer of non-standard speech-forms, that he took pains to teach what he had observed to the actor playing the part in question, and that he made systematic use of non-standard spellings in the course of his teaching. It seems reasonable to assume that other dramatists also took pains to inculcate the kind of pronunciation they wanted, and that some of them, at least, devised non-standard spellings to suit their purpose. It is worth noting that the first Irish actor known to have played Irish parts was William Bowen, who created the parts of Teague in *The Twin Rivals* (1702) and Foigard in *The Beaux' Stratagem* (1707). In the seventeenth century Irish parts were apparently played by English actors, normally by actors who specialized in character parts. Anthony Leigh, who created the part of Bartoline, had previously created that of the villainous Irish priest Tegue O'Divelly in *The Lancashire Witches* (1681), and was to play the same part in *The Amorous Bigot* (1689); he also played the Welsh-

175

man Jinkin in Edward Ravenscroft's *Dame Dobson* (1683) [Bartley (1954) 242–3]. English character-actors would no doubt take pains to observe the speech of Irishmen for themselves, but they would probably rely fairly heavily on the indications given to them by the writers of the plays they acted in, so that there was a real need for non-standard spellings. Not all our texts are from plays, of course, but the use of non-standard spellings in the plays would establish a precedent for the non-dramatic pieces.

The next point we have to consider is the opportunity that dramatists and actors would have had to observe Irishmen, and here we must draw a distinction between writers who had Irish connections and those who, so far as we know, had none. Of the twenty-seven texts printed here, ten are anonymous, or at least of disputed authorship. One of them, *Páirlement Chloinne Tomáis* (X) was certainly written by an Irishman, since apart from the few words of English printed above (pp. 109–10) the text is in Irish. Two of the political pieces, XXI and XXIV, are presumably the work of Irishmen : XXI is concerned with a purely local event, an election riot at the Tholsel in Dublin, and XXIV would hardly be intelligible outside Ireland. The third political piece, *The Irishmen's Prayers* (XVII), might well be the work of an Englishman : it belongs to the same genre as Lord Wharton's *Lilli Burlero*, and is one of a large number of pieces inspired by the stirring events of 1688 and 1689. The two versions of the *Fingallian Burlesque* (XIII and XVI) show a detailed knowledge of Irish history and legend, and some acquaintance with the Irish language; with these is to be associated *The Fingallian Dance* (XI). The unknown author of the Hiberno-English scene in *Captain Thomas Stukeley* (I) seems to have been well acquainted with the geography of the district round Dundalk, and uses a number of Irish phrases with propriety. The remaining two anonymous pieces, *The Welsh Embassador* (VII) and *Bog-Witticisms* (XV), may well be the work of Englishmen, though it is worth remembering that the latter of these is connected with the name Farewell, the name of the putative editor of *The Irish Hudibras* (XVI).

Of the authors whose names are known only one, Peadar O Doirnín (XXV) was a native Irishman, but four others were Irish at least by birth and education—Maurice Cuffe (IX), George Farquhar (XIX), Jonathan Swift (XXVI), and Thomas Sheridan (XXVII). Of the English writers three are known to have spent a considerable period of time in Ireland—Richard Head (XII), John

Dunton (XVIII), and John Michelburne (XX); a fourth, Susanna Centlivre (XXII), may have been born in Ireland and certainly spent her childhood there. The remaining writers, Munday and his collaborators (II), William Shakespeare (III), Thomas Dekker (IV and V), Ben Jonson (VI), Thomas Shadwell (XIV), and John Durant Breval (XXIII), were Englishmen with no known Irish connections, and we have to consider the opportunities that they and other writers would have had for familiarizing themselves with the speech and manners of Irishmen.

An important piece of evidence for the presence of a large number of Irishmen in England in the early seventeenth century is a dialogue in Dekker's *Honest Whore* Part II, a dialogue so interesting and significant that it is worth printing with only a few trifling omissions [Bowers (1953–61) ii 138] :

> *Lodovico.* Mary, England they [the Irish] count a warme chimny corner, and there they swarme like Crickets to the creuice of a Brew-house; but Sir, in *England* I haue noted one thing. . . . In *England*, Sir, troth I euer laugh when I thinke on't : to see a whole Nation should be mark't i'th forehead, as a man may say, with one Iron : why Sir, there all Costermongers are Irishmen.
>
> *Carolo.* Oh, that's to show their Antiquity, as comming from *Eue*, who was an Apple-wife, and they take after the Mother. . . .
>
> *Lodovico.* Why then, should all your Chimny-sweepers likewise be Irishmen? answer that now, come, your wit.
>
> *Carolo.* Faith, that's soone answered, for Saint *Patricke* you know keepes Purgatory, hee makes the fire, and his Countrymen could doe nothing, if they cannot sweepe the Chimnies. . . .
>
> *Lodovico.* Then, Sir, haue you many of them . . . Footmen to Noblemen and others, and the Knaues are very faithfull where they loue, by my faith very proper men many of them, and as actiue as the cloudes, whirre, hah. . . . And stout! exceeding stout; Why, I warrant, this precious wild Villaine, if hee were put to't, would fight more desperately than sixteene Dunkerkes.

Confirmation of the statement that "all Costermongers are Irishmen" is plentiful. In *Old Fortunatus* (IV) two jokers disguise themselves as Irish costermongers; in *The Irish Masque* (VI) the leader of the Irishmen is a costermonger (vi 5); in *Hey for Honesty*

177

(VIII) there is a reference to an Irish costermonger (viii 21). As early as the 1530's Skelton in his *Speke, Parott* (ll. 85–6) has a somewhat obscure reference to Irish avocations [Kinsman (1969) 79]:

"Moryshe myne owne shelfe," the costermonger sayeth;
"Fate, fate, fate, ye Irysh water-lag."

In 1598 Gilpin wrote "He cries oh rare, to hear the Irishmen/Cry pippe, fine pippe, with a shrill accent", and in 1601 Marston used very similar terms when he wrote "Hee whose throat squeakes like a treble Organ, and speakes as smal and shril, as the Irish-men crie pip, fine pip" [*NED* s.v. *pip* sb.³]. In Beaumont and Fletcher's play *The Coxcomb* (1612) there are two references so indirect as to make it certain that any audience which could pick up the meaning must be very familiar with the Irish as costermongers [Bowers (1966) 297, 309]:

This rebbell tonge [Irish] sticks in my teeth worse then a tough hen; sure it was nere knowne at Babell, for they soul'd no apples, and this was made for certaine at the first planting of Orchards, 'tis so crabbed.

By my trot I will give dye Worship two shilling in good argott [Ir. *airgead* 'silver'], to buy dy Worship pippines.
—This rogue thinks all the worth of man consists in Peepins.

Jonson in *The Alchemist* (1610) refers to "an Irish costar-mongar", and in *Christmas his Masque* (1616) to "Mac-pippin . . . a Costermonger" [Herford & Simpson (1925–52) v 361, vii 44]. Dekker's anecdote about the chimneysweeps also appears in very similar words in the anonymous *Welsh Embassador* (vii 83–6) which has been attributed to Dekker (above, pp. 39–40). Much the commonest employment for Irishmen in England was as footmen, grooms, or body-servants. In our texts they appear in such capacities in II, V, VI, VII, XII, XV, XIX and XXII. There are Irish footmen also in Thomas Heywood's *Four Prentices of London* (1592) and in Beaumont and Fletcher's *Coxcomb* (1612); *Bog-Witticisms* is full of them. Two references in *Purgatorium Hibernicum* (pp. 6, 124) to *rebells' plush* as the proper wear for Irish rebels may conceal allusions to Irish footmen, since plush was recognized as the standard material for footmen's liveries [*NED* s.v. *plush*]. Dekker's testimonial to the loyalty of Irish servants is confirmed by an anonymous *Discourse of Ireland* written about 1599

[Quinn (1941–2) 164–5] : "in England wee find the Irish seruant very faithfull and Louing." This testimony is the more surprising in the light of the belief then current that a favourite occupation of Irishmen was the cutting of Englishmen's throats : in our texts there are four references to this practice (i 30, iii 50, iv 40, xx 92), and in Wharton's *Lilli Burlero* (l. 8) we learn that the Irishman "will cut de Englishman's troat" [Crump (1968) 309]. Plainly any English writer would have had ample opportunity of observing the speech and habits of Irish footmen, if not in their own service in that of their friends or patrons.

It is not clear in what circumstances the Irish costermongers, chimneysweeps and footmen came to England. No doubt some of the Englishmen who visited Ireland on professional business of one kind or another brought back Irish servants with them, but these could have accounted for only a small part of the total. According to Dekker, as we have seen, the Irish swarmed to England "like Crickets to the creuice of a Brew-house"; that is, they came to better themselves, as many hundreds of thousands of Irishmen have done since Dekker's time. In particular, it seems likely that periodic strife and warfare in Ireland, endemic through most of our period, meant that many Irishmen were deprived of their means of livelihood and had to seek their fortunes in England. After the rebellion of 1641 a specially large number of Irishmen found their way to England, and many were enrolled in the Royalist army; after the defeat of the Royalist cause they would have to seek another way of life. In Sir Richard Howard's play *The Committee* (1662) the Irish servant Teague is seeking employment because his master had been killed in the Civil War; he is reduced to beggary, and is taken on by a certain Colonel Careless, whom he serves thenceforth with great devotion. In 1688 a number of Irish regiments were sent to England to support the doubtful cause of James II, and created great alarm [Simms (1969) 45–8]; in Portsmouth drunken Irish soldiers assaulted and robbed the citizens, and there was a riot after one of them had fired into a Protestant church. In London, too, there was rioting when the Irish soldiers attacked a crowd of jeering boys. After the collapse of the Stuart cause the Irish regiments had to be disbanded; some were sent to the Continent, some got back to Ireland, but some no doubt stayed in England, either to enter service, or just to live by their wits.

From the 1680's onwards we find another figure appearing in the plays, that of the villainous Irish priest fomenting treason and inculcating idolatry. How far such Irish priests really existed it is now difficult to determine, but there is no doubt about the widespread belief in their existence. In 1678 Titus Oates had begun his fabrication of the "Popish Plot", and though the details of this were so improbable that no dispassionate observer could have believed them, they were welcomed by a public opinion already alarmed at the relaxation of the Penal Laws, the activities of the Jesuits, and the military menace of France. In October the murder of Sir Edmundbury Godfrey, before whom Oates had sworn an affidavit of his charges, lent colour to the idea of the plot, and an Irish priest named Kelly was supposed to have had a hand in it. By 1680 belief in Oates had waned, but for the time being he was allowed to live unmolested in retirement; as late as 1682 some Catholic gentlemen in Munster were accused of complicity in the Plot, though they were acquitted by the Protestant Chief Justice [MacErlean (1910–17) ii pp. xiii–xxxix]. It was not until 1685, after the accession of James II, that Oates was eventually convicted of perjury, and condemned to be flogged and pilloried. However exaggerated the anti-Catholic panic may have been, it is likely enough that some Irish priests were at work in England.

Once the Protestant succession was assured by the "Glorious Revolution" of 1688, anti-Catholic and anti-Irish feeling began to die down, and there is little trace of it after 1700. During the eighteenth century Ireland remained relatively peaceful, and travel to England became a normal undertaking for the better-off. It is now that we meet for the first time a new figure in the plays, that of the Irish fortune-hunter, whose philosophy is succinctly described in the autograph manuscript of Thomas Sheridan's *Brave Irishman* (p. 52):

> Like many other Gentlemen of that Country I was fool enough to think I had nothing to do to make my Fortune, but to go to London, & that the bare Name of an Irishman was a Sufficient Recommendation to any Lady that I should make my Addresses to. I spent all my little Fortune in this vain Pursuit.

The first of our texts to introduce the figure of the Irish fortune-hunter is J. D. Breval's *The Play is the Plot* (XXIII); the whole point of *The Brave Irishman* (XXVII) is that Captain O'Blunder is not, in spite of all expectation, a fortune-hunter.

Evidence of the familiarity of Englishmen with Irish manners and speech is to be found in the extraordinary frequency with which, in the plays at least, they are able to undertake successful masquerades as Irishmen; sometimes they are even able to deceive real Irishmen. The plays must not be taken too seriously, of course, and we must allow for the convenience of the successful masquerade as a dramatic device; but even as a dramatic device the masquerade would lack plausibility if no Englishmen, or very few, had had the opportunity of observing the Irish. The earliest piece of evidence is the more convincing because it is indirect. In *Sir John Oldcastle* (II) an Irish servant is arrested in the mistaken belief that he is one Harpoole, steward to the heretic Lord Cobham : he protests his innocence, and claims that he is "Mack Chane of Vlster", but the judge dismisses his claim with the words "You cannot blinde vs with your broken Irish." Obviously criminals habitually used "broken Irish" to conceal their identities, and the judge was determined not to be taken in again. In *Old Fortunatus* (IV) Andelocia and his servant Shadow disguise themselves successfully as Irish costermongers. In Beaumont and Fletcher's *Coxcomb* (1612) Antonio disguises himself as an Irish footman and (at first) successfully deceives his wife Maria. In *The Welsh Embassador* (VII) Edmond, disguised as an Irish footman, successfully deceives his own brother. In Jonson's *New Inn* (1629) the distressed Lady Frampul disguises herself as a one-eyed Irish beggarwoman, and is able to speak a few words of Irish. After this there are no more masquerades for half a century, but in George Powell's play *A Very Good Wife* (1693) the malicious Venture disguises himself as an Irish doctor "Sir Feezil Mackafarty", so as to embarrass Squeezewitt by an accusation of venereal disease; he is only discovered when he loses his "mustachoes" in a scuffle. In Farquhar's *Beaux' Stratagem* (1707) Archer, masquerading as an Irishman, tricks Foigard into revealing himself as an Irish priest, and precisely the same device is used in *The Play is the Plot* (XXIII), where the servant Jeremy, also masquerading as an Irishman, tricks Machone into revealing himself as a deserter from the army. In the autograph manuscript of *The Brave Irishman*, though not in the printed texts, Schemewell comes in "disguised as an Irishwoman with a Child in his Arms", and claims to be O'Blunder's wife; O'Blunder knows he has no wife, but fails to detect the imposture.

Throughout our period there were plenty of Irishmen in England for writers to observe, and frequent masquerades show that close observation was common; what we do not know, unfortunately, is

181

the part of Ireland from which the exiles came. It is true that a number of sources do specify particular parts of Ireland. In *Sir John Oldcastle* (II), as we have seen, the Irishman claims to be "Mack Chane of Vlster"; in *The Irish Masque* (VI) the costermonger Dennis says that he was "borne in te English payle" (vi 55); in *The Welsh Embassador* (VII) the supposed Irish footman says that he had been in the service of the king of Leinster (vii 6–7); *Bog-Witticisms* (XV) is attributed to "Mac O Bonniclabbero of Drogheda", and in the passage printed above the footman comes from Tredagh, i.e. Drogheda (xv 34); Teague in *The Twin Rivals* (XIX) comes from Carrickfergus (xix 11); in *Ireland Preserved* (XX) the rapparees live within twelve miles of Derry (xx 111); the speakers in the poem about the riot at the Tholsel (XXI) must be Dubliners; in *The Play is the Plot* (XXIII) Machone has relatives in Tipperary (xxiii 78–80); in *The Pretender's Exercise* (XXIV) the recruit comes from Glenmalure in Co. Wicklow (xxiv 9); in *The Brave Irishman* (XXVII) Captain O'Blunder comes from Ballyjamesduff in Co. Cavan (xxvii 23). In addition certain texts are associated with certain places. The action of the scene from *Captain Thomas Stukeley* (I) takes place in Dundalk; *The Siege of Ballyally Castle* (IX) happened in Co. Clare; *Páirlement Chloinne Tomáis* (X) is connected with north Kerry; *The Fingallian Dance* (XI) and the two versions of the *Fingallian Burlesque* (XIII and XVII) are of course connected with Fingall north of Dublin, and so too apparently is the first scene from *Ireland Preserved* (XX); the action of *Hic et Ubique* (XII) takes place in Dublin, and that of *Muiris O Gormáin* (XXV) on the road to Drogheda. Unfortunately we cannot be certain that the writers of all these pieces had necessarily observed the Hiberno-English of speakers from the places they found it convenient to name in their works.

Nevertheless it is a striking fact that, of the nineteen associations with specific places, only four refer to places in the West of Ireland (Clare, Kerry, Derry, Tipperary); one to Ballyjamesduff, rather in the East than in the West; one to Ulster, stretching from West to East; and no less than thirteen to places actually on or within a few miles of the east coast of Ireland. No doubt the Irishmen who crossed the sea at various periods to seek their fortunes in England might have come from any part of Ireland, especially from any district where there was war or civil disturbance, but it seems likely that a high proportion of them would have come from the east coast, where English influence was strongest and the journey to England least exacting. Certainly those Englishmen who took Irish servants back with them to England would probably have taken them into their service in the Pale, and English visitors who observed the Irish on their native ground would have had most opportunity for observation in the same district. The conformity between historical probability and the evidence of the texts seems to justify us in assuming that most of our sources reflect the Hiberno-English of the east coast. If, therefore, we wish to examine the probable influence of the Irish language on this type of Hiberno-English, we shall have to take into account the peculiarities of the Irish spoken in the same districts.

Unfortunately the Irish of the east coast is the worst documented of any of the dialects of Irish. No mediæval dialect is well documented : the strength of the Irish literary tradition meant that the dialect features of spoken Irish were rarely recorded in written texts; the rhymes and assonances of bardic poetry continued to be used long after sound-change had made them inaccurate. A few scraps of Irish in anglicized spelling throw some light on pronunciation, but these are naturally few in number, and none can be located with confidence on the east coast. The short Irish phrase-book compiled by Andrew Boorde about 1540 [Furnivall (1870) 133–5] may, according to Lloyd [(1914) 18], reproduce "the speech of some part of the north of the ancient Laighin (Leinster) bordering on Meath. . . . There is some likelihood of these numbers and phrases having been drawn from the Irish then spoken in the city and county of Dublin." The five lines of verse printed by Murphy [(1953–5) 118], which refer to Fingall, may reproduce "the dialect spoken in Elizabethan times in some district near Dublin". [ibid. 118–9]

The modern dialects of the east coast are no better documented. Irish had ceased to be spoken in most of Leinster and eastern Ulster before the Census of 1851, but the Census of 1891 recorded the existence of 1,500 Irish-speakers in Co. Meath, 2,500 in Co. Louth, and nearly 10,000 in Cos. Cavan, Monaghan and Armagh. As late as 1931 Professor Wilhelm Dögen of Berlin was able to make recordings of the Irish of a number of places in eastern Ulster, and transcripts of some of his recordings were printed by Wagner [(1958–69) iv 283–305]. However, when Wagner began collecting material for his *Linguistic Atlas and Survey of Irish Dialects* in the the early 1950's he could find only one speaker in Co. Louth, one in Co. Monaghan, and two in Co. Cavan, and these had almost forgotten the Irish they had spoken as children [ibid. i 29–31]; a more substantial body of material was collected in Co. Tyrone, where there were still twelve speakers [ibid. i 32]. For the Irish of Co. Meath and Co. Louth we have to rely mainly on the unsystematic and unscientific work of Laoide [(1905) 123–6; (1914) 123–32]. Fortunately, however, there is evidence to suggest that the Irish of eastern Ulster and north Leinster had much in common with Manx Gaelic, about which we know a good deal (see below, §§ 46, 100). Since the seventeenth century Manx has had its own distinctive orthography, based on the orthographies of English and perhaps of Welsh [Thomson (1960) 118], so that many important features of pronunciation are discernible from written sources. Furthermore, the spoken language was relatively well documented before the last native speakers died in recent times. About 1890 Sir John Rhys spent some time in the Isle of Man, and in 1894 he published his *Outlines of the Phonology of Manx Gaelic*. About 1930 the Norwegian scholar Carl Marstrander visited the island and collected material, most of which remains unpublished, though some of it was used by Wagner [(1958–69) iv p. viii], who collected further material in the early 1950's; the material used by Jackson in his *Contributions to the Study of Manx Phonology* (1955) was collected in 1950.

Evidence of the close relationship between Manx Gaelic and the Irish of the adjacent coast is of various kinds. Historically such a relationship is very plausible : in the early Middle Ages Dublin, Man and the western isles of Scotland formed part of a single Scandinavian kingdom; the king of Man was often resident in Dublin [Kinvig (1950) 50–58]. Travel by water between Ireland and Man was a commonplace until recent times. Compelling evidence is provided by Rhys, and what he wrote is worth quoting rather fully [Rhys (1894) 163–4] :

> The course of the herring fishery brings Manxmen in contact with Irishmen chiefly on the coast of Munster, especially at the town of Kinsale. . . . The Manx fishermen who go there, and also to the west of Scotland, never have any hesitation in declaring that the Gaelic of the western Islands of Scotland is far more intelligible to them than Irish. . . . On the other hand a Manxman who speaks and reads his own Gaelic well has told me, how he was once in the habit of visiting the shores of

Carlingford Lough, and that he could understand the Gaelic of that district best, much better in fact than any Gaelic he had ever heard in Scotland.

Carlingford Lough divides Co. Louth from Co. Down, and therefore marks the boundary between the modern provinces of Leinster and Ulster; it lies in the heart of the coastal strip from which the majority of the Irishmen in our texts seem to have come. Of course Rhys's evidence does not prove identity or near-identity between Manx and east-coast Irish; he may be right in thinking that the lost Gaelic of Galloway would have been even closer to Manx than any form of Irish [Rhys (1894) 164]. According to Jackson [(1951) 78], in the thirteenth century or thereabouts Common Gaelic split up into two dialects, Eastern Gaelic and Western Gaelic, the former giving rise to Scottish and Manx Gaelic, the latter to Irish. In view of the number of important features shared by Scottish and Manx Gaelic but not found in Irish it is hardly possible to question Jackson's hypothesis; it seems likely, therefore, that the features shared by Manx Gaelic and the Irish of the eastern seaboard are the result of direct influence from Manx Gaelic, just as the features shared by Scottish Gaelic and the Irish of Ulster are due to direct influence from Scottish Gaelic [O'Rahilly (1932) 164, 260–61].

In seeking to explain the peculiarities of the Hiberno-English represented in some of the texts I shall often have occasion to refer to Manx Gaelic, not of course because any direct influence of Manx on Hiberno-English is at all probable, but because of the likelihood that features found in Manx may also have existed in the Irish of parts of the east coast. That this approach is not unprofitable is demonstrated by the fact that an unusual development of the verbal noun in Manx Gaelic, which so far as I am aware is not paralleled in any dialect of Irish, provides a satisfying explanation of certain Hiberno-English syntactic constructions which would otherwise be quite inexplicable (§§ 193–8, 201).

PHONOLOGY

CONSERVATISM AND INTERFERENCE

§1. The two basic peculiarities of Hiberno-English that we shall need to consider are conservatism and "interference" from the Irish language. Conservatism needs no special comment : it is a matter of observation that once a language becomes separated from its source it tends to stagnate—its rate of change slows down. It is easy enough to understand how the English spoken by Irishmen, who had little opportunity of hearing the speech of native Englishmen, should have been unaffected by changes taking place in England; it is less easy to understand why their English remained (apart from "interference" from Irish) so little changed. Nevertheless, parallel situations (such as the development of the French language in Canada) show that this is the normal pattern : once a language becomes isolated it tends to remain stable. "Interference" from the Irish language is a function of bilingualism, and needs further discussion. There are various types of bilingualism, but in every case it is convenient to speak of a "primary" and a "secondary" language [Weinreich (1963) 14] : the primary language is normally the native language, the mother tongue, the one which is learnt first; but in some bilingual situations the secondary language may be learnt soon after or even simultaneously with the primary language, and the difference is not one of priority but of allegiance. Language acquisition in infancy involves the learning of a number of unconscious "rules" which enable the speaker to frame new utterances : interference happens when the speaker transfers the "rules" of the primary language to the secondary language and frames an utterance which, in one way or another, would not be acceptable to a monoglot speaker of the secondary language : to put it crudely, the speaker is thinking in the primary language while speaking in the secondary language.

§2. The effects of interference in a bilingual situation may be direct or indirect, short-term or long-term. The direct, short-term effect of interference is that the bilingual speaker uses forms of speech which are imperfect attempts at the forms of the secondary language; there may be no stability at all in his imperfections, which may vary from utterance to utterance. If, however, the same imperfection is often enough repeated, either by the same speaker or by a number of speakers, it may become stabilized : that is, it may become an integral part of what is in effect a new form of language. This new form of language will depend on a number of "rules", some of which are proper to the primary language, others to the secondary language, and others again to neither language in its pure form; but the unsophisticated speaker will have no idea which is which, and all the "rules" he observes will for him have the same status. In such a case the indirect, long-term effects of bilingualism will last long after the bilingual situation has ceased to exist, and successive generations of monoglot speakers will use a language which, though historically it owes something both to the original primary and to the original secondary languages, now exists in its own right. A simple example of the process can be seen in the realm of vocabulary. There may be various reasons why a bilingual speaker using his secondary language will introduce a word or a phrase from his primary language (below, §§ 124, 142); but if enough speakers introduce the same word it may acquire the status of an inherited loanword [Weinreich (1963) 11], persisting after the bilingual situation has ceased to prevail and without consciousness of its origin; it may even in certain circumstances be taken over by native speakers of the secondary language.

§3. It is important not to make the error of assuming that evidence of interference at a given period is necessarily evidence of the existence of bilingualism at the same period, or that a period of bilingualism was necessarily followed by permanent monoglot speech. The linguistic history of the east coast of Ireland is very complex : as we have seen (above, pp. 23–9), periods of bilingualism in various languages have been interspersed with periods of monoglot Irish speaking. Even as far as English is concerned, historical circumstances were such that we cannot exclude the possibility of fluctuation between monoglot English speaking, monoglot Irish speaking, and bilingualism. In favourable circumstances it may be possible to deduce from the evidence the approximate date of the acquisition of English by Irish-speakers, but we cannot feel confident that this was the first, last, or only acquisition of English.

187

§4. Any attempt to reconstruct the phonology of seventeenth-century Hiberno-English must be based very largely on the evidence of non-standard spellings in the texts. The rhymes in verse texts can tell us no more than that two sounds were pronounced in the same way, without giving any clue to the quality of the common sound; such evidence is certainly important, but it is very limited in its significance, and the number of verse texts is in any case rather small. The assonances in *Muiris O Gormáin* (XXV) are slightly more rewarding, since they establish a relationship between English and Irish vowels; but this is a short text, and the number of assonances is small.

§5. Only one of our texts, *Ballyally Castle* (IX) is the work of what we may call a "native" writer—that is, a speaker of Hiberno-English—and it is important to note that the kind of non-standard spelling likely to be found in such a text is very different from the kind of spelling to be found in the work of an "external" writer—that is, one who is making a deliberate attempt to represent a type of speech which is not his own. If we leave aside mere slips and illiteracies, the "native" writer is likely to use non-standard spellings only when two sounds, originally distinct, have fallen together; and in such a case he is likely to err in both directions—that is, he is likely to use a spelling appropriate to one sound when a spelling appropriate to the other would be "correct"—with approximately equal frequency. In seventeenth-century Hiberno-English, ME $\bar{\imath}$ and $\bar{e}$ had fallen together in /i:/ (below, §§ 40, 65). In such circumstances a "native" writer is likely to use *i* for *ee* just as often as he uses *ee* for *i*, and this is in fact precisely what we find in the *Aphorismical Discovery*. An "external" writer, however, will do no such thing: he is likely enough to use *ee* for *i*, to show that the reflex of ME $\bar{\imath}$ is not a diphthong but /i:/, but he will certainly not use *i* for *ee*, since this could only suggest that the reflex of ME $\bar{e}$ was some such diphthong as /əi/. Since the reflex of ME $\bar{e}$ in the case we are envisaging would not differ from its reflex in Standard English, no non-standard spelling is required.

§6. The activities of the "external" writer involve what Weinreich [(1963) 21] calls "double interference":

> When a lay unilingual hears his language spoken with a foreign "accent", his perception and interpretation of the accent is itself subject to the interference of his native phonic

system. A bilingual attempting to speak language S, for example, renders the sounds of S by reference to the system of language P, which to him is primary; the unilingual speaker-listener of S then interprets this distorted speech by reference to the S system as the primary one.

In our particular case, the Irishman renders the sounds of English by reference to the system of Irish; the English-speaker listening to him perceives and interprets his utterance by reference to the system of English. Our case is in fact more complicated than the one envisaged by Weinreich, since some of the writers of our texts were themselves Irishmen, and may have spoken a type of English which was not identical with the Standard English of the time; but the principle is the same. For instance, the consonant /θ/ does not occur in Irish, and the speaker of Hiberno-English renders it by the pure dental stop /т/, which shares with /θ/ its dental articulation, though not its spirant quality (below, §82); the English-speaker is likely to interpret this /т/ as /t/, which shares with /т/ its stop quality, though not its dental articulation. Thus, though English /θ/ and /t/ are hardly ever confused in Hiberno-English, the English-speaking listener may think that they are, and may use the symbol t to represent the Hiberno-English articulation of both. Even if we could be sure what the writer intended by his symbol, we could not be sure that what he intended was identical with what was in fact used by the Hiberno-English speaker.

§7. In practice we can seldom be sure exactly what is intended by the writer. If the writer used a scientific phonetic notation we could indeed be sure, but of course he does not; he has to use the ordinary English alphabet, and he is bound by the conventions of ordinary English orthography, which alone is familiar to his readers; and English orthography is remarkably unsystematic, and therefore ambiguous, even in comparison with that of other European languages. Even if a writer had an ear acute enough to avoid the "double interference" described above, there is no way in which he could represent the finer differences between sounds. If, for instance, he was able to observe that Hiberno-English /т/ (substituted for English /θ/) was not identical with /t/, there is no way in which he could convey the difference between them to the reader. Some sounds cannot be indicated at all, since there is no appropriate graphy for them. The phoneme /ʒ/ is not very rare in English; it occurs in words like *leisure* and *vision*, and in foreign words like *rouge*; yet neither s nor g would in any way suggest the sound. The reader cannot tell whether the writer's perceptions and interpretations are entirely governed by "double interference", or whether he has been able to observe some of the finer differences; in either case he may have been debarred by the deficiencies of English orthography from accurately representing his perception, and may have had to resort to some potentially misleading approximation. For this reason, non-standard spellings cannot be interpreted at all except in the light of the reader's expectations.

§8. It may be useful to illustrate this important point by an example which has nothing to do with Hiberno-English. Boswell tells us [*Life of Dr Johnson*, 23rd March 1776] that Dr Johnson never entirely rid himself of his Lichfield accent :

> Garrick sometimes used to take him off, squeezing a lemon into a punch-bowl, with uncouth gesticulations, looking round the company, and calling out, "Who's for *poonsh*?"

We have to ask ourselves how Johnson (or rather Garrick imitating Johnson) actually pronounced the word *punch*. The graphy *oo* has three values in English : the most common is /u :/, as in *food*, but it may also stand for /u/, as in *good*, or /ʌ/, as in *blood*. We can eliminate the last value without more ado, since this is the vowel used in Standard English, and there would be no point in devising a variant spelling for a standard pronunciation; we have to decide, then, between the values /u :/ and /u/. Our decision will be based on our knowledge, however vague, that words which in Standard English have /ʌ/ are pronounced in northern dialects with /u/, and that such words are not pronounced with /u :/ in any dialect of English [Wright (1905) §98] : we shall conclude that Johnson (or Garrick) said /punʃ/, and no doubt we shall be right. Our conclusion will be based, not exclusively on the spelling, nor exclusively on our expectations, but on a combination of the two. If our expectations are ill-founded, our conclusion is likely to be wrong. In interpreting the spelling *poonsh* we have assumed that the distribution of sounds in Standard English and the dialects was approximately the same in the eighteenth century as it is today, and this is probably true, at least as far as the sounds in question are concerned; but if it had not been so, our conclusions might have been entirely wrong.

§9. The difficulty facing us in the interpretation of the non-standard spellings in our texts is that it is not obvious that we can have any rational expectations at all, since we start by knowing nothing about the pronunciation of early modern Hiberno-English; and if we have no rational expectations we shall not be able to interpret the spellings. The only way to by-pass this difficulty is by constructing a number of hypotheses consistent with the known historical circumstances affecting the development of the English language in Ireland; if we are lucky, the spellings will enable us to eliminate all but one of our hypotheses, or at least to modify one of them in a way which does not violate historical plausibility. Whatever this spelling may mean (we may be able to say to ourselves), it cannot mean *that*, or *that*, or *that*; whatever is left over must give us the right answer, provided the remaining possibility is one which might reasonably have been represented in this way; if it is not, we must see whether we can modify our hypotheses.

§10. Our first task, therefore, is to consider the probable nature of Hiberno-English pronunciation in the light of what we know about its origin. The history of the English language in Ireland would lead us to expect that each variety of Hiberno-English would be descended from some type of English acquired by Irish-speakers and modified to conform more closely to the structure of the Irish language. As we have seen (above, §3), it is important not to over-simplify: the special circumstances of each part of the country need to be considered separately. If, as is usually the case, the historical evidence is not sufficient to establish the linguistic history of a district in detail, we must establish a number of hypotheses based on different dates for the acquisition of English, and different processes of accommodation to the Irish pattern; in favourable circumstances the spellings will tell us which of the hypotheses is valid. Vowels and consonants have had very different histories, and will need to be considered separately; but first there are a few general points to be disposed of.

NON-SIGNIFICANT SPELLINGS AND RHYMES

§11. A number of spellings in our texts are of no phonological significance, even though they cannot be called standard. In *Bally-ally Castle* (IX) such spellings are merely a function of the general mild illiteracy of the text: *pewritan* 'puritan' (5), *excamenation* 'examination' (31), *exsamen* 'examine' (32), *one* 'on' (54 &c.), *dimetrie* 'diameter' (85), *hadgard* 'haggard' (92). In other texts such spellings are normally of a kind which, though seldom used by printers in the period in question, still survived among writers: *forgeats* 'forgets' (i 34), *weare* 'were' (vii 160), *jeast* 'jest' (xiii 77), *yong* 'young' (xv 27), *cople* 'couple' (xv 27), *fese* 'fees' (xv 52), *enuff* 'enough' (xviii 23 &c.), *feaver* 'fever' (xviii 81), *poiet* 'poet' (xviii 109), *shud* 'should' (xxi 40 &c.); in the spellings *eleavent* 'eleventh' (xviii 150), *trew* 'through' (xxi 36), the use of *t* for *th* is significant, but the representation of the stressed vowel is not. About half of these spellings are in texts printed here from manuscripts; the other half are from printed editions, but no doubt a printer instructed to take pains with intentional non-standard spellings would be more than usually likely to preserve mere eccentricities. In a few instances the spelling may reflect a non-standard pronunciation: *jeast* is rhymed with *beast*, and some of the orthoepists record a long vowel in *jest* [Dobson (1968) §8 (2)]. Since such pronunciations are not specifically Hiberno-English, little is lost by not considering them in detail. Two spellings in *Bog-Witticisms* (XV) are in a different category: the word *scrivener* is spelt *skrivishner* (7) and *skriviwnar* (48); neither of these is explicable in terms of any probable sound-change or sound-substitution, and (if they are not merely misprints) they reflect the speaker's ignorance of the sound of a rare word. The rhyme *come* : *Rome* (xvii 19) may be merely an eye-rhyme, but it may be accurate: *Rome* normally has /u:/ in this period [Dobson (1968) §154], and *come* may have [ibid. §18].

VARIANT FORMS

§12. As far as one can tell from the spellings, some of the forms in our texts have developed from variant forms current in an earlier period of the English language; that is, from forms different from those which gave rise to the forms current in Standard English. It seems convenient to deal with these all together at this point, though it will mean anticipating some later conclusions in the interpretation of the spellings.

§13. First of all, there are a number of forms characteristic of the western dialects of English. In the eastern dialects of Middle English, OE *y* developed into *i* or *e*, but in the western dialects it developed into *ü*, which in certain circumstances could become *u*. The spellings *shurt* 'shirt' (i 13), *bult* 'built' (ix 55 &c.), *bourying* 'burying' (xviii 6) seem to reflect this western development of OE *scyrte*, *byldan*, *byrgan*. Other western dialect forms show the development of ME *a* into a diphthong *ai* before /ndʒ/ in *daingeroes*

192

'dangerous' (ix 3) [Dobson (1968) §63] and the lengthening of ME *a* before intervocalic /r/ in *mawrry'd, mawrried* 'married' (xv 51, 54) [ibid. §§ 44, 55 n.2]. A number of ME words had variation between *a* and *ā*, and in the word *water* the survival of *ā* seems to be a western dialect feature; this is reflected in the spellings *vayter, vaiter* (vi 48 &c., xii 89); in *waaterman, vaaterman* (xv 10, 63) the StE lengthening and retraction of ME *a* has not taken place. In other words the survival of *ā* seems not to be limited to any dialect in particular; here belong the spellings *faather, faader* 'father' (xiv 14, xviii 11 &c.), *auny* 'any' (xv 33) [Dobson (1968) §6], and perhaps *rauvish* 'ravish' (xx 100), though there seems to be no direct evidence of ME *ā* in *ravish*. Other dialect features which are not specifically western are the development of forms of the word *master* from forms which had ME *ai* (below, §52), and the development from OE (Anglian) *nēr* rather than OE (WS) *nēar* implied in the spelling *neere* 'near' (ix 83) [Dobson (1968) §119 (a)].

§14. Variation between ME *e* and *a* occurred in a number of words, and seventeenth-century English did not always prefer the form preferred in present-day English. The words *then, when* and *thresh* had common forms with *a* (and the pronunciation of *thresh* preserves this form); on the other hand *than* and *gather* had common forms with *e*. Variation before /r/ is also frequent, since the lowering effect of /r/ did not operate uniformly. The spellings *teere* 'dear' (iv 13), *heere* 'hear' (ix 19), *cleere* 'clear' (ix 75) and *deer* 'dear' (xx 23) reflect forms in which ME *ē* was not lowered before /r/ as in Standard English; the spelling *bear* 'beer' (xxvi 13) reflects a form in which non-standard lowering took place; the rhyme *beares : yeares* (xiii 33) implies one or other of these changes. The spelling *foreces* 'forces' (ix 17) reflects a ME variant with *ǫ* rather than *o* [Dobson (1968) §13]; *foremarly* 'formerly' (ix 37) is probably due to the association of this word with *fore* [ibid. §47]. The spelling *daury* 'dairy' (xv 36) implies the smoothing of ME *ai* to *ā* before /r/ [ibid. §231]. The spelling *turd* 'third' (i 42, xviii 1 &c.) reflects the sound-change whereby metathesis of *ri* in ME *pridde* resulted, not in *ir* as might have been expected, but *ur* [ibid. §84]; the effects of the change can no longer be discerned in Standard English, in which both *ir* and *ur* have given /ə:/, but present-day Hiberno-English still retains the reflex of *ur*. The rounding influence of /w/ is reflected in *wut* 'wilt' (v 13 &c.).

§15. Words which are sometimes used in stressed and sometimes in unstressed positions tend to develop distinctive forms according to the stress; in course of time it may happen that an original un-stressed form is stressed again, so that a new stressed form different from the original one is developed. This is what has happened in Standard English in the words *have, hath, shall, shalt,* now pro-nounced with short *a* instead of the original ME *ā* or *au*; the original stressed forms are implied by the spellings *hauve* (xv 43 &c.), *hate* (xviii 8 &c.), *shaul* (xv 55), *shaut* (xv 47), and by the rhyme *have her : favour* (xiii 105). Some unstressed forms not now heard, or heard only in very informal speech, are implied by spellings in our texts. Reduction of prepositions is particularly common in the earliest texts, up to about 1625 : *a* 'on' (v 16, vi 27, vii 32), *o* 'on' (vi 65), *a* 'of' (v 32, vi 87, vii 23). In other prepositions and in pro-nouns a long vowel or diphthong may be reduced to a short and perhaps obscure vowel : *be* 'by' (ii 5, iii 47, vi 8 &c., xi 5, xii 21, xiii 21 &c., xv 8 &c., xix 4 &c., xxiii 61 &c., xxv 7); *me* 'my' (ii 20 &c., vi 4 &c., xi 5, xii 21, xiii 37 &c., xv 8 &c., xix 4 &c., xxiii 61 &c., xxv 7); *de* 'thee' (v 45 &c., xii 117, xx 77 &c.); *de* 'they' (xi 9).

STRESS

§16. As early as 1577 Stanihurst described a non-standard type of accentuation to be heard in Wexford (and probably in Fingall too, though his wording is not entirely clear on this point) [Holinshed (1577) f. 3*r* col. 1] :

> Most commonly in wordes of two sillables, they giue the last the accent. As they say, Markeate, Baskeate, Gossoupe, Pus-soate, Robart, Niclase, &c., which doubtlesse doth disbeautifie their Englishe aboue measure.

The accuracy of Stanihurst's observation, at least as far as Wexford is concerned, is confirmed by more recent observers of the dialect of Forth and Bargy [Barnes (1867) 13]. There is a striking parallel, which has not passed unnoticed, between the aberrant accentuation of Wexford and Fingall and the accentuation of the southern dialects of Irish.

§17. In general the stress falls on the first syllable of polysyllabic words in all varieties of Gaelic. In the Munster dialects, however, the stress falls on the second syllable whenever that syllable is long, and even on the third syllable of trisyllabic words if that syllable is long and the first two syllables are short; this accentuation has been attributed with some plausibility to the influence of Norman French,

194

in which a similar accentuation prevailed [O'Rahilly (1932) 87–9]. In northern dialects of Irish the original stress remains; in Ulster Irish and in Scottish Gaelic the long vowel of an unstressed final syllable is shortened. According to O'Rahilly [ibid. 87] the southern accentuation prevailed in south Leinster as well as in Munster, and extended as far north as north Co. Dublin; it is not clear, however, what kind of evidence he relied on, and his conclusions have been vigorously contested by Piatt [(1933) 21–2]. The accentuation of Manx Gaelic is curious and distinctive; it combines elements of both the southern and the northern stress-systems. The stress is shifted to a long second syllable only if the first syllable too is long; if the first syllable is short it retains the stress, and the long vowel of the second syllable is shortened as in Ulster Irish and Scottish Gaelic [Jackson (1955) 19–20]. There seems to be no evidence to show whether or not a similar system prevailed in east-coast Irish.

§18. The evidence for the occurrence of postponed stress in Hiberno-English consists partly of rhymes and partly of non-standard spellings. In verse texts the rhyming of a word normally stressed on the first syllable with a monosyllable, or with a poly-syllable invariably stressed on the final syllable, is conclusive evidence of postponed stress. A rhyme between two disyllables with the same ending, which would not provide a good rhyme if they were stressed on the first syllable, is strong but not conclusive evidence of postponed stress, since allowance must be made for the possibility of approximate or defective rhyme; metre may also suggest postponed stress, but again allowance must be made for the possibility of irregular metre. Spelling is an insecure guide, since there is no way of indicating the position of the stress in standard orthography : the best that can be done is to use a spelling which suggests the length which probably accompanied the postponed stress, as Stanihurst does in the passage quoted in §16. An additional device is the insertion of a hyphen : since the second element of all compounds retains some degree of stress, the hyphen (suggesting as it does that the word is properly a compound) ingeniously suggests some degree of stress on the second syllable. Where the standard orthography suggests a long vowel in the second syllable, as in *picture*, the hyphen is the only orthographic device which can suggest postponed stress.

§19. All seventeenth-century texts which purport to be Fingal-lian contain evidence of one kind or another that certain words have postponed stress. The explicitly Fingallian texts printed below

195

are *The Fingallian Dance* (XI), *Purgatorium Hibernicum* (XIII) and *The Irish Hudibras* (XVI). As it happens, no instances of postponed stress occur in the passage from *Purgatorium Hibernicum* printed above, though there are some in other parts of the work; but there are plentiful instances in the other two pieces. Postponed stress appears to occur also in *Stukeley* (I), *Hic et Ubique* (XII) and *Ireland Preserved* (XX), though since these are prose texts the evidence consists exclusively of spellings, and is not entirely conclusive; these three pieces may also represent Fingallian, even though they do not claim to do so (below, §21). The instances in *The Fingallian Dance* (XI) are *daunceirs* 'dancers' (: *hairs*) (3), *plack-keet* 'placket' (9*) and *rac-keet* 'racket' (12) [an asterisk indicates that the form cited is due to an emendation]; the last two instances rhyme together, but this does not help us, since the two words would rhyme no matter what the stress. In *The Irish Hudibras* (XVI) a number of instances are confirmed by rhymes with monosyllables : *pray-ere* 'prayer' (: *hear*) (6), *mak-keer* 'maker' (: *swear*) (16), *quar-teer* 'quarter' (: *here*) (32), *pic-ture* (: *whore*) (68) *shoul-deer* 'shoulder' (: *swear*) (98). The rhyme *question'd* : *postpond* (41) seems to leave no doubt that in *question'd* the stress is on the second syllable. Other rhymes are less conclusive, since both words appear to have postponed stress : *a-ceers* 'acres' : *fa-deers* 'fathers' (47), *va-teer* 'water' : *fa-deer* 'father' (93, 105). So far all the words in question have been English words, but the next rhyme introduces an Irish word : *par-doon* 'pardon' : *gar-soon*, Ir. *garsún* 'boy' (91). Other Irish words rhymed with English words are *clampeer*, Ir. *clampar* 'noise' (: *dear*) (74) and *cro-naan*, Ir. *crónán* 'song' (: *profane*) (78). Finally, there is one instance in this text of a trisyllabic word with postponed stress, *mi-ra-cles* 'miracles' (71); since the word occurs within the line the position of the stress is indicated only by the metre and the hyphens, but there can be no serious doubt of what is intended. In *Stukeley* (I), *Hic et Ubique* (XII) and *Ireland Preserved* (XX) we have to rely entirely on the spelling, a dangerous guide; but the fact that each text contains at least two spellings suggesting postponed stress is reassuring. The instances of English words are *ovare* 'over' (i 10), *blankead* 'blanket' (i 14), *sougare* 'soldier' (xii 32), *michear*, *micheer* 'micher, thief' (xii 39, 121), *bacoan* 'bacon' (xx 8 &c.), *minishteer* 'minister' (xx 129); there is also one instance of an Irish word apparently stressed on the second syllable, *moistere*, *moistare*, Ir. *máighistir* 'master' (xii 1, 8 &c.).

196

§20. In those varieties of Gaelic which display a shift of stress the stress is never shifted unless the second syllable is long. Of the four Irish words listed above two (*garsún, crónán*) meet this qualification, and both would be stressed on the second syllable in Munster Irish and Manx Gaelic; but the other two words (*clampar, máighistir*) do not meet the qualification, and would not have postponed stress in any variety of Gaelic. The Hiberno-English phenomenon, therefore, cannot be directly related to any Gaelic antecedent. Many of the English words affected are of Norman-French origin, and in all but one of these the postponed stress might in theory be due to the survival of the original stress; but in the native words the second syllable had never been stressed. The words of French origin are *dancer, placket, prayer, quarter, picture, questioned, pardon, miracles, blanket, soldier, micher, bacon,* and *minister.* Some of these words have been borrowed into Irish, and it is particularly interesting to compare Ir. *blaincéad* with the *blankead* used in *Stukeley.* In the native words *maker, father, water* and *over,* the vowel of the second syllable was always short and unstressed in the historic period; *acre* and *shoulder* were originally monosyllabic, the second vowel being introduced merely to facilitate the pronunciation of the /r/; *racket* is of uncertain origin, and is perhaps onomatopœic. The Hiberno-English tendency seems to go far beyond anything discernible in any variety of Gaelic, and reflects a general desire to stress any polysyllabic word on the final rather than on the first syllable; the only Irish parallel known to me is the existence of a form *ministéar* 'minister' (stressed on the final syllable in Munster Irish) beside the more usual *ministir.*

§21. *Stukeley* (I), *Hic et Ubique* (XII) and *Ireland Preserved* (XX) do not purport to reflect the Fingallian dialect : the action of the first takes place in Dundalk, that of the second in Dublin; though the first scene of *Ireland Preserved* printed here may be connected with Fingall by the instruction "*Fingall* Dance" in the introductory stage-direction, one of the two words with postponed stress occurs in the third scene, the action of which takes place in Derry. There are two possible explanations of the occurrence of postponed stress in these three texts. One possibility is that the authors of the plays happened to be acquainted with Fingallian and used it in their plays without being aware of or concerned about its inappropriateness. The other possibility is that the Hiberno-English of the towns shared certain features with Fingallian. There is, unfortunately, no direct evidence at all about the nature of the

English spoken in the towns; neither Stanihurst nor any other writer so much as mentions it. Historically it is likely enough that wherever Mediæval Hiberno-English survived it would have much the same development, so that a likeness between urban Hiberno-English and the dialects of Wexford and Fingall is perhaps to be expected. Dublin and Dundalk in particular might be expected to show features in common with Fingallian, partly because of their geographical contiguity (Dublin on the southern edge of Fingall, Dundalk not far from its northern limits), partly because of the probable migration of the people of Fingall to the towns to seek employment as servants or tradesmen.

Theoretical expectations

§22. The Common Gaelic vowel system consisted of five short vowels, *i e a o u*, and five long vowels, *í é á ó ú*; there were also certain diphthongs resulting from the vocalization of spirants, but with these we are not now concerned. The short vowels in general remained; in Irish, however, the five short vowel phonemes were reduced to three at some date not easily established, but probably towards the end of the seventeenth century, and therefore too late to concern us (below, §74); only scanty traces of this development are found in Scottish and Manx Gaelic [Jackson (1955) 44]. The long vowels have in general remained to the present day, but in Manx Gaelic (and in the Irish of parts of the east coast—§46) there was a substantial change : long *á* was fronted and raised to /ɛ:/, and new long vowels /a:/ and /ɔ:/ were developed from short *a* and *o* respectively by various processes of lengthening and contraction. The result was a seven-phoneme system [Thomson (1976) 258], the relationship of which to the phonemic system of Common Gaelic can be shown by a diagram :

Common Gaelic :	*í*	*é*	*á*	*a*	*o*	*ó*	*ú*
Manx Gaelic :	/i:/	/e:/	/ɛ:/	/a:/	/ɔ:/	/o:/	/u:/

Manx Gaelic also has a front rounded phoneme /œ:/, but this seems to be of recent origin and need not concern us. What we have to consider is the inter-relationship of these various systems with various English vowel-systems from the Middle English period onwards; and it is the long vowels which are crucial.

§23. Middle English had seven long vowels *ī ē ę̄ ā ǭ ō ū*, and what we have to examine is the probable reception and pronunciation of these by speakers of various kinds of Irish. For the speaker of a variety of Irish which retained the five long vowels of Common Gaelic, the problem would not be a simple one : he would have had difficulty in distinguishing the seven long vowels of Middle English, and would have tended to run two pairs of them together. There can be little doubt that ME *ā* would be equated with CG *á*, but after this the doubt begins. Our clearest guide is to be found in the many words, originally of Norman-French origin, which entered Irish either directly from Norman French, or more probably from Middle English : among the front vowels, *ę̄* and *ē* were both equated with CG *é*, and *ī* was equated with CG *í* [Risk (1968–75) §§ 1, 12]. On the basis of these equivalences it would be natural to assume that our hypothetical bilingual speakers would also equate ME *ę̄* and *ē* with CG *é*, and ME *ī* with CG *í*. This need not necessarily be so, however : the equivalences established for the Norman-French words belong to an early period, and different equivalences might have prevailed if the acquisition of the English language did not occur until the transitional period between Middle and Modern English, when the beginnings of the "Great Vowel Shift" had already begun to affect the quality of the long vowels. There must have been a stage during this transitional period when ME *ē* was already a very close vowel, and the diphthongization of ME *ī* had proceeded no further than to [ɪi]; the two vowels, though still perfectly distinct to a speaker of English (as they must have remained, since they never fell together), might have seemed very similar or possibly indistinguishable to an Irishman, who might then equate them both with CG *í*. The same considerations are applicable to back vowels : if the acquisition of English was early, ME *ǭ* and *ō* might both be equated with CG *ó*, but if it happened in the transitional period ME *ō* and *ū* might both be equated with CG *ú*.

§24. If a bilingual community had made such an accommodation between the phonemes of their English and their Irish, and their Irish was subsequently affected by the fronting and raising of CG *á* to /ɛ:/, it is likely that they would adjust their pronunciation of ME *ā* in the same way (cf. §119); similarly, it is probable that ME *a* and *o* would tend to be lengthened, though not necessarily in the same contexts as provoked lengthening of CG *a* and *o*; certainly the English lengthening of the same short vowels would have been very readily accepted. If, on the other hand, the Irish spoken by a bilingual community had already undergone the changes in question, the result would have been quite different. The speaker of east-coast Irish would naturally equate his own seven long vowel phonemes with the seven long vowel phonemes of Middle English; the English of such speakers, provided it was not complicated by acquaintance with a later form of English, would have remained extremely conservative but not otherwise distinctive. If the acquisition of English happened so late that ME $\bar{\imath}$ and $\bar{u}$ had been fully diphthongized to /əi/ and /əu/ respectively, the problem would again have been different. There would now have been only five long vowels, those developed from ME $\bar{e}$ $\bar{ę}$ $\bar{a}$ $\bar{ǫ}$ $\bar{o}$, and Irish-speakers who had preserved the five long vowels of Common Gaelic unchanged would naturally equate the two sets of vowels. Irish-speakers whose language had been affected by the east-coast changes described above would have been able to make a choice of the equivalences they established, the choice being dictated by the precise realization of the English vowels at the crucial time.

§25. These, then, are some of the rational expectations we should bear in mind when interpreting non-standard spellings; but there are further considerations based on the fact that English pronunciation in the period covered by our texts was neither homogeneous nor stable. If we exclude types of speech which were dialectal or vulgar, we are still left with a range of pronunciations varying from the very "conservative" pronunciations of the older dignitaries to the very "progressive" pronunciations of the young and fashionable. There would be no point in using non-standard spellings (even if there were any unambiguous ways of doing it, which seems unlikely) to indicate pronunciations in use among any substantial body of speakers of Standard English. As we have seen (§1), there is reason to suppose that Hiberno-English was very conservative, and it must no doubt have been amusing for an Englishman to hear an Irish peasant using pronunciations appropriate to a bishop or a judge; but it is difficult to see how such pronunciations could be suggested by non-standard spellings if they were in accordance with one accepted interpretation of the standard spelling. Furthermore, standard pronunciation was in a constant state of flux, so that the progressive pronunciation of one generation became the conservative pronunciation of the next; if, as seems likely, Hiberno-English pronunciation was very stable, features of it which would be noteworthy and therefore worth indicating at one period might

200

be standard at another. For this reason it is necessary for us to look briefly at changes in pronunciation in the course of the seventeenth century; it is impossible to give accurate dates for the changes that took place, because they took place at different dates in the speech of different classes of speaker, and the account which follows must be considered as no more than a rough outline [see also Dobson (1955) 36–8].

§26. The ME short vowels underwent relatively little change, and two of them, *i* and *e*, are still pronounced much as they were in Middle English. ME *a* was probably still mainly /a/ at the beginning of the century, but it was soon raised to /æ/. ME *o* was lowered a little to its present value of /ɒ/. ME *u* was generally lowered and unrounded to something like the present /ʌ/, but in some words in which it was preceded by a labial consonant the original quality remained; this distinction was merely allophonic until the middle of the century, when a further shortening of /u:/ from ME *ō* gave a new vowel of the same quality [ʊ], not conditioned by a labial context; the result was a new phoneme /u/. Later seventeenth-century English therefore had six short vowel phonemes /i e æ ɒ ʌ u/.

§27. The history of the seven ME long vowels is more complicated. Late Middle English saw the beginning of the raising of ME *ē* and *ō* towards /i:/ and /u:/ respectively and of the diphthongization of ME *ī* and *ū* towards /əi/ and /əu/ respectively. The precise chronology of these changes is uncertain (below, §§ 65–8), but they were certainly complete before the end of the sixteenth century, so that about 1600 English had five long vowel phonemes /i: ɛ: a: ɔ: u:/. The earliest seventeenth-century change was that of ME *ā* to /æ:/. In the course of the century ME *ę̄* and *ǭ* were raised to /e:/ and /o:/ respectively. The number of long vowels was increased by the monophthongization of ME *ai* and *au* to /ɛ:/ and /ɒ:/ respectively; before labial consonants and /n/ the latter had a front allophone [a:]; about the middle of the century the allophones [ɒ:] and [a:] became phonemic when they coincided with allophones of ME *o* and *a* lengthened before voiceless spirants and /r/. At this time, therefore, there were eight long vowel phonemes in Standard English, /i: e: ɛ: æ: a: ɒ: o: u:/. These eight phonemes were unevenly distributed, five of them representing front vowels and three back vowels, and this disproportion was eliminated by further raising of the front vowels. In particular, the reflex of ME *ai* did not long retain a separate identity: it fell together either with ME $\bar{a}$ or occasionally with ME $\bar{\e}$; late in the century ME $\bar{a}$ was itself raised to identity with ME $\bar{\e}$. About 1700 a dialectal pronunciation with /i :/ was substituted for /e :/ in all but a few of the words with ME $\bar{\e}$. At the end of the seventeenth century there were therefore six long vowel phonemes /i: e: a: ɒ: o: u:/.

§28. As well as ME *ai* and *au*, ME *ou* also underwent smoothing to identity with ME $\bar{\varrho}$, whose subsequent development it shared. ME *eu* and *iu* fell together in /iu/, which developed in the second half of the seventeenth century to /ju :/. Words written with *oi* had two pronunciations, one with ME *oi* and the other with ME *ui* : when ME *u* was lowered to /ʌ/, ME *ui* became [ʌi] and fell together with /əi/ from ME $\bar{\i}$; ME *oi* remained as /ɔi/. Later seventeenth-century English therefore had three diphthongal phonemes /əi əu ɔi/.

The stressed vowels in detail

ME *i*

§29. In present-day Hiberno-English, ME *i* is often realized as a close [i] rather than the StE [ɪ]. Spellings suggesting a similar pronunciation are not uncommon in our texts : *peepin* 'pippin' (iv 2 &c.), *peeps(h)* 'pips' (iv 2 &c., vi 6 &c.), *sheet* 'sit' (v 7 &c.), *leetell* 'little' (ix 86), *geeven* 'given' (xv 63), *cheester* 'sister' (xxiii 106). The only one of these words in which lengthening of ME *i* is at all likely is *given* [Dobson (1968) §10]. The spelling *preeson* 'prison' (xxiii 130) may be a further instance of the same phenomenon, or it may be a reflex of Ir. *priosún*, which preserves the original ME long vowel. Spellings with *ee* occur in the *Aphorismical Discovery* : *breeke* 'brick', *reede* 'rid'. However, the more frequent non-standard spellings suggest lowering rather than raising : *hest* 'hist' (i 7), *lettle* 'little' (i 15), *heter* 'hither' (vi 101), *fether* 'whither' (viii 80 &c.), *tell* 'till' (ix 62), *drenk* 'drink' (xv 6), *untel* 'until' (xv 41), *breng* 'bring' (xv 63), *bremston(e)* 'brimstone' (xviii 95 &c.), *fell* 'will' (xx 71 &c.). Lowering of ME *i* to *e* is attested from the ME period onwards [Dobson (1968) §80], and persists in the dialects [Wright (1905) §68]. In Ireland, lowering is characteristic of Ulster dialects [Adams (1948) 16], and is no doubt to be associated with the similar lowering in Scotland. Some Ulster dialects have marked lowering to [æ], or lowering and retraction to [ʌ] [Adams (1948) 22; Gregg (1964) §2.1], and this is no doubt what is intended by *fafteen*

'fifteen' (xx 7 &c.), and perhaps by *feadar* 'whither' (xxv 8), since
this text is in Irish, and in Irish orthography *feadar* would imply
/f'adər/; however, since lowering of ME *i* to *e* in *whither* is
exceptionally early [Dobson (1968) §80], this form may rather show
lowering of *e* to *a* (below, §31).

ME *e*

§30. One of the best-known features of present-day Hiberno-
English is the raising of /e/ to /i/ before nasals, and occasionally
before other consonants. Raising of ME *e* to *i* is well documented
in seventeenth-century English [Dobson (1968) §77]; raising of /e/
to /i/, especially before nasals, is also common in Irish, though its
operation is often concealed by a change in the spelling, as when
MIr. *teine* 'fire' is now spelt *tine*. The first of our texts to show this
sound-change systematically is *Teigue and Dermot* (XXI), which
has *whin* 'when' (22 &c.), *min* 'men' (23), *wint* 'went' (30), *thin*
'then' (34), *lift* 'left *v.*' (37), *gitt* 'get' (52), *ilse* 'else' (56). Other
instances are *virmine* 'vermin' (vii 148), *lift* 'left *n.*' (xxiv 26 &c.),
phin 'when' (xxvii 136); the rhymes *forgiven* : *Heaven* (xvii 61),
gitt : *Sit* (xxi 52) provide further evidence of the same phenomenon. Significant spellings occur in the *Aphorismical Discovery*, which
has *inter* 'enter', *inuious* 'envious', *trincher* 'trencher'. The form
fither 'whether' (xix 149) cannot be included here, since the word
has *i*-forms from an early date [*NED* s.v. *whether*; Dobson (1968)
§85 and n.2.]. The word *devil* had ME *ē*, which might be shortened
to either *e* or *i*; forms with *i* are common in our texts, and the long
vowel survives in *deevil* (xv 14 &c.), *deefil* (xxiii 103), and (with
northern loss of /v/) *deel* (xix 18 &c.) and presumably *deole* (xii 10).

§31. Some spellings seem to indicate a lowering of ME *e*. In
Standard English a number of words show lowering of ME *er* to
ar, and words not affected in Standard English may show the same
development in dialectal and sub-standard speech: *consharning*
'concerning' (xv 18 &c.), *sharvish* 'service' (xv 58), *prefarment*
'preferment' (xxiii 87), *parson* 'person' (xxiii 132). The spelling
clarke 'clerk' (vi 8) corresponds to the StE pronunciation. The
ear-spellings in *cleark* (xii 91), *vearse* (xviii 2 &c.) may represent
variants with ME *ę̄* in borrowings from French [Dobson (1968) §8
(2)], but they may merely reflect such StE spellings as *heart, hearth*.
Lowering before intervocalic /r/ in *farie* 'very' (iv 12), *arrands*
'errands' (xxii 61), is uncommon, but is documented from late
Middle English onwards [ibid. §67]; the form *har* 'her' (ix 12 &c.)

may show the same change [ibid. §68], but it may merely reflect the tendency of this text to use *ar* for unstressed *er* (below, §61); *Darry* 'Derry' (xx 108) probably belongs below. There is no general lowering of ME *e* in England; in Ireland it is characteristic of Ulster dialects, where a lowered pronunciation is general [Adams (1948) 16] and some dialects have [a] or [ɑ] [ibid. 22; Gregg (1964) §2.1]. Instances in our texts are *ham* 'hem' (xv 12), *tall* 'tell' (xv 22, xxi 8), *bad* 'bed' (xx 24), *Franch-man* 'Frenchmen (xx 143), *shantleman* 'gentleman' (xxv 47). The form *togadder* 'together' (xv 45) may, but need not, be an instance of the same change; such forms as *togadir* are common in Mediæval Hiberno-English [McIntosh & Samuels (1968) 5]. The spelling *affuction* 'affection' (xv 59) is no doubt intended to be obscenely suggestive, but it is worth noting that the probable origin of the StE word *ruction* is an Ulster pronunciation of *(insur)rection*, with reference to the rising of 1798. Lowering seems to be implied by the rhyme *fellows* : *gallows* (xvii 43); lowering may have occurred in an unstressed syllable in *supjack* 'subject', *upjack* 'object' (xii 9).

ME *a*

§32. In discussing words with ME *a* it will be convenient to deal first with those which have StE /æ/, and then with the few cases which have StE /ɑ:/ or /ɒ:/. In the first group—those in which the vowel remains short in Standard English—the commonest non-standard spelling is *aa*: *faat* 'what' (v 28 &c.), *phaat* 'what' (xiv 6 &c.), *caatholick* 'catholic' (xiv 14 &c.), *gaallant* 'gallant' (xiv 16), *Phaatrick* 'Patrick' (xiv 27), *daat* 'that' (xiv 38, xv 15 &c.), *vaat* 'what' (xv 19 &c.), *maatre* 'matter' (xv 19), *blaake* 'black' (xx 11), *daamask* 'damask' (xx 104); here also belong *waaterman, vaaterman* 'waterman' (xv 10, 63), *daan* 'then' (xv 18), *thraash* 'thresh' (xx 27), *aal* 'all' (xv 20 &c.), *vaal* 'wall' (xv 50)—see §§ 13, 14, 54. The interpretation of the graphy *aa* is difficult for two reasons : first, it is not used in StE orthography, so that its significance to those who used it is more than ordinarily conjectural; secondly, it is used not only for ME *a* but also for ME *ę̄* (§45) and *ā* (§46). The use of a doubled vowel-symbol would suggest a long vowel : *aa* was in fact occasionally used in Middle English in such words as *caas* 'case'; among the orthoepists, the spelling reformer John Cheke used it about 1550 for ME *ā* [Dobson (1968) 44], and Sir Isaac Newton used it about 1660 for a dialectal lengthening of ME *a*, probably to /a:/ [Elliott (1954) 10]. It seems natural to assume that for those who used it *aa* stood for "lengthened *a*", but the precise implications of this remain very vague.

§33. Lengthening of ME *a* in Hiberno-English is a plausible enough sound-change. As we have seen (§22), lengthening of CG *a* (*ai, ea*) occurs in Manx Gaelic [Rhys (1894) 3, 9–10; Jackson (1955) 9]; lengthening of *a* (*ai, ea*) is regular in the Irish of Cois Fhairrge [de Bhaldraithe (1966) §§ 415, 421, 427], and sporadic in other dialects. In some varieties of present-day Ulster English all open and half-open vowels are lengthened [Gregg (1964) §2.1]; in other varieties lengthening is dependent on the nature of the following consonant [Adams (1948) 16–17]. Nevertheless, we cannot exclude the possibility that those who used *aa* intended to represent a short vowel, since there are other instances in which a doubled vowel-symbol is used to represent a short vowel: we have already seen (§29) that *ee* is used to suggest a close [i] rather than the normal [ɪ] as the realization of /i/, and we shall see below (§39) that *oo* is used for the phoneme /u/ in words where /ʌ/ might have been expected. The spelling *aa* is used in anglicizations of Irish words with *ea* in which lengthening is not very likely: *laat*, Ir. *leat* 'with you' (v 45*), *shaad*, Ir. *sead* 'louse' (xx 10). It seems possible, therefore, that *aa* might be used to suggest a short vowel with the same quality as that of ME *a* lengthened in words like *pass, staff*; that is, /a/ as distinct from /æ/. It may be significant that the use of *aa* for ME *a* does not become common until after 1680; as long as /a/ was a possible reflex of ME *a* in Standard English, HE /a/ would not be remarkable; only when /æ/ became universal in Standard English in the second half of the seventeenth century would it be worth noting. The only occurrence of *aa* before 1680 is in the repeated use of *faat* 'what' in *The Honest Whore* (V); in the word *what* it is likely enough that the preceding labial and the following dental would have produced early lengthening [Dobson (1968) §53], so that here, at least, *aa* is likely to represent a long vowel.

§34. Where ME *a* stands before /nd/, *The Welsh Embassador* (VII) and *Bog-Witticisms* (XV) have spellings with *au/aw*: *stawnd* 'stand' (vii 21), *hawnd* 'hand' (vii 22 &c.), *aund* 'and' (xv 12 &c.). These spellings suggest /ɒ:/, but /ɑ:/ is a more likely value in these words (see also §47); the spelling *lond* 'land' (viii 63) and the rhymes *land* : *demand* (xvi 89) and *disbanded* : *commanded* (xxi 47) probably imply a similar pronunciation. Newton in 1660 shows a dialectal lengthening before /nd/ [Elliott (1954) 10], and pronunciations with /ɑ:/ are recorded for southern Scotland and Ulster

[Wright (1905) §81]. There are a few other instances of *au* for ME *a*; the single occurrence of *aut* 'at' (xv 50) is no doubt due to some kind of error; *Pautrick* 'Patrick' (xv 32) may have a long vowel due to the influence of Ir. *Pádraig*, as the anglicized name still has in Cois Fhairrge [de Bhaldraithe (1953–5) §13].

§35. The only non-standard spelling of a word in which ME *a* has given StE /ɑ:/ is *aufternoons* 'afternoon' (xv 49) : this suggests that when ME *a* was lengthened before voiceless spirants, Hiberno-English accepted a more retracted vowel than Standard English. The only non-standard spelling of a word in which ME *a* has given StE /ɒ:/ is *faarme* 'warm' (xx 28 &c.); since in this text *aa* normally corresponds to StE /æ/, the StE lengthening and retraction has presumably not taken place.

§36. A dialectal lowering and fronting of ME *o* to *a* has left some traces in Standard English, as in *strap* beside *strop*. Spellings in our texts show a more widespread acceptance of this variant, perhaps encouraged by the similar lowering in northern dialects of Irish : *cashter-monger* 'costermonger' (vi 5), *farced* 'forced' (ix 46), *beyand* 'beyond' (ix 92), *shat* 'shot' (xxi 36). Here also belong *becash* 'because' (vi 91) with shortening of ME *au* to *o* (§54), *trat(h)* 'troth' (iv 9 &c., xxv 7), with shortening of ME *ou* to *o*, and *van* 'one' (xxi 23) with non-standard shortening of ME *ǭ* to *o* (§59).

§37. Some apparent instances of the raising of ME *o* to *u* are less easy to explain. The spelling *ludging* 'lodging' (ii 29) is isolated, and in this badly-printed text may be an error; possibly, however, it may be intended to suggest a non-standard articulation of ME *o*, since Irish *o* is centralized and only lightly rounded, and therefore has affinities with English /ʌ/; but one would not expect to find /ʌ/ as early as this. *Purgatorium Hibernicum* (XIII) and *The Irish Hudibras* (XVI) consistently write *Good* 'God' (xiii 99, xvi 95); the significance of *Gud* (xxi 26) is doubtful; the dialect of Forth also has *Gud* [Barnes (1867) 43]. Probably there is an association here between *God* and *good*; compare the Scottish use of *Gudesake*, etc. *NED* s.v. *Gud* cites three instances of *Gud* in oaths, but in these the deformation may be euphemistic.

§38. Lengthening of ME *o* before a voiceless spirant may be implied by the rhyme *trote* 'troth' : *groate* (xiii 101); the vowel of *groat* often underwent shortening [Dobson (1968) §33] and later lengthening to /ɒ:/. It is difficult to know what to make of *trath* (xxv 7) assonating on *á*; we seem to have both fronting as in §36 and lengthening before a voiceless spirant, and it is not easy to see

206

how these two changes could have been combined. Jonson's (*shea-*) *moynshter* 'monster' (vi 81) is also curious and difficult to explain : if it is not an error the *y* may indicate a glide-vowel likely to develop in Irish pronunciation between a back vowel and a palatal consonant-group such as /nʃt/; compare the spelling *cloysh* 'clothes' (vi 76 &c.) discussed in §49.

ME *u*

§39. There are few non-standard spellings of words with *u*. Spellings with *oo* in the work of "native" writers (§5) are probably not significant, since they may reflect the use of *oo* for /ʌ/ in such words as *blood*, *flood*; thus *goon* 'gun' (ix 83), and such spellings as *boode* 'bud' in the *Aphorismical Discovery*. Similar spellings in the work of other writers indicate the dialectal survival of /u/ in words which in StE had /ʌ/ : *hoondrad* 'hundred' (xv 57), *goon* 'gun' (xxvii 3 &c.). The same pronunciation is presumably indicated by the rhymes *chooseing* : *cousin* (xiii 103), *Summ* : *room* (xvi 45). Two spellings in John Dunton's *Sermon* (XVIII), *woordy* 'worthily' (14) and *mooder* 'mother' (16 &c.) are of doubtful significance : they may indicate pronunciations with /u/ instead of /ʌ/, but a long vowel is possible in each of these words, and similar spellings occur in the works of English writers (cf. §59).

ME *ī*

§40. The evidence suggests that ME *ī* remained undiphthongized with the value /i:/ until about 1700. All our texts, up to and including XIX, with the exception of VIII, IX, X, XVII and XVIII, have spellings with *ee*. The words in question are *by*, *child*, *Christ*, *cry*, *Dido*, *die*, *dry*, *find*, *fine*, *five*, *Irish*, *lie* n., *lie* v., *life*, *like*, *my(self)*, *pikeman*, *pipe*, *price*, *right*, *side*, *splice*, *spy*, *thy*, *time*, *white(-livered)*, *wife*, *wise*. The same pronunciation is probably indicated by *ie(e)* in *sie(e)gne* 'sign' (i 3 &c.), *Ierish* 'Irish' (xvii 8 &c.,) and by *ea*, *ei* in *feat* 'white' (i 20), *sheild* 'child' (xviii 11); the use of the spelling *ea* for /i:/ before 1600 is very curious indeed, since at that date it should have stood for /ɛ:/ or perhaps /e:/, but it is not easy to see what other pronunciation could be intended. Numerous spellings with *ee* occur in the *Aphorismical Discovery* : *beseede* 'besides', *heedes* 'hides', *meetre* 'mitre', etc. As one might expect, there are also numerous inverted spellings : *bride* 'breed', *gyre* 'jeer', *pipe* 'peep', etc.

§41. An entirely different pronunciation is indicated by a number of spellings in *The Irish Masque* (VI): *phoit*, *phoyt* 'white' (11 &c.), *deuoish* 'device' (83), *phoyle* 'while' (146). Here the first element of a diphthong /əi/ has been rounded by a preceding labial consonant; similar pronunciations can be heard at the present day, but these are plainly inconsistent with the /i:/ indicated by Jonson in other words, since they presuppose diphthongization.

[For shortening of ME *ī* see §§ 58, 59.]

ME *ē*

[For shortening of ME *ē* see §§ 58, 59.]

ME *ę̄*

§42. The earliest non-standard spellings for ME *ę̄* are in *The Irish Masque* (VI): *phair* 'where' (1 &c.), *entrayt* 'entreat' (28). Jonson's evidence is especially important, since in the rhymes in his poetry he is careful to distinguish ME *ę̄*, ME *ā*, and ME *ai*. For ME *ę̄* he probably used /e:/, for ME *ā* probably /æ:/; for ME *ai* he probably used /ɛ:/, but even if he used a diphthongal pronunciation himself, as some of his contemporaries did, he must have been familiar with the monophthongal pronunciation /ɛ:/. Since there is no reason to suppose that ME *ę̄* could have been diphthongized in Hiberno-English, it seems that the pronunciation he was indicating must have been /ɛ:/, a pronunciation lower than his own. Spellings with *ei/ey/ai/ay* also occur in later texts: *greyshy*, *greisie* 'greasy' (xii 33 &c.), *meynyng* 'meaning' (xii 87), *feir* 'where' (xii 89), *deir* 'there' (xviii 63), *raison* 'reason' (xx 54). By the later part of the seventeenth century ME *ai* and *ā* had fallen together in /ɛ:/, so that the same pronunciation is presumably intended by the spellings *phare* 'where' (xiv 17), *dare* 'there' (xv 28), *crame* 'cream' (xv 40) *grate* 'great' (xv 53); similar spellings from after 1700 are discussed below.

§43. The evidence shows that ME *ę̄* was pronounced as /ɛ:/ in certain words; it must not be assumed that it was so pronounced in *all* words. In all but one of the words listed above the *ę̄* is either preceded or followed by /r/, which has a well-known lowering effect on vowels [Dobson (1968) §§ 201–10]. It is probably no coincidence that in two of the words (*break*, *great*) in which ME *ę̄* is now pronounced as /ei/ in Standard English the vowel is preceded by /r/. The evidence suggests that in Hiberno-English ME *ę̄* was either lowered, or else resisted raising, when it was either preceded or followed by /r/, so that it became identical with ME $\bar{a}$; for the probable value of ME $\bar{a}$ in Hiberno-English see below, §§ 46–7. The one word which contains no /r/, the word *meaning*, seems to be a special case, since Wyld [(1936) 211 fn.] cites a spelling *maneing* (1639) which has no connection with Ireland; we may conjecture that such forms may show the effect of the East Saxon sound-change by which OE $\bar{æ}$ gave ME $\bar{a}$ [Jordan (1934) §50], but evidence is lacking.

§44. About 1700 all but a few words with ME $\bar{ę}$ were replaced by forms of a different dialectal type with ME $\bar{e}$ [Dobson (1968) §116], in England but not in Ireland. Henceforward pronunciations derived from ME $\bar{ę}$ were to be considered especially characteristic of Hiberno-English. Boswell tells us [*Life of Dr Johnson*, 27th March 1772] about Johnson's opinions on the pronunciation of English. Having pointed out that, as a writer on pronunciation, Sheridan suffered from "the disadvantage of being an Irishman", Johnson embarked on an anecdote which is relevant to our purpose :

> When I published the Plan for my Dictionary, Lord Chester-field told me that the word *great* should be pronounced so as to rhyme to *state*; and Sir William Yonge sent me word that it should be pronounced so as to rhyme to *seat*, and that none but an Irishman would pronounce it *grait*. Now here were two men of the highest rank, the one, the best speaker in the House of Lords, the other, the best speaker in the House of Commons, differing entirely.

Lord Chesterfield's has become the standard pronunciation; Sir William would allow no exceptions to the general rule.

§45. The use of *a*-spellings in those of our texts which are later than 1700 no doubt reflects the general tendency of Irishmen to preserve the older pronunciation, since only one of the words in question contains an /r/ : *bate* 'beat' (xx 8), *dare* 'there' (xx 20), *pace* 'peace' (: *case*) (xxi 7), *spake* 'speech' (: *make*) (xxi 29). Such spellings probably represent a pronunciation with /e :/, the value which ME $\bar{a}$ had generally reached by this time (§48), but there are other spellings from after 1700 which seem to impliy a different pronunciation : *spaake* 'speech' (xx 14 &c.), *graat* 'great' (xxiii 59 &c.). As we have seen, *great* is one of the words in which ME $\bar{ę}$ early became identical with ME $\bar{a}$; *speak* is probably also a special case, since Wyld [(1936) 211 & fn.] cites *spake*-spellings from texts which have nothing to do with Ireland; possibly there was interaction between the verb and the East Saxon form of the noun, *spache*, which occurs several times in the ME *Vices and Virtues* [Holthausen (1888) Glossary]. We have already seen (§§ 32–3) that the graphy *aa* is used in some texts to represent the reflex of ME *a*, and that it probably represents the short vowel /a/ as distinct from /æ/. When *aa* stands for ME *ẹ̄* a short vowel seems out of the question, and it is therefore more relevant that the same graphy is also used to represent ME *ā*, and that its value in this usage is probably /ɛ:/ (below, §46). It seems likely that the use of *aa* to represent ME *ẹ̄* shows yet again the falling together of ME *ẹ̄* and *ā*, but in a value which, though normal in the seventeenth century, was no longer so in the eighteenth.

[For shortening of ME *ẹ̄* see §§ 58. 59.]

ME *ā*

§46. The earliest non-standard spelling for ME *ā* is *ai/ay*, used systematically in *The Irish Masque* (VI) and occasionally in XII, XIII, XVI, XVII and XIX. In VI the spelling is found in the words *face, grace, Pale, pate, sake, take, tale*; here also belongs *water* (§13). The other instances are *vaiter* 'water' (xii 89), *pail* 'pale' (xiii 10), *tail* 'tale' (xvi 81), *Wailesh* 'Wales' (xvii 28), *Paishtry-Cooks* 'pastry-cook's' (xix 13). As we have seen (§42), the most probable value of the spelling *ai/ay* is /ɛ:/. In most dialects of Irish, CG *á* appears as /ɑ:/, with front allophones in certain contexts, but in Manx Gaelic it appears as /ɛ:/ [Rhys (1894) 3–4; Jackson (1955) 24–6]. A similar development of CG *á* probably took place in the Irish of parts of the east coast: it is recorded for Brefney [Laoide (1905) 124, 126; (1914) 124–5], and occurs in surviving dialects in north Donegal [Wagner (1958–69) i Maps 8, 110, 181, 206, 233, 270, 298]. The spelling *ai* is used for Irish *á* in *suggain*, Ir. *súgán* 'straw-rope' (xiii 14*). About 1680 a different spelling makes its appearance, the spelling *aa*: it is used systematically in XIV, XVIII, XIX, XX, XXIII and XXVII. The words in question are *brave, consideration, estate, face, fornication, grace, haste, inclination, jakes, make, made, meditation, name, occupation, page, place, plague, plate, Quaker, recreation, sake, salvation, same, spake* v., *take, vacancy*; here also belongs *father* (§13). The form *vaaking* 'waking' (xv 16) is isolated, since XV normally uses *au* for ME *ā* (below, §47). We have already seen (above, §32), that *aa* must stand for "lengthened *a*". By 1680 the normal reflex of ME *a* was /æ/, so that "lengthened *a*" should stand for /æ:/, not very far removed from /ɛ:/. Even if the east-coast Irish pronunciation of CG *á* had been precisely [ɛ:], the implication of the spelling would not have been very inaccurate; in fact the Manx pronunciation is somewhat lower than [ɛ:] [Jackson (1955) 10], and Rhys [(1894) 3] heard it as [æ:], so that the inaccuracy is negligible. It appears, then, that the spellings with *aa* most probably represent a continuation of the same type of pronunciation as was earlier indicated by the use of *ai/ay*. At the beginning of the seventeenth century, ME *ā* was still /æ:/, so that a HE /ɛ:/ would have been closer than the StE pronunciation, and could only be represented by *ai/ay*; at the end of the century ME *ā* had been raised as far as /e:/, so that if HE /ɛ:/ had remained unchanged it would now be more open than the StE pronunciation, and a new spelling would be called for; it is difficult to see what spelling could be used other than a spelling denoting "lengthened *a*". The only argument against continuity of pronunciation is the fact that there is a chronological overlap in the use of the two types of spelling; but this is to be attributed to the heterogeneity of Standard English (above, §25), in which both "conservative" and "progressive" pronunciations might be used at one and the same period. Some confirmation of the above hypothesis is to be found in the use of *aa* for Irish *á* in the anglicization of Irish words : *garraane baane*, Ir. *gearrán bán* 'white horse' (xii 112), *cro-naan*, Ir. *crónán* 'song' (xvi 78), *ruscaan*, Ir. *rúscán* 'bark vessel' (xx 4). The rhymes *shade : head* (xiii 7) and *jade : dead* (xiii 15) can hardly be accurate, but are consistent with the hypothesis that ME *ā* was realized as /ɛ:/.

§47. The first indication of a pronunciation of ME *ā* quite different from the one we have considered so far is to be found in *The Honest Whore* (v 78–80), where Bryan's pronunciation of *wares* is seen to be liable to confusion with the StE pronunciation of *wars*. ME *a* in *war* had been lengthened and retracted through the combined influence of preceding /w/ and following /r/ to something like /ɑ:/ or /ɒ:/ [Dobson (1968) §49]. If Bryan's pronunciation of *wares* had been /wɛ:rz/ or the like, confusion with *wars* would be incomprehensible; we have to assume that he said /wɑ:rz/— that is, in his type of Hiberno-English ME *ā* followed the general Irish development of CG *á* rather than the special east-coast development. It is no doubt the same type of pronunciation which is intended by the spelling *au/aw*, used systematically in *Bog-*

Witticisms (XV) and occasionally in *The Twin Rivals* (XIX) and *Ireland Preserved* (XX). In XV the words spelt with *au/aw* are *face*, *make*, *mare*, *paper*, *place*, *take*; here also belong *any*, *dairy*, *have*, *married*, *Patrick* (§§ 13–15, 34). Instances in the later texts are *tauk(e)* 'take' (xix 18 &c.), *laubour* 'labour' (xx 98), *tauble* 'table' (xx 104), *plawgy* 'plaguy' (xx 109); here also belongs *rauvish* 'ravish' (xx 100) (§13). The use of *tauk(e)* 'take' in XIX is puzzling, since we also find *taaking* 'talking' in the same text; see further below, §54. The four instances of *au/aw* in *Ireland Preserved* all occur in the short scene drawn from Part II; in the two scenes from Part I *aa* is regular. Possibly Michelburne was attempting to represent two different varieties of Hiberno-English; if so, he did not carry out his intentions systematically, since *aa* also occurs in the scene from Part II. The spelling *pace* 'pass' in the *Aphorismical Discovery* may be an inverted spelling reflecting the pronunciation of ME *ā* as /α:/. The spelling *aw* occurs in some texts to represent Irish *á* in the anglicization of the Irish words: *slawne*, Ir. *slán* 'farewell' (v 45), *frawhawn*, Ir. *fraochán* 'bilberry' (xxvi 22), *garrawn*, Ir. *gearrán* 'horse' (xxvi 30), *sougawn*, Ir. *súgán* 'straw saddle' (xxvi 31), *puckawn*, Ir. *pocán* 'he-goat' (xxvi 41).

§48. The eighteenth century saw the development and dispersion of a new type of Hiberno-English in which ME *ā* was represented by /e:/, as it is in present-day Hiberno-English. In *Muiris Ó Gormáin* (XXV) all but one of the words with ME *ā* assonate on *é*: *ale*, *apron*, *brave*, *comrady*, *favour*, *halfpenny*, *lady*, *name*, *race*, *soulvation*. The one exception is *kas* 'case' (16), which assonates on *á*; since the same sequence of assonances includes the word *kal* 'call' (8), the realization of *á* must be [α:]. Though it is not written in Gaelic script, and in spite of the spelling with *k*, it seems that *kas* must represent Irish *cás* rather than English *case*.

[For shortening of ME *ā* see §58.]

ME *ǭ*

§49. Spellings suggest that ME *ǭ* has undergone a number of non-standard developments. The spelling *abrode* (xix 140) suggests the historical development of this word rather than the StE development with shortening and re-lengthening to /ɒ:/ [Dobson (1968) §53 (2)]; the historical development survived concurrently with the other until the eighteenth century. The spelling *doos* 'those' (iv 18) suggests non-standard raising of ME *ǭ* to *ō*; the similar spelling in *foo* 'who' (xix 141) merely indicates the StE raising after a labial, not recorded in the StE spelling. The development whereby ME *ǭ* before /l/ became a diphthong identical with the one derived from ME *ū* [Dobson (1968) §169] is indicated by the spelling *sould* 'sold' (xxiii 97), and no doubt by *auld* 'old' (xix 164), though the choice of the graphy *au* is curious; the *Aphorismical Discovery* has *could* 'cold'. The spelling *gow* (i 43) is strange : it is perhaps just possible that it stands for *go we*, i.e. 'let us go'—an identical form is recorded by the orthoepist Smith [Dobson (1968) §49]—but the context suggests the imperative *go!* If *wees me* (ii 20) stands for 'woe is me', the form *wee* must reflect the Scottish and northern development of OE *wā*. Jonson's spelling *cloysh* 'clothes' (vi 76 &c.) may suggest the glide-vowel likely to develop in Irish pronunciation between a back vowel and a palatal consonant-group; compare the spelling *moynshter* 'monster' (vi 81) discussed in §38.

[For shortening of ME *ǭ* see §§ 58, 59.]

ME *ō*

§50. There are few non-standard spellings of ME *ō*. The most interesting is *dowres* 'doors' (ix 60) : in the work of a "native" writer of Hiberno-English (§5) this might suggest that ME *ō* and *ū* had fallen together, in accordance with the theoretical possibility mentioned in §23; but if this had happened one might have expected that there would be more non-standard spellings of a similar or opposite kind. The spelling *ploud* 'blood' (viii 22) is not significant since, for whatever reason, *bloud* was a common spelling in the Standard English of the time. The spelling *gued* 'good' (xx 96), if it is not a misprint, presumably reflects a Scottish type of pronunciation likely enough to be heard in Ulster.

[For shortening of ME *ō* see §§ 58, 59.]

ME *ū*

§51. In contrast with the development of ME *ī*, retention of ME *ū* without diphthongization seems to be very rare. Spellings with *oo* occur mainly in Stukeley (I), in *about, house, our, out, proud, thou, house*; the only other instances are *cooncel* 'council' (xiv 51 &c.), *noo* 'now' (xix 89), *croon* 'crown' (xix 116), *hoose* 'house' (xix 159). The spelling *trooses* 'trousers' (vii 32 &c.) cannot with confidence be taken as an example of ME *ū*, since the word is from Ir. *triús*, and late borrowing is always a possibility; but the

213

rhyme *mouth* : *youth* (xiii 61) seems to suggest /u :/ in *mouth*, if it is not merely an eye-rhyme. It is noteworthy that in *The Twin Rivals* (XIX) the Irish servant Teague claims to be a native of Carrickfergus in Co. Antrim; since this is an area of Scottish settlement, and since in Scottish ME *ū* is not diphthongized, the forms in this text cannot be considered relevant to the general development of ME *ū* in Hiberno-English. In *Bog-Witticisms* there are two spellings which might perhaps indicate some kind of non-standard diphthong, *noow* 'now' (26 &c.), *coow* 'cow' (35 &c.); the *Aphorismical Discovery* has *shoowre* 'sour', and the rhyme *bow* v. : *know* (xvii 35) suggests a similar pronunciation. In Manx Gaelic CG *ú* is sometimes diphthongized to something resembling /ɔu/ [Jackson (1955) 46]; if ME *ū* had been equated with CG *ú* and then undergone a diphthongization similar to that of Manx, the result might indeed have been some non-standard diphthong; but it might have been so close to the StE /əu/ that most writers would not bother to indicate it.

ME *ei, ai*

§52. The spelling *ale* 'ail' (xii 10) no doubt indicates the falling together of ME *ai* and *ā*; *alwash* 'always' (xv 60) may indicate the same change, or it may indicate a reduction due to lack of stress. The spellings *(n)eder*, *(n)edder* '(n)either' (vi 35 &c., viii 17 &c.) suggest forms with ME *e* due to lack of stress [Dobson (1968) §§ 4, 8 (c) (i), 129 (a)]. The forms of *prithee* show ME *e* and *i* as in Standard English. ME *maistre* 'master' is a word of dual origin, since OE *mægester* and OF *maistre* fell together; smoothing of OF *ai* to *ę̄* is not well documented in this word, but it seems to be reflected in *mester* (ii 5 &c.) and *(school-)measther* (xxv 31); forms with *oi, oy* are derived, not from Middle English, but from Irish *máighistir*, and are discussed in §57. The form *sent* 'saint' (ii 52) is probably due to lack of stress.

§53. The word *faith* presents a puzzling problem. The spellings include *fet, fete, feat, fat, fate* and *faat*. Spellings with *e* and *ea* no doubt reflect the smoothing of OF *ei* to *ę̄*. A form with ME *a* is attested as early as 1450 in the romance of *Sir Amadace* : "Hi-fath, ther will him non mon butte I" [*NED* s.v. *faith* 12.b., *MED* s.v. *feith* 8 (c)]. If *fate* in the lines from Skelton quoted above, p. 178, means 'faith', this is another early instance; but it may mean 'what'. No doubt the use of the word in oaths and ejaculations led to early reduction and alteration of the vowel. The most puzzling feature of all is the occurrence of the spelling *faat* in *The Honest Whore* (V) and *The Welsh Embassador* (VII); the same spelling is used for 'what' in *The Honest Whore* (§33), but apart from this neither text uses the spelling *aa* at all; the implication would seem to be that the vowel used in 'faith' and 'what' was not used in any other word. Possibly this is an early instance of the lengthening of ME *a* to /a:/: the preceding labial and the following dental consonant are both favourable to lengthening [Dobson (1968) §53], and forceful pronunciation in an ejaculation might contribute to the same result.

ME *au*

§54. ME *au* includes both the original diphthong and the *au* developed from *a* before /l/; in words of the latter type the spelling in Standard English is usually *al(l)*, but some *au*-spellings occur in our texts, especially in *Bog-Witticisms* (XV): *aul* 'all' (12), *cauf* 'calf' (41), *shaut* 'shalt' (47), *shaul* 'shall' (55). In a small number of words the development of ME *a* to *au* seems not to have taken place: thus *val(s)* 'wall(s)' (xxiv 60 &c.) and, since in XV *aa* normally represents ME *a*, *aal* 'all' (xv 20 &c.), *vaal* 'wall' (xv 50). A fairly common vulgarism reduced ME *au* before /l/ to *ā* [Dobson (1968) §104 (3) and n.4], and traces of this appear in our texts, especially in forms of the word *wall*: *wale(s)* (ix 62 &c.), *vales* (xiii 69). Other instances of the same change, the forms *taalk* 'talk' (xiv 22) and *taaking* 'talking' (xix 117), are reinforced by two spellings in *Purgatorium Hibernicum* (pp. 30, 118), *take* 'talk'. The use of *taaking* 'talking' in *The Twin Rivals* is particularly strange, since the same text also uses *tauke* 'take' (§47); possibly the words *take* and *talk* were pronounced alike—by a well-known linguistic phenomenon, when in a dialect two distinct forms have fallen together the unsophisticated speaker of a different dialect is likely to hear each as the other. The form *drae* 'draw' (ix 1 &c.) is unique: it may possibly reflect an English vulgarism [Dobson (1968) §104 (3)]. The spelling *athorety* 'authority' (ix 27) suggests lack of stress, but the same spelling occurs under stress in *athor* 'author' in the *Aphorismical Discovery*. The spelling *becash* 'because' (vi 91) shows the same shortening as is found in Standard English, with fronting of the resulting short vowel (§36).

215

§55. Where ME *au* was followed by /n/ the commonest pronunciation in Standard English is /ɑ:/. Many such words are still
written with *au* in our texts : *daunsh, daunch* 'dance' (vi 72 &c.),
daunceirs 'dancers' (xi 3), *aunswer* 'answer' (xv 47), *chaunce* 'chance'
(xvi 83).

ME *ou*

§56. A number of spellings suggest early monophthongization of
ME *ou* to identity with ME *ǭ* : (*k*)*no* 'know' (i 5, xxiv 26 &c.), *one*
'own' (vi 55, xviii 13 &c.), *s*(*h*)*ole* 'soul' (xi 5, xiii 22), *do*' 'though'
(xiii 101), *tro* 'trow' (xvi 81); the conjectural spelling *oan* 'own'
(xxv 7*), if correct, would also belong here, and the rhyme *tro*
'trow' : *so* (xvi 81) is based on the same type of pronunciation. The
development whereby ME *ou* from ME *o* before /l/ gives a diphthong identical with that derived from ME *ū* [Dobson (1968) §169]
is illustrated by the spellings *poul* 'poll' (xxi 2) and *Toulsill* 'Tholsel'
(xxi 30); compare the similar development of ME *ǭ* discussed in
§49. The spellings *soujer, sougare* 'soldier' (xii 22, 32) reflect ME
forms without /l/; in the spelling *souldars* (ix 7) the representation
of the vowel is probably not specially significant. The spelling
taught 'thought' (xxi 5 &c.) is no doubt due to confusion with
taught the past tense of *teach*; the StE pronunciation of *thought* is
derived from a form with ME *au*. The isolated spelling *awn* 'own'
(xv 19) is difficult to explain, and may be a misprint; it is perhaps
worth noting, however, that in parts of *Purgatorium Hibernicum*
not printed here there are a number of rhymes between ME *ou*
and ME *au*. Some of these involve the word *straw*, which may have
ME *ǭ* from ON *á*, but no such objection can be made to the
rhymes *cause* : *knowes, know* : *law* (pp. 86, 120).

ME *iu, eu, oi*

§57. There are no non-standard spellings of ME *iu, eu* or *oi*,
but a rhyme and an assonance throw some light on the pronunciation of the last. The word *joyn* (xxi 46) rhymes with the river-
name *Boyne*, Irish *Bóinn*, and *joy* (xxv 6) assonates on *ó*; it would
seem that the pronunciation of ME *oi* must have been /o:i/. In
present-day Hiberno-English ME *oi* is often pronounced /ɑ:i/,
and there is some indirect evidence for the currency of a similar
pronunciation in the seventeenth century. Some of the forms of the
word *master* cannot be explained in terms of any English antece-

216

dent, and must be derived from Irish *máighistir* : these are *mawhis-deer* (v 61*) and *moister(e)* (xii 1 &c.), *moistare* (xii 8 &c.), *moyster* (xii 68 &c.). The first of these is plainly the anglicization of the Irish word : the use of the spelling *oi/oy* in the other forms suggests a likeness between the English diphthong and the Irish /ɑ:/ followed by the normal glide before palatal consonant-group.

The shortening of long vowels

§58. A characteristic feature of MHE scribal practice was the doubling of consonants which were historically single; where this is found after a long vowel it is a reasonable assumption that the vowel had undergone shortening [Heuser (1904) 34, 63; Zettersten (1967) 15–16; McIntosh & Samuels (1968) 4]. Spellings suggesting the shortening of long vowels are very common in *Ballyally Castle* (IX) : with ME *ī*, *lickwaies* 'likewise' (44 &c.), *lick* 'like' (65 &c.), *firres* 'fires' (89), *sid* 'side' (98); with ME *ē*, *wickes* 'weeks' (35), *bin* 'been' (70); with ME *ẹ̄*, *lest* 'least' (7), *revell* 'reveal' (43), and per-haps *shwering* 'swearing' (2); with ME *ā*, *mad* 'made' (52 &c.); with ME *ǭ*, *rogges* 'rogues' (5), *nott* 'note' (13); with ME *ō*, *luck* 'look' (13), *ruffe* 'roof' (60), *huckes* 'hooks' (61), *tuck* 'took' (97). It is true that in so ill-written a text one has to allow for the possibility of random mis-spellings, but such spellings as *luck* and *ruffe* are so far from the standard *look* and *roof* that accident seems out of the question; in any case, many similar shortenings took place in Standard English, and others are widely attested by the orthoepists [Dobson (1968) §§ 24–39].

§59. Further attestation of shortening is rather scanty. There is only one instance of the shortening of ME *ī*, *whil* 'while' (xxv 24), though the *Aphorismical Discovery* contains numerous instances such as *licke* 'like', *picke* 'pike', etc. Shortening of ME *ē* is rather fully attested : *shit* 'sweet' (viii 17 &c.), *suit* 'sweet' (xiii 37*), *belived* 'believed' (xiii 53), *bin* 'been' (xx 70). The spelling *dis* 'these' (iv 31, xx 48 &c.) may reflect a ME variant with *i*, as may *wickes* 'weeks' (ix 35) cited above. The spellings *presht* 'priest' (xv 29), *des* 'these' (xx 46 &c.) may show early shortening of ME *ẹ̄* to *e*. The word *devil* has early shortening in Standard English; a number of spellings in our texts show either retention of the long vowel or later shortening to /i/ (above, §30). Shortening before /v/ and /f/ is regular in *Purgatorium Hibernicum*. As well as *belived* 'believed' (xiii 53) cited above, the following instances occur : *belive* 'believe' (pp. 28, 78), *live* 'lieve' (p. 41), *chifest* 'chiefest' (p. 40). Corres-

217

ponding spellings *reliue* 'relieve', *reliver* 'reliever', occur in the *Aphorismical Discovery*, but there they may be inverted spellings based on the falling together of ME $\bar{e}$ and $\bar{\imath}$ (above, §5). Shortening of ME $\bar{\varrho}$ occurs only in *del* 'deal' (xv 25). Shortening of ME $\bar{a}$ is not certainly attested outside *Ballyally Castle* (IX). The word *slats* (xvii 55) is a dialectal variant of *slates* [*NED* s.v. *slat, slate*]. The spellings *fash* 'face' (iv 30 &c., viii 19, xvi 69, xxiv 63 &c.), *grash* 'grace' (viii 17 &c., xix 165), *plash* 'place' (viii 18, xvii 13, xxiv 22) seem designed to avoid the awkwardness of the spelling -*ashe*, and need not necessarily imply shortening; the significance of the rhyme *fash* 'face' : *Mass* (xvi 69) is not entirely clear. Shortening of ME $\bar{\varrho}$ occurs in *holly(ness)* 'holy, holiness' (xviii 20, &c.); the spellings *on* 'one' (xv 28), *von* 'one' (xvii 11, xxiv 10 &c.), *won* 'one' (xviii 1) and the rhyme *von* 'one' : *gone* (xvii 11) show non-standard shortening; the spelling *van* (xxi 23 &c.) shows the fronting of the resulting short vowel (above, §36). Shortening of ME $\bar{o}$ is not certainly attested outside *Ballyally Castle* (IX). Dunton's *Sermon* (XVIII) has three spellings with *oo* for standard *o*, *woordy*, 'worthily' (14), *mooder* 'mother' (16 &c.) and *boosom* 'bosom' (133); these might indicate lack of shortening and the pronunciation /u:/; lack of shortening in *bosom* is common in northern dialects of English [Wright (1905) Index], but unknown in *mother*; the significance of the Irish borrowing *múdar* is not entirely clear. Alternatively, *oo* might indicate the pronunciation /u/, as in *good* (compare §39): in *mother* this is the most probable explanation, but it is difficult to see the point of such a spelling in *bosom*. The spellings *odder* 'other' (viii 62) and *nodder* 'nother' (viii 17) may suggest an early shortening to ME *o*, recorded by the orthoepist Hart in the same two words [Dobson (1968) §4], but this is improbable in *moddar* 'mother' (xv 12 &c); possibly *dd* here is merely a graphy for HE /ᴅ/ (below, §84). The significance of *sonar* 'sooner' (ix 40) is doubtful, since early shortening is unlikely; it may be merely a slip.

§60. If *Ballyally Castle* (IX) is representative, non-standard shortenings of ME long vowels were characteristic of certain types of Hiberno-English. On the other hand, the extreme scarcity of relevant spellings in the other texts suggests that shortening was not a very conspicuous feature of the types of Hiberno-English with which the writers were familiar : shortening would have been so easy to indicate (by the doubling of consonants and other obvious means) that the absence of such indications amounts to strong negative evidence.

Unstressed vowels

§61. Non-standard spellings of unstressed vowels are unlikely to be very significant, since in informal speech the majority of ME unstressed vowels had been reduced to /ə/; unskilled writers therefore often interchanged the vowel-symbols, since they were not sufficiently well versed in the standard orthography, and their own pronunciation was no guide to the choice of the correct symbol. It is not at all surprising, therefore, that well over half of the non-standard spellings of this type in our texts are to be found in *Ballyally Castle* (IX), the only text written by a speaker of Hiberno-English. The commonest non-standard spelling in this text is *ar* for *er* in *after, alter, better, commander, cover, divers, formerly, further, hinder, lesser, leather, lever, lower, minister, outer, over, powder, reader, recover, shelter, sooner, timber, warder, water*. The spellings *abell* 'able' (18 &c.), *axell* 'axle' (53), *dubell* 'double' (67) reflect the substitution of /əl/ for earlier vocalic /l/. Other non-standard spellings in final syllables are *en* for *on* in *summon*, *esh* for *ish* in *banish* and *finish*, and the curious *oes* for *ous* in *desirous* and *dangerous*. The spelling *lickwaies* 'likewise' (44 &c.) does not represent an alteration of the unstressed syllable but a different formation current in the seventeenth century [*NED* s.v. *likeways*].

§62. There are few non-standard spellings in medial or initial syllables. The spelling *cathelick* 'catholic' (17) shows reduction of the unstressed medial vowel to /ə/. In *minstar* 'minister' (47) the medial vowel has been syncopated; *unhapely* (36) is of doubtful significance, since it might reflect reduction or loss of the medial vowel in *unhappily*, but more probably represents the variant form *unhaply*. In initial syllables the spellings *athorety* 'authority' (27) and *accation* 'occasion' (84) show reduction of the unstressed vowel; on the first see above, §54. The spelling *cumishon* (33) is probably of no special significance.

§63. In other texts, non-standard spellings of unstressed vowels are few. There are some *ar* spellings comparable to those of *Ballyally Castle* in *buttar* 'butter' (xv 40), *souldar* 'soldier' (xix 7), *micharr* 'micher' (xx 5), *trooparr* 'trooper' (xx 6 &c.), *shouldar* 'shoulder' (xx 11). In *cashtell* 'castle' (vi 78) the *el* is etymological; *hoondrad* 'hundred' (xv 57) is perhaps a northern dialect form influenced by ON *hundrað*. The spelling *gossop* 'gossip' (xii 16, xvi 55) is particularly interesting because it is clearly related to the form *gossoupe* (with shift of stress) used by Stanihurst in the passage quoted above, §16; the *Aphorismical Discovery* has *goshope*. Spellings with *op* occur from Middle English onwards [*MED* s.v. *god-sib*], but are always very rare; retraction and rounding of unstressed /i/ was presumably encouraged by the following labial consonant. The name *Toumaish* 'Thomas' (vi 63 &c.) is puzzling; possibly the spelling indicates shift of stress, as in the Munster pronunciation of Irish *Tomás*; if so, the form belongs in §19. The spelling *Toulsill* (xxi 30) for the word which in Ireland is spelt *Tholsel* is not significant; *NED* records many spellings with *ill*, and the word underwent a variety of changes when its origin ceased to be recognized. The spelling *Wirginny* 'Virginia' (xxvii 105) represents (as far as the final syllable is concerned) a type of pronunciation still to be heard in the United States, no doubt based on the French *Virginie*. The spelling *evidaunsh* 'evidence' (xvi 114) is of doubtful significance : it cannot represent a shift of stress, since the metre precludes this; but words of this type often retained some degree of secondary stress on the final syllable, and this is perhaps what is intended. The spellings *matre, maatre* 'matter' (xv 19) probably represent attempts to suggest vocalic /r/, as distinct from the more usual sequence /ər/. The only non-standard spelling of a medial unstressed vowel is *catalick* 'catholic' (xxiv 12); presumably the vowel is /ə/, normal after 1700. There are two non-standard spellings of initial unstressed vowels, *imbasheters* 'ambassadors' (vi 10 &c.) and *axshept* 'except' (xx 98); the first is of no significance, since spellings with initial *i* (and medial *t*) were common [*NED* s.v. *ambassador*]; the second may reflect the Ulster lowering of ME *e* to a sound resembling /a/ (above, §31). Loss of an initial unstressed vowel was not uncommon in earlier English, and most of the instances in our texts are not very significant : *pon* 'upon' (xii 122, xxii 28 &c., xxiv 21 &c.), *scape* 'escape' (xviii 96), *long* 'along' (xxiv 57); however, *NED* cites only one instance of *buse* 'abuse' (xii 30).

§64. Spellings suggesting the addition of unstressed vowels not found in Standard English are rare. In all varieties of Gaelic it is usual for an epenthetic vowel to develop between a liquid or nasal and certain following consonants. In Munster Irish [O'Rahilly (1932) 202] and in Manx Gaelic [Jackson (1955) 60–61] an epenthetic vowel may also develop between a consonant and a following liquid or nasal, and this phenomenon seems to be reflected in the spellings *Ingaland* 'England' (xvii 38 &c.) and *Ingalish* 'English' (xvii 3 &c.); though the phenomenon appears only in a single text, and only in two closely related words, the parallel with such an

Irish word as *eaglais* 'church' (in Munster pronounced /agəliʃ/)
is so close that it must be accepted as genuine. A somewhat similar
phenomenon occurs in English when a vocalic liquid or nasal is
replaced by a consonantal liquid or nasal : the result may be a kind
of metathesis, whereby such a sequence as /rən/ may be replaced
by /ərn/ and vice versa [Dobson (1968) §§ 327–9]. This metathesis
is common in present-day Hiberno-English, and is reflected in the
spelling *peternell* 'petronel' (ix 99). The spelling *letheren* 'leathern'
(ix 22) is unrelated to this phenomenon : it represents the historical
form descended from OE *leþeren*. Non-standard spellings of the
name *James*, *Yamish* (vi 4 &c.), *Yeamus* (xvii 18 &c.), *Jamish*
(xix 87), reflect pronunciations influenced to varying degrees by the
Irish form *Séamas*, or its vocative (*a*) *Shéamais*; see also below, §99.

Conclusions about the vowels

§65. The crucial developments are those of ME *ī*, *ū*, *ā*, and to
a lesser extent *a*. The evidence shows conclusively that ME *ī* and *ē*
had fallen together in many varieties of Hiberno-English. The
Aphorismical Discovery has not only many *ee*-spellings for ME *ī*
but also many inverted spellings with *i-e* for ME *ē*. Most of our
texts have *ee*-spellings for ME *ī*; inverted spellings are not to be
expected, but the complete absence of any spellings suggesting a
non-standard pronunciation of ME *ē* makes it certain that the two
sounds must have fallen together. This conclusion is further confirmed by a number of rhymes : *and bee!* : *eye* (xiii 85), *neare* : *fire*
(xiii 87), *Nees* : *spleece* 'splice' (xiii 97), *Teef* 'thief' : *Leef* 'life'
(xvi 7), *dee* 'die' : *see* (xvi 101). There seems to be no likelihood
that the two sounds had fallen together in any English dialect;
attempts have been made to prove that they did indeed fall together
in a small area of West Somerset [Luick (1896) §§ 27–8; (1914–40)
§482 Anm.2; Palmer (1969) §4.23], but the arguments are uncon-
vincing, and even if the point were to be proved it is difficult to see
why or how so small an English dialect-area could have had such
an extensive influence on Hiberno-English. If ME *ī* and *ē* were
distinct in the form of English which reached Ireland, their falling
together must have been the consequence of the influence of the
Irish language. No doubt it is possible, as suggested above (§23),
that in the transitional period between Middle and Modern English,
when ME *ē* must have been a very close vowel and ME *ī* had not
yet been fully diphthongized, the two sounds might have been

221

heard as one by the Irish ear; but, if so, it might be expected that ME ō and ū (the corresponding back vowels) would also have fallen together. The evidence for the falling together of ME ō and ū is scanty, and most of it has to be discounted as representing the Ulster dialect, which may well have been influenced by varieties of northern English in which ME ū was never diphthongized (§51). One possible explanation of the different treatment of ME ū is to be found in the fact that in Manx Gaelic CG ú is sometimes diphthongized to some kind of /ɔu/ diphthong (§51); if the same development had occurred in east-coast Irish, and had affected words with ME ū, the resulting sound might not have differed sufficiently from StE /əu/ to make it either desirable or possible to indicate the difference. The difficulty here is that, if ME ō and ū had fallen together and the resulting sound was diphthongized, a diphthongal pronunciation in words with ME ō would have been well worth noting; yet there is little trace in our texts of any such pronunciation. There are no spellings at all, and only a single rhyme, *too : below* (xvi 95); the rhymes in *The Irish Hudibras* are too free for much reliance to be placed on them.

§66. Another and more plausible explanation of the different treatment of ME ī and ū in our texts is to be found in a hypothesis that the diphthongization of ME ū began earlier and proceeded more rapidly than the diphthongization of ME ī; if this had happened there would have been a stage at which ME ī might still be apprehended as a pure vowel identifiable with CG í, while ME ū was already pronounced in a way which could only be apprehended as diphthongal, so that it would be identified with one of the CG diphthongs resulting from the vocalization of voiced spirants. There is some evidence to support such a hypothesis: in particular, a number of orthoepists (Palsgrave, Smith, Bullokar, Waad, Lodwick) recognize the diphthongal quality of ME ū but classify ME ī among the pure long vowels [Dobson (1968) §§ 137, 160]. Other explanations are available for this difference of treatment, the most plausible being that the standard spelling of ME ī as i, y would suggest analysis as a pure vowel, whereas the standard spelling of ME ū as ou, ow would suggest analysis as a diphthong. Nevertheless, the possibility remains that some, at least, of these orthoepists were describing a stage in the development of ME ī and ū comparable with the one we are envisaging. We can exclude Lodwick, who was a Dutchman, and was writing at a date when ME ī was quite certainly a full diphthong; and Waad, whose principles have to be

222

deduced from the eighteen words of an inscription in a book he presented to the Bodleian Library. The remaining three orthoepists, all of the sixteenth century, need to be considered with some care : their statements, though ambiguous, seem perfectly consistent with our hypothesis.

§67. In his *Lesclaircissement de la Langue Francoyse* (1530) Palsgrave compares the pronunciation of English vowels with that of French and Latin. ME $\bar{e}$, he tells us, is almost the correct pronunciation of *i* in French and Latin, but these sounds are "a little more sounding towardes i, as we sounde i with us." This statement would make very good sense if ME $\bar{e}$ had been raised as far as [ɪ:], but not yet as far as [i:], and ME $\bar{\imath}$ had been diphthongized only as far as [ɪi], perhaps with the second element longer than the first. Smith in 1568 classifies long and short vowels together, pairing on the one hand ME $\bar{\imath}$ and *i* and on the other hand ME $\bar{e}$ and *e*; for ME $\bar{e}$, which he describes as a sound between the other two, he has to devise a new symbol. Again, this statement would make very good sense if the sounds conformed to our hypothesis. Bullokar in 1581 also says that ME $\bar{e}$ is a sound between $\bar{e}$ and $\bar{\imath}$; moreover, in his translation of *Æsop's Fables* (1585) he uses a number of rhymes between ME $\bar{e}$ and ME $\bar{\imath}$. These cannot be accurate rhymes, since in English the two sounds never fell together, and indeed many of Bullokar's rhymes are plainly inaccurate; but they would be more intelligible if the sounds he used were the ones postulated by our hypothesis. All three writers appear to recognize the diphthongal quality of ME $\bar{u}$, though their wording is not always as clear and unambiguous as one would wish.

§68. Fortunately there is no need to insist on any one specific interpretation of the evidence : what is important for our purpose is the documentation of the fact that there existed in the sixteenth century pronunciations of ME $\bar{\imath}$ and $\bar{u}$ which could be apprehended by educated Englishmen as representing a simple long vowel and a diphthong respectively. If Englishmen could apprehend the sounds in this way, it can hardly be doubted that Irish-speakers could do likewise; and if they did so, they might have identified the first with their own vowel *i* and the second with one of the diphthongs developed from the vocalization of voiced spirants. We have to conclude that the majority of our seventeenth century texts reflect a type of Hiberno-English spoken by Irishmen whose ancestors had acquired their English at some time in the sixteenth century, and probably not later than the middle of the century. Such a con-

223

clusion is historically in no way surprising : it was in the first half of the sixteenth century that the despotism of the Tudors led to the imposition of a new, strong, English-speaking government in Ireland (above, pp. 14–18), a government with which the native Irish would have had to come to some kind of terms, and whose language some of them, at least, would have had to acquire.

§69. As we have seen (§§ 46–7), there seem to be two quite different developments of ME $\bar{a}$, one to /ɛ:/ and the other to /ɑ:/. We have no information about the development used in I, II, III, IV, VII, VIII, IX, X XI, XXI, XXII and XXIV; the development to /ɛ:/ is found in VI, XII, XIII, XIV, XVI, XVII, XVIII, XIX, XX, XXIII and XXVII; the development to /ɑ:/ is found in V, XV, XIX, XX and (if we can rely on the anglicization of Irish words) XXVI; XXV uses the later English development /e:/. There is a small overlap in the distribution of the two major developments : in *The Twin Rivals* (XIX), which usually has /ɛ:/, there is a single apparent instance of /ɑ:/ (§§ 47, 54); in *Ireland Preserved* (XX) there seems to be an attempt, not very systematically carried out, to represent two different varieties of Hiberno-English. The difference between the two developments might in theory be either chronological or regional : that is, the acquisition of English by bilingual speakers might have occurred at different dates, or the two varieties of Hiberno-English might belong to different districts. More than half the texts using /ɛ:/ for ME $\bar{a}$ also have spellings implying a monophthongal pronunciation of ME $\bar{i}$ and a diphthongal pronunciation of ME $\bar{u}$, so that the ancestors of speakers of this dialect must have acquired their English in the sixteenth century. The history of /ɑ:/ for ME $\bar{a}$ is less clear : of the five texts which use it three (V, XV, XIX) have spellings suggesting /i:/ for ME $\bar{i}$, but two of these (XV, XIX) also contain spellings suggesting pronunciations derived from /u:/ for ME $\bar{u}$. The only text in this group which plainly reflects an English acquired in the sixteenth century is *The Honest Whore* (V).

§70. The speech of those who used /ɛ:/ for ME $\bar{a}$ must have been affected by the change of CG $\acute{a}$ to /ɛ:/ after the date of their acquisition of English (above, §24); since the acquisition can be placed in the sixteenth century, the change of CG $\acute{a}$ to /ɛ:/ must be dated later than that—though obviously earlier than the earliest texts which show its effects. The English of those who used /ɑ:/ for ME $\bar{a}$ cannot have been acquired later than the middle of the sixteenth century, since otherwise the reflex of ME $\bar{i}$ would

224

certainly have been a full diphthong; if their language was un-affected by the change of CG *á* to /ɛ:/, this can only have been because this change did not take place at all in the Irish they spoke. We can be sure, then, that the difference between the two varieties of Hiberno-English was regional; we cannot be sure that it was not also chronological, since for most of the texts with /ɑ:/ we cannot pin down the date of the acquisition of English with any accuracy. As we might expect, the major Fingallian texts, and in general most of the east-coast texts, have /ɛ:/. The texts with /ɑ:/ are less easy to categorize : there is no evidence for the localization of *The Honest Whore* (V) or *Hybernian Stile* (XXVI); in *Bog-Witticisms* (XV) the Irish footman is supposed to come from Drogheda, where we might have expected a dialect not very different from Fingallian; in *The Twin Rivals* (XIX) the speaker is from Carrickfergus, and the scene in *Ireland Preserved* (XX) in which the *au*-spellings occur takes place outside Derry. The localizations, however, are not very significant : in present-day Irish the preservation of CG *á* as /ɑ:/ is normal, and fronted and raised realizations are rare : we might expect that ME *ā* would be /ɑ:/ everywhere except along the east coast, and the scarcity of texts reflecting this sound is confirmation of the conjecture that the Hiberno-English with which writers were most familiar was that of the east coast (above, p. 183).

§71. There is no correlation between the use of *aa* to reproduce ME *a* and either of the reflexes of ME *ā*. Probably /a/ for ME *a* was normal in all types of Hiberno-English, but because of the absence of any simple and unambiguous way of denoting the sound, most texts did not bother to indicate this feature.

CONSONANTS

Theoretical expectations

§72. Throughout its history the Irish language has been in-fluenced by a continuing process of palatalization. During the pre-historic period consonants were progressively palatalized by follow-ing front vowels; for the details see Greene (1973). The resulting palatalization was at first allophonic, but it became phonemic with the alteration or loss of the vowel which had caused it. In con-sequence of these developments, Classical Old Irish had two complete sets of consonants, one neutral set and one palatal set : though the difference of quality was phonemic, the distribution of

225

the phonemes still very largely reflected the conditions which had caused palatalization, in so far as a palatal consonant was never followed by a back vowel or a neutral consonant by a front one. A consonant normally had no influence on a preceding vowel (such forms as *meic(c)*, *mic*, genitive of *mac(c)* 'son', are quite exceptional), except in so far as a non-phonemic glide might develop between a vowel and a consonant of unlike quality. In traditional Irish orthography an appropriate vowel-symbol was inserted between such a vowel and consonant; possibly the orthographic device was based on the audible glide, but it was primarily a mechanical way of indicating the quality of the consonant.

§73. The regular pattern was first disrupted by a change in the articulation of the original diphthongs. During the Middle Irish period OIr. *éo, íu* underwent a shift of stress with consequent absorption of the first element of the new rising diphthong into the preceding palatal consonant, so that *éo* became /o:/ and *íu* became /u:/, each preceded by a palatal consonant. OIr. *áe* and *óe* fell together and eventually developed into a simple long vowel, in Ulster Irish and Scottish Gaelic an unrounded back vowel, but in most dialects of Irish one or other of the front vowels /e:/ and /i:/; these were, of course, preceded by neutral consonants. As a result of these developments all the long vowels except /ɑ:/ came to be preceded by consonants of unlike quality; /ɑ:/ came to be preceded by palatal consonants only later, when the endings *-éal*, *-éan* (earlier *-él*, *-én*) came to be replaced by *-eál*, *-eán*.

§74. Short vowels were so far unaffected, but at some date in the early modern period consonants began to have an influence on preceding vowels; long vowels were stable enough to resist the influence, but short vowels tended to change their articulation to conform with that of a following consonant, so that a short back vowel before a palatal consonant was replaced by the corresponding front vowel, and a short front vowel before a neutral consonant was replaced by the corresponding back vowel. This change hardly affected Scottish or Manx Gaelic, but it affected all dialects of Irish to a greater or lesser degree. The result of the change is that most dialects of Irish now have only three short vowel phonemes, one close, one mid and one open : the rules governing the realization of the close and mid phonemes are complex [O Siadhail & Wigger (1975) 81-2]. There has been no need for a change in the orthography, since the traditional spelling is as appropriate to the new pronunciation as to the old : thus, whereas the graphy *ui* originally

226

represented /u/ followed by a palatal consonant, as it still does in Scottish Gaelic (Manx Gaelic is not relevant here, since it uses a different orthography), it now represents /i/ preceded by a neutral consonant. The date of this fundamental change is difficult to determine, since it is not reflected in the orthography. It is plainly later than the lengthening of short vowels before *r*, since in such words as *múirnín* the lengthened vowel is a back one; but since this lengthening is itself of uncertain date we are no further forward. O'Rahilly [(1932) 141] says that "this change seems to have gained ground in Irish in the seventeenth century", but the evidence is scanty and no certainty is possible.

§75. The changes which resulted in a breaking of the link between the quality of a consonant and the articulation of a following vowel had an important effect on the treatment of loanwords. Sound-substitution in loanwords affects not only single sounds but also sequences of sounds : that is, a speaker pronouncing a foreign word will avoid not only unfamiliar sounds but also unfamiliar sequences of familiar sounds [Weinreich (1963) 23]. Every foreign consonant was identified with some Irish consonant, which had to belong either to the palatal or to the neutral set : it might therefore happen that (from the Irish point of view) a foreign word contained a sequence of palatal consonant and back vowel, or a sequence of neutral consonant and front vowel. Until the time of the changes described above, such a sequence was unacceptable, and had to be avoided by changing either the consonant or the vowel : that is, either a palatal consonant was replaced by the corresponding neutral consonant (or vice versa), or a front vowel was replaced by the corresponding back vowel (or vice versa). Both processes are illustrated by the variant forms in Irish of ME *sisour* 'scissors' : either *siosúr* /ʃisu :r/ with change of consonant, or *sosúr* /sosu :r/ with change of vowel. After the changes described above this constraint no longer existed, and we therefore find free combination of consonant and following vowel as in present-day /se :t/ 'seat' [de Bhaldraithe (1953–5) §49] contrasted with earlier *séala* /ʃe :lə/ 'seal'. What is not entirely clear is why in the earlier period a final consonant is usually made to conform in quality to the *preceding* vowel : there seems to be no phonological reason why this should be so. Yet in such a word as *seirbhís* /ʃer'ivi :ʃ/ from *service*, English /s/ has been replaced by Irish /ʃ/ at the end as well as at the beginning of the word.

§76. In more recent loanwords a different constraint operates.

In Irish, consonant-clusters consist of consonants of like quality—that is, every cluster consists either entirely of palatal or entirely of neutral consonants, not of a mixture of the two; there are very few exceptions to this rule, and none is relevant to the argument. Since every foreign consonant was identified with some Irish consonant, either palatal or neutral, it might often happen that a foreign consonant-cluster might consist, from the Irish point of view, of consonants of unlike quality. Such a cluster would be unacceptable, and would be adjusted to conform with Irish speech-habits by the alteration of one or more of the consonants. Thus, for example, English /s/ was identified with Irish neutral /s/ (the palatal variety being reserved for English /ʃ/), and English /t/ was identified with Irish palatal /t'/ (the neutral variety being reserved for English /θ/). Thus the English cluster /st/ was unacceptable, and needed to be adjusted by the alteration of one or other of the two consonants. Both possibilities can be observed : English *still* 'distilling apparatus' appears in present-day Irish dialects as both /stil'/ and /ʃt'il'/. However, since the influence of Irish consonants is generally retrogressive rather than progressive, it is more usual for the first consonant to be influenced by the second : English /st/ in loanwords is regularly replaced by /ʃt/, and, since English /l/ and /n/ are generally represented by Irish /l'/ and /n'/, English /sl sn/ are replaced by /ʃl' ʃn'/ [de Bhaldraithe (1953–5) §49].

§77. It is reasonable to expect that bilingual speakers or their descendants when speaking English would make accommodations similar to those to be observed in loanwords, the nature of the accommodations depending on the date of the acquistion of English. However, since the date of the Irish development described above remains uncertain (§74), we cannot foretell which of our texts will follow the pattern of the earlier loanwords and which the pattern of the later loanwords. In favourable circumstances it might happen that the evidence of the texts could help us to fix a more accurate date for the Irish development, and such favourable circumstances do in fact exist, as we shall see in §119.

The consonants in detail

/p/

§78. The occurrence of *ph* for /p/ in the names *Pha(a)trick* (vi 37 &c., xiv 27), *Kilphatrick* (xii 17) is puzzling : it should stand for /f/, and though occasional interchange of *p* and *f* does occur in Irish, it is not at all likely in this well-known name. Possibly there is influence here from the vocative (*a*) *Phádraig*, though the only actual vocative in our texts is in *The Irish Masque* (vi 94) (cf. §99); but the lenition appropriate to the vocative is not often reproduced in Hiberno-English (below, §136).

[For voicing of /p/ see §111.]

/b/

[For unvoicing of /b/ see §107.]

/ʍ/

§79. There is a long-standing equivalence between English /ʍ/ and Irish neutral /f/ (realized as [Φ]), an equivalence which operates in both directions, and which it is easy to illustrate : on the one hand there are Irish place-names, like *Fuineadh* (Co. Mayo), anglicized as *Whinnoo*, and personal names like *O Faoláin*, anglicized as *Whelan*; on the other hand there are such English words as *whip*, *whiting*, borrowed into Irish as *fuip* and *faoitín* respectively. We might expect that at an earlier period English /ʍ/ might have been replaced by Irish neutral /f/ or palatal /f'/ according to the articulation of the following vowel. The English words for which non-standard spellings appear in our texts (including some in which Standard English has substituted /h/ for historical /ʍ/) are *what, when, where, whether, which, while, whip, white, whither, who, whole, whom, whore, whose, why*. Seven texts (III, IV, VII, IX, X, XXII, XXVI) contain no non-standard spellings of such words. By far the commonest non-standard spelling is *f*, which appears systematically in I, V, XI, XIII, XVI, XIX, XXI, XXIII, XXIV and XXV; the spelling *ph*, found systematically in VI, XIV and XXVII, is presumably an arbitrary variation without special significance. Special interest attaches to the spellings *fu*, which appears systematically in XII (beside one instance of *f*), and *fw*, which appears systematically in XVIII. These spellings may possibly be designed to suggest the sound [Φ], which shares its spirantal quality with [f] and its bilabial quality with [w], but it is also possible that the spelling is intended to represent the labial glide which is sometimes to be heard after Irish /f/. In some Irish dialects this glide is more prominent than in others : according to Laoide [(1905) 125, (1914) 124] it was especially prominent in Meath, even before back vowels, except *ó*.

Since Dunton in his *Sermon* (XVIII) uses *fw* before ME ǭ in *who*, *whom*, *whose*, it seems less likely that he intended to suggest a labial glide; see, however, the discussion of his use of *vw* (below, §80). Whatever the precise meaning of *fu* and *fw*, it seems clear that they must denote Irish neutral /f/ rather than palatal /f′/; it is therefore interesting to note that in XII *fu* is used exclusively before front vowels, and in XVIII *fw* is used before front as well as back vowels; the complex implications of these facts are discussed below (§§ 117–9).

[For voicing of /ʍ/ see §112.]

/w/

§80. Non-standard spellings for /w/ are much less common than those for /ʍ/ : as well as the seven texts which have no non-standard spellings for /ʍ/, II, V, XI and XXIII have none for /w/, and it must be assumed that the non-standard pronunciation, presumably with Irish /v/ realized as [β] (or perhaps in the earlier period also by Irish palatal /v′/ before a front vowel), must have been less noticeable than that of /ʍ/. The words in question are *once, one, wag, waking, wall, war, ware, warm, warrant, was, watch, water, waterman, way, we, wear, weary, weather-cock, wedding, welcome, well, wench, went, were, wicked, wild, will* n., *will* v., *wilt, win, wind, wiser, with, within, without, woman, wonder, wont, word, work, world, worship, worst, worth, would; away, unworthy.* The commonest non-standard spelling for /w/ is *v*, used systematically in I, VI, VIII, XII, XIII, XIV, XV, XVI, XIX, XXI, XXIV and XXVII, and beside other spellings in XVIII, XX and XXV. In his *Sermon* (XVIII) Dunton uses a most sophisticated spelling system. Before the front vowels *i* and *e*, and in no other place, he uses the spelling *vw* : *vwel*(*l*) 'well' (86, 126), *vwicked* 'wicked' (92), *vwill* 'will' (93 &c.), *vweare* 'wear' (129), *vwent* 'went' (130). In the words *was, with, woman, world, worship, would*, he uses the spelling *v*; it is unfortunate that there are no examples of ME ā̆, since otherwise we might have been able to deduce whether its reflex was a front or a back vowel. For the words *one* and *with* he systematically uses the spellings *won* and *wid*; the reason for this usage is not apparent. The use of *vw* only before front vowels is evidence of a sensitive ear and careful notation : it seems likely that Dunton intended to indicate a labial glide, since it is before front vowels that this is most apparent, and if so this may be what he intended by the spelling *fw* (§79). Again we note that the quality of the consonant is not influenced by the articulation of the following vowel, but at this late date the fact is not surprising. The spelling *vw* was later used by Henry Brooke in his *Contending Brothers* (1778), an adaptation of Farquhar's *Twin Rivals* (XIX); but Brooke uses it in all positions, not merely before front vowels. The spelling *vrite* 'write' (xv 7) is probably a mechanical substitution of *v* for *w*, since /w/ was no longer pronounced in the combination *wr* at the end of the seventeenth century [Dobson (1968) §416]; it is perhaps just possible that Hiberno-English preserved the reflex of /w/ in this position as an archaism, but if so it is surprising that no other writer noticed it.

[For unvoicing of /w/ see §108; for loss of /w/ see §§ 89, 115.]

/f/

§81. Irish palatal /f'/ and /v'/ were probably originally bilabial, like neutral /f/ and /v/; in present-day dialects they are often labio-dental, but older speakers may use bilabial realizations. On the analogy of /w/ for English /v/ (below, §82) one might have expected the spelling *wh* for English /f/, but no such spelling appears in our texts; the only *wh*-spellings known to me occur in the nineteenth-century MSS 23.B.19 and 23.E.18 in the library of the Royal Irish Academy, where *fine* (xxv 37) is written *whine*.

[For voicing of /f/ see §112.]

/v/

§82. In Mediæval Hiberno-English the writing of *w* for *v* was very common [Heuser (1904) 65, 73, 74; Zettersten (1967) 15; McIntosh & Samuels (1968) 5], though the writing of *v* for *w* seems to have been unknown; presumably the sound used was bilabial. In present-day Hiberno-English, intervocal /v/ is often replaced by /w/, and in his *Sermon* (XVIII) Dunton regularly writes *w* for intervocal /v/: *all-dewoureing* (62), *dewotions* (65), *owercome* (66), *cowers* (139); in each case the /v/ is either followed or preceded by a back vowel. The form *abow* 'above' (xii 40) is less significant, since many English dialects show loss of /v/ in this word [Wright (1905) §279]; the dialect of Forth has *aboo* [Barnes (1867) 22]. For initial /v/ Dunton writes *w* only in the Latin words *wia* and *witæ* (xviii 78); there is, of course, no likelihood that the so-called

"Classical" pronunciation of Latin is intended here. Two later instances of initial *w* are *waacancy* 'vacancy' (xx 72 &c.) and *Wirginny* 'Virginia' (xxvii 105). In the word *salvation*, *w* is used in two texts : *soulwation* (xii 121), *shalwashion* (xv 21 &c.). The use of *b* for /v/ in *scrib(o)ner* (xii 86) is difficult to explain. According to Bartley [(1954) 284] "the bilabial [*v*] was indicated by spelling b in four plays, in 1636, 1763, 1772, and 1776"; unless 1636 is a misprint for 1663, *Hic et Ubique* cannot be one of the four plays, and in any case the explanation does not seem very probable.

[For unvoicing of /v/ see §108; for loss of /v/ see §115.]

/θ/

§83. In present-day Hiberno-English /θ/ is equated with Irish neutral /t/, and is therefore replaced by the dental (not alveolar) stop /т/. We might expect that at an earlier date English /θ/ might be replaced by Irish neutral /t/ or palatal /t′/ according to the articulation of the following vowel; if so, it is difficult to see how the two sounds could have been differentiated by the use of non-standard spellings, since only the one symbol *t* is available in English orthography. If the rhyme *about* : *Mout* 'mouth' (xvi 79) is accurate it shows that English /t/ and /θ/ were pronounced alike in these two words, but does not tell us what the common sound was. All but seven of our texts (III, IX, X, XI, XXII, XXV, XXVI) have instances of *t* for *th* : the words in question are *thank, thief, thing, think, third, thought, thousand, three, throat, through, throw, thrust, thunder; Catholic, mouthful, nothing; both, cloth, death, doth, earth, eighth, eleventh, faith, (one-and-)fortieth, hath, loth, month, mouth, North, strength, teeth, troth, truth, worth.*

[For loss of /θ/ see §115.]

/ð/

§84. Non-standard spellings for /ð/ are even more frequent than those for /θ/. In addition to the texts which have non-standard spellings for /θ/, XI, XXII and XXV also have non-standard spellings for /ð/. The words in question are *than, that, the, thee, their, them(selves), then, there, thereby, therefore, these, they, thine, this, thither, those, thou, though, thus, thy(self); although, another, brother, either, father, gathering, grandfather, hither, mother, neither, nother, other, prithee, smothering, together, tother, whether, whither, withdraw, within, without, (un)worthy; with.* The normal non-standard spelling is *d*, as might be expected; there is no way to tell whether it always stands for the dental (not alveolar) stop /ᴅ/, or whether before front vowels it sometimes stands for /d/. In the words *mother, nother, other* some texts use *dd*, but this is unlikely to be specially significant (§59).

[For unvoicing of /ð/ see §109; for loss of /ð/ see §115.]

/t/

§85. In Mediæval Hiberno-English there are occasional instances of the writing of *th* for *t* as well as *t* for *th* [Heuser (1904) 64], and there are a few instances of *th* in our texts : these presumably imply a pronunciation with /ᴛ/, since this is the sound which Irishmen normally substitute for English /θ/. The substitution of /ᴛ/ for /t/ in *fath* 'what' (xxv 28 &c.) is unparalleled and difficult to explain. In present-day Hiberno-English, as a consequence of the influence of Irish consonant-clusters (§76), English /t/ is replaced by /ᴛ/ before a following /r/ or /ər/; this change is reflected in the spellings *Kilpathrick, Pathrick* 'Patrick' (xii 109, 116) and *school-measther* 'schoolmaster' (xxv 31); the *Aphorismical Discovery* has *conthriuers* 'contrivers'.

[For voicing of /t/ see §111; for loss of /t/ see §114.]

/d/

§86. The sequence /dj/ has become /dʒ/ in *soujer, sougare* 'soldier' (xii 22, 32); the forms *soldering* (xvi 113) and *souldars* (ix 7) show loss of /i/ or /j/ with consequent preservation of /d/ [Dobson (1968) §391]. There are no instances of the present-day HE change of /d/ to /ᴅ/ before /r/ or /ər/ : the spelling *powthar* 'powder' (ix 104) reflects a pronunciation once found in Standard English and still common in the dialects [*NED* s.v. *powder*; Wright (1905) §297].

[For unvoicing of /d/ see §107; for loss of /d/ see §114.]

/s/

§87. The spelling *sh* for /s/ occurs in all but a few of our texts. It is of no special significance in cases where Standard English eventually accepted the pronunciation /ʃ/ : *conshence* 'conscience' (vi 3), *comishon, cumishon* 'commission' (ix 15 &c.), *shalwashion* 'salvation' (xv 21 &c.), *shure(ly)* 'sure(ly)' (xviii 23, xxi 11), *relashon* 'relation' (xx 65 &c., xxiii 66 &c.), *absolushon* 'absolution' (xx 124), *nashion* 'nation' (xxiv 52); *shuperasque* 'superasque' (xviii 108) is based on a pronunciation with /sju :/. The reduction of /sj/ to /ʃ/ was widely accepted after the middle of the seventeenth century [Dobson (1968) §388]; the earlier spellings indicate a vulgarism and the later ones are otiose.

§88. Our texts differ widely in their use of *sh*-spellings other than these. None appear in II, VII, XIII, XXV and XXVI: in XIII the absence of such spellings is accidental, since they occur occasionally in parts of the work not printed here; XXV is written by an Irish scribe; in XXVI there are effectively no indications of pronunciation. In two more texts, XI and XXII, *sh*-spellings occur only in the word *soul*, a special case which is discussed below (§91); IX has *sh*-spellings of a special type, also discussed below (§89). The remaining nineteen texts can be divided into two clear-cut groups, those which have *sh*-spellings only in the neighbourhood of front vowels, and those in which the occurrence of such spellings is not limited in this way; ME *a* and *ā* must be counted among the front vowels, since texts which never have *sh*-spellings in the neighbourhood of *o*- and *u*-sounds have them freely in the neighbourhood of ME *a* and *ā*. The texts which have *sh*-spellings only in the neighbourhood of front vowels are I, III, IV, V, X, XII, XVI, XXIII, XXIV (with a limitation discussed below, §89); the texts which have *sh*-spellings also in other contexts are VI, VIII, XIV, XV, XVII, XVIII, XIX, XX, XXI, XXVII. The words in question can be divided into a number of groups, between which there is necessarily some overlap; I list the simplest cases first, leaving the complications for later discussion. Words with /s/ before a front vowel: *ceremony, city, civil, sad, saddle, sadness, saint, sake, salvation, same, save, say, sea, seamonster, secretary, see, seed, seek, self, sell, send, serpent, servant, serve, service, set, sick, sickness, silly, silver, sign, sin, sing, sinking, sinner, sir, sister, sit, six(pence)*, and the Latin *sempiterna*; *besides, concerning, consider, decease, except(ing), gossip, himself, itself, Kinsale, myself, themselves, thyself, yourself,* and the Latin *descensus*. Words with /s/ after a front vowel: *bless, case, cresses, decent, Dennis, device, face, glass, grace, ambassador, justice, kindness, kiss, lice, Mass, message, mistress, pastry(-cook), peace, place, price, this, Thomas, witness, yes*, and the Latin *facilis*. Words with /s/ before a back vowel: *saw, so, some, son, sore, sorrow, sort, subject, sucking, suffer, Suffolk, summer*. Words with /s/ after a back vowel : *house-keeping, purpose, us*. Words with /s/ not next to a vowel : *advance, dance, didst, distance, elements, evidence(-place), parents, pips, pox, sixpence, thinks*.

§89. We are now in a position to look at some more complicated situations. In present-day Hiberno-English, /s/ may be replaced by /ʃ/ in a number of consonant-clusters. One of these we have already looked at, the cluster /st/ (above, §76), and there are others. In the Irish consonant-cluster *rs* the *r* may induce in the *s* a retroflex articulation which gives it an acoustic resemblance to /ʃ/ [de Búrca (1958) §150; de Bhaldraithe (1966) §171; Mhac an Fhailigh (1968) §140], and this articulation may be transferred into Hiberno-English [Henry (1957) §73]. When /s/ is followed by a labial consonant, especially /w/, the lip-protrusion of the labial may induce in the /s/ an articulation which has something in common with that of English /ʃ/. The first of these three developments is not reflected at all in our texts, the other two only sparsely. If we examine words containing /st/ we find that the texts can be divided into the same groups as before, according to whether the /st/ is preceded by a front or a back vowel; in no case can we feel confident that the use of *sh* is dependent on the following /t/. The words in question are : *Bastille, best, biggest, cast, castle, Christ, distance, fast, hast, honest, liest, master, minister, pistol, priest, saist, wrested; cost, costermonger, dost, must, penny-post, trust; sea-monster*. The only word with initial /st/ is *stay*. Only one text has *sh*-spellings which seem to be the consequence of the cluster /rs/ : *The Pretender's Exercise* (**XXIV**) writes *horsh* 'horse' (35 &c.), *firsht* 'first' (19), and since this text does not otherwise use *sh* except in the neighbourhood of a front vowel, the conclusion seems certain. On the other hand *curshed* 'cursed' (xvii 30 &c.) and *forsht* 'forced' (xvii 29 &c.) are not significant, since *The Irishmen's Prayers* uses *sh* freely in all positions. The only *sh*-spellings in *Ballyally Castle* (**IX**) are in words with the cluster /sw/, *shwering* 'swearing' (2) and *anshwerd* 'answered' (28), and these no doubt reflect /ʃ/ induced by the following labial consonant. In the words *smell, speak, spend, squire* and *sweet*, *sh*-spellings occur only in texts which have *sh* in all positions, and are therefore not significant. In *shit* 'sweet' (viii 17 &c.) the /w/ has apparently been absorbed (the *Aphorismical Discovery* has *shiftnesse* 'swiftness'); the significance of *suit* 'sweet' (xiii 37*) is not clear.

§90. In the light of the features of the historical phonology of

Irish discussed above (§§ 72, 75) it is not at all surprising to find indications of /ʃ/ for /s/ in the neighbourhood of front vowels; it is very surprising to find such indications in the neighbourhood of back vowels, where there is no other contributory factor, and no obvious explanation presents itself. There seem to be four possibilities.

(1) In some variety of Hiberno-English every /s/ became /ʃ/, presumably because the same development had taken place in some variety of Irish; but there is no evidence at all of such a change in any variety of Irish, and in default of such evidence it is difficult to see why or how such a change could have taken place in Hiberno-English.

(2) In some variety of Hiberno-English /s/ was realized in some way which suggested /ʃ/ to English ears, presumably because the same realization existed in some variety of Irish; in this case the graphy sh would conceal the difference between two sounds, true /ʃ/ in the neighbourhood of front vowels and some other sound in other positions; but no such development is known in Irish. Irish /s/ is pronounced with the tip of the tongue against the lower teeth-ridge, and with some degree of velarization; it may have a slightly lisping quality, or before a rounded vowel it may have a slightly whistling quality; neither of these realizations is much like /ʃ/.

(3) Writers had observed pronunciations with /ʃ/ for /s/, failed to notice the limited contexts in which they had occurred, and wrongly assumed that they occurred in all contexts. This explanation might seem plausible if the anomalous sh-spellings were found in the works of one or two writers only, but it seems inadequate to explain the occurrence of such spellings in the works of ten writers spread over a period of more than a century. At least two of the writers were Irishmen, Farquhar (XIX) and Sheridan (XXVII); Michelburne (XX) knew Ireland well; the writer of the political satire XXI, if not himself an Irishman, must have been deeply involved in the Irish scene.

(4) The use of sh-spellings was quite mechanical, as if the printer had been instructed to insert an h after every s. Mechanical alteration of the spelling is no doubt a possibility, but the use of sh where the StE spelling uses c can hardly be mechanical.

Of these four possibilities the second is perhaps the least unlikely; but no certainty is possible (cf. §118).

§91. The word *soul* is a special case, since it appears with *sh*-spellings not only in texts which use *sh* in all positions, but also in XI and XXII which have no other *sh*-spellings, and in XVI which otherwise uses *sh*-spellings only in the neighbourhood of front vowels. It seems certain that a pronunciation with /ʃ/ must have been widespread. Substitution of /ʃ/ for /s/ is uncommon in Irish, but it does occasionally occur; in northern Irish the word *sórt* regularly appears as *seort* with /ʃ/. Substitution of /ʃ/ for /s/ in *soul* may have been influenced by the curious formation *soulvation* (xii 121, xiv 56, xxi 35, xxv 31), apparently a portmanteau word based on the idea of "salvation of one's soul"; /ʃ/ before ME *a* would be intelligible in *salvation*, and *sh*-spellings do in fact occur in this word (§88); /ʃ/ might perhaps have been transferred to *soulvation* and thence to *soul*.

§92. In a few instances /s/ is represented not by *sh* but by *ch*, which presumably indicates a pronunciation /tʃ/. The forms *daunch* 'dance' (vi 85 &c.) and *advanch* 'advance' (xxiv 30) offer no difficulty, since /ntʃ/ could readily develop from /nʃ/ : a glide-consonant /t/ between /n/ and /ʃ/ is not uncommon in present-day Standard English in such words as *ancient*, and similar pronunciations are recorded in the seventeenth century [Dobson (1968) §435]. A similar development is reflected in the rhyme *sences : vench is* (xiii 11), and the *Aphorismical Discovery* has *fenche* 'fence'. Forms in which the *ch* is initial are less easy to explain : *cheester, chister* 'sister' (xxiii 106, xxvii 122), *chergeant* 'sergeant' (xxvii 2 &c.). In Irish, *t* may be prefixed to words beginning with *s* after the definite article *an* in circumstances where other consonants undergo lenition; in such cases the *s* is not pronounced. If the *s* is palatal the *t* will also be palatal, and in northern Irish /tʃ/ is a possible pronunciation of palatal *t*; thus such a form as *an tséipéil* 'of the chapel' may be pronounced with initial /tʃ/. In Tyrone Irish "some nouns beginning with 's' have 't-' prefixed to them when not preceded by the singular article" [Stockman & Wagner (1965) 211]; the examples with palatal *s* are *séipéal* 'chapel', *seomra* 'room', *simleoid* 'chimney'. The first and last of these are to be found also on Maps 168 and 203 of the *Linguistic Atlas* [Wagner (1958–69) i], and forms with /tʃ/ are recorded for Louth, north Leitrim, and the Isle of Man. None of the instances is entirely satisfactory, since all are derived from Norman French or English forms with initial /tʃ/, which might have survived unchanged or been re-introduced; the forms of *séipéal* are particularly unsatisfactory, since they might be due to the influence of *teampall* '(Protestant) church', and the forms with *t* have been written *tea'pall, téa'pall* [Dinneen, s.v. *teampall*; Laoide (1905) 73]. Nevertheless, the fact that words with neutral *s* (*snáth, snáthaid, súiste*) also acquire a *t* in Tyrone Irish makes it probable that the instances with palatal *s* are genuine. It is a striking fact that Thomas Sheridan, the author of *The Brave Irishman* (XXVII), was brought up within a few miles of the district of north Leitrim in which the Irish development is known to have taken place : it seems probable that his *ch*-forms reflect the local HE usage he had heard as a child. The same development may be reflected in "Mack Chane of Vlster" (for Irish *Mac Seáin*), the name of the Irish servant in *Sir John Oldcastle* (II).

[For voicing of /s/ see §113.]

/z/

§93. Many of our texts have *sh*-spellings of words with /z/, and the interpretation of these is difficult; since English orthography provides no graphy to represent /ʒ/, we cannot be sure whether *sh* stands for /ʃ/ or /ʒ/. For possible unvoicing of /z/ see below, §110. In general, *sh*-spellings for /z/ occur in the texts which also have *sh*-spellings for /ʃ/, but there are some interesting exceptions. As might be expected, the two texts which have *sh*-spellings for /s/ only in the word *soul* (XI and XXII) have none for /z/. Dekker's two pieces, IV and V, together with XVI and XVIII, have numerous *sh*-spellings for /s/ but none for /z/ (for a possible exception in XVI see §95 below). If the pronunciation of /z/ was /ʒ/ rather than /ʃ/ the absence of *sh*-spellings in some texts would be understandable; in Dekker's time there was no /ʒ/-phoneme in Standard English, and although the phoneme existed towards the end of the century there was, as we have seen, no really satisfactory way of representing it.

§94. There are no instances in our texts of initial /z/. Medial /z/ is common, and since in every instance the /z/ is either preceded or followed by a front vowel, palatalization is not unexpected. The words in question are *business, cousin, desire, dozen, greasy, isn't, present, presently, preserve, prison, prisoner, wiser*. Final /z/ is also common, both as an integral part of the word and as the plural or possessive ending. Final /z/ as an integral part of the word is preceded by a front vowel in *always, as, has, his, is, please, 'tis, was*. Here we should probably include *becash* 'because' (vi 91); see §54. The only instance of final /z/ as an integral part of the word preceded by a back vowel is *nosh* 'nose' (viii 21), and since this text has *sh*-spellings for /s/ in the neighbourhood of a back vowel the form need cause no surprise. Where final /z/ is the plural or possessive ending it is usually but not always preceded by a consonant. The vast majority of instances are to be found in *The Irish Masque* (VI) : *pomwater'sh* 'pomewaters' (6), *pearsh* 'pears' (48), *newesh* 'news' (60), *cloysh(s)* 'clothes' (76 &c.), *vindsh* 'winds' (100), *cornersh* 'corners' (102), *heelsh* 'heels' (118), *cowesh* 'cows' (119), *rebelsh* 'rebels' (123), *knauesh* 'knaves' (123), *deputish* 'deputy's' (133); following the same pattern we also find *here'sh* 'here's' (35). In other texts the only forms are *fadersh* 'father's' (xv 13), *nailesh* 'nails' (xvii 27), *pieceish* 'pieces' (xix 116). Forms in which final /z/ is integral to the word but is none the less preceded by a consonant are *Yamish* 'James' (vi 4 &c.), *Wailesh* 'Wales' (xvii 28), *Jamish* 'James' (xix 87). There are two forms in which /z/ would presumably be unvoiced to /s/ next to the voiceless /t/ : *Gotsh* 'God's' (vi 27), *isht* 'is't' (vi 147).

§95. One *sh*-spelling of doubtful significance is *performsh* (xvi 104) : the context shows that the meaning is 'performance', but it is not clear whether the form is a contraction of *performance* (in which case *sh* probably stands for /ʃ/), or the plural of a non-standard noun *perform* (in which case *sh* probably stands for /ʒ/).

[For unvoicing of /z/ see §110.]

/ʃ/

§96. There are not many instances of *s*-spellings for StE /ʃ/, but there are a few. They occur most frequently in the word *shall* (i 9 &c., viii 40 &c., xx 40 &c.); *sal* 'shall' was normal in the northern dialect of Middle English, and frequent in Mediæval Hiberno-English [Heuser (1904) 30, 38, 46]. It is less easy to explain the form *seep(s)* 'sheep' (xviii 121, xx 31 &c.); the same form occurs in *Purgatorium Hibernicum*, which also has *see* 'she', *seet* 'shite', *sitten* 'shitten', *sow'd* 'shown'. Orthographical confusion does not allow us to determine whether such forms existed in Mediæval Hiberno-English. It is particularly curious that /ʃ/ should have been replaced by /s/ (if that is what the spelling *seep* implies) before the front vowel /iː/, a position in which /s/ is often replaced by /ʃ/. Nevertheless, the fact that the same word is so written in *Purgatorium Hibernicum*, Dunton's *Sermon*, and *Ireland Preserved*, texts which are in general very trustworthy, seems to guarantee that this is a genuine form. The only other *s*-spellings are in *Sir John Oldcastle* (II), which has *Irisman* 'Irishman' (11 &c.) and *famise* 'famish' (30). These spellings are paralleled in the MHE *English Conquest of Ireland* [Heuser (1904) 62] : the form *Englismen* is a particularly close parallel to our *Irisman*.

/tʃ/

§97. The Irish language originally had no affricate /tʃ/; in northern Irish an affricate has developed in modern times from the assibilation of palatal /t'/. In loanwords from Norman French and Middle English, initial and postconsonantal /tʃ/ were replaced by /ʃ/, as in *seans* 'chance', *seomra* 'chamber', *áirseoir* 'archer', *stáinse* 'stanchion', but intervocalic /tʃ/ was interpreted as a consonant-cluster and underwent metathesis to /ʃt/, as in *róiste* 'roach'; native words show the same metathesis, as in *báisteach* 'rain' from earlier **báitseach*. Since post-mediæval borrowings from English words with a final consonant are often given a final *-e*, *-a* [Mac Eoin (1974) 63–4], metathesis is also found in such words as *laiste* 'latch', *maiste* 'match', *paiste* 'patch'. In our texts, initial and postconsonantal /tʃ/ are regularly written *sh* in *chain*, *chamber*, *champion*, *chance*, *chapter*, *charge*, *charity*, *cheat*, *cheek*, *chief*, *child*, *choke*, *choking*; *porch*. In contradistinction to Irish practice, *sh* also appears for medial and final /tʃ/ in *preaching*, *Richard*; *breech*, *fetch*, *much*, *pitch(-fork)*, *rich*, *such*. The contrast between *Rishard* 'Richard' (ii 5) and Irish *Risteárd* is particularly striking. There is only one instance of the Irish metathesis, *coasht* 'coach' (xviii 130); compare Irish *cóiste*.

/dʒ/

§98. The treatment of the Norman French and Middle English voiced affricate /dʒ/ in Irish is very similar to that of voiceless /tʃ/; but, since there is no /ʒ/ in Irish, unvoicing is universal. Initial and post-consonantal /dʒ/ were replaced by /ʃ/, as in *seighléir* 'gaoler', *stróinséir* 'stranger'; intervocalic /dʒ/ underwent unvoicing and metathesis to /ʃt/, as in *páiste* 'child'. Manx Gaelic seems to have had a different treatment, since the word for 'child' is *paitchey*; see, however, Jackson (1955) 84. In our texts, initial /dʒ/ is written *sh* in *gentleman*, *gentry*, *Jesuit*; postconsonantal

/dʒ/ is written *sh* in *shubshect* 'subject' (vi 52 &c.). Intervocalic /dʒ/ is written *sh* in *relishion* 'religion' (xxiv 11); unvoicing without metathesis appears in *beseech'd* 'besieged' (iii 46). A different development altogether appears in forms of the name *James*, *Yamish* (vi 4 &c.), *Yeamus* (xvii 18 &c.), and in the word *mayesty* 'majesty' (vi 4 &c.); these spellings seem to indicate a pronunciation /j/ for /dʒ/.

§99. In seeking an explanation for this pronunciation, it is necessary to distinguish between initial and medial position. In loanwords in Irish, initial /dʒ/ is occasionally represented by *i-* or *gi-*, as in *iúistís, giúistís* 'justice', *giota* 'jot'; no pronunciation corresponding to the *i*-spellings is now in use, but *gi-* is pronounced /g'/; it seems unlikely that these rare forms could be relevant here, though they have to be mentioned for the sake of completeness. After /d'/ became assibilated to /dʒ/ in some dialects of northern Irish and in Scottish and Manx Gaelic, a new substitution for English /dʒ/ became available; it was little used in Irish, but in Scottish Gaelic it was substituted for earlier /ʃ/ in a few words. Thus, Ir. *seaicéad* 'jacket' is replaced in Scottish Gaelic by *deacaid*; more to the point, Ir. *Seoirse, Seorsa* 'George' is replaced in Scottish Gaelic by *Deorsa*, just as *Séarlas* 'Charles' is replaced by *Tearlach*. There seems to be no evidence of the replacement of *Séamas* 'James' by **Déamas*; but, if this had happened, the vocative **(a) Dhéamais* would correspond very closely to Jonson's *Yamish*. It is true that, although *Yamish* is vocative in the majority of instances, it is not so in all; but proper names are so often used in the vocative that there is always a chance that this may replace the nominative, and there is a very exact parallel in the Scottish name *Hamish*, representing (a) *Shéamais* the vocative of *Séamas*. The form *Yeamus* seems to represent some kind of a compromise with the more normal form *Séamas*.

§100. The above explanation will not do for medial /j/ in *mayesty*. In Manx Gaelic, medial palatal *d* regularly becomes /ʒ/, which may be further reduced to /j/ [Jackson (1955) 81]; a close parallel to Jonson's *mayesty* is to be found in Manx *madjey* 'stick' (corresponding to Ir. *maide*), which may be pronounced /ma:jə/ [ibid. 84]. A similar development of medial palatal *d* seems to have taken place in the Irish of parts of the east coast: Ir. *bídeach, baoideach* 'tiny' appears in an Oriel poem as *buidheach* [Laoide (1905) 96]; this very form, anglicized as *booygh*, is used in *Captain Thomas Stukeley* (I) (below, §161).

/l/

§101. All dialects of Irish have at least two *l*-phonemes, palatal /l′/ and neutral /l/; in present-day Hiberno-English, English /l/ is generally equated with the palatal rather than the neutral variety. All northern dialects of Irish have at least one additional *l*-phoneme, a strongly palatal sound for which the conventional symbol is /ʟ′/; this is lacking from Munster dialects, and probably did not occur in the lost dialects of Leinster. Speakers of those dialects which have the phoneme /ʟ′/ use it to replace the English sequence /lj/, which does not occur in Irish. For speakers of Munster Irish this sequence offers difficulty, and it is often replaced by simple /l/ : thus, *will you* may be pronounced /wilu :/. There is little evidence of a similar development in the early modern period, but there is one clear instance in *Willam* 'William' (xvii 62); the *Aphorismical Discovery* has *fayler* 'failure'. The forms *soujer*, *sougare* 'soldier' (xii 22, 32) reproduce earlier forms of the word without /l/; loss of /l/ in *shaut* 'shalt' (xv 47) is rare but not unparalleled in Standard English [Dobson (1968) §425], and loss of /l/ in *wut* 'wilt' (v 13 &c.) may be due to a similar process.

/r/

§102. Loss of postvocalic /r/ is implied by the rhymes *Case* : *Ars* (xvi 9) and *Cluster* : *F[orste]r* (xxi 30); this loss had happened by assimilation already in Middle English [Jordan (1934) §§ 166, 251], but remained dialectal or vulgar [Dobson (1968) §401 (c)]. The spellings *conferrmant* 'preferment' (xv 38), *micharr* 'micher' (xx 5) and *trooparr* 'trooper' (xx 6 &c.) may be intended to suggest an articulation of /r/ different from the one current in England.

/j/

§103. In *looky* 'look ye' (xii 49) /j/ is lost before unstressed /i :/, as often in (colloquial) Standard English [*NED* s.v. *look* 4 a]; in *pleshy* 'bless ye' (x 14) the change is not standard, and may have been encouraged by the preceding /ʃ/. For loss of /j/ in the sequence /lj/ see above, §101.

/k/

§104. In the sequence /kn/ the /k/ was first weakened to /h/ and eventually disappeared [Dobson (1968) §417]; complete loss of /k/ remained dialectal and vulgar until after 1700. The spelling *kanave* 'knave' (ii 9) is surprising at this early date; perhaps Munday and his collaborators used the pronunciation /hn/. Such spellings are frequent in representations of the speech of Welshmen [Bartley (1954) 293], and there is an example in *kanaveries* 'knaveries' (vii 121); it need occasion no surprise that Hiberno-English too was conservative in this respect. The spelling *no* 'know' (xxiv 26 &c.) seems pointless, since by the date of this text the pronunciation /n/ was standard.

/ŋ/

§105. Reduction of the unstressed ending /iŋ/ to /in/ or /ən/ has been a feature of English dialects since the ME period [Dobson (1968) §377 (iii) & n.2], and is normal in present-day Hiberno-English. There are a few instances in our texts : *shuttene* 'shutting' (i 37), *coggin* 'cogging' (vii 137), *housh-kepin* 'house-keeping' (xv 44), *livein* 'living' (xv 44), *stockins* 'stockings' (xx 57). The same pronunciation is implied by the rhymes *babling* : *Mabline* (xiii 47), *chooseing* : *cousin* (xiii 103); the rhyme *King* : *sin* (xvii 59) is probably merely inaccurate. Reduction of /ŋ/ to /n/ in the sequence /ŋθ/ is found from the Middle English period onwards, and is common in Mediæval Hiberno-English [Heuser (1904) 35, 68, 73–4; McIntosh & Samuels (1968) 4]; in present-day Hiberno-English the ultimate result is /nT/; in our texts it occurs only in *strent* 'strength' (xviii 61).

The unvoicing of voiced consonants

§106. There is in the Gaelic languages no general tendency towards the unvoicing of voiced consonants. In Irish it is normal for voiced consonants to be partially unvoiced in initial and final position :

> Voiced consonants are fully voiced when they occur in intervocalic position; they are not fully voiced in initial or in final positions. Initially articulation may begin before voicing, and finally voicing may cease before articulation is finished. [Mhac an Fhailigh (1968) §106; cf. O Cuív (1944) §104, de Bhaldraithe (1966) §141.]

In most dialects of Scottish Gaelic the voiced stops have undergone complete unvoicing to the corresponding voiceless stops, while the original voiceless stops are distinguished by postaspiration in initial position and preaspiration in final position [O'Rahilly (1932) 146–50]. There are a few scanty traces of a similar development in Irish and Manx Gaelic, but nothing systematic. In Manx Gaelic there is a tendency for intervocal voiceless stops to become voiced [Jackson (1955) 65]. No such change occurs in native Irish words, but a similar phenomenon is to be observed in loanwords from Norse and Norman French [Risk (1968–75) §132], as in *cábún* 'capon', *spidéal* 'hospital', *bagún* 'bacon'. Individual consonants may be subject to voicing or unvoicing because of their absence or rarity in the consonant inventory of Irish; these are discussed below.

§107. The unvoicing of voiced stops is relatively common in our texts. Unvoicing of initial /b/ to /p/ occurs in *pelly* 'belly' (v 3), *ploud* 'blood' (viii 22), *preed* 'breed' (viii 43), *pleshy* 'bless ye' (x 14), *ponds* 'bonds' (xii 89), *podyes* 'bodies' (xii 122), *proges* 'brogues' (xxv 37*). A similar unvoicing occurs in certain loanwords in Irish : *péist* 'beast' from Latin *bestia*, *praiseach* 'kale' from Latin *brassica* [Risk (1968–75) §113]. The unvoicing in *upjack* 'object' and *supjack* 'subject' (xii 9) is due to mis-hearing, and can have no phonological significance. Unvoicing of initial /d/ to /t/ occurs in *tie* 'die' (ii 30), *Tamasco* 'Damascus' (iv 1 &c.), *teere* 'dear' (iv 13), *teale* 'deal' (iv 28, vii 159), *tevil, tivel, tivil,* 'devil' (xii 91, xvii 56, xxiv 5 &c.). The significance of the spelling *Tuchland* 'Dutchland' (vi 116) is not clear; it may possibly reflect the High German form *Teutsch*, though no comparable forms are recorded by *NED*. Final /d/ is regularly unvoiced in *The Irish Masque* (VI) in the words *and, God, good, hand, heed, hundred, word*; the only instances in other texts are *lort* 'lord' (ii 55) and *Got* 'God' (xii 78). The spelling *imbasheters* 'ambassadors' (vi 10 &c.) is not an instance of the unvoicing of medial /d/ : *NED* cites numerous instances of forms with *t*. There are no instances of the unvoicing of /g/ to /k/. The significance of the unvoicings of voiced stops is far from clear. All of them are of the same type as occurs in Scottish Gaelic, but the relevance of this fact is dubious. Possibly the partial unvoicing of initial and final voiced consonants in Irish may have been apprehended as voicelessness, in contrast to the fuller voicing of English.

§108. The unvoicing of voiced spirants is a more complex matter, and the individual consonants need to be discussed separately; unlike the stops, many of the spirants underwent some change of articulation in Hiberno-English. The phoneme /w/ is not, strictly speaking, a spirant, but it must be included here because it was replaced in Hiberno-English by the Irish neutral /v/ phoneme, of which the normal articulation is [β]; since English /v/ was replaced in Hiberno-English by the Irish palatal /v′/ phoneme, English /w/ and /v/ correspond to phonemes which in Irish are very closely related, and their treatment is similar. As we have seen (above, §80), the normal spelling in our texts for English /w/ is *v*; the spelling *f* presumably indicates unvoicing of /w/, just as it indicates unvoicing of /v/. Nearly all the instances of *f* for /w/ are to be found in *Ireland Preserved* (XX): *fee* 'we' (2), *fill, fell* 'will' (2 &c.), *fid* 'with' (3), *faarme* 'warm' (28 &c.), *fell* 'well' (41 &c.). The only other *f*-spelling is *feather-cock* 'weather-cock' (xxv 24), but the spelling *phit* 'with' (vi 11 &c.) presumably has the same significance. The only word in which our texts have *f*-spellings for /v/ is *very* (iv 12, xix 47, xx 28 &c.). Though it is not very widely attested, unvoicing of initial /w/ and /v/ is a plausible enough sound-change, since in Irish neither /v/ nor /v′/ is found initially in the basic form of any word : these phonemes occur only as lenited forms of /b b′/ or "nasalized" forms of /f f′/. A similar substitution occurs in such loanwords as *féan* 'wain', *fuinneog* 'window', *feithicil* 'vehicle', *fionntar* 'venture'; Mediæval Hiberno-English has *fortyn* 'worts' [Zettersten (1967) 15]. Unvoicing of medial and final /v/ cannot be explained in terms of the phonology of Irish. In *efry* 'every' (xii 122) a ME sound-change may be the explanation [Jordan (1934) §216.3]; *lofe* 'love' (xv 14) may reflect a northern dialect sound-change [ibid. §217]; *starfing* 'starving' (xii 127) is difficult to explain. The only text to show unvoicing of inter-vocalic /v/ is *The Play is the Plot* (XXIII), which has *Cofentry* 'Coventry' (90) and *deefil* 'devil' (103); these remain inexplicable.

§109. The next phenomenon to be discussed is of doubtful status. As we have seen (§§ 83–4), the English consonant phonemes /θ ð/ are normally replaced in Hiberno-English by /т D/, written *t d* : if, therefore, we find spellings like *tat* 'that', in which *t* is used for English /ð/, we cannot tell whether /ð/ was unvoiced to /θ/ which was replaced by /т/, or whether /ð/ was replaced by /D/ which was unvoiced to /т/. The problem is further complicated by the fact that English initial /ð/ is always derived from earlier /θ/, so that we might have to deal with the survival of an earlier stage of development, rather than with any kind of unvoicing. Spellings with *t* for English /ð/ are very limited in their occurrence, and appear in only seven of our texts, I, V, VI, VII, VII, XII and XIX. *The Honest Whore* (V) has *t* only in the combination *wut tow* 'wilt thou' (13 &c.), a reflection of the ME assimilated form

245

wiltou and the like; *Hic et Ubique* (XII) also uses *wilt tow* (107); *hast tow* 'hast thou' (vii 73) is not significant, since this text invariably has *t* in *tow*, though not in any other word. *Stukeley* (I) has *t* in *too* 'thou' (7) and *tat* 'that' (22), but *der* 'there' (32) and *de* 'the' (42). The development of StE /ð/ from earlier /θ/ in pronouns and comparable words is due to lack of stress, and we have to accept the possibility that, in spite of the scantiness of present-day dialect attestation, the stressed form with its voiceless consonant may have survived. There is no clear evidence of the use of forms with an initial voiceless consonant in Mediæval Hiberno-English : *The English Conquest of Ireland* has a number of instances of *day* 'they', and inverted spellings like *onther* 'under' presuppose the use of a voiced consonant in some words written with *th* [Heuser (1904) 64]. Final /ð/ is rare in English, and the only common word in which it occurs is *with*; strong forms of this word, with voiceless final /θ/, are frequently recorded by the orthoepists [Dobson (1968) §4] and still survive in the dialects [Wright (1905) §317 and Index]. The form *wit* 'with' occurs in *Hic et Ubique* (xii 20), which otherwise has *t* only in *wilt tow*, and the *The Twin Rivals* (xix 166), which has no other instance of *t*. The problematic texts are *The Irish Masque* (VI) and *Hey for Honesty* (VIII), which invariably have *t* for initial /ð/. *The Irish Masque* (VI) also has *t* for medial /ð/ in *faters* 'father's' (95), *heter* 'hither' (101), *pretee* 'prithee' (120 &c.), *anoter* 'another' (148); the only instances of *d* for medial /ð/ are *pre dee* 'prithee' (31 &c.), *neder noder* 'neither' (35) and *eder oder* 'either' (36). Because medial /ð/ has been voiced since the earliest times, and since unvoicing of a medial consonant is improbable, it seems certain that Jonson's spellings represent a mechanical substitution of *t* for StE *th*; and if so, we can have no confidence that initial *t* for /ð/ represents a voiceless rather than a voiced sound. The *t*-spellings in *Hey for Honesty* (VIII) are probably of no independent significance : Randolph, as an avowed disciple of Jonson's, would in any case be likely to imitate his usage in the rendering of Hiberno-English (§221).

§110. Since the voiced spirants /z ʒ/ are lacking from the inventory of Irish consonant phonemes, it might be expected that they would be difficult for Irish-speakers to pronounce, and that they might therefore undergo unvoicing to /s ʃ/; in loanwords of all periods /z/ is regularly replaced by *s*. In early loanwords *s* represents /s/ or /ʃ/ according to the nature of the following vowel [Risk (1968–75) §145], in recent loanwords always /s/ [de

Bhaldraithe (1953–5) §50], unless influenced by neighbouring consonants; compare §75 above. Yet, because the absence of /z ʒ/ from the Irish inventory represents a "hole in the pattern" [Weinreich (1963) 22], it is not in fact very difficult for Irish-speakers to pronounce /z ʒ/, since all they have to do is to apply voicing to the phonemes /s ʃ/ which they already possess; and in fact the inventory of consonant phonemes in present-day Hiberno-English includes /z ʒ/, with a distribution-pattern closely parallel to that of /s ʃ/. As we have seen (§§ 93–4), English /z/ is frequently written *sh* in our texts; since English orthography provides no graphy for the representation of /ʒ/, we cannot be sure whether this *sh* is intended to represent /ʃ/ or /ʒ/. On the basis of the early loanwords we might assume that it probably represents /ʃ/; but on the basis of present-day Hiberno-English we might assume that it probably represents /ʒ/. Since /s/ does not invariably become /ʃ/ in all our texts, one might expect that /z/ would not always become /ʒ/; and that, if unvoicing was regular, unchanged /z/ would be unvoiced to /s/. The effect of such a development would be very easy to represent orthographically by the use of such spellings as *pleace* 'please', *chooce* 'choose' etc., and in fact spellings of this type are common in representations of the speech of Welshmen, whose language also lacks the phoneme /z/ [Bartley (1954) 293]. The *Aphorismical Discovery* includes many spellings which unambiguously indicate the unvoicing of /z/ : *ussed* 'used', *vissibly* 'visibly', *decease* 'disease', *frencie* 'frenzy'; the inverted spelling *zeudo* 'pseudo' and the frequent *-ize* for *ish* point in the same direction. Yet none of our texts contains a single spelling which unambiguously indicates the unvoicing of /z/, and such spellings as *weeze* 'wise' (i 12) seem definitely to exclude it; furthermore, as we shall see below (§113), there are spellings which seem to indicate the opposite change, the voicing of /s/ to /z/. Similarly, there is an almost complete absence of unambiguous indications of the unvoicing of /ʒ/ to /ʃ/ : the only one is *accation* 'occasion' (ix 84), paralleled by *perswation* 'persuasion' in the *Aphorismical Discovery*. We have to conclude that if unvoicing of /z/ and /ʒ/ existed in early modern Hiberno-English, our authors made very little effort to record it.

The voicing of voiceless consonants

§111. Spellings suggesting the voicing of voiceless consonants are much rarer than those suggesting the unvoicing of voiced con-

247

sonants. There are only two instances of the apparent voicing of voiceless stops, *blankead* 'blanket' (i 14) and *ub* 'up' (xxiv 14) : the first of these is exactly paralleled by Ir. *blaincéad*, and in fact the English ending *-et* normally appears as *-éad* in Irish, as in the recent *ticéad* 'ticket'. Voicing in such cases is no doubt due to the fact that final unsupported voiceless stops do not occur in native Irish words, though northern Irish and Manx Gaelic have frequent unvoicing of final unsupported *g* in unstressed syllables, as in the name *Pádraig* [O'Rahilly (1932) 147 & fn.1]. Though *ub* 'up' is an isolated instance, there seems to be no reason why it should not be genuine. The *Aphorismical Discovery* has *kide* 'kite'. The form *pottados* 'potatoes' (xvi 53) is not an instance of the voicing of medial /t/ : forms with *d* are common in the seventeenth century [*NED* s.v.].

§112. The voicing of voiceless spirants is less rare, though still not common. Some of our texts seem to show voicing of initial /ʍ/. As we have seen (§79) the normal spelling for /ʍ/ is *f*, reproducing the Irish neutral /f/ realized as [Φ]; but we also find the spelling *v*, used systematically in II, XV and XVII, and once each in VI (beside *ph*), VIII (beside *f*) and XX (beside *f*) : *vat* 'what' (vi 19, viii 20, xx 128). It would seem that this must reproduce Irish neutral /v/, realized as [β]. It seems impossible that voicing could reflect an Irish sound-change : as we have seen (§108), English /v/ tends to be unvoiced in Irish to *f*; we must rather look for an English explanation of the phenomenon. Simplification of OE *hw* to /w/ is attested in southern dialects of English from the twelfth century onwards [Jordan (1934) §195]; this pronunciation gradually made its way into Standard English, but in the seventeenth century was still dialectal or vulgar. The pronunciation /w/ seems to have been common in Mediæval Hiberno-English, where we find such spellings as *wat* 'what', *wy* 'why', etc. [Heuser (1934) 31–2], and the pronunciations indicated by the *v*-spellings in our texts might represent survivals from the Middle Ages. Alternatively, some bilingual speakers might have learned their English from speakers of a sub-standard dialect. The spelling *vh* in *vhile* 'while' (xvii 21 &c.), *vhen* 'when' (xvii 41 &c.) is probably a mechanical substitution of *v* for *w*, and does not imply voicing. The spelling *deveat* 'defeat' (xvii 29) shows voicing of intervocalic /f/; in Irish, medial /f'/ and /f/ are very rare, and in the modern language intervocalic /f'/ and /f/ are always the result of late assimilations (as in *scríobhtha* /ʃkr'i:fə/ 'written'), so that it is not surprising that corresponding voiced sounds should be substituted. The significance of the spelling *vfrow* 'Frau, German woman' (vi 116) is not clear; the word is from Dutch *vrouw*, but no *v*-spellings are recorded by *NED*; possibly Jonson's spelling is a kind of compromise between Dutch *vrouw* and German *Frau*. Voicing of /f/ in *Carick-vergus* 'Carrickfergus' (xix 11) is difficult to understand or explain.

§113. Voicing of /s/ to /z/ seems an improbable sound-change, since /z/ is lacking from the inventory of Irish consonant phonemes, and unvoicing of /z/ to *s* is normal in loanwords in Irish (above, §110); nevertheless, a number of spellings seem to suggest just this. The forms in question are *Creez(e)* 'Christ' (iv 21 &c.), *preez* 'price' (iv 24), *advies* 'advice' (ix 88), *sacrifize* 'sacrifice' (xx 119); no explanation suggests itself.

Lost and added consonants

§114. Loss of final /t/ and /d/ was common in seventeenth-century English [Dobson (1968) §398], and there are a number of instances in our texts. Loss of final /t/ after /s/ is found in the early texts I, III, IV, V, VI in the word *Christ*; Jonson has it also in the words *trush* 'trust' (vi 7), *didsh* 'didst' (vi 26), *honesh* 'honest' (vi 122); loss of *t* after *s* is found in Irish in the loanword *foraois* 'forest'. Loss of /t/ after /k/ is found in *supjack* 'subject', *upjack* 'object' (xii 9). Loss of final /d/ after /n/ was common already in Mediæval Hiberno-English in such words as *fyne* 'find', *undirston* 'understand' [McIntosh & Samuels (1968) 5]; in our texts it is found in *an(e)* 'and' (i 36, xix 109, xxii 12) and *Hollen* 'Holland' (v 84). Loss of medial /d/ after /n/ occurs (as often in colloquial Standard English) in *granfader* 'grandfather' (xix 69) [cf. Dobson (1968) §410 (i)]. The addition of /d/ after final /n/ is rare in English [ibid. §436]. MHE spellings like *wand* 'when', *sonde* 'soon' are usually interpreted as inverted spellings based on the loss of /d/ after /n/ [Heuser (1904) 31; McIntosh & Samuels (1968) 5], but it is possible that an excrescent /d/ developed in this position. The spelling *womands* 'woman's' (xiv 70) is unlikely to be merely scribal. The spelling *cunt—stable* (xii 47) is no doubt intentionally obscene. Loss of final /d/ after /r/ occurs in *alarbor* 'to larboard' (xiii 5).

§115. Loss of consonants other than /t/ and /d/ is rare in our texts. There are two instances of the loss of initial /w/ before a back rounded vowel, *oord* 'word' (xiv 57) and *urship* 'worship' (xxiii 104); such spellings are more usual in the representation of the speech of Welshmen [Bartley (1954) 292]; they occur in our texts in *vdcocks* 'woodcocks' (vii 121) and (improbably) in *ymen* 'women' (vii 78) and *enches* 'wenches' (vii 122); corresponding pronunciations can be heard in Wales to the present day. Both XIV and XXIII were written by Englishmen, and the two spellings are no doubt due to error or confusion. For loss of /w/ in the sequence /sw/ see above, §89. Early texts show loss of final /v/ in *have* (ii 52, vi 138) and *save* (iii 48 &c., v 2 &c., vi 138, vii 25 &c.); loss of final /v/ in *have* is common in Scottish and northern English dialects, but loss in *save* is not documented, and may be a HE feature—it occurs only in oaths. Loss of medial /v/ in *never* (vi 80) and *devil* (xii 10, xix 18 &c.) reflects developments in Scottish and northern English dialects [Jordan (1934) §216.1; Wright (1905) §279]. Final /θ/ (or perhaps its HE equivalent /τ/) is lost in *tro* 'troth' (ii 28); loss of /ð/ in *cloysh(s)* 'clothes' (vi 76 &c.) reflects a pronunciation recorded in the seventeenth century [Dobson (1968) §401 (c)] and still common in colloquial Standard English. Loss of medial /k/ in *posh* 'pox' (viii 41) no doubt reflects the absence of the sequence /ks/ in Irish, where loanwords usually undergo metathesis (as in *bosca* 'box'). Loss of initial /h/ in *ish* 'his' (xxiv 55) is due to lack of stress [cf. Heuser (1904) 31].

Conclusions about the consonants

§116. It is somewhat surprising that there is so little trace in our texts of a feature conspicuous in the earlier loanwords in Irish, the attribution to foreign consonants of palatal or neutral quality according to the articulation of the following vowel. No doubt the effect of "double interference" (§6) would have been to efface many of the resulting distinctions : the English listener, unaccustomed to the difference between palatal and neutral consonants, would have failed to hear it, and therefore could not have indicated it in his spellings even if appropriate graphies had been available. However, the secondary articulations of some of the Irish consonants had led bilingual speakers to identify the members of certain palatal and neutral pairs with separate English consonants; in these cases the English listener might have been expected to have been able to hear the differences, and appropriate graphies would be readily available. However, the evidence of our texts is fraught with difficulties, difficulties the more frustrating because this evidence ought to enable us to date more accurately the important Irish phonological development whereby the influence of consonants on preceding short vowels finally brought to an end the constraint by which the quality of each consonant was effectively dictated by the articulation of the following vowel (§74).

§117. The difficulties referred to can easily be illustrated by the usage of *Hic et Ubique* (XII). On the one hand this text uses *sh*-spellings for English /s/ only in the neighbourhood of front vowels (§88), so that the older constraint would seem to be still operative. On the other hand, the spelling *fu* (which, however it is interpreted in detail, certainly reflects Irish neutral /f/ rather than palatal /f'/) is used before front vowels in *fuat(e)* 'what' (10 &c.), *fuy* 'why' (35 &c.), and the ejaculation *fuillilaloo* 'alas!' (28), as if the constraint had ceased to operate; in fact this spelling is used *only* before front vowels. It seems impossible to resolve this conflict of evidence in any entirely satisfactory way. It would not help to assume that the Irish change affected certain words before others : if this had happened, it would have been differences in the consonant which followed the vowel which affected the date of the change; but the usage in *Hic et Ubique* apparently depends on differences in the consonant which precedes the vowel, and this plays no part in the process. We are entitled to assume (what is in any case intrinsically probable) that the change took place gradually, in the sense that there must have been a period during which forms appropriate to the earlier and the later system coexisted in the language; to some extent such a coexistence can still be observed in present-day Irish, where there may be random variation in the realization of short vowel phonemes between consonants of unlike quality. During such a period a bilingual speaker would have the opportunity of rendering an English word in terms of either the earlier or the later system of the Irish language.

§118. Though this theoretical consideration seems to offer some hope of explaining the observed facts, the details remain obscure. It is not immediately obvious why a bilingual speaker should choose to render words with English /s/ according to the earlier system and words with English /ʍ/ according to the later system. We may conjecture that, to the Irish ear, the acoustic difference between English /f/ and /ʍ/ seemed greater than the difference between English /ʃ/ and /s/, so that the inaccuracy involved in rendering /s/ before front vowels by an Irish palatal sound would seem less significant than the inaccuracy involved in rendering /ʍ/ before front vowels by an Irish palatal sound. Some support for this conjecture may be found in the fact that many of our texts use the spelling *sh* for /s/ even in the neighbourhood of back vowels : one

251

possible explanation for this fact assumes that in some variety of Irish the realization of neutral /s/ had an acoustic resemblance to /ʃ/ (above, §90.2). For speakers of such a variety of Irish the difference between English /ʃ/ and /s/ might indeed seem relatively unimportant, and they would see no harm in continuing the older Irish constraint by which a palatal consonant should be used before a front vowel; but the difference between English /f/ and /ʍ/ might seem so substantial that they would find it necessary in this case to follow the newer system and use neutral /f/ before a front vowel in words with English /ʍ/.

§119. In attempting to correlate the evidence of Hiberno-English texts with Irish phonological developments it is important to remember that the significant date is not the date of the text in which crucial spellings occur, but the date of the acquisition of English by the bilingual speakers whose language it reflects : though the *realization* of phonemes might be influenced by changes in the Irish language (§24), it is unlikely that their *distribution* would be affected. *Hic et Ubique* (XII) is not the only text in which spellings reflecting Irish neutral consonants are used before front vowels : in Dunton's *Sermon* (XVIII) the use of such spellings is even more extensive. As we have seen (§§ 79–80), Dunton uses *fw* for English /ʍ/ in all positions, even before front vowels, and *vw* for /w/ exclusively before front vowels. Both *Hic et Ubique* and the *Sermon* must reflect the language of bilingual speakers whose English had been acquired at a date when short vowels had begun to be influenced by the quality of the following consonant, but when that influence was not yet paramount. *Hic et Ubique* has *ee*-spellings for ME *ī* but no *oo*-spellings for ME *ū*, and it must therefore reflect the language of those whose English was acquired in the sixteenth century (§68); Dunton's *Sermon* has no *ee*-spellings, but ME *ā* is consistently represented by *aa*-spellings which reflect the fronting and raising of CG *á* to /ɛ:/ (§46), and this too must be a sixteenth-century change (§69). It seems, therefore, that in spite of O'Rahilly's opinion the redistribution of the Irish short vowel phonemes under the influence of a following consonant must have been well under way in the sixteenth century.

VOCABULARY

INTRODUCTORY

§120. Since the youngest of our texts was written nearly 250 years ago, and the oldest nearly 400 years ago, it is to be expected that they will use many words which have either become altogether obsolete, or which (if they still exist) are now used in different senses; the meanings of such words are given in the Glossarial Index, but they are not discussed here. Since nearly all the texts either consist of dialogue, or at least are written in a highly colloquial style, it is also to be expected that they will use a great many slang terms. Slang changes very rapidly, and if any slang term happens not to be used in a literary work while it is still fresh it will escape the net of the dictionaries; in such cases the meaning may be doubtful, or sometimes wholly obscure. In §§ 168–9 I have tried to elucidate as much of the slang as possible, but I have sometimes had to confess defeat. The most interesting part of the vocabulary of the texts is the part which is in one way or another peculiar to the Irish scene : it includes words and phrases borrowed directly from the Irish language, words and phrases influenced in some way by the Irish language, and words relating to specifically Irish things or customs; and it is to such words and phrases that I have given most attention in the following paragraphs.

§121. The effect of bilingualism on vocabulary is always complex and sometimes paradoxical, and it may be useful to refer briefly to the effects of bilingualism in England in the years following the Norman Conquest. For about 150 years after the Conquest the French words borrowed into English referred almost exclusively to things and concepts for which there was no native word : legal and administrative concepts unknown to the Anglo-Saxons, and features of the new luxurious living introduced by the Norman aristocracy. It was not, in fact, until the use of the French language began to decline after the loss of Normandy by King John in 1204 that any large number of French words entered English, and it was then for the first time that French words began to be used when there was a perfectly good native word available. It may seem paradoxical that when the French language was strong it had little effect on English, and that when it became weak its effect was very great, but in fact the explanation is simple. As long as the French language was strong, French-speakers had little occasion to use English, but as the currency of French diminished, those who had been brought up to speak it were obliged to make more and more use of the English language, in which they were far from expert : it often happened that they did not know, or had temporarily forgotten, or were too careless to use the appropriate English word or expression, and substituted the French equivalent instead. If this happened often enough, native speakers of English might become so accustomed to hearing French words and expressions that they would begin to use them themselves, the more so since those who used French were generally of a higher social status and therefore apparently worthy of imitation.

§122. It seems likely that similar conditions prevailed in Ireland. As long as the Irish language was strong and under no serious threat from English, few words passed from Irish into English : there are, for instance, only five Irish words in the whole of the *Kildare Poems* [Heuser (1904) 12]. Until about 1600 the only Irish words with any wide currency in English were those which referred to specifically Irish concepts and things, for which there was no English word : aspects of the political and cultural organization of the Irish people, details of their dress and food, and so on. When in the later sixteenth century the English language took on a new lease of life and began to spread, we find a different situation. More and more Irish-speakers found it necessary to use what little English they knew, and existing bilingual communities found the balance tilting more and more towards English until sooner or later the English language prevailed and the Irish language was lost. It is at this stage that we should expect to find Irish words beginning to enter Hiberno-English in relatively large numbers, and on the whole our texts confirm this expectation.

§123. The actual transfer of a word from the primary language into the secondary language is not the only way in which interference between two languages can affect the vocabulary : it is also possible for the choice and use of a word in one language to be affected by the usage of the other, or for a phrase to be constructed out of words belonging to one language while it reflects an idiom peculiar to the other [Weinreich (1963) 48]. Very few words in any language have a single easily definable meaning : most have a wide "semantic field", a range of meanings any of which it may reflect in an appropriate context. The semantic fields of words in different languages rarely coincide exactly, so that the same word in one language will need to be translated by different words in another language according to the context; this is why two-language dictionaries offer more than one rendering of the same word. In a bilingual situation it is easy for an unsophisticated speaker to imagine that there is one word in the secondary language which corresponds exactly to each word in the primary language : if only he can learn it and remember it he will never be at a loss to express his ideas. If he invariably uses the same word in the secondary language to render a word in the primary language, he will sometimes be right, but often he will be wrong—he will use the word in a sense outside its accepted semantic field in the secondary language. Similarly, he will tend to assume that the idiomatic phrases he uses in the primary language can be transferred into the secondary language by translating each word separately; in fact this is rarely so, since idioms are usually peculiar to the language in which they occur.

§124. A speaker's ability to cope with the difficulties of a secondary language varies according to his state of mind, and it is well known that any kind of emotional stress, favourable or unfavourable, tends to promote a reversion to the primary language in one way or another [Weinreich (1963) 78, 82]. For this reason interjections, ejaculations and oaths, all used at moments of emotional stress, are very readily transferred from one language into another. Such expressions may be used for either of two reasons : on the one hand, to relieve an emotional tension building up inside the speaker, and on the other hand to persuade the listener of the speaker's sincerity and good faith. In the first case the primary language will be more efficacious, but in the latter case the purpose of the ejaculation will be frustrated unless it is understood by the listener, so that here we should expect the words of the secondary language to be used, though the way they are put together may be influenced by the idiom of the primary language. This is in general what we find in Hiberno-English, and our texts provide ample illustrations. In the following discussion the spelling of the texts is usually ignored unless it is of special interest, and ejaculations are cited in a normalized Irish or English form.

255

§125. The earliest Irish ejaculation in our texts, and one of the most popular, is the cry of lamentation *ochón*, usually written as two words, as if it consisted of the interjection *oh!* followed by a word *hone* (ii 60 &c., xvi 97, xviii 35 &c., xix 60, xxi 3 &c., xxvii 92 &c.). The number of ejaculations in *Hic et Ubique* (XII) is very large indeed, and most of them occur also in later texts. Among the most popular are extended forms of the Irish ejaculation *obó*, expressing apprehension : *ub, ub, ub, boo* (xii 107), *aboo! boo!* (xiv 69); *hub-bub-boo* (xx 12 &c.), *who-bub-boo* (xx 83), *hub, bub, bub, bu* (xxii 11), *ubbo bo-boo* (xxiii 116). It is uncertain whether the repeated *hub* of xxiv 33 &c. represents this interjection; it may perhaps represent Ir. *hob*, a cry used to a horse. Another lamentation reflects Irish *puililiú*, *fuililiú : *fuillilaloo* (xii 28), *who-la-loo* (xx 12 &c.), *pulilillew* (xxi 57). Other ejaculations are no more than mild expletives. The most popular is Ir. *ara* (xii 18 &c., xiii 29, xvii 2, xix 38, xx 37, xxii 12 &c., xxiii 77 &c., xxvii 33 &c.). Probably *arrow* (xii 107) also represents *ara* rather than the alternative Irish ejaculation *arú*, since representation of Irish final -*a* by -*ou*, -*ow* is confirmed by *yerrou* (xxi 4) representing Ir. *dhera*; *arú* appears as *rhoo* (xii 10). The autograph manuscript of Sheridan's *Brave Irishman* repeatedly uses *orrow*, no doubt also representing Ir. *ara*. Another mild ejaculation is Ir. *ó dhe* (xii 8 &c., xxi 26). More substantial ejaculations include *m'anam do'n Diabhal* 'my soul to the Devil' (xii 120, xxvii 5 &c.), *fuil Dé* 'God's blood' (xiii 15*) and (*a*) *Mhuire* 'Mary!' (xxiv 52). One ejaculation which is hard to explain is *ceann gránna* 'ugly head' (xxvii 32 &c.). This phrase is used as a term of abuse in two late eighteenth-century plays, John O'Keeffe's *Wicklow Gold Mines* and William Macready's *Bank Note*, both produced in 1795 [Duggan (1937) 149, 257], but outside *The Brave Irishman* there is no instance of its use as a mere expletive, and it is difficult to see how it could come to be used in this way. Since it does not appear in Sheridan's autograph it may represent an ignorant addition by some actor (above, p. 74).

§126. It is not surprising that there are very few English interjections, or that all of those which do occur are onomatopœic to a greater or lesser extent. The earliest is *owe* (i 2), documented by *NED* [s.v. *ow*] in Middle English, and again from 1768 in Scottish (our instance falls between the two periods); the context is generally one of surprise. In later texts *uf uf* (xix 11) is an attempt to represent the sound of sniffing; *foh* (xxi 28), *phugh* (xxvii 132), *pugh* (xxvii 150) and *phoo* (xxvii 162) are variant forms of an interjection still in use. The only form which is in any way problematic is *swoop, swoop* (xiii 97), not elsewhere recorded; it has some similarity in form and meaning to *whoop*, recorded by *NED* from 1568 as "an exclamation . . . expressing excitement, surprise, derision, exultation, incitement, etc."

§127. In our texts the only Irish oath of the type designed to convince the listener of the speaker's sincerity and good faith is *(dar an) leabhar so* 'by this book' (xxi 40); with this should be compared the English expressions *vpon hish booke* (vi 9) and *I'le swear de Book* (xxi 15). As might be expected, nearly all the oaths are in English : some of them are translated from Irish expressions, others are of purely English origin. There is ample contemporary evidence of the tendency of Irishmen to interlard their discourse liberally with oaths. The Jesuit William Good gives a useful list of the oaths used [Camden (1610) 145] :

> At every third word it is ordinary with them to lash out an oth, namely *by the Trinity, by God, by S. Patrick, by S. Brigid, by their Baptisme, by Faith, by the Church, by my Godfathers hand, and by thy hand.*

Later accounts seem to be dependent on Good, though each adds something new. Gainsford [(1618) 150] tells us that

> they commonly intermix othes with their speeches, as by the Trinitie, God, his Saints, St. Patrick, St. Briget, faith, and troth, the Temple, your hand, O Neales hand, and such like.

Eachard [(1691) 21] is even closer to Camden :

> At every third word it is ordinary with them to rap out an Oath, as by the *Trinity*, by *Christ*, by St. *Patrick*, by St. *Brigid*, by their Baptism, by their Godfathers hand and suchlike.

A shorter list of oaths is given in Dunton's *Sermon* (xviii 114–5).

§128. The most unusual and (as we shall see) the most characteristic of these oaths are those which invoke some person's hand. They are not unique : *NED* [s.v. *hand* 6] quotes instances from 1300 onwards in contexts which have no Irish connection. Nevertheless, Matheson [(1956–7) 247–8] has shown that "swearing by hands" had a special significance for the Gaelic peoples, and Spenser remarked on the peculiar solemnity it had for Irishmen [Renwick (1934) 77] :

The Irish vse now to sweare by there lordes hand, and to forsweare yt, hold yt more Cryminall then to sweare by god.

Swearing by hands is not even yet extinct : the current Irish ejaculation *ambasa* is based on *bas* '(palm of the) hand'. An oath by a gossip's [i.e. godfather's] hand was particularly sacred. The Irish formula, *dar láimh mo chairdios Críost*, occurs in *Páirlement Chloinne Tomáis* (x 28), and an anglicized version of it was noted by Dineley in 1681 [Shirley (1856–7) 180] :

> One of the greatest protestations that they think they can make, and what they hold an oath very sacred amongst them, and by no means to be violated, is deralauve ma hardis criste, by my gossips hand.

Moffet [(1716) 12] refers to this in passing as a standard oath : "By *Gossip's Hand*, he oft did swear." The oath *by my gossip's hand* is frequent in our texts (vi 44, vii 22, xii 16, xvi 55, xviii 115, xx 1); there is one instance of the more elaborate formula *by the hand of my good gossip* (xx 141). There are numerous other "hand" oaths, but (with one exception) they all belong to the first quarter of the seventeenth century : *by this hand* (i 20 &c., vii 42 &c.) and the extended form *by this hand and body* (v 31*), *by my hand* (iii 26 &c., vi 131), *by St Patrick's hand* (iv 13 &c.), *by my father's hand* (vi 95), and a number of fanciful variants—*by Justice Dillon's hand* (vi 132), *by my Lord Deputy's hand* (vi 133), *by the hand of Gilarnoo* (xiii 21*). Other oaths involving possessives are *by (my) father's soul* (iii 27, xiii 22), *by the shoes of Patrick* (viii 25), *by my father's saddle* (xii 16), and *by the hem of my mother's smock* (xv 12).

§129. Swearing by God and the saints was naturally common enough, but commoner in the earlier part of the period than in the later. Oaths invoking the name of God are few in number : *by God* (vi 2 &c., xii 78), and the altered form *begog* (x 38), *by the grace of God* (vi 111), *by Christ* (iii 47, vi 119, xv 36 &c.); for the curious word *la* in MacMorrice's *by Chrish Law* (iii 25) see below, §130. As one might expect, the saint most commonly represented in oaths is St Patrick, and we find *by St Patrick* throughout the period (ii 5 &c., v 37, vi 96, xii 35 &c., xiv 26, xv 32, xxii 30, xxiii 112 &c.). The only other oaths by saints are both in *Hic et Ubique* (XII) : *by St Sonday* (19) and *by St Shone Batty* (116). The first of these seems eccentric but is not really so : *St Sunday* is an equivalent of *St Dominic* [*NED* s.v. *Sunday* 2]. The second apparently means 'by St John the Baptist', but it may involve a crude pun : the name normally given to St John the Baptist in Irish is *Eoin Baiste*, and Patrick may be alluding, either intentionally or in error, to the Irish idiom *ná déan Seán báidhte de* 'don't add too much water to the whiskey.' There are a few instances of a mild oath of a common type : *Christ bless us* (i 22), *St Patrick bless us* (i 23), *Christ bless him* (vi 20), *Christ bless thy sweet face* (vi 22).

§130. Other popular oaths are *by my faith* (vi 43, xii 21, xiv 15, xx 5 &c., xxiii 61), *by my troth* (ii 28, iv 9 &c., xiv 42, xx 71) with its variant *by my own troth* (xxv 7*), and the combined *by my faith and troth* (vi 24). After the middle of the seventeenth century we meet a fashion for *by my soul* (xi 5, xiv 23 &c., xv 8 &c., xix 4 &c., xxi 1 &c., xxii 13 &c., xxiv 15, xxvii 47 &c.) and *by my salvation* (xiii 39, xv 21), varying with *by my soulvation* (xii 121, xiv 56, xxv 31); the curious form *soulvation* may be a consequence of the interchange of *soul* and *salvation* in oaths (see also §91). A popular oath of a different kind, not found after 1630, is *Christ save me* (vii 25 &c) with its variants *so Christ save me* (iii 43 &c., v 2 &c.), *so God save me* (iii 48), and the anomalous *by Christ save me* (vi 40 &c.). In *Henry V* (III) *so Christ save me* (29, 51) is followed by a mysterious *law*; in *Old Fortunatus* (IV) *as Christ save me* (21, 39) is followed by *la*. As we shall see (§131), *la* is also used with the oaths *faith!* and *i' faith!*, though it does not occur after 1630. There is indeed an English interjection *la!*, but it is a very mild one, and it seems inappropriate in the context of an oath. However, in *Love's Labour's Lost* (V ii 114) Shakespeare uses *law* in a context precisely similar to the ones we have been considering, and the form is guaranteed by the rhyme :

> And to begin Wench, so God helpe me law,
> My loue to thee is sound *sans* cracke or flaw.

It is perhaps worth noting that *la* occurs twice in the context of an oath in the *Kildare Poems* [Heuser (1904) 146, 155], though it precedes and does not follow the oath itself : *la, god it wote.* We may reasonably conclude that *la, law* is a variant of the English interjection *la, lo,* with a stronger meaning and a vowel influenced by rhetorical emphasis, widely current in Ireland but known also in England.

§131. Another kind of oath consists of a mere ejaculation. The most popular ejaculation is *faith!* or *i' faith!* The earlier texts prefer *i' faith!*, which occurs in only two texts later than 1630 (i 5

259

&c., iv 6 &c., v 10* &c., vi 67, vii 18 &c., xv 21 &c., xvi 55); there are also instances of *i' faith la!* (v 29 &c., vii 10 &c.). The simple ejaculation *faith!*, though it is found before 1630, is much better represented in the later texts (iv 12 &c., vi 37 &c., xii 51 &c., xiii 88, xiv 48, xvi 36 &c., xx 15 &c., xxi 45, xxii 5 &c., xxvii 100); there are also instances of *faith la!* (v 7*, 65). The compound ejaculation *faith and troth!* occurs only once (xiv 65).

§132. Oaths of the type *the devil take me* (*you, her*, etc.) occur very occasionally at the beginning of the century (vi 46), but do not become common until after 1680 (xiv 16 &c., xv 14 &c., xxiv 5 &c.); the form *devil take me* (*you, her*, etc.), without the definite article, hardly appears before 1700 (xviii 114, xix 18 &c., xxiv 58). The list of oaths in Dunton's *Sermon* includes *devil break my neck* (xviii 114), but this is not recorded elsewhere. Captain O'Blunder's *devil split it* (xxvii 75) is paralleled by *the devil may thy collar splice* (xiii 98), where *splice* has the obsolete sense of 'split' (§168). A variant of *devil take it* is *pox take it* and the like (xx 44 &c., xxiv 44). The formula (*a*) *pox* (*up*)*on* appears early: *a pox on the horse's nose* (v 16), *a pox on thee* (v 83), *pox on the gardens, and the weeds* (v 92), *a pox upon thine eyes* (vii 132), *pox on her lice* (viii 41), *pox on thy tale* (xvi 81) [glossed in a footnote by the Irish phrase *breall ar an scéal*], *pox* (*up*)*on you* (xxi 7, xxii 57). After 1700 we find *upon my soul* (xxii 28 &c., xxvii 1 &c.) and *upon my soulvation* (xxii 35) instead of the earlier *by my soul, by my soulvation*.

§133. Among the minor oaths or expletives, the most interesting is the very frequent *and be!* (vi 2 &c., xii 21, xiii 23 &c., xiv 65 &c.). Jonson's spelling *an't be* (vi 2, beside *ant be* vi 61, *andt be* vi 72, etc.) makes it clear that *and be!* stands for *an*(*d*) *it be* 'if it be'. This expletive seems to be a rendering of Irish *muise*, based on a mistaken derivation of *muise* from *má 'seadh* 'if it be'. This derivation still has some currency (it is given, for instance, by Dinneen), but it is much more likely that *muise* represents an arbitrary alteration of *Muire* 'Mary'; this latter derivation is made effectively certain by the existence of the form *mhuise* parallel to (*a*) *Mhuire* 'Mary!' with the lenition appropriate to the vocative; the present-day Hiberno-English forms are *musha* and *wisha* respectively. The supposed derivation of *muise* from *má 'seadh* is not implausible in the light of the use of *má 'seadh* as a kind of concessive expletive 'in that case . . .'—in the Book of Ballymote it glosses Latin *igitur* [*Contributions* s.v. *má* II (a)]; nevertheless, the meaning of *muise* as normally used is quite different—it is a mild asseveration, 'indeed, really, to be sure'; and the usage of *and be!* in our texts is precisely the same.

§134. A very curious oath or expletive, and one which it is difficult to explain, is *by dis chees* (xiii 70); there are two more occurrences in *Purgatorium Hibernicum*, two in *The Irish Hudibras*, but none in any other text so far as I am aware. The phrase is therefore peculiar to the type of Fingallian dialect represented in the *Fingallian Burlesque*. It may, of course, have been invented by the unknown author of the *Burlesque*, but in view of the general accuracy of his usage this seems unlikely. It is perhaps possible that the basis of this phrase is a confusion between the two Irish words *cás* (genitive *cáis*) 'case' and *cáis* (genitive *cáise*) 'cheese'; one possible Irish basis for the idiom is *do réir an cháis seo* 'according to this case', i.e. 'in these circumstances'.

§135. A special type of ejaculation is the one addressed directly to the person spoken to, and containing or implying a verb in the imperative. Some of these are neutral in character, but others are abusive and insulting. Among the neutral ejaculations are the terms for 'farewell!' Irish has two such terms, *slán agat* (used by the person who is going) and *slán leat* (used by the person who is staying). These are correctly used in *Stukeley* (i 48* and 49*), but the latter is incorrectly used by the person who is going in *The Honest Whore* (v 45*); in *Stukeley* the form *slane lets* (i 49*) represents Ir. *slán leatsa*, abbreviated as in Manx Gaelic [Rhys (1894) 172]. Other ejaculations are *féach* 'look!' (i 18) and *éist do chlampar* 'hush your noise' (i 17). Some ejaculations are abusive, and these show an interesting chronological progression. The earliest texts use *marbhthásc ort* 'a curse on you', literally 'death-tidings on you', which appears in the forms *marafastot* (i 24) and (much corrupted) *marragh frofat* (v 46). [The usual Irish spelling is the unsatisfactory *marbhfhásc* 'death-shroud'; I owe the above convincing etymology to Professor Breandán O Buachalla.] Next comes the curious expression *siubhail go croich* 'walk to the gallows', i.e. 'get hanged!', which appears in the forms *sholl de crow* (vii 179), *shulecrogh* (viii 80) and *shoole a crogh* (xii 120). One expletive which it is difficult to explain is *spereen . . . upon it* (xvi 83); *spereen* is glossed in the printed text as "Despair", and it no doubt possible that *spereen* is a contraction of *despairing*, with substitution of Ir. *-in* for English *-ing*, as often in the dialect of Forth; but it would seem that such an expression should be applicable only to a human being, not (as here) to an inanimate thing. No convincing

Irish etymology presents itself. Finally there is the mild ejaculation *croidhe cráidhte ort* 'vexation to you!' (xxiv 52).

§136. Terms of abuse and terms of endearment also tend to be used at moments of emotional stress, and therefore to reflect the influence of the primary on the secondary language. When Irish words are transferred into English, either as terms of abuse or as terms of endearment, the characteristic forms of the Irish vocative (lenition of the initial consonant and usually palatization of the final consonant) are very rarely reproduced. The same omission is to be found in the Irish-English phrasebook compiled by Andrew Boorde in the early sixteenth century, where we find, for example, *benyte* and *farate*, representing Irish *bean an tighe* 'woman of the house' and *fear an tighe* 'man of the house', instead of the appropriate vocative forms (*a*) *bhean an tighe* and (*a*) *fhir an tighe* [Furnivall (1870) 134]. Lloyd [(1914) 22–3] suggests that Boorde in his ignorance added words he had heard in another context to fill out his phrases; but it seems possible that he and the later writers thought it undesirable in some way to record these particular changes. It is perhaps worth mentioning that in anglicized forms of Irish place-names the normal lenition of the second element is usually not reproduced, perhaps in order not to obscure the significance of the element. At all events, the reproduction of the true vocative form is the exception rather than the rule in our texts.

§137. *Captain Thomas Stukeley* (I), short though it is, includes a generous selection of terms of abuse : *bodach* 'lout' (18) and its extension *bodach bréan* 'rotten lout' (9), *mac diabhail* 'son of a devil' (24), *cana* 'cur' (25), *striopach* 'whore' (33). The only parallel to this richness is in the splendid catalogue of abuse in *The Pretender's Exercise* (xxiv 52–3) : *Mhuire! croidhe cráidhte ort! scraiste, (a) bhodaigh bhréin, gráineach, cliútach!* 'Mary! vexation to you! sluggard, rotten, loathsome, deceitful lout!' The phrase *bodach bréan*, which occurs in both these texts (in the latter in its true vocative form) is found also in *The Honest Whore* (v 46); it must have been a standard combination. The noun *striopach* from the first text and the adjective *gráineach* from the second are put together in *Hic et Ubique* (xii 127); *bodach* occurs also in Swift's *Dialogue* (xxvi 25). The only other Irish abusive terms are *a c(h)ailleach* 'O hag' (xiii 97*) and *sead* 'louse' (xx 10). Curiously enough there are very few English terms of abuse which in any way seem to reflect Irish usage, though (as we shall see) there are a number of distinctive Hiberno-English terms of endearment; one such is *thief* (vii 179, xvi 7, xxiii 55, xxiv 7 &c.), which may reflect Ir. *gadaidhe* 'thief', used also in the more general sense of 'rogue'. The term *strapp* 'whore' (xiii 3), still in use in Ireland, is of unknown origin; it may possibly be related to Ir. *stríopach*, itself of unknown origin.

§138. There are a few other abusive terms which seem to be of very limited distribution. The term *guddy hang* 'gallows-bird' (xii 33 &c.) is of special interest : it occurs also in *Purgatorium Hibernicum* (nine times) and in *The Irish Hudibras* (eight times), where it is glossed "Fit for nothing but the Gallows"; in the form *gooudee hang* it occurs in the dialect of Forth, where it is glossed "A good-for-nothing person" [Barnes (1867) 42]. An adjective associated with this noun is *greyshy* (xii 33 &c), *greisie* (xii 120); this is the word *greasy*, but in the dialect of Forth *greezee, grizee* has the special meaning 'ugly' [ibid. 43]. The term *Monaghan* (xvi 60, xxvi 32) occurs twice more in *The Irish Hudibras*, where it is glossed "Clowns, Inhabitants of the County of Monaghan"; it also occurs six times in *Purgatorium Hibernicum*. Apart from the fact that Monaghan was at this time a remote rural district, isolated from the centres of culture in Ireland, no reason is known why its inhabitants should be considered classic clowns.

§139. Terms of endearment are numerous, and their range extends from phrases expressing true affection to mere ingratiating or polite forms of address. The earliest Irish term of endearment is *a chroidhe* 'O heart!', which appears without lenition as *a cree* (ii 60) and (exceptionally) with lenition as *achree* (xii 8 &c.). Next comes the compound endearment *a mháighistir a ghrá(i)dh* 'O master dear' (v 61*); the simple *a ghrá(i)dh* recurs in xii 35 and xix 142. The two words *grádh* and *croidhe* are commonly combined in the phrase *grádh mo chroidhe* 'love of my heart', and this appears in the form *gra-ma-cree* (xiii 82), not here in the vocative, and in the form *cram-ma-cree* (xvi 29), in the vocative but lacking lenition, and glossed "Dear Heart". The initial *c-* in the latter form is by no means unique, and the still more perverted form *Cran a Cree* appears in Beaumont and Fletcher's *Coxcomb* (1612) [Bowers (1966) 297]. An exceptional endearment is *rogha* 'sweetheart', literally 'choice', which appears in the form *ro* (xiii 15); it occurs repeatedly throughout *Purgatorium Hibernicum*, but nowhere else in English. A common endearment which occurs only once in our texts in (a) *rú(i)n* 'darling', literally 'secret' (xvii 1). Many common Irish endearments happen not to occur at all in our texts : thus, for instance, the frequent *a mhúirnín* 'darling', which appears in Sheridan's autograph of *The Brave Irishman* (p. 47) as *a Vurney*, with appropriate lenition.

§140. As well as using Irish endearments, Irishmen seem to have been addicted to the use of extravagant forms of address in English; though the general floweriness of the phrases may be a reflection of Irish usage, it is curious that none of them can be explained as a direct rendering of an Irish phrase. The earliest instances involve the word *sweet*. This was in general use in England in the seventeenth century, and such forms of address as *sweet lord* (v 21) and *sweet heart* (vi 37, xiii 37*) are in themselves not remarkable—though the latter may perhaps reflect Irish *a chroidhe*. We shall see below (§§ 178–9) that Irishmen tended (and still tend) to substitute *my (own) self* and the like for the simple personal pronouns, and we need not therefore be surprised at the use of *thy (own) sweet self* (iv 60, xv 18) as a form of address. When the verb is *see* (v 60, xvi 25), or *show* (vi 2), or *kiss* (xv 57) it is not unreasonable to substitute *sweet face* for *sweet self*; so with the more elaborate forms *thy own sweet countenance* (iv 32) and *that sweet face of thine* (vii 23). The formula *thy (own) sweet face* becomes mechanical when the verb is *send for* (v 12) or *bless* (vi 22), and this mechanical usage leads to the use of *sweet face* as a direct vocative (v 24, vi 72 &c.). An alternative development from *thy (own) sweet face* is the use of *sweet-faced* as a complimentary adjective (vi 89); the same usage occurs a little earlier in Beaumont and Fletcher's *Coxcomb* (1612) [Bowers (1966) 306]. As we shall see below (§188), seventeenth-century Hiberno-English tends to omit the inflection of the past participle, and this is probably the basis of the adjectival use of *sweet face* (iv 76) or *sweet countenance* (iv 63) in the meaning 'handsome'. The same meaning seems to be intended in iv 43; if so, we should perhaps read *dee sweete countenance* rather than *di sweete countenance*.

§141. From 1660 onwards we find repeated use of *joy* as an endearment or polite form of address (xii 65 &c., xiv 6 &c., xvi 29, xx 5 &c., xxiii 54 &c., xxvii 115). A similar usage is sparsely represented in English, as for instance in Titania's speech to Bottom (*A Midsummer Night's Dream* IV i 1–4) :

Come, sit thee down vpon this flowry bed,
While I thy amiable cheekes do coy,
And sticke muske roses in thy sleeke smoothe head,
And kisse thy faire large eares, my gentle ioy.

Nevertheless, the great frequency of the word in Hiberno-English leaves no doubt that it represents an arbitrary substitution for some such Irish endearment as *a chroidhe* or *a ghrá(i)dh*; in *The Irish Hudibras* it is several times substituted for the *ro(e)*, Ir. *rogha* (§139), of *Purgatorium Hibernicum*. From the late 1680's onwards we find the extended form *dear joy* (xv 46 &c., xvi 5 &c., xix 9 &c., xx 23 &c.). So popular was this form of address supposed to be among Irishmen that the phrase, usually hyphenated, came to be used as a name for an Irishman (xv 61, xvi 1, xvii 5 &c.) : Eachard [(1691) 17] remarked, as of something well established, that the Irish "are vulgarly called by the names of *Teague* and *Dear-Joy*" (for *Teague* see below, §143). *Dear Joy* is given a prominent place on the title-page of *Bog-Witticisms* (p. 52). In spite of its popularity, the phrase does not appear in any of our texts after 1700, though there is one instance of the variant *sweet joy* (xxv 6). Later forms of address are *honey* (xxii 78) and *my dear* (xxvii 59); both are used in standard English, and need occasion no remark except in so far as their effusiveness may seem un-English. However, *my (dear) jewel* (xxvii 100 &c.) is in a different category, since *NED* records no instance of the use of *jewel* as an endearment : *my jewel* is perhaps a rendering of Irish *a stó(i)r* 'O treasure'.

THE IRISHMAN AND HIS CUSTOMS

The Irishman

§142. So far we have considered cases in which a bilingual speaker reverts under the stress of emotion to his primary language, or at least uses the secondary language in a way suggested by the primary language, but there are other circumstances in which a word from the primary language may be used in the course of an utterance in the secondary language. In many respects Irish culture differed from English culture : many Irish customs and things had no counterpart among the English, and therefore there was no name for them in English. In such circumstances bilingual speakers would have no alternative but to draw on the primary language, and their descendents would no doubt cease to be aware of the origin of the word, which would become what Weinreich [(1963) 11] calls "an inherited loanword"; even Englishmen wishing to avoid awkward circumlocutions would have to use the Irish word, and the majority of the words we have to discuss now were in fact used by Englishmen writing about Ireland from the fifteenth century onwards. In surveying these we may start with the people of Ireland, in general and in particular.

§143. In the sixteenth and seventeenth centuries three different types of Irishman could be distinguished: the native Irish, the "New English" who had recently settled in the country, and in between them the "Old English", descended from the settlers of the Middle Ages, linked with the native Irish by their religion and with the "New English" by their loyalty. In the later seventeenth century the current term for a native Irishman was *Teague*, an anglicization of the northern Irish pronunciation of the name *Tadhg*, sometimes equated with the English name *Timothy*. This term did not become common until the latter part of the century, but it was already in use before 1650: "When a protestant official wished to denigrate the old English members of parliament in 1641, he called them 'Teigs', and they duly took offence" [Clarke (1969) 25]. On the title-page of *Bog-Witticisms* Ireland is called *Teague-Land*, and *Teague-Land Jests* became the title of subsequent editions of the same work (above, p. 53). In 1690 the Irish poet David O Bruadair entitled one of his poems *Caithréim Thaidhg* 'The Triumph of Tadhg', and elsewhere he speaks of those who *adubhairt Téigs is Diarmaids riamh go tarcuisneach* 'kept calling us "Teagues" and "Dermots" derisively' [MacErlean (1910–17) iii 126, 102]. In 1691, as we have seen (§141), Eachard gives *Teagues* as one of the names by which the Irish are "vulgarly" called. The term occurs as a generic name for an Irishman only once in our texts (xxiii 30), but *Teague* is the commonest personal name for an Irishman: it occurs in this function six times (XIV, XVII, XIX, XX, XXI, XXII), compared with *Dermot* four times (VI, VIII, XX, XXI), *Bryan* twice (V, XV) and *Patrick* twice (VI, XII); no other name occurs more than once.

§144. The first type of Irishman with which the English became acquainted was the soldier, and the terms *kerne* and *galloglass* entered the English language early. These represent Irish *ceithearn* and *gallóglach* respectively: *ceithearn* is properly a collective noun, meaning 'troop of foot-soldiers', and *kerne* is sometimes used in the same sense, though it early came to refer to a single foot-soldier;

266

gallóglach properly means 'mercenary', and indeed the literal meaning is 'foreign soldier'. In our period the words *kerne* and *galloglass* are applied to lightly and to heavily armed foot-soldiers respectively. Fynes Moryson in 1617 gave the following account of their functions [Falkiner (1904) 287]:

> Divers kinds of foot use divers kinds of arms. First, the Galliglasses are armed with morions and halberts. Secondly, the Kerne and some of their footmen are armed with weighty iron mails and jacks, and assail horsemen aloof with casting darts, and at hand with the sword.

A similar account is given by Eachard [(1691) 25]:

> Their Warfare consists of Horsemen, of Soldiers set in the Rereguard, whom they call Galloglasses, who fight with sharp Hatchets; and of light-armed Footmen called *Kernes*, whose service is with Darts and Skeanes.

The Irish words occur together in *Stukeley* (i 44), the latter in the spelling *gallinglasse* with intrusive *n* as in English *nightingale* from earlier *nightegale*.

§145. In the later seventeenth century many of the dispossessed Irish went on the run and acted as irregular soldiers or guerrillas; some of their activities were not far removed from banditry. They were known by two names, both of Irish origin, *rapparees* and *tories*. The origin of the word *rapparees* is discussed by Story [(1691) 16]:

> Some of them were murthered by the *Rapparees*; a word which we were strangers to till this time. Those are such of the *Irish* as are not of the Army, but the Country people armed in a kind of an hostile manner with Half-Pikes and Skeins, and some with Sythes, or Musquets. For the Priests the last three or four years past would not allow an *Irishman* to come to Mass, without he brought at least his Rapparee along; that they say in *Irish* signifies an Half-stick, or a Broken-beam, being like an Half-pike; from thence the Men themselves have got that name.

In spite of some confusion, Story is in the main right: Ir. *rapaire* 'rapparee' is a kind of compromise between the native word *ropaire* 'snatcher, stabber' and the loanword *rápaire* 'rapier, short pike'. The plural of *rapaire* is *rapairí*, and English *rapparees* is therefore a double plural. The word *tory* is from Ir. *tóraidhe*, which originally meant 'pursuer' rather than 'hunted man'; it ultimately became the recognized name of the political party opposed to the Whigs. In our texts *tory* appears the earlier of the two words (vii 88, xiii 75), much earlier than the earliest record in *NED* (1646); later we find the plural *tories* already applied to the members of a political party (xxi 13); *rapparees* appears in its strict sense in the context of the siege of Derry (xx 95).

§146. There are fewer names in our texts for Irish civilians. One such is *culleen*, glossed "Bore" (xvi 14), representing Ir. *coilín*, which means something like 'yokel'. According to Stanihurst [Holinshed (1577) f.2*v* col. 2] it was applied specifically to Fingallians :

> Fingall especially from tyme to tyme hath bene so addicted to all the poyntes of Husbandry, as that they are nicknamed by their neighbors, for their continuall drudgery, Collonnes of the latin word *Coloni*, wherunto the clipt English worde, Clowne, séemeth to be aunswerable.

Another word is *spalpeen* (xxvi 32, xxvii 16 &c.), representing Ir. *spailpín*, a late word of doubtful origin meaning 'migratory labourer' and applied to those peasants, mainly from the West of Ireland, who spent the summer working in the more fertile country of eastern Ireland, Scotland, or England. Later the word acquired the meaning 'rascal', but this hardly appears in our texts, unless there is some trace of it in Swift's usage (xxvi 32). It was widely believed that many Irishmen made a living by giving perjured evidence for a fee, so we may perhaps include here the word *evidence* (xix 108, xxiii 123) in the seventeenth-century sense 'witness'; employment as a professional witness was an *evidence-place* (xvi 114).

Clothing and weapons

§147. A number of words refer to the distinctive clothing of the Irish. Their nether garments were unlike English breeches or hose, and were referred to as *trouses* (i 13, vii 32 &c., xvi 12), representing Irish *triús* with added plural *-es* as in *breeches*. The nature of this garment was fully described by Gernon in 1620 [Falkiner (1904) 356–7] :

> The trowse is a long stock of frise, close to his thighes, and drawne almost to his waste, but very scant, and the pryde of it is, to weare it so in suspence, that the beholder may still suspecte it to be falling from his arse. It is cutt with a pouche

before, which is drawne together with a string; he that will be counted a spruce ladd, tyes it up with a twisted band of two colours like the string of a clokebagge. An Irishman walking in London a cutpurse took it for a cheate [i.e. 'something to steal'], and gave him a slash.

On their feet the Irish wore *brogues* (xiii 90, xvi 12, xxiv 47 &c., xxv 37*, xxvii 63); the Irish form is *bróg*, a borrowing of OE *brōc* 'trousers', and therefore cognate with English *breeches*. Again a useful description is provided by Gernon [ibid. 357]:

His brogues are single soled, more rudely sewed then a shoo but more strong, sharp at the toe, and a flapp of leather left at the heele to pull them on.

§148. The relationship of the word *brogue* 'Irish way of speaking' to *brogue* 'shoe' has given rise to much speculation, not all of it very sensible; but in fact there is no doubt that the two words are the same, and the sense-development, though unusual, is clear. An investigation carried out by the Irish Folklore Commission, and reported by Gerard Murphy [(1941-2) 231-6], showed that two widely separated Irish dialects, those of the Rosses in Co. Donegal and of Dingle in Co. Kerry, use the idiom *tá bróg ar a theangaidh* 'there is a shoe on his tongue' to describe some form of defective speech. This idiom corresponds precisely to the seventeenth- and eighteenth-century English idiom *a brogue on his tongue* to describe an Irish way of speaking. The earliest instance seems to be in *The Irish Hudibras* (p. 47):

A Dish-clout round his Neck was hung,
And wore his *Brogue* upon his Tongue:
For Tongue a *Brogue* supply'd the Strain;
And yet he had more Tongue than Brain.

Nearly contemporary with this is a usage by Samuel Mullenaux [(1690) 22]: at the siege of Limerick, he tells us, the Williamite forces could hear the enemy talking "with their damned Irish brogue on their tongues." The phrase is used by J. D. Breval in 1718 (xxiii 128), and by Defoe in his *Complete English Tradesman* (1726) [cited by *NED*], to look no further. Probably this curious idiom originated in some story or anecdote now lost and irrecoverable; but the existence of the idiom, and the origin of the linguistic significance of *brogue*, is beyond doubt. The word occurs in three of our texts (xix 16, xxiii 12 &c., xxvii 62), but not in the mouths

269

of Irishmen; in the last instance Captain O'Blunder fails to understand the meaning.

§149. The arms used by Irishmen included the *skene* (vii 133, ix 2, xii 74, xx 118) and the *meddoag* (xviii 83). The first represents Ir. *scian* 'knife', and it is described by Gernon in 1620 as follows [Falkiner (1904) 357]:

> And for his weapon he weares a skeyne which is a knife of three fingers broad of the length of a dagger and sharpening towards the poynt with a rude wodden handle.

The second word represents Ir. *meadóg* 'dagger'. A very characteristic weapon of the Irishman was the *dart* (vii 29 &c.), referred to in the two passages quoted in §144 above: this was a light spear of great length, so that when held upright it was considerably taller than the man who held it. The dart is very often referred to in the literature of the sixteenth and seventeenth centuries, and is shown in many drawings and engravings of Irishmen; see, for instance, the frontispiece to this book, and the illustrations in Quinn [(1966) Plates 2, 4, 7–9, 11, 20, 21]. A less warlike but nonetheless dangerous weapon was the *shillela* (xxvii 48), the oak cudgel named after the oak-groves of Síol Ealaigh in Co. Wicklow. Two words are used to refer to the typical horse ridden by the Irishman, though no doubt the same type of horse is intended. The first is *garron*, representing Ir. *gearrán* (vi 77*, vii 127, xx 111, xxvi 30); this word also appears qualified by *bán* 'white' (xii 112), *dubh* 'black' (xii 112) or *riabhach* 'roan' (xxiii 93 &c.). The second is *hobby* or *hobby-horse* (v 20). The *hobby* is described by several writers. Fynes Moryson [Falkiner (1904) 223] tells us that "Their horses, called hobbies, are much commended for their ambling pace and beauty." Eachard [(1691) 6] gives a fuller description:

> Here are likewise excellent good Horses, (which we call Hobies) which have not the same pace with others, but a soft and round Amble, setting one Leg before another very finely.

The same word *hobby-horse* is also used in the sense 'buffoon' (v 94).

Housing

§150. The Irishman's house is sometimes referred to as a *crate* (xvi 13, where it is glossed "Cabbin, or Irish Hut"). This was a temporary habitation constructed of hurdles: *Purgatorium Hibernicum* (p. 4) refers to "a moveing crate/In place of tent raise[d] in

270

a heat." The word may be the English word *crate* in the rare and obsolete sense 'hurdle', or it may be from the Irish loanword *creat(a)* 'frame, ribs of a house-roof'; but neither origin would explain the common spelling *creaght* [*NED* s.v.]. Prendergast [(1854–5) 130] quotes two documents, one of 1654 referring to "small crates", the other of 1655 referring to "Cabins and Creaghts". The word *creaght* properly refers to a herd of cattle with its drivers, and represents Ir. *caoraidheacht*, which originally referred to sheep and was subsequently extended to include cattle; the practice of "booleying" cattle—taking them to summer pasturage on high ground—survived until quite recent times in Ireland, and it was easy to confuse the temporary dwellings accommodating the *caoraidheacht* with the *crates* of the peasants. The problem is still further complicated by yet another use of the word *creaght*. Story's account of the rapparees, quoted above in §145, continues as follows :

> Some call them *Creaughts*, from the little Huts they live in : these huts they build so conveniently with Hurdles and long Turf, that they can remove them in Summer towards the Mountains, and bring them down to the Vallies in Winter.

Archbishop King in his *Diary* refers to the rapparees as *Creaght men* [Lawlor (1903) 75]. No doubt there is confusion here with some other Irish word, perhaps with *creachtóir* 'plunderer'.

Food and drink

§151. The foods most commonly referred to in our texts are dairy products. Probably the most frequently used Irish word in English writings of the seventeenth century is the word which *NED* gives as *bonny-clabber* and defines as 'milk naturally clotted or coagulated on souring.' The familiarity of the word to English readers is attested by the attribution of *Bog-Witticisms* to "oour laurned Countree-maun *Mac O Bonniclabbero* of *Drogheda*" (above, p. 52). The forms of the anglicized word are very various, and its origin in Irish is doubtful. According to Dinneen the Irish form is *bainne clabair*, in which the first element is *bainne* 'milk' and the second is the genitive of a word *clabar* defined as 'sour thick milk'— the same meaning as that of the whole phrase. A word of the same form, *clabar*, means 'mire, mud'; a variant *clábar* means 'thick mud'. Malone [(1960) 142] suggested that the second element of *bainne clabair* was not originally Irish at all, but represented

271

English *clapper*; some of the details of his explanation are un-acceptable, but it is worth further consideration. English *clapper* is normally represented in Irish by *clabaire*, one of the meanings of which is 'the invested cup through which the churndash passes', and this meaning seems to have been influenced by the Irish word *clab* 'mouth', of which the diminutive *claibín* also has the meaning 'perforated cup for the churndash'. There is no evidence at all that either English *clapper* or Irish *clabaire* ever had the meaning 'churndash', but such a semantic development is not at all im-probable, since the form and motion of the clapper or tongue of a bell are not unlike those of a churndash; and the anglicized forms of *bainne clabair* give some support to such a hypothesis. In our texts the forms are *bonny clabbe* (vi 92), *bonny clabbo* (vii 126), *bony clabber* (xii 110, xv 40), and *banniclabber* glossed "Butter-milk" (xvi 53); Gainsford (1618) has *bonniclaboch*; William Wood's *New Englands Prospect* (1634) has *boniclapper*; *Purgatorium Hiber-nicum*, in passages not printed here, has *bannyclap*, *bonny-clapp* and *bonny clapbagh*; *The Irish Hudibras*, in passages not printed here, has (as well as the normal form) *bannaclab* "Sower-Milk" and *banna-clab* "Thick-Milk". These representative spellings show that some forms substitute *p* for *b*, as if they were based on English *clapper* rather than Irish *clabair(e)*; others lack the -*er* ending, or have an aberrant ending, as if they showed the influence of Irish *clab* or one of its derivatives. The problem of the form cannot be said to be fully solved, but at least Malone's hypothesis throws some light on it. If English *clapper* and Irish *clabaire* could indeed mean 'churndash', the meaning of *bonny-clabber* would offer little difficulty : as Malone says, "the phrase would make excellent sense if it originally meant 'milk of the dasher' (i.e. at a stage fit to be churned)"; though cream can be churned straightaway, whole milk cannot be churned until it has begun to acidify and coagulate. The description given by Gainsford [(1618) 151] fits this stage exactly : "*Bonniclaboch*, which is milke strangely put into a tub a sowring, till it be clodded, and curded together."

§152. Another important dairy product is cheese, and the Irish relished a kind of cheese made of buttermilk and known as *mulchán*. This is referred to in conjunction with bonny-clabber in *Hic et Ubique* (xii 111) : ". . . de Cow dat make de buttermilk, and de bony clabber for dy child and my shelf, and de mulaghane." There is a similar reference in a part of *Ireland Preserved* not printed here (p. 83) :

I fill be after dig my Potato,
And drink my good Bonny Clabber.
I maake de Rye Bread, and Grind de Quarne,
Shurning de Milk, and Roasting de Malahaune.

The nature of *mulchán* is described by Gernon (1620) [Falkiner (1904) 359–60]:

> You shall have no drink but Bonyclabber, milk that is sowred to the condition of buttermilk, nor no meate, but mullagham (mallabanne), a kind of choke-daw cheese, and blew butter.

The descriptive word *choke-daw* is not recorded by *NED*, but it is presumably a variant of the dialectal word *choke-dog* [*NED* s.v. *choke-* 2] applied to a kind of hard cheese. A very similar account is given by the anonymous *Brief Character of Ireland* [(1692) 26]:

> *Bonny-Clabber* and *Mulahaan*, alias *Sowre Milk*, and *Choak-Cheese*, with a Dish of *Potatoes* boiled, is their general Entertainment, to which add an *Oat-cake*, and it compleats their *Bill of Fare*.

Again, in a funeral lament the *Brief Character* inquires [ibid. 33]:

> Hadst thou not some Sheep and a Cow, Mulahaan and Oat-cake, and good Usquebaugh to comfort thy heart, and put Mirth upon thy Friends?

The word *mallabanne*, added by Gernon as if a synonym of *mullagham*, is puzzling but not unique, since it is used much later in the century by Thomas Dineley [Shirley (1856–7) 186]:

> Dyet generally of the vulgar Irish are potatoes, milk, new milk, which they call sweet milk, bonny clobber, mallabaune, whey, curds . . .

It seems impossible that *mallabanne* and *mallabaune* can represent *mulchán* : possibly they represent *meall bán* 'white lump' (with a glide vowel developing between *l* and *b*) or the plural *mealla bána* 'white lumps'; such expressions, appropriate enough to hard cheese, might easily be confused with *mulchán* by English writers.

§153. Gernon's reference to "blew butter" is obscure, but there is plenty of evidence that the Irish had a habit of burying butter in a bog, and using it after the lapse of a number of years. Dineley [ibid. 186] refers to

273

Butter, layd up in wicker basketts, mixed with store of [. . .], a sort of garlick, and buried for some time in a bog, to make a provision of an high tast for Lent.

The butter to be buried was usually enclosed in a vessel made of bark, called a *rúscán*; this appears in our texts as *ruscaan* (xx 4) [*NED* s.v. *ruskin²*]. Apart from these dairy products the only items of food mentioned in our texts are to be found in Swift's *Dialogue* (XXVI): *stirabout* 'porridge' (21), *sowins* 'flummery' (21) representing Ir. *súghán*, and *frawhawns* 'bilberries' (22) representing Ir. *fraochán*.

§154. The drink most often referred to in our texts is *usquebaugh* (vi 93, vii 96, xv 13, xvi 64, xxiii 54 &c.), representing Ir. *uisce beathadh* 'aqua vitæ'. This word is the ancestor of the modern word *whiskey*, but the drink itself differed from modern whiskey in so far as it was flavoured with herbs and other substances. In 1617 Fynes Moryson [Falkiner (1904) 227] remarked that

> the usquebagh is preferred before our aqua vitæ, because the mingling of raisins, fennel-seed, and other things mitigating the heat, and making the taste pleasant, makes it less inflame, and yet refresh the weak stomach with moderate heat and a good relish.

In 1620 Gernon [ibid. 361] gave similar testimony:

> The aquavitæ of Ireland is not such an extraction, as is made in England, but farre more qualifyed, and sweetened with licorissh. It is made potable, and is of the colour of Muscadine.

The Irish word survives with a similar meaning in French *Scubac*, the name of a liqueur made in Lorraine and flavoured with cinnamon, nutmeg and cloves. The characteristic Irish drinking-vessel was the *maddor* (xxvi 33). Ir. *meadar* was applied to a square vessel carved out of a single block of wood. In English the word seems to have been first used in *Purgatorium Hibernicum*, in which it occurs a number of times, and in *The Irish Hudibras*, which not only defines the word in its alphabetical Table as "A hollow square piece of Wood, to drink out of", but also adds a couplet about it (p. 3):

> Meddar, which is a pretty Knack,
> A deep round foursquare wooden Jack.

274

Moffet [(1716) 24], perhaps imitating the *Hudibras*, also refers to "A wooden large four corner'd Cup."

Recreation

§155. There is not much in our texts about recreations, and nothing at all about any recreation other than singing and dancing. The Irish *cro-naan* (xvi 78), representing Ir. *crónán,* is described by Dunton (p. 21) as follows :

> Even our landlady was brought in to sing an Irish Cronaan, which is so odd a thing that I cannot express it, being mostly perform'd in the throat, only now and then some miserable sounds are sent through the nose.

There is no native Irish word for dancing : the two words in current use, *rinnce* and *damhsa*, are from OF *renc* and *dance* respectively. However, in the seventeenth century the Irish were much given to dancing, and five names of dances occur in our texts. The district of Fingall seems to have been particularly well known for dancing : apart from the title of No. XI and the stage direction at the beginning of No. XX, two of the names of dances refer to towns in Fingall. The name *Ballrootherie* (i 45*) is applied to a tune, but there can be no doubt that it properly refers to a dance, since it frequently occurs in conjunction with the *Whip of Dunboyne* (vi 87). Balrothery and Dunboyn are towns in Fingall, and the dances to which they gave their names are described by Fynes Moryson [Falkiner (1904) 322] :

> They delight much in dancing, using no arts of slow measures or lofty galliards, but only country dances, whereof they have some pleasant to behold, as Balrudery, and the Whip of Dunboyne, and they dance about a fire commonly in the midst of a room holding withes in their hands, and by certain strains drawing one another into the fire.

In *Purgatorium Hibernicum* (p. 39) we are told that the piper MacShane "Cou'd play Mageen,/Whepp of Dunboyn, and Dance a Myeen,/And Dance Balruddery"; elsewhere (p. 135) we are told of the harpist Hugh O'Darsy that "Mageen, yea, and be !, he did play,/Fipp of Dunboyn and Irish Hay." The Irish Hay, referred to in vii 57, seems to have been some kind of reel : originally *hay* or *hey* meant merely a country dance, but from the middle of the seventeenth century the Irish Hay is referred to as a distinctive type of dance [*NED* s.v. *hay, hey* 1. a].

§156. Two mysterious dances are referred to in *The Irish Masque* (VI), *fading* (72) and again *te fading and te fadow* (87). The dance *fading* was well known from the beginning of the seventeenth century, and is often referred to [*NED* s.v.]; it seems to have had some kind of indecent connotation, since *with a fading* was the refrain of an indecent song, and Shakespeare [*A Winter's Tale* IV iv 195] links *fading* with *dildo* in an obvious *double entendre* :

> He has the prettiest Loue-songs for Maids, so without bawdrie (which is strange,) with such delicate burthens of Dildo's and Fadings : Iump-her, and thump-her.

The origin of the word is unknown. The origin of *fadow* (not recorded elsewhere) is equally unknown, unless it might reflect the name of a song the refrain of which included the Irish word *fadó* 'long ago'; a number of Irish refrains are quoted by seventeenth-century dramatists, like the mysterious *calmie custure me* of *Henry V* IV iv 4 and elsewhere, which may represent Irish *Cailín ó Chois tSiúire mé* 'I am a girl from beside the Suir' [Murphy (1939–40)]. Another possible Irish refrain is *kara ma gus* (vii 109*) if, as seems likely, this represents *cuirim mo chos* 'I place my foot'.

IRISH WORDS AND IRISH MEANINGS

§157. There remain a number of Irish words and phrases which are less easily classified than those we have discussed so far. Some refer to characteristically Irish things and customs, and these are often used by English writers too; others seem to be due to ignorance or forgetfulness—the speaker either does not know, or cannot for the moment remember, the appropriate English word. Ir. *seamróg* 'shamrock' (vi 47) here refers, as usually at this period, to shamrock as a foodstuff rather than as a national emblem. Ir. *súgán* appears with two different meanings : *suggain* 'straw-rope' (xiii 14*) and *sougawn* 'straw saddle' (xxvi 31). Ir. *go leor* 'in plenty' appears as *gillore* (xvii 52), the *i* in the first syllable reproducing the quality of the Irish unstressed vowel before a palatal consonant; the currency of the word in present-day English is probably due to its use by Sir Walter Scott, who took it from Scottish Gaelic. The Irish noun *cóisir* 'banquet, festive party' appears in English as a verb meaning 'to live at free quarters upon

276

dependents' [*NED* s.v. *cosher*]; *ycoshere* (xvi 31) is glossed as "Lodge", and the same meaning would suit *cosher* (xxvi 25). Ir. *loch* appears as *lough* (xviii 95), *loough* (xxvi 18); the word entered English early—the form *luh* is found in the Northumbrian dialect of Old English. Ir. *cliabh* 'basket' appears as *cleave* (xxi 17). Ir. *seach* is another noun which appears in English only as a verb (xxvi 27) meaning 'take turn and turn about at a single pipe'; for its complicated history see Bliss [(1977) 86–7]. Ir. *cadódh* 'wrapping' usually refers in English to a blanket or coverlet, but as *caddow* (xxvi 34) it seems to mean rather a rough frieze cloak. All of these are in a sense technical terms, and are used by English writers too.

§158. The use of other words and phrases is less clearly justifiable, and seems to be the result of ignorance or forgetfulness. We can exclude from consideration such personal names as *Shuane* (xii 52), *Juane* (xii 109), representing Ir. *Siobhán* 'Joan', since personal names are not really translatable; we can exclude, too, Ir. *beag* 'little' and *mór* 'great' when they are used in the formation of personal names like *Rorie beg* (i 49), *Maghloghan Moor* (xxiii 64). There remain, however, a large number of words and phrases, and the different texts vary considerably in the number and type of these that they use: *Hic et Ubique* (XII) and *The Irish Hudibras* (XVI) are particularly interesting, and are worth discussing separately.

§159. *Hic et Ubique* (XII) is distinguished by the use of a number of phrases consisting of several words. The longest is *Sha, sha, ta tuggemi Moistare* (25), which appears to reproduce Irish *'s eadh, 's eadh, tá, tuigim é, a Mháighistir* 'yes, yes, it is, I understand it, Master' (on the form of the word *master* see above, §57). This long utterance is perfectly correct, but other phrases seem to be the result of misunderstandings. Thus, in lines 36–7 the original has *I will tell dee tale if thou wilt Glunt amee*. In the text printed above *Glunt amee* has been emended to *Glun ta mee*, on the assumption that it stands for Irish *(an) gcluin tú mé?* 'do you hear me?'; but in the context of the whole sentence a question is inappropriate. It seems that Head may have heard the question *(an) gcluin tú mé?*, misinterpreted it, and therefore used it wrongly. In lines 48–9 the original has *this chvereeh craveRauge make run away for himself*; the use of a capital letter in the middle of a word shows that something has gone wrong with the printing, and in the text printed below *chvereeh craveRauge* has been tentatively emended to *chureeh crave Ruagh*, on the assumption that it stands

for Irish (a) *churaidh craobh-ruaidhe* 'O Red Branch knight!'. It is plausible enough that an arrant coward should be ironically referred to as a Red Branch knight, but in the context of the whole sentence the vocative is inappropriate; again it seems that Head had misinterpreted something he had heard. An expression correctly used by Head is *arraball* (23), reproducing Irish *ar ball* 'soon'. A final word of great interest is *donny* 'wretched, miserable' (30), reproducing Ir. *donaidhe*. This appears to be a Fingallian word : it occurs also in xiii 26, and repeatedly in parts of *Purgatorium Hibernicum* and *The Irish Hudibras* not printed here; at the present day it is widely used in north Leinster and the extreme south of Ulster, but not elsewhere.

§160. Some of the words and phrases in *The Irish Hudibras* (XVI) have already been discussed in different contexts. Thus, the postponed stress in *clam-peer*, Ir. *clampar* 'noise' (74) and *gar-soon*, Ir. *garsún* 'boy' (92) was discussed in §19. The ejaculation *brauler a skeal*, Ir. *breall ar an scéal*, glossing *Pox on dy Tail* (81), was discussed in §132. Ir. *scéal* also appears as *skeal* (24) in the special sense 'news' which it often has in Irish. The most interesting Irish expression is found in lines 103–4,

> And I meeself great Eye have still,
> To make performsh upon his Will,

where *great Eye* is glossed "DEULMORE IRICISM, Great Eye, great desire." Among the Irish words which can mean 'hope' there are two which are very like each other, *súil* and *dúil*; *súil* properly means 'eye', and the normal meaning of *dúil* is 'desire, expectation'. *Deulmore* is a reasonable anglicization of *dúil mhór*, which could correctly be glossed 'great desire', but 'great eye' seems to presuppose *súil mhór*; it is difficult to see quite how this confusion could have come about.

§161. Irish words in other texts can be briefly disposed of. The word *booygh* (i 15), representing Ir. *buidheach* 'tiny', an Oriel variant of *bídeach*, *baoideach*, shows the Oriel development of /d'/ to /j/ (§100). Ir. *bánóg* 'enclosed field' appears as *bannoke* (vi 111). Ir. *póg* 'kiss' appears as *poge* (xiii 80). The form *muck(e)* 'pigs' (xx 31, 46) reproduces the Irish plural *muca*. The phrase *in connaugh* (xxvi 28) is difficult : it seems to represent Ir. *ar ceannach* 'for sale', so that *a cow in connaugh* might mean 'the value of a cow'; but it would be difficult to find a close parallel in Irish. Finally *puckawn* (xxvi 41) represents Ir. *pocán* 'he-goat'.

§162. Two of our texts are written in Irish, and naturally enough the Irish words occurring in the English dialogue are written in traditional Irish orthography. In *Páirlement Chloinne Tomáis* (X) there is only one such word, *órdlach* 'inch' (22). In *Muiris O Gormáin* (XXV) there are a number of words and phrases : *bláth na finne* 'flower of beauty' (6), *cárta* 'quart' (13), *fáilte* 'welcome' (14), *póg* 'kiss' (14), *ór* 'gold' (22), *cóir* 'true, truly' (30), *go deóigh* 'for ever' (32), *aig ól* 'drinking' (46), *ród mór* 'highroad' (48). In two places Ir. *dar* 'by' (used to introduce an oath) is pleonastically prefixed to an English oath : *dar be me o[a]n trath* (7), *dar bi my soulvation* (31).

§163. Another group of words is perhaps even more interesting : English words of which either the form or the meaning has been influenced by some Irish word. There are three words whose form has been influenced by Irish. Many European languages have forms of the word *tobacco* without a final vowel, like French *tabac* and German *Tabak, Tobak*, but such forms are of the greatest rarity in English : *NED* lists a few such spellings, but gives no quotations. It is highly probable, therefore, that *toback* (xvi 20) is influenced by Ir. *tobac*; and it is perhaps worth noting that *Purgatorium Hibernicum* has forms *tomback* (p. 10) and *tombacco* (pp. 21, 58) which are certainly influenced by the Irish variant *tombac*, since forms with *m* are quite unknown in English. The form *corp* 'corpse' (xviii 7) is paralleled in Scottish and northern English dialects, but here is probably due to the influence of Ir. *corp*. The form *comrady* 'comrade' (xxv 46), unparalleled in English, is certainly influenced by Ir. *comrádaidhe*, in which the English ending -*ade* has been assimilated to the Irish agent-ending -*ádaidhe*; *comrady* cannot represent an actual borrowing of Ir. *comrádaidhe*, since it assonates with Ir. *é*, not Ir. *á*. [The form *comrague* (vii 162) is not influenced by Irish but represents a compromise between *comrade* and *comrogue* 'fellow-rogue'.]

§164. Irish influence on the meaning of English words is less easy to demonstrate, but there are four reasonably certain instances. The verb *let* in the sense 'allow to escape' was always rare in English and is now obsolete except in the phrase *to let blood*. In present-day Hiberno-English, *let* is the normal word for 'utter (a sound)' or 'emit (a breath, etc.)', and there is no doubt that this usage reflects the use of Ir. *leigim* 'I let' in precisely the same senses. The reference in vii 130 to *all de farts lett in Ireland* is probably an instance of the same usage, but certainty is impossible : *NED* [s.v. *let* v.[1] 7] cites a precisely comparable usage, *she chanced to let a wind backwards* (1662); the author, Sir John Davies, spent much of his life in Ireland, and may have used a hibernicism, but this is no more than a conjecture. In *A Wife Well Managed* (XXII) the word *now* (13 &c.) is repeatedly used in the sense 'indeed', unknown in English; this usage seems to reflect the use of Ir. *anois* 'now' in similar contexts. The word *pet* (xxvi 7), though familiar in present-day English, is in fact of Irish origin; it is recorded in English from the early sixteenth century, but not in the sense 'darling, favourite' used by Swift, which must still have been a hibernicism based on Irish usage [Bliss (1977) 79]. Finally, *warrant* (xxvi 19) is used in a sense not found in English, 'authority by inheritance'; since this is one of the meanings of the Irish loanword *baránta(s)*, Swift's usage is presumably due to Irish influence [ibid. 80].

§165. Some words, though not directly influenced by Irish, have acquired meanings or uses found only in Ireland, or in Ireland and other limited areas. Thus *haggard* 'stack-yard', from ON *heygarðr*, is found only in Ireland and the Isle of Man [*NED* s.v.]; it is mis-spelt *hadgard* in ix 92. The word *spa(a)ke* 'speech' (xx 14 &c., xxi 29) is found only in Ireland, Scotland, and northern English dialects [*NED* s.v. *speak*]; the precise meaning found in our texts is not readily paralleled outside Ireland. The word *unwell* (xxvi 6) is of particular interest, since it has entered Standard English and is not felt to be in any way dialectal; yet it is not found in any edition of Johnson's *Dictionary* published during his lifetime, and according to *NED* it only came into general use about 1785. *Unwell* was introduced into English as a hibernicism by Lord Chesterfield [Bliss (1977) 78-9]. In Standard English and in most dialects the word *garden* (xxvii 18) means a flower-garden; in Ireland however, unless the word is qualified in some way, it refers to a small field, usually used for the cultivation of vegetables, and this is the sense used by Sheridan.

§166. A relatively short passage in *The Irish Hudibras* (xvi 39-44) contains a number of technical terms connected with the Restoration Settlement in Ireland, by which the Stuart kings tried to satisfy the just claims of the dispossessed Irish without entirely alienating the Protestant settlers whose loyalty they wished to retain. Thus *restord* (39) means 'reinstated (in one's former property)', and *Reprisal* (39) refers to the compensation exacted from the former owner restored to his estates and paid to the settler who had to hand them over. *Court of Clamper* (40), glossed "Court of

Claims", refers to the Courts of Claims set up to try and disentangle the complicated problems of title resulting from the Settlement. The word *Clamper* is interesting. It appears to be a reflex of Ir *clampar* 'noise' (§§ 19, 160); but in the seventeenth century *clamper* was used as a noun meaning 'a botched up charge' and as a verb meaning 'to patch up an accusation'. *NED* suggests that these meanings are derived from the verb *clamp*, but this seems scarcely possible, since *clamp* appears much later than *clamper*. Ir. *clampar* can also mean 'wrangling, dispute', and this is no doubt the meaning intended in *The Irish Hudibras*; the precise relationship between the Irish and English words remains obscure. The word *postpond* (42) has the obsolete meaning 'kept waiting'; *Debenturers* (43), not elsewhere recorded, means 'holders of debentures', and refers to those of Cromwell's soldiers who had been paid with debentures instead of cash (p. 18).

MALAPROPISMS

§167. The name of Mrs Malaprop in Richard Brinsley Sheridan's *The Rivals* (1775) is derived from the French phrase *mal à propos* 'irrelevant'; but her particular talent lay in the misapplication of long and learned words, and this is what is meant by the term *malapropism*. Most of the malapropisms in our texts are to be found in Thomas Sheridan's *Brave Irishman*, but there are a few in earlier texts : *turne* 'return' (iv 71), *conferrmant* 'preferment' (xv 38), *knuckle-bones* 'huckle-bones, hip-bones' (xx 55). These instances were no doubt intended by the writers in question as mere blunders, characteristic of the Irish, but in *The Brave Irishman* (XXVII) the malapropism emerges fully-fledged : *creation* 'recreation' (7), *magnifies* 'signifies' (13 &c.), *burrough* 'warren' (21), *conversation* 'company' (71), *bandy-shoulder'd* (126), *huckle-backs* 'humps' (127), *dissuade* 'persuade' (154). It is interesting to speculate how much Richard Brinsley Sheridan owed to his father's example.

SLANG

§168. Determination of the precise elements in the vocabulary which can properly be characterized as slang is extremely difficult, partly because of rapid fluctuation in the status of colloquial expressions, and partly because of the deficiencies in the record of informal speech. The following analysis must be considered purely tentative. The earliest probable slang word in our texts is *pashes* 'fragments' (viii 27); *NED* gives no literary record, but the word is documented in *EDD*. *Purgatorium Hibernicum* (XIII) is particularly rich in slang words, most of which were eliminated from the later *Irish Hudibras* : *snuffe* 'fit of passion' (63), *give mee . . . de bagge* 'dismiss me, give me the sack' (68), *foile* 'frustration' (70*), *belching an oyster* 'expectorating a gob of phlegm' (91), *spleece* 'split' (98), *rosted* 'arrested' (100). Of these, *foile* occurs also in the *Aphorismical Discovery*; *spleece* is recorded [*NED* s.v. *splice* v. 5] only in the works of John Evelyn the diarist, in 1664; *rosted* is apparently a form of *roasted* in the slang sense of 'arrested', cited by *NED* [s.v. *roast* v. 4.a] from a dictionary of cant, without supporting quotations. Next in chronological sequence come *sirreverence* 'lump of excrement' (xiv 72), *tiff* 'cheap liquor' (xv 41), *buttons* 'lumps of excrement' in the slang phrase *make buttons* 'be in great terror' (xvi 2), *ready* 'cash' (xvi 19), *feisting* 'farting' (xx 10), *bodderd* 'deafened' (xxvi 3), *twig* 'look at' (xxvii 35), *smoke* 'take note of' (xxvii 36), *humbuggs* 'hoaxes' (xxvii 137*). The last four of these require further comment. The word *bodderd* might well have been included under another heading, since it is ultimately of Irish origin : it is derived from Ir. *bodhar* 'deaf', or from the related verb *bodhraim* 'deafen'. The fact that the Irish phoneme /ð/ had become silent before 1300 [O'Rahilly (1930)] shows that *bodhar* or *bodhraim* had entered Mediæval Hiberno-English before this date, and survived in the spoken language until the eighteenth century [Bliss (1977) 77–8]; the complete absence of any literary record before 1700 suggests that the word was wholly colloquial, and had the status of slang. Of the three words in *The Brave Irishman* (XXVII) the first two, *smoke* and *twig,* occur in the speech of the London "mob", and are presumably not Hiberno-English; *twig* is not recorded by *NED* until 1764. The word *humbugg* came into vogue about 1750 [*NED* s.v. *humbug*]. It is a curious fact that all the early editions of *The Brave Irishman* have the spelling *bumbugg* : either the compositors were so unfamiliar with the word that they made or perpetuated a mistake, or perhaps this is an otherwise unrecorded variant form, having the same relationship to *humbugg* as *bumble-bee* has to *humble-bee*.

§169. A number of obscure words and phrases in *Purgatorium Hibernicum* (XIII) may also represent unrecorded slang. In the phrase *burne-breech hacknes* (72) both words are obscure; the context suggests a sexual connotation, but is not sufficiently perspicuous to provide a definite meaning. The word *grist* (92) seems in the context to mean 'flattery'; elsewhere in the poem (p. 36) *unlawfull grist* seems to refer to bribes; perhaps the basic meaning is 'inducement'. The phrase *pole bushell* (102) is wholly obscure. Finally, the word *crangore* (49) may perhaps represent unrecorded Irish slang. The context demands the meaning 'sexual encounter', and the word looks more Irish than English. One possibility (suggested to me by Mr N. J. A. Williams) is that the word represents an Irish *craitheadh an ghabhair* 'shaking of the goat'; the phrase is unrecorded, but would make a plausible instance of sexual slang.

UNEXPLAINED WORDS

§170. A few words remain wholly obscure, especially in the texts which reproduce something approaching broken English. Thus, *dow* (ii 8) should mean 'thou', but the context seems to demand 'I'; the syntax is so obscure that almost anything is possible (§196). The word *leufter* (ii 12) is meaningless as it stands, and it is probably misprinted. If *f* has been substituted for long *s*, *leuster* is a possible form of *lewdster* 'lewd person', but this seems an improbable term for a man to apply to himself. Alternatively, *leufter* might be an error for *leuterer* 'vagrant' [*NED* s.v. *loiterer*]; the meaning would suit the context well, but the change of form is considerable. The phrase 5 *stroke nailes* (ix 68) is puzzling. A possible meaning for *stroke* is 'bushel' [*NED* s.v. *stroke* sb.[1] 23], but five bushels of nails seems too many. *Stroke nailes* could perhaps stand for *strake-nails* [*NED* s.v. *strake* sb.[1] 9], but five nails seems too few. A meaning 'five-inch nails' would suit the context well, but no variant of *stroke* seems to have the required sense. The broken English words *ta* (x 33) and *fart* (x 34) defy interpretation. The form *bot* (xx 105) could stand either for *but* 'only' or for *both*, but neither gives very good sense. The spelling *ball* (xxi 18) could stand for *bawl*, but the context requires a noun with the meaning 'shouting, uproar', and no such form is documented. Finally, for *se* (xxv 8) the context seems to require the meaning 'you'; *se* could perhaps be an Irish orthographic variant of *she*, which in the English of the Scottish Highlands may stand for 'you' [*NED* s.v. *she* 1.d.], but this seems a remote possibility.

283

MORPHOLOGY AND SYNTAX

§171. It is not always possible to distinguish morphological from syntactic abnormality. If we find in a Hiberno-English text a form which, though it exists in Standard English, would not in Standard English be the form required by the context, there is no certain way of telling whether it is an instance of a non-standard form or of a non-standard construction. For this reason the sequence of the following paragraphs is dictated more by practical convenience than by theoretical exactitude. I have dealt first with abnormalities which are probably morphological, then with those which are fairly clearly syntactic, and finally with usages which are idiomatic rather than governed by rule. So as not to confuse the issue many of the examples are presented in normalized spelling.

§172. Two tendencies are at work in the development of languages, a tendency towards "irregularity" resulting primarily from sound-change, and a tendency towards "regularity" resulting from the analogical reformation of "irregular" forms. It is well known that analogical reformation most strongly affects the less frequently used forms; any word used with great frequency is likely to resist reformation, since the "irregular" forms are familiar through constant repetition. Thus, in present-day English the forms of the strong verbs, most of which are very frequently used, are in general stable; but the relatively rare past tenses *crew* and *throve* are being replaced by the more "regular" *crowed* and *thrived*. Children often apply the "rules" they have learned too rigidly, and use "regular" (though incorrect) forms instead of correct (but "irregular") forms. Bilingual speakers have the same kind of difficulty, and (like children) may use incorrect "regular" forms. Unlike children, however, bilingual speakers may be aware of the danger of making mistakes, and may show a preference for constructions which will enable them to avoid the risk of error: they may, for instance, prefer periphrastic verbal tenses to the more natural inflected tenses because they are uncertain of the appropriate inflected form (below, §§ 188, 207).

§173. Syntactic abnormalities usually reflect the transference of the "rules" of the primary language to the secondary language, what Weinreich [(1963) 30] calls "the application of a grammatical relation of language *A* to *B*-morphemes in *B*-speech." A prolonged period of bilingualism followed by the ultimate loss of the original primary language may indeed lead to the permanent transfer of some of the "rules" of the primary to the secondary language, which now becomes a new form of speech in its own right (cf. §2); this kind of permanent transfer can readily be observed in present-day Hiberno-English.

PRONOUNS

Demonstrative and relative pronouns

§174. The use of *dem* 'those' (xxiv 25 &c., xxvi 1) is found in all English dialects [Wright (1905) §420 (1)], and is a common vulgarism in the speech of the illiterate [*NED* s.v. *them* 5]. The form *dis* 'these' (iv 31, xx 48 &c.) might represent a phonological development (§59), but *this* for *these* is very common in the northern and western dialects of English, especially when it is followed by a plural noun denoting time, as it is in xx 48 and xx 112 [Wright (1905) §419 (5)]. The use of *whome* 'who' (ix 42 &c.) must be due to hypercorrection, since *whom* is hardly used in any of the dialects, even in its proper oblique functions [ibid. §422].

Personal pronouns

§175. Non-standard uses of personal pronouns are common in our texts, especially in those which represent something like "broken English". Confusion between nominative and oblique forms may have been assisted by the fact that in Irish the oblique and disjunctive forms of the pronoun are identical in the second and third persons; in the first person there is in any case only one form for each number, *mé* singular and *sinn* plural. The phrase *me is* (ii 22, xxv 13 &c.) agrees closely with the Irish *tá mé* 'I am'; other instances of *me* as the subject are *me make* (xii 115), *me . . . has* (xxv 16), *me let* (xxv 23) and *me can't* (xxv 38*). In the second person *dee* 'thou' (xv 48, xx 106) represents a dialectal usage rein-

285

forced by the influence of the Quakers, who used *thee* on principle [*NED* s.v. *thee* 3]; *you* 'your' (xxv 28) seems to be unparalleled.

§176. The use of third-person pronouns presents a more complicated problem. It is a well-known though unexplained feature of the English of Scottish Highlanders that they use *her* as an all-purpose pronoun, and *her* is also to be found in representations of the speech of Welshmen [*NED* s.v. *her* 2.b; *Bartley* (1954) 73–4]; in our texts the use of *her* by Welshmen is found in *The Welsh Embassador* (vii 71, 92). The origin of the usage is obscure : some non-standard usages of *her* are listed by Wright [(1905) §§ 403 (a), 406 (b), 411], but none is really comparable with what is found in our texts, where *her* stands for 'me' (ii 30), 'his' (viii 24) and 'their' (xvii 27). The use of *him* 'it' (xix 6, xxiv 5) is paralleled in English dialects [ibid. §405 (b)]; *him* 'you' (xxv 22) is difficult to parallel, but this is broken English, and perhaps no detailed explanation is necessary. Non-standard uses of *it* occur only in versions of the *Fingallian Burlesque* : *it* 'her' (xiii 30), 'me' (xvi 98, 102). Finally we may note the vulgarism *him and I* 'him and me' (xix 167); the earliest occurrence of this solecism known to me is in *Bog-Witticisms* (p. 22, second pagination).

§177. So far all the pronominal forms discussed occur in Standard English, though not in the functions called for by the context. In addition to these there are two pronominal forms which do not occur at all in Standard English, *'ame* 'them' (xi 7 &c.) and *zee* 'I' (i 30 &c.). The first of these, *'ame*, is fairly easy to explain. It is a Fingallian form, and occurs three times in *The Irish Hudibras* in passages not printed here (pp. 16, 105, 141); it caused difficulty to the scribe of *Purgatorium Hibernicum*, who was obviously unfamiliar with it; at the corresponding points in his text he avoided it, either by changing it to *'em* at the cost of spoiling the rhyme, or by leaving a blank. It is no doubt derived from MHE *ham* [Heuser (1904) 36; Zettersten (1967) 16; McIntosh & Samuels (1968) 4], and corresponds to the *aam* of the dialect of Forth [Barnes (1867) 21]. The form *zee* 'I' is much more difficult. *Stukeley* (I) is printed in black-letter type, so that *z* has the shape of *ʒ*; it is perhaps possible that the author of the Hiberno-English scene used *z* to represent /j/, as the early Scottish printers did [*NED*, *SND* s.v. *Z*], and that *zee* should be read as /ji:/ rather than /zi:/. In the sixteenth century a type of pronunciation in which some Middle English front vowels were preceded by a prosthetic /j/ was widespread in England, and affected educated pronunciation [Dobson (1968) §429]; ME *ĭ* was not affected, since diphthongization had begun before the onset of prosthesis. In those dialects of Hiberno-English (such as the one reflected in *Stukeley*) in which ME *ĭ* remained undiphthongized (§40), the pronoun *I* could perhaps have developed a pronunciation /ji:/, which a Scotsman might perhaps have written *zee*. This explanation is highly speculative, and depends on the assumption that the author of the Hiberno-English scene was a Scotsman (a conjecture for which there is no other evidence); it fails to explain why *you* (i 40) is not also written with *z*, or why no comparable forms are found in any other text.

Possessive and reflexive pronouns

§178. In Irish it is not possible to stress a possessive pronoun: where emphasis is required it is achieved by adding the emphatic suffix *-sa, -se* to the noun qualified by the possessive. Thus the Irish for 'my coat' is *mo chóta mór*, and the Irish for '*my* coat' is *mo chóta mórsa* [de Bhaldraithe (1970) 164]; like other emphatic constructions, this one is often used where there is no real need for emphasis. It seems likely enough that bilingual speakers accustomed to the Irish construction would feel the need for some English equivalent, and there are a number of instances in our texts in which *own* is added to a possessive in contexts where it would not be appropriate in Standard English: in the earlier texts *thine own* (v 12 &c., vi 104 &c., vii 18, xii 108, xv 25 &c.), *mine own* (xv 45), in later texts *thy own* (xvi 25), *my own* (xiii 37, xv 45, xxv 7*, xxvii 76). In earlier English the final /n/ of *mine, thine* was sometimes transferred to the beginning of the following word, as in *dy nyes* 'thine eyes' (vii 132), and accordingly we find *di none* 'thine own' (iv 32 &c.), *my nown* 'mine own' (xix 10); the form *nown* was abstracted from this construction, and could be used after possessives which did not end in /n/, as in *his nown* 'his own' (xxiii 103). These developments are in no way characteristic of Hiberno-English, but are well documented in other forms of English; see *NED* s.v. *own*, *nown(e)*, *nain*. A comparable transference of final /n/ probably underlies the curious form *narsum* (xii 45), plainly a fanciful variant of *arse*.

§179. In Irish the personal pronouns may be emphasized in two different ways, either by adding the word *féin* 'self' as in *mé féin*, *tú féin*, etc., or by the use of the emphatic suffix already described, as in *mise, tusa*, etc.; the two methods may be combined, as in *mise féin, tusa féin*, etc. The obvious English equivalent for the first construction is the use of *myself, thyself*, etc.; these are used in Standard English for emphasis, but only in conjunction with the normal personal pronoun, as in *I myself*, etc.; in Hiberno-English they stand on their own either for the subject or for the object pronoun. Thus we find *myself* meaning 'I' (xii 22 &c., xx 3 &c.) or 'me' (xii 9 &c., xxiv 24 &c.); *thyself* meaning 'thee' (xii 2 &c.); *yourself* (xx 45) and *yourselves* (xviii 26 &c.) meaning 'you'. The English equivalent of Ir. *mise féin*, etc. is *my own self*, etc. : *my own self* 'me' (xv 19, xx 98), *thy own self* 'thou' (xii 42), 'thee' (xii 51); there is an interesting analogical form in *him nown self* 'him' (xix 46), which is to *himself* as *my nown self* is to *myself*. It will be noted that the number of texts in which the emphatic pronoun occurs is very limited : it is found only in XII, XV, XVIII, XIX, XX and XXIV. Either the phenomenon was limited in its occurrence, or (more probably) only the more acute of the observers noticed this not very conspicuous feature.

§180. Instances of abnormality in the use of conjunctions are not very numerous; most of them merely reflect obsolete usage, and therefore illustrate the conservatism of Hiberno-English. The form *but* 'than' (iv 43) should probably not be included here, since the use of *but* rather than *than* after such phrases as *no less* was not yet wholly obsolete in the seventeenth century, though it was becoming rare. There are three instances of the use of conjunctions followed by *that, if that* (xvi 111), *because that* (xvii 7) and *although that* (xvii 51); the use of *that* with conjunctions had been common in Middle English, but it became obsolete about 1600 [*NED* s.v. *that* 7]. The use of *for because* (xviii 8) and *for why* (xviii 44) also became obsolete about 1600 [*NED* s.v. *because* B.1, *forwhy* 1.b]. The use of *nor* 'than' (xviii 48), apparently a different word from the familiar negative *nor*, is limited to the dialects of Scotland and northern England. The use of *while* 'until' (xxv 24) was standard until the end of the seventeenth century, but is now limited to northern English dialects [*NED* s.v. *while* 3.b]. Swift italicized *without* 'unless' (xxvi 36) as a hibernicism; the use of *without* as a conjunction was originally standard, but by the eighteenth century it had become colloquial and even vulgar [*NED* s.v. *without* C.2]. Swift also italicized *till* 'so that' (xxvi 37); this is not an English usage at all, but is dependent on the fact that the Irish conjunction *go* can mean both 'till' and 'so that'.

NOUNS

§181. A substantial number of English nouns have "irregular" plurals, and bilingual speakers tended to substitute incorrect "regular" plurals for these (§172): *foot(e)s* 'feet' (iv 45, xx 12), *mans* 'men' (xx 69 &c.), *womans* 'women' (xx 101), *tiefs* 'thieves' (xxiv 63 &c.), *gooses* 'geese' (xxiv 63). There are also some instances in which the correct "irregular" plural is used, but with an *s* added to it, as if the plurality were insufficiently indicated without it: *seeps* 'sheep' (xviii 121), *shildrens* 'children' (xx 119), *shentlemens* 'gentlemen' (xxiv 19 &c.), *mens* 'men' (xxiv 54 &c.); we may perhaps include here *peoples* 'people' (xviii 62, xx 135).

§182. It was at one time permissible or customary to use an endingless plural after a numeral, as in *three mile* or *five pound*; this usage can still be heard from old people in England, and is widespread in Ireland. Curiously enough, the only one of our texts in which this usage appears is *Ireland Preserved* (XX): *egg* 'eggs' (7 &c.), *lambs* 'lambs' (75), *year* 'years' (88), *day* 'days' (112), *mont* 'months' (126). The same text also uses a number of endingless plurals *not* preceded by a numeral, and this usage is not sanctioned by custom: *relashon* 'relations' (65), *Jesuite* 'Jesuits' (135); in *Franch-man* 'French-men' (143) the abnormality could perhaps be phonological (§31). The *s* of the possessive is omitted in *priest* 'priest's' (35). Possibly the omission of *s* in *allway* 'always' (93) should be included here, since the form *alway* was certainly obsolete when the play was written: *NED* records no instances between the *Authorized Version* of 1611 and the deliberate archaisms of the nineteenth century. The only instance of an endingless plural in any other text is *vare* 'wares' (vi 28). The opposite phenomenon, the addition of *s* where it is inappropriate, is very common in *The Pretender's Exercise* (XXIV): *Killamountains* (4), *countys* (5), *Wicklows* (6), *troops* (15), *vaters* 'water' (18 &c.), *vords* 'word' (20), *Englishes* (20), *val(l)s* 'wall' (23 &c.), *vays* 'way' (64), *mans* (66), *hearts* (67). Instances in other texts are *rascalls* 'rascal' (vii 137), *podyes* 'body' (xii 122), *aufternoons* 'afternoon' (xv 49), *owns* 'own' (xx 2) and *betters and betters* (xxiii 65). It is difficult to find an explanation for this curious phenomenon, other than a general lack of familiarity with the English language; there is nothing in Irish which could lend support to it.

289

§183. In Irish the adjective normally follows the noun, and it might be expected that the same sequence would occasionally occur in Hiberno-English. In fact there are only two instances in our texts, *peeps feene* 'fine pippins' (iv 2 &c.) and *night last* 'last night' (xxv 46). The first of these instances is particularly interesting, since two nearly contemporary accounts of the "shrill accent" of the Irish costermonger (quoted above, p. 178) use the sequence *fine pip*; the second instance is an example of broken English. The use of *thirteen* (xx 110) as the ordinal adjective 'thirteenth' presumably displays unfamiliarity with the English numerical system. In most dialects of English it is common to use an adjective where an adverb is called for [Wright (1905) §444], but the only instance in our texts is *woordy* 'worthily' (xviii 14). The adverb *again* is twice used in senses which, though not unparalleled in older and dialectal English [*NED* s.v. *again* 2], are perhaps reinforced by senses of Ir. *arís* 'again' : 'back' (xx 88), 'in return' (xxiv 7).

§184. There are a number of instances of non-standard forms or uses of negative adjectives and adverbs. The non-standard forms are *no* 'not' (xii 115, xiii 18), *none* 'no' (viii 23, xv 55). Non-standard uses sometimes involve a double negative, as in *none* 'any' (xviii 25), *no* 'any' (xxii 60); sometimes the double negative is only implied, as in *vidout no* 'without any' xvi 57. The erroneous use of a negative in a positive clause is found only in *The Brave Irishman* (XXVII), and should perhaps be classed with the malapropisms (§167) : *no* 'any' (104), *never* 'ever' (135). There are several instances of the use of a negative adverb with a verb without the normal auxiliary *do* : *not no* 'do not know' (xxiv 25 &c.), and in the imperative *dou not maake* 'don't make !' (xx 77); here also belongs *me no howle* 'I am not howling' (xii 115), with the use of *no* for *not* referred to above.

VERBS

Verbal forms

§185. One feature of the morphology of verbs which appears to be specifically Fingallian is the survival in the form *y-* of the Old English collective and perfective prefix *ge-*, used with most past participles and with the infinitive and finite forms of some verbs [for a very full account see *NED* s.v. *y-*]. In our texts it appears only in *The Fingallian Dance* (XI) and *The Irish Hudibras* (XVI); curiously enough, it does not occur at all in *Purgatorium Hibernicum*, apart from the conventional archaism *ycliped, iclipt* 'called'. There are only two past participles with *y-*, *ycome* and *ygo* (xvi 23); with the latter compare *ee-go* in the dialect of Forth [Barnes (1867) 37]. There are three infinitives, *y-cree* 'cry', *y-rore* 'roar' (xi 11) and *y-make* (xi 12). To the two finite forms, *yknows* '(who) knows' (xvi 34) and *yfeel* (xvi 100) must be added *ycoshere* 'lodge' (xvi 31), based on an Irish stem (§157). Finally, there is an unparalleled use of *y-* with an adverb in *y-yore* 'old times' (xi 10). The survival of the prefix *y-* is a feature of the south-western dialects of English [Wright (1905) §438]. Another archaism which may be mentioned here is the use of *be* 'are' (vi 51, xx 34 &c., xxiii 62).

§186. In the present tense of verbs the *s* of the third person singular is often omitted, and an obtrusive *s* is added to forms of the other persons. The omission of *s* is particularly common in the earliest texts; *sound* 'sounds' (iii 26), *call* 'calls' (iii 47), *say* 'says' (iv 12), *cut* 'cuts' (iv 40), *loue* 'loves' (iv 41), *bring* 'brings' (vi 70), *ale* 'ails' (xii 10), *do* 'does' (xx 33 &c.). The *st* or *t* of the second person singular is also occasionally omitted : *like* 'likest' (vi 142), *know* 'knowest' (xiii 87), *do* 'dost' (xx 106), *will, vil(l)* 'wilt' (xvi 5 &c., xx 128). An obtrusive *s* is less common, but occurs in *brings* 'bring' (ix 22), *sendes* 'send' (ix 23), *tells* 'tell' (xxvii 2), *catches* 'catch' (xxvii 6); the first two of these instances are in fact historic presents. That we really have to do here with the substitution of the third person singular for other forms is suggested by *is(h)* 'are' (iii 50, xxiv 25 &c., xxvi 1), *was, vash* 'were' (ix 54, xxi 51, xxiv 3), where the change does not consist merely of the addition of an *s*. In Irish the third person singular of the verb is used with plural noun subjects, and (in the analytic form of the verb) with pronouns of all persons; this may be the origin of the Hiberno-English usage. The form *says I* (xxvii 140) is hardly an instance of this usage, since it is common in most dialects of English. The form *be* 'is' (xx 36 &c) is possibly influenced by Ir. *bídh* 'is'; *is* 'am' (xxv 31), 'have' (xxv 37) is merely broken English. The curious imperative *gave* 'give!' (xiii 80) occurs elsewhere in *Purgatorium Hibernicum,* and is difficult to explain. The only instances of the use of *will* where present-day Standard English requires *shall* are in *The Lancashire Witches* (xiv 23 &c.); *shall you vill* (xxiv 54) is broken English.

§187. In the past tense and past participle there are a few incorrect "regular" forms like *blowed* 'blown' (iii 28), *know'd* 'knew' (xix 46). Many apparently incorrect forms would not have been so in the seventeenth century, when the forms of strong verbs were much less firmly standardized than they are now : so, for instance, the past tenses *come* 'came' (vi 65, vii 13), *run(ne)* 'ran' (vii 6, ix 54, xxvii 91), *speake, spaake* 'spoke' (vii 11, xx 63), *bid* 'bade' (vii 42), *rid* 'rode' (xx 111), and the past participles *began* 'begun' (ix 40), *spoke* 'spoken' (xxv 38). A complex error is illustrated by *borning* 'being born' (xviii 79) : Farquhar's *Beaux' Stratagem* uses the form *borned* 'born', and it seems that a dental suffix was added to the strong past participle *born*, giving rise by back-formation to a new infinitive from which a new present participle was formed; in American English *aborning* is used in the same sense [Burchfield (1972) s.v.].

§188. A number of texts use endingless past participles of weak verbs : *rob* 'robbed' (ii 21), *ashame* 'ashamed' (xi 14, xxiv 69), *devoure* 'devoured' (xviii 8), *grieve* 'grieved' (xviii 26), *desheas* 'deceased' (xviii 70), *bridle and sadle* 'bridled and saddled' (xx 112), *cristan* 'christened' (xxv 30). Loss of /d/ or /t/ in some of these forms could in theory be phonological (§114), but in early texts there are also a number of instances in which the past participle of a strong verb is replaced by the infinitive form : *hang* 'hung' (i 14, xxiv 54), *vndoo* 'undone' (ii 22), *giue* 'given' (iii 26 &c.), *shit* 'sat' (vi 146), *fight* 'fought' (viii 23), *break* 'broken' (xii 44). It appears, therefore, that these endingless participles illustrate the reluctance of a bilingual speaker to be bothered with the inflectional niceties of his secondary language—he uses one form for all. There are also a number of endingless forms of the past tense of weak verbs : *touch* 'touched' (v 38), *knoke* 'knocked' (vi 65), *serve* 'served' (vii 6), *clap* 'clapped' (xii 45), *dye* 'died' (xviii 132), *call* 'called' (xxi 34). Again in some cases the loss of /d/ or /t/ could be phonological, but again there are instances of the use of the infinitive form where phonological change seems out of the question : *tell* 'told' (vii 13), *stawnd* 'stood' (vii 21), *make* 'made' (xiii 30, xxiv 39 &c.). The form *gives* 'gave' (ix 88) doubtless represents a historic present; the historic present is possible but not likely in some of the other instances quoted. The use of the past for the present in *vas, was* 'is' (xxiv 19 &c., xxv 28) is unparalleled.

The consuetudinal present

§189. In Irish the verb "to be" has a special consuetudinal present tense *bidheann sé* 'he usually is', distinct from the punctual present *tá sé* 'he is'; present-day Hiberno-English also has a special consuetudinal present *he does be* distinct from the punctual present *he is*. It is probable that the use of the verb "to do" as a consuetudinal auxiliary results from an association between this verb, as used in English in negative, interrogative, and negative-interrogative sentences, and the Irish present ending *-(e)ann* used in similar contexts [Bliss (1972) 75–81]. In the course of the seventeenth century the use of the ending *-(e)ann* was extended into affirmative sentences even in literary texts [O'Rahilly (1932) 132], and in speech this development had probably happened much earlier; the use of the auxiliary "to do" in Hiberno-English would no doubt have been extended into affirmative sentences at the same time. The present tense of most verbs has in any case a consuetudinal meaning; in the Irish verb "to be" the ending *-(e)ann* is found only in the consuetudinal present *bídheann*, not in the punctual present *tá*; the auxiliary "to do" would therefore come to be associated with a consuetudinal meaning. With verbs other than the verb "to be" the auxiliary is otiose, since the present tense is in any case consuetudinal, and for this reason it is rare in present-day Hiberno-English except with the verb "to be"; but we might expect that in early usage it would be common with verbs other than the verb "to be".

§190. Some care is needed in interpreting instances of the auxiliary "to do" in our texts, since throughout most of the seventeenth century it was in common use in Standard English as a meaningless auxiliary. In such a usage as *Der Canons against us do make such a noise* (xvii 15) the meaning is hardly consuetudinal, and the construction is of no special significance. In fact only one of our texts, *Ireland Preserved* (XX), contains any clear instances of the consuetudinal auxiliary, but there they are plentiful. In one speech of fifteen lines (22–36) there are no less than twelve instances of the auxiliary "to do", and the meaning is plainly consuetudinal in every case; in no case is the main verb the verb "to be". Later in the piece there are four more instances, one of which is *do be* : *you do be mauke de Rauvish upon de young Womans* (100); the remaining instances are in lines 41, 71, 103. It need occasion no surprise that this construction does not appear until after 1700. The Irish change which generated it (the extension of the use of the present ending *-(e)ann* into affirmative sentences) seems to have spread gradually northward over the country; it reached Ulster late, and the older ending *-(a)idh* can still be heard in Donegal [O'Rahilly (1932) 132]; and it would presumably take some time for the influence of an Irish change to make itself felt in Hiberno-English. It is perhaps somewhat surprising that the construction should appear at all in *Ireland Preserved*; however, the majority of the instances occur in the first of the three scenes printed here, and its action is not, apparently, located in Derry.

The perfect

§191. The Irish verb has in general no perfect tense, though (as we shall see below, §199) there is a compound tense equivalent to a kind of "progressive" perfect. In many cases where the perfect is used in English the present tense is used in Irish, and this usage is sometimes reflected in Hiberno-English, as in *he's dead and buried these ten years* 'he has been dead and buried for ten years' (xxvii 115). The only verbs which in Irish have a (compound) perfect tense are verbs of motion, and (as in many other languages) the perfect is formed, not with the verb "to have" as in English, but with the verb "to be" and the past participle. This usage is several times reflected in our texts : *di Lady is runne away from dee* (v 10), *I am come a great vay of miles* (vi 23), *Duke Scomberg and his Army is come* (xvii 19), *'tis come burying you are de corp* (xviii 6), *the wind is turn'd, the wind was turn'd* (xxvii 148 &c.)

"PROGRESSIVE" TENSES

The is writing *construction*

§192. English differs from the other Germanic languages in using a large number of "progressive" tenses formed from some part of the verb "to be" and the present participle—*he is writing*, and the like. Similar "progressive" tenses are found in the Celtic languages, and it is likely enough that their frequency in English is the result of Celtic influence. In the history of Gaelic the progressive tenses have tended to spread at the expense of the inflected tenses : thus, in Scottish Gaelic the original present tense has been fused with the future, and the "progressive" present is the only present tense in use. In Manx Gaelic the process has gone still further [Wagner (1958) 16] :

> spoken Manx uses scarcely any finite forms of ordinary verbs, but circumscribes them by means of auxiliary verbs ("to be" for durative, "to do" for terminative action) plus the verbal noun of the verb in question.

294

As might be expected, there are in our texts some instances of the *is writing* construction where Standard English would prefer an inflected form of the verb :

> *Are you not mad fwen you will be giving yourshelves and sweet*
>   *shouls to Divel?* (xviii 112)
> *I fill be going home* (xx 75)
> *How sall I be getting de Money?* (xx 75)

Equally, however, there is at least one instance of an inflected verb where a "progressive" form would seem more natural in Standard English :

> *My shelf no howle, me make speak for you* 'I am not howling,
>   I am speaking to you' (xii 115)

The is write *construction*

§193. The Celtic languages have no inflected present participle, but a kind of compound participle is formed from the verbal noun preceded by some preposition; in Gaelic the preposition is normally *ag* 'at', so that the Irish for 'he is writing' is *tá sé ag scríobhadh*. In Manx Gaelic no distinction is made between the participle and the verbal noun in its other functions : generally the preposition *ag* is suppressed, but with verbs beginning with a vowel or with *r* it is permanently incorporated into the form of the verbal noun, as the following table shows :

Ir. *cur* 'put' *ag cur* 'putting'	— Manx *cur* 'put(ting)'
Ir. *ithe* 'eat' *ag ithe* 'eating'	— Manx *g'ee* 'eat(ing)'
Ir. *rádh* 'speak' *ag rádh* 'speaking'	— Manx *g'ra* 'speak(ing)'

The nearest English equivalent of the Gaelic verbal noun is the infinitive; if, therefore, any form of Irish had undergone developments similar to those of Manx, we might expect to find "progressive" tenses formed with the infinitive instead of with the present participle; we might also expect to find such "progressive" tenses used to replace the normal tenses, even when the concept of continuing action (the normal implication of the "progressive" tenses) is lacking. In some of our texts we do indeed find such formations. Many of

295

the instances are complicated by other features, and will be discussed later : to start with we will consider some of the simpler instances.

> *Kilphatrick will be mush fear by and preshently* 'will fear, will be afraid' (xii 17)
> *De scald child, fate!, is feare de fire* 'fears' (xiii 88)
> *You do be mauke de Rauvish upon de young Womans* 'you make' (xx 100)
> *She vas go lame since she loose her too fore Broge* 'she went' (xxiv 46)

In all these instances the verb "to be" is otiose and does not change the meaning in any way (except that in the last the use of *vas* gives *go* a past meaning); its use seems not very different from the use of the verb "to do" as a meaningless auxiliary, very common in the seventeenth century, and indeed in some cases we could substitute the verb "to do" for the verb "to be" and make good seventeenth-century English; *the scalded child does fear the fire* and *she did go lame* would have been quite acceptable. In other instances, however, the meaning is plainly that of the "progressive" tense, so that it would not be possible to substitute the verb "to do" for the verb "to be" : *I am point* 'I am pointing' (xxiv 22), *I am tell* 'I am telling' (xxiv 61), *I am break* 'I am breaking' (xxiv 67). In one instance the meaning is future : *I am exercise* 'I will exercise' (xxiv 18).

§194. So far the origin of the construction seems clear, but there are a few instances in which another origin, or at least a complex origin, seems possible. It is a rule of Gaelic syntax that the verb normally comes first in the clause : if it is desirable that another element in the clause should be placed first for emphasis, this element is preceded by the unstressed form of the verb "to be" known as the copula, and the remainder of the clause is recast as a relative clause. The initial position of the verb in Irish is rarely imitated in Hiberno-English, though it does occur in *is none of you strong enough . . . to owercome him* (xviii 65), but a construction based on the Irish inversion for emphasis is very common at the present day, and there is one example in our texts, *'Tis come bourying you are de corp . . . of a verie good woman* (xviii 6–7). Here *'tis* corresponds to the Irish copula *is*, the element *come bourying* is emphasized, and the rest of the clause is recast as a relative clause, though the relative pronoun is omitted, as it usually is at the present day. There seems to be some relationship between this construction and the form of the *is write* construction in which *is* comes before the subject and the infinitive follows it :

Is de old hawke have de old eye (xiii 86)
And here is Nees beg dy Par-doon (xvi 91)

If the verbs had been *has* and *begs*, we should have had no hesitation in interpreting these clauses as meaning 'It is the old hawk (that) has . . .' and 'here is Nees (who) begs . . .'; but the verbs are *have* and *beg*, and it seems more natural to take *is . . . have* and *is . . . beg* as meaning 'has' and 'begs' respectively, in accordance with the *is write* construction. Yet, as we saw in §186, the *s* of the third person singular is often omitted, so perhaps the first explanation was right after all, especially since there is otherwise no obvious reason for the inversion of verb and subject; at least we can say that in such cases two quite different constructions would have led to very similar sequences of words.

§195. The interpretation of the *is write* construction is further complicated by the frequent omission of pronouns, both relative and personal. In our texts the omission of the relative pronoun is not uncommon : *yknows* 'who knows' (xvi 34), *made* 'that made' (xviii 51), *crys* 'who cries' (xxiv 34), *cry* 'who cry' (xxiv 35), *be* 'who are' (xxiv 38). When the *is write* construction is used in a relative clause the relative pronoun seems always to be omitted :

Comanded bee superior powers, / Is make me h[a]unt dese donny bowers 'who make' (xiii 25–6]
Good rest his Shoul, and Body too, / Is ly vidin de ground below 'which lies' (xvi 95–6)

When the personal pronoun is omitted the verb is always in the third person, irrespective of the person of the omitted pronoun. This phenomenon is particularly frequent in the broken English of *Sir John Oldcastle* (II): *is* 'I am' (11, 12, 28), *bee* 'I am' (8); instances in other texts are *ish* 'it is' (iii 61, vi 29), *shal* 'I shall' (xxv 6), 'you shall' (xxv 24). Omission of the personal pronoun is very common in the *is write* construction, and it may sometimes lead to ambiguity. Thus, doubt about the precise connotation of the word *varm* leaves us uncertain whether *is tink it varm enough* (xiii 64) means 'I think it warm enough' or 'you think it warm enough'. As before, omission of the personal pronoun is especially frequent in *Sir John Oldcastle* (II), as in *Is haue no mony* 'I have

no money' (29), *Is thanke my mester* 'I thank my master' (36);
so also in lines 6, 8, 21, 28, 29, 30. Instances from other texts are :

> *Is may as vel kisse my breesh* 'You may as well . . .' (xiii 84)
> *Vas carry it on his Shoul-deer* 'He carried me . . .' (xvi 98)
> *Vas give it charge to come to see* 'He charged me . . .' (xvi 102)

§196. The remaining instances of the *is write* construction are
characterized by other peculiarities. There are three instances in
which the verb "to be" is followed, not by an infinitive, but by a
finite form of the verb :

> *Fo ish tat ishe coughes* 'who is that who is coughing?' (i 22)
> *Vas he soe hot is cou'd no quench / De flame?* '. . . that he
> could not . . .' (xiii 18)
> *Dey dereby were lost Paradis* 'they thereby lost Paradise'
> (xviii 22)

With these should be compared three instances in which the
auxiliary verb *did* is used with an inflected past tense :

> *Dat fwich deir Holy Maker did forbade 'em* (xviii 20)
> *I did tought she cou'd not know me agen* (xix 146)
> *Who Fir'd vid Balls . . . / And did shat van Man trew de Head*
> (xxi 36)

There are two instances of the *is write* construction in which the
pronoun of the first person is expressed, but the verb is none the less
in the third person :

> *Ise kill me mester* 'I kill [? have killed] my master' (ii 20)
> *Me is go to Draeidheacht Aath* 'I am going to Drogheda'
> (xxv 13)

Finally there is a sentence in *Sir John Oldcastle* (II) so obscure that
the construction cannot be identified with certainty, *Now dow be
kil thee* (8) : the words *be kil* look like an instance of the *is write*
construction, but it seems impossible to fit them into the rest of the
sentence (cf. §170).

§197. The basic origin of the *is write* construction seems clear
enough, but the origin of some of the peculiarities which accompany
it is not so clear. The omission of the relative pronoun is intelligible
in terms of Irish usage, since the Irish relative pronoun *a* is regularly
elided in speech; most of the instances cited above involve the
present of the verb "to be", and the Irish relative form *atá* 'which
is' differs little from the form *tá* 'is', from which it is not normally

298

distinguished in speech. The omission of the personal pronoun is less easy to understand. In Irish there are two conjugations of the verb, the synthetic and the analytic. With synthetic forms of the verb the pronouns are of course not needed, since the person and number are sufficiently indicated by the inflection. With synthetic forms of the verb a pronoun subject is always added to the first verb in a clause (though it may be omitted with subsequent verbs or in answers to questions), so that the ambiguity of reference found in some of our texts can never arise.

§198. The *is write* construction occurs in less than a third of our texts, and it is interesting to examine which these are. If we leave aside the anomalous variants discussed in §196, the construction is found in eight texts. It is particularly common in the two explicitly Fingallian texts, *Purgatorium Hibernicum* (XIII) and *The Irish Hudibras* (XVI), and it occurs with great frequency in the parts of these works not printed here. It is found in the two texts linked with Fingallian by the occurrence of postponed stress (§19), *Stukeley* (I) and *Hic et Ubique* (XII). It is found in *Muiris O Gormáin* (XXV), which deals with a journey to Drogheda; the poet, Peadar O Doirnín, was born near Dundalk. These five texts are all associated with the coastal district extending north from Dublin, and it is precisely here that the Irish language is likely to have undergone developments comparable with those of Manx Gaelic; in some details such developments are in fact documented (§§ 46, 100). Of the remaining texts, *Sir John Oldcastle* (II), in which the *is write* construction is very frequent, is not localized; *The Pretender's Exercise* (XXIV) is also not localized, though it is worth noting that the only recruit whose place of origin is named comes from Co. Wicklow, also on the east coast. The solitary instance of the construction in *Ireland Preserved* (XX) occurs in the scene set in Derry, and there are two possible explanations of this fact. The other scenes printed here are not localized, though the reference in a stage-direction to a *"Fingall* dance" makes it possible that Fingall was intended; perhaps Michelburne confused two dialects, and transferred a Fingallian feature to Derry. Alternatively it is possible that the *is write* construction was actually used in Derry: at least one development comparable with Manx Gaelic can be observed in north Donegal (§46).

The after writing *construction*

§199. In English the perfect of the "progressive" form of the

verb consists of the perfect of the verb "to be" followed by the present participle of the verb in question : *he has been writing.* In Gaelic there is no true perfect, but a comparable "progressive" tense is formed with the present of the verb "to be" linked to the verbal noun of the verb in question by some preposition meaning 'after'. In Irish the preposition was once *iar* (often reduced to *ar*), but is now usually *tar éis*, so that the form is *tá sé tar éis scríobhtha*; this construction is imitated in present-day Hiberno-English by the literal translation *he is after writing* 'he has (just) written.' Constructions in which *after* is followed by the present participle are fairly numerous in our texts, but only one of them is precisely comparable with the present-day usage :

> *You shee here de cause dat is after bringing you to dis plaace* 'which has brought you' (xviii 5)

In every other instance the reference is either certainly or probably to the future, not to the past. Such usages have generally been ridiculed as due to the ignorance of English writers, who have not the sense to understand the construction used by Irishmen [see, for instance, Bartley (1954) 130; Greene (1966) 49]; but not all the writers are English, and in other respects they reflect Hiberno-English usage with such accuracy that it seems more profitable to accept their evidence as trustworthy and to seek an explanation for it. It is worth noting that *SND* records an identical usage for Scotland, and quotes an instance from a magazine of 1929 [*SND* s.v. *efter* 3; cf. *EDD* s.v. *after* 6].

§200. We may begin with a list of the instances in which the verb "to be" is actually in the future tense (in present-day usage these could only represent a future perfect, a tense which is not only intrinsically unlikely but which would not suit the context) :

> *You vill be after being damn'd* (xiv 37)
> *I vill be after absolving you for it* (xiv 63)
> *I'll be after telling dee de Raison* (xx 53)
> *I fill be after doing fell for my shelf* (xx 64)
> *I fell be after keeping my Cow and my Seep* (xx 73)
> *An will you be after giving me the Moidore indeed?* (xxii 12)
> *Well, fat will you be after Drinking?* (xxiii 52)
> *He will not be after hanging his Countryman* (xxiii 124)

In all these instances the *after* is strictly otiose : *be after writing* seems exactly equivalent to *write*, which could be substituted for it

300

in each case. There are two further instances in which the verb "to be" is not in the future, but the reference is none the less to the future, and the same substitution could be made :

Fen beggars must be after chooseing (xiii 103)
I can be after maaking twenty thirty of my Fadders and my followers . . . (xx 83)

In a further instance the meaning is not self-evident, and can only be elucidated by the parallelism with the instances at which we have already looked :

Dere be non, dat be after coming in de Nort, but get . . . (xx 97)

There can be no serious doubt that the meaning here is 'none who come into the North' rather than 'none who have come'. Finally, there is a curious instance in which the verb "to be" is in the perfect :

He has been after wearing dem [scil. *brogues*] *himself* (xx 52)

Plainly the reference here is to the past, but equally plainly this is not the present-day use of *after writing*, in which the verb "to be" would be in the present; again the *after* is otiose, and *been after wearing* is equivalent to *worn*.

The after write *construction*

§201. There are several instances of a similar construction in which the main verb is not a present participle, as in the other instances we have looked at so far, but an infinitive; there is an obvious likeness to the *is write* construction, and it will be convenient to call this the *after write* construction. There is only one instance in which the verb "to be" is in the future :

De Priest fill not be after give us de Absolution without dem (xx 123)

Here *be after give* is equivalent to *give*. In two further instances the reference is rather to the present than to the future :

Itching | She's after bee to run a-bit[c]hing (xiii 32)
Der fell be no Waacancy, unless I be after buy de Plaash (xx 72)

301

One instance in *The Irish Hudibras* (XVI) is genuinely ambiguous. Nees, planning to visit his father Anchees in the Other World, says that

> *. . . when he was after dee,*
> *Vas give it charge to come to see.* (101–2)

There are two possible meanings here : 'My father charged me to come and see him when he had died', with the present-day meaning of *after*, or 'When he was dying my father charged me to come and see him.' The latter meaning seems the more likely, for a number of reasons, not least that it gives better sense; it is also worth noting that there is no instance (unless this is one) of the *after write* construction referring to the past.

§202. There is a single instance in which *after* is followed, not by either a present participle or an infinitive, but by a past participle : *Barrels of de Money, dat have been after hid* (xx 107). There is no doubt a parallel here to the use of the verb "to be" followed by an inflected verb (§196), but nevertheless it is difficult to understand the construction : *after* seems to be wholly superfluous here, since the meaning must be 'barrels that have been hidden'. A final instance is again ambiguous : *His Graash . . . has great kindness for dose dat be after first come* (xx 62). The ambiguity lies in the fact that *come* might be an infinitive, as in the normal form of the *after write* construction, or a past participle like *hid* in the previous instance. It seems most likely that *come* is an infinitive, that *be after come* is the equivalent of *come*, and that the meaning of the whole is 'His Grace has great kindness for those that come first.'

§203. The origin of the *after writing* and *after write* constructions is far from clear. In the single instance where the *after writing* construction refers to the past, it is no doubt derived from Ir. *iar*, *ar* (ScG. *air*, Manx *er*) 'after', used with the verbal noun in all dialects of Gaelic, but this could never refer to the future. It seems that when it refers to the future the *after writing* construction must have some quite different origin, in which *after* reflects some other preposition. The preposition in question may perhaps be *ar* 'on', rendered *after* by association or confusion with *ar* the reduction of *iar* 'after'. The preposition *ar* 'on' is frequently used with verbal nouns, and sometimes gives a passive meaning, as in *ar díol* 'for sale', i.e. 'being sold'. Even when the meaning is passive the verbal noun preceded by *ar* can often be rendered by the English present participle, as in *ar maothas* 'being soaked' or 'soaking'; and the passive meaning is often absent, as in *ar siubhal* 'walking', *ar sodar* 'trotting', *ar marcaidheacht* 'riding', *ar seachrán* 'straying', *ar snámh* 'floating', *ar lasadh* 'burning', *ar crochadh* 'hanging'. This preposition causes no initial mutation in the verbal noun which follows it; *ar* 'after' properly caused nasalization or "eclipsis", but in the spoken language this was commonly replaced by lenition. There is thus a contrast in the spoken language between *ar siubhal* 'walking' and *ar shiubhal* 'gone away', i.e. 'having walked'. Only seven consonants are liable to eclipsis, the stops (voiced and voiceless) and the voiceless spirant *f*; all other consonants remain unaffected. It follows that with the majority of verbal nouns *ar* 'on' and *ar* 'after' would not be distinguishable, as long as eclipsis rather than lenition remained the rule after *ar* 'after'; a bilingual speaker seeking a rendering for *ar* with the verbal noun might perhaps choose *after* even when the meaning was present or future (there is a probable instance of the opposite "mistranslation" in *Y cannot be upon vaaking* (xv 16), where *upon vaaking* seems to reproduce Ir. *ar múscailt* 'awake', with *ar* 'after'). If this is indeed the origin of the *after writing* construction there must have been a good deal of analogical extension of the use of *after*, since in many of the instances quoted in §§ 199 and 200 the Irish preposition would be *ag* rather than *ar*.

The for writing *construction*

§204. Yet another "progressive" construction is attested in one of our texts, *Bog-Witticisms* (XV). In this construction the present participle (never the infinitive) is preceded, not by *after*, but by *for*:

> *Y vill be for mauking Child upon dy Body* (23 &c.)
> *Vee vill shet up Housh-kepin and be for livein aul togadder* (44)
> *Dou shaut be for sending Aunswer to vaat Y hauve sent dee* (47)

In colloquial Standard English, *for* can be used with a present participle (or gerund) in the sense of 'in favour of' one or other alternative, as in *I'm for waiting till he comes*, but this is hardly the meaning found in *Bog-Witticisms*. This is not a text which inspires much confidence, and these three sentences may be the result of some error or misunderstanding. If the use of *for* with the participle is genuine it may perhaps reflect the Irish use of *do* 'to, for' with the verbal noun to express "the idea of entering upon or continuing a state or action" [*Contributions* s.v. *do* IV]; in each of

303

the three sentences quoted above the idea of entering upon a course of action is clearly present. Though the most natural English equivalent of Ir. *do* is *to*, we shall see below (§208) a further series of cases in which it seems to have been rendered by *for*.

VERBAL PERIPHRASES

The put fear *construction*

§205. Many English verbs can be rendered in Irish by variations on an idiom in which the verb *cuirim* 'I put' is followed by some noun and the preposition *ar* 'on'. Thus 'I frighten' can be rendered by *cuirim eagla ar* 'I put fear on', 'I delay' by *cuirim moill ar* 'I put delay on', 'I lock' by *cuirim glas ar* 'I put a fastening on', and so on. Literal translations of this idiom are to be found in our texts :

> *To put sheat upon my moyster* (xii 98)
> *I will vatch de vales, Nees, / And putt foile on dee*
>   (xiii 69–70*)
> *Y vill put kish upon dy faush indeede* (xv 22 &c.)

In a further series of instances the noun is preceded by the definite article, though this is not in accordance with Irish idiom :

> *He put de fuckation upon my weef* (xii 35)
> *De English vil put de sheat pon efry podyes* (xii 122)
> *. . . just as we were going to put the fight upon the Rebels*
>   (xxiii 92)

In the phrase *to put the Kill upon my shelf* (xii 65) the word *Kill* seems more like a verb than a noun, but the use of the definite article, as well as the juxtaposition with *put*, certifies that it is after all a non-standard noun. In a final series of instances the noun is preceded by the adjective *great* :

> *I did see putting the great fuck upon my weef . . .* (xii 41)
> *. . . Lest vid a Fart dou blow it from me, / And put de great*
>   *Moccage upon me* (xvi 75–6)
> *. . . For der putting on ush dat curshed great Sheat* (xvii 30)

§206. In a limited number of cases the verb used in the Irish idiom is not *cuirim* 'I put' but *déanaim* 'I make, I do'. Thus, 'I deceive' can be rendered by *déanaim feall ar* 'I make deceit on',

'I clean' by *déanaim glanadh ar* 'I make cleaning on', and so on. Literal translations of this idiom, too, are to be found in our texts :

> *It will make cure upon dee* (xiv 73)
> . . . *aund aul de People to mauke Witnesh upon it* (xv 30)
> *And I meeself great Eye have still, | To make performsh upon his Will* (xvi 104)
> *I make speech pon you* (xxiv 21)

In the sentence *poor Kilpatrick will be made Kil upon* (xii 69) the word *Kil* might seem to be a verb, if it were not for the analogy of *to put the Kill upon my shelf* (xii 65), discussed above; and this analogy makes it probable that in the sentence *Nees vill . . . | Make hang upon himself indeed* (xvi 17–18) the word *hang* is also a non-standard noun. As before, there are some instances in which the noun is qualified by the definite article or an adjective :

> *I'll make much Prayer upon dee* (xvi 30)
> *He will maake de Fornicaation upon dy Wife* (xx 18)
> *You do be mauke de Rauvish upon de young Womans* (xx 100)

There is an obvious parallelism between the second of these examples and *He put de fuckation upon my weef* (xii 35), discussed above, and no doubt the nonce-word *fuckation* is due to association with *fornication*.

The make write *construction*

§207. There is another and entirely different construction which also uses the verb "to make", one which reflects the Irish use of *déanaim* 'I make, I do' as an auxiliary. This auxiliary is used with the verbal noun in such phrases as *déanaim marcaidheacht* 'I ride', *déanaim caoineadh* 'I weep', *déanaim snámh* 'I swim', and the construction is of considerable antiquity [*Contributions* s.v. *do-gní* I (d) (iii), (e)]. In Manx Gaelic the use of the corresponding auxiliary greatly extended its scope, so that together with the "progressive" tenses it effectively displaced all the historic inflected tenses (above, §192). The attraction of such a construction for a bilingual speaker needs no emphasis, since it enables him to avoid the use of "irregular" inflected forms about which he may be doubtful (cf. §172). It might have been expected that if the construction was imitated in Hiberno-English the auxiliary used would be "to do", particularly in view of the extensive use of this verb as a meaningless auxiliary in seventeenth-century English (cf. §193);

but in fact the auxiliary used in our texts is regularly "to make". In the following examples the word following "to make" is an infinitive :

> *May her fader's shild make dye in de prishon* (xii 128)
> *De fox, fwen he makes scape from de hounds . . .* (xviii 96)
> *. . . if you will give me your Permission to maake swear against you* (xix 110)
> *The Micharr of a Trooparr, did maake Force my Fadders House* (xx 6)
> *She make run away Vith a shantleman brave* (xxv 47)

As we have seen (§193), the nearest English equivalent to the Gaelic verbal noun is the infinitive, but it is not the only equivalent. Any abstract noun related to a verb fulfils some of the functions of a verbal noun, and in the following examples the word following "to make" is such an abstract noun :

> *. . . to see my Moistare make conjuration* (xii 18)
> *'Tis ill kind for dy Faders shild, to be making speech wit dy shelf* (xii 20)
> *He did make intention to cut off my head* (xii 80)
> *Be me shoul Y vill not mauke staying sho long* (xv 31)

There are also two instances in which the abstract noun *spaake* 'speech' is preceded by the definite article :

> *I fill maake de spaake to hish Graash* (xx 14)
> *. . . and ware dou maake de spaake wid him* (xx 90)

§208. One of our texts, *Hic et Ubique* (XII), contains a number of instances of a construction not documented elsewhere, in which "to make" is followed by an infinitive and the preposition *for* :

> *Here is one . . . would make speak for dy shelf* (2 &c.)
> *The donny fellow make buse for my Moister* (30)
> *I did make sharge for him in the Kings name* (46)
> *For Christis shake, make help for my shelf moyster* (67)
> *If I make tell so for him before, he will not come for me afterward* (93)
> *Fuat de Devil must my shelf go make fetch for de Clark* (97)
> *. . . de garrane dough, thou didst make promise for me* (113)

In some of these examples the word following "to make" might be either a verb or a noun (*abuse, charge, help, promise*), but the analogy of the remaining cases seems to guarantee that the verb is what is intended. The preposition *for* seems to function as an indicator of the object, either (as in most cases) the direct object, or (as in the first, the last, and perhaps the fifth) the indirect object. In sentences which do not use the *make write* construction there is one example of *for* as an indicator of the direct object, *My moistare will make mad for my shelf* 'My master will drive me mad' (9), and one as the indicator of the indirect object, *Dere is one wu'd fain be speaking for dee* 'There is someone who wishes to speak to you' (27). In Irish the indirect object is most commonly preceded by the preposition *do* 'to, for'; the most natural English equivalent in such a context would be *to*, but we have already seen (§204) that *for* might be preferred in Hiberno-English. No such explanation is available for the use of *for* as an indicator of the direct object, and we should have to assume a rather surprising analogical transference; we have already seen (§159) that Head was not always an accurate observer, so perhaps the use of *for* is due to some kind of error on his part. *This chureeh crave Ruagh make run away for himshelf* (48) is not an example of this use of *for*: it is comparable rather with such Irish expressions as *d'imigh sé leis* 'he went off with himself'; the use of *make run away* is identical with the use quoted in §207.

§209. Though the two types of verbal periphrasis discussed above have very different origins, the variant of the *put fear* construction which uses the verb "to make" can be very similar to the *make write* construction, and no doubt there has been mutual influence between the two. In §206 the phrase *make speech pon* was listed as an instance of the *put fear* construction, and in §207 the phrases *making speech wit*, *maake de spaake to* and *maake de spaake wid* were listed as instances of the *make write* construction; yet the difference between these patterns is minimal. There has probably been influence, too, from constructions which bear a superficial resemblance to these, but which are not in fact periphrases. Thus, *Y vill be for mauking Child upon dy Body* (xv 23) reflects the Irish idiom *déanaim clann ar* 'I beget a child on' [*Contributions* s.v. *do-gní* II (m)], but there is no periphrasis. So with other examples :

> *My shelf make no meyning for Dat at all* 'I am unable to attach any meaning to that' (xii 87)
> *My shelf will make no servant for de* 'I will not act as [*or*, continue to be] your servant' (xii 116)

I make English upon you, you make English upon me again
'I speak English to you . . .' (xxiv 6–7)

In *dou not maake de trouble* (xx 77) the only anomaly lies in the use of the definite article, and this is discussed below (§213). In *dare musht be mauking upon the great Sherimony of de Presht* (xv 28) it is possible that some word has been accidentally omitted after *mauking*; but it is also possible that *mauking upon* reproduces the Irish idiom *déanamh ar* 'going to, approaching' [*Contributions* s.v. *do-gní* III (d)], so that the general meaning of the whole sentence would be something like 'they must go to a religious ceremony.'

INVERSION OF VERB AND SUBJECT

§210. There is a curious idiom, well documented in our texts, by which verb and subject are transposed after an oath or expletive. The examples are *Marafastot art thou a feete liuerd kana* (i 24), *I by St. Patrick vill tey* (vi 96), *Yfaat hast tow* (vii 73), *No, indeed, would he not* (xviii 117), *Yesh, fet would I* (xix 33), *Fet am I* (xix 69*), *Fet have I* (xix 79). In addition there are no less than eleven instances in *A Wife Well Managed* (XXII), in lines 11, 20, 27, 29, 46, 50, 55, 59, 61, 78, 81; in every instance the expletive is *Faith*, except in line 55 where it is *pon my Shoul*. Other examples can be found in texts not printed here : Beaumont and Fletcher's *Coxcomb* (1612) has *no by my trot and fait can'st thou not man* [Bowers (1966) 297]; Crowne's *City Politiques* (1688) has *Ay, by Shaint Patrick, am I!* [Crowne (1874) 206]. I have found no entirely satisfactory explanation of this idiom. In colloquial Standard English inversion is possible in an enthusiastic acceptance of an invitation : *Will you come to the theatre tonight? Will I!* Here the words *Will I!* form a rhetorical question : the inversion would not be used after an expletive, where something like *Indeed I will!* would be the formula. In any case, the great majority of the instances of inversion in our texts are spontaneous utterances; there are a few questions, but no invitations. In comparable utterances in Irish the formula would be something like *m'anam go mbéidh!* 'my soul that I will!'; the pronoun would not normally be expressed. The verb is subject to eclipsis, and if there is a distinct dependent form, that is the form used, as in *m'anam go bhfuil!* 'my soul that I am!' By far the most common position in which the dependent form of the verb is subject to eclipsis is in a question, positive or negative : *an bhfuil?* 'am I?', *nach bhfuil?* 'am I not?' It is perhaps possible

that the eclipsis of the dependent form of the verb might have led
a bilingual speaker to substitute the interrogative for the affiirmative
form of the verb in the relevant contexts.

§211. Among all the parts of speech, prepositions give most
difficulty to learners of a second language, because their semantic
fields vary widely from language to language; a bilingual speaker
is very likely to transfer details of the use of prepositions from his
primary to his secondary language. We have in fact already seen a
use of the English preposition *upon* dictated by Irish idiom (§§ 206,
207), and there are many comparable cases involving this and other
prepositions. The Irish for 'what is your name?' is *cé'n t-ainm atá
ort?* 'what name is upon you?', and there are in our texts several
instances of this idiom : *Fat Naam ish upon him?* (xix 30 &c.),
Fat Name upon you dere? (xxiv 1). Ir. *ar* is often used to indicate
detriment or disadvantage of various kinds, and there are a number
of instances of this usage :

> *There was no sharge powder upon the pishtol* (xii 80)
> *Wilt tow . . . leave noting upon me poor Kilpathrick* (xii 108)
> *You . . . make trouble pon my shelf* (xxiv 51)
> *He's sometimes pretty smart upon me with his humbuggs*
>   (xxvii 137)

Other constructions are less easily paralleled in Irish, but do not
seem entirely out of keeping with Irish idiom : *Y did pray him to
shend it upon Ursula* (xv 9), *what was the first Prefarment that was
upon you in England?* (xxiii 88). Two different constructions used
with the word *care* can both be paralleled in Irish : *have a care
upon your shelf* (xix 51) reflects the use of Ir. *áird* 'attention, heed'
with *ar* 'upon', *de Jesuite take care for dem* (xx 135) reflects the use
of Ir. *aire* 'care, attention' with *do* 'to, for'. In Irish the preposition
used with *éistim* 'I listen' is *le* 'with', and this idiom is exactly
reproduced in *listen wid me, and I'le tell you . . .* (xviii 119).

§212. Other non-standard forms and uses of prepositions owe
nothing to Irish : most of them represent obsolete, dialectal, or
vulgar English. The earliest and most difficult instance is the use
of *be* in *tell ty tale, ty shelfe, and be all tree* (vi 57–8); the meaning
seems to be 'tell your story yourself, and on behalf of all three (of
us)', but no suitable meaning of the preposition *by* is recorded since

Old English; the suggestions that *be* is here the imperative of the verb "to be" [Herford & Simpson (1925–52) x 543] lacks plausibility. In older English the preposition *on* was often used where present-day usage calls for *of* (vi 90, xvi 84, xxiv 69) [*NED* s.v. *on* 27]; here also belong *on's* (xiii 11) and *on't* (xxvii 22). The use of *vidin* 'within' as a mere substitute for *in* (xvi 96) is now obsolete [*NED* s.v. *within* B. 1 (a)], as is the use of *for to* with an infinitive (xvii 22 &c.) [*NED* s.v. *for* 11]. The use of *of* (xxii 60) where present-day usage requires *on* is dialectal or vulgar [*NED* s.v. *of* 55], as is *again* 'against' (xxvi 2) [*NED* s.v. *again* B*].

VARIOUS IDIOMATIC USAGES

§213. As might be expected, there are in our texts a number of idioms literally translated from the Irish. The possibility of coincidence of idiom must not be ignored : the interjected *thou knowest* (v 18, xii 38 &c.), for instance, might perhaps reflect Ir. *tá a fhios agat* used in a precisely similar way, but the phrase is in no way alien to English usage. All the instances discussed below, however, are so distinctive that Irish influence seems certain. The most frequent is *thy (his, her) father's child* (xii 19, 128, xiv 13, xxvi 11), literally translating Ir. *mac a athar* in such contexts as *tá fáilte annseo roimh mhac a athar* 'his father's son is welcome here', i.e. 'he is welcome here for his father's sake.' The connotation of the Irish phrase is correctly reproduced in Swift's *Dialogue* (xxvi 11), and in the extended form *the child of her father and mother* (xviii 11), but in *Hic et Ubique* (xii 19, 128) and *The Lancashire Witches* (xiv 13) it has been weakened, so that *thy father's child* comes to mean no more than *thee*. This weakened form of the idiom may be the result of poor observation by Head and Shadwell, but it is possible that the weakening had taken place in Hiberno-English. Though there are verbs in Irish with the meaning 'die', the idiom commonly used is *bás a fhagháil* 'get death'; this usage is clearly reflected in *I vil be a Cardinal before I vill have death* (xiv 27–8). Irish, like many other languages, sometimes uses the definite article where English has either no article at all, or the indefinite article. The only one of our texts which reflects this Irish usage is *Ireland Preserved* (XX), in which there are a number of instances : *you be de great Fool* (34), *to maake de piece of Money to buy de English Cloaths* (47), *day be de great Mans now* (69), *dou not maake de trouble* (77), *mauke de Rauvish upon de young Womans* (100–101),

Chests full of Plaat, Barrels of de Money (107), *de Priest fill not be after give us de Absolution* (123), *You be de Fool* (134). In the question *how does he get his health?* (xxvi 5) Swift italicized the word *get* to indicate a hibernicism : the idiom literally translates Ir. *cé'n chaoi a bhfaigheann sé an tsláinte?* 'what kind of health does he enjoy?', and the meaning is quite different from that of the English *get one's health* 'recover one's health' [*NED* s.v. *get* 12]. The idiom *it is kind father for you* (xxvi 19) literally translates Ir. *is dual athar duit*, in which *athar* 'father' is in the genitive : the meaning of the Irish idiom is 'you have inherited that tendency from your father', a meaning which accords well with the previous clause *a good warrant you have*, where *warrant* seems to mean 'authority by inheritance' (§164).

§214. There are other non-standard idioms in our texts for which there seems to be no basis in Irish. If *by and preshently* (xii 17) is a genuine usage, and was not merely invented by Head for comic effect, it must depend on a confusion of the English synonyms *by and by* and *presently*. *What for a Message is it?* (xxii 6) uses *what for* in the sense 'what kind of', a usage which is rare but not unparalleled [*NED* s.v. *for* 19 c.]. The use of *so you are* (xxii 45), *so I do* (xxii 65) to reinforce a previous statement is common in present-day Hiberno-English, but there is no obvious basis for it in Irish. The most interesting idioms are those which are neither English nor Irish, but are closely paralleled in French. There can be little doubt about the origin of *grash a* 'thanks to' (viii 42), corresponding to French *grâce à*, or *vith a grash* 'please, I beg you' (xxiv 31), corresponding to French *de grâce*. In *a poor shilly bitt of apple dat vas not of woort tree straws* (xviii 21), the phrase *of woort* seems to owe something to French *de valeur*. A sentence in *Ireland Preserved* has a curious use of the infinitive, *I have been dis seven days to learn to wear de English Brogue* (xx 47–9); there is a parallel here to the French construction *j'ai passé sept jours à apprendre . . .* French influence on Hiberno-English may seem surprising, but it has to be remembered that many Irishmen were educated abroad. Irish colleges were founded from the sixteenth century onwards, at Douai in 1596, at Toulouse in 1660, and at Paris in 1677, to mention only foundations in French-speaking countries. These colleges were intended primarily for aspirants to the priesthood, but not all the aspirants actually became priests; both priests and others might well be concerned with the education of the laity when they returned to Ireland.

311

SUMMARY AND CONCLUSIONS

§215. The twenty-seven texts analysed above provide a great mass of information about all aspects of Hiberno-English; it remains to consider first, how reliable that information is likely to be, and secondly, what general conclusions can be drawn from it. The most obvious danger, already briefly considered above (p. 174), is that our texts might represent some kind of "Stage Irish" only remotely related to the speech of real Irishmen. The term "Stage Irish" is used to denote a conventional form of language, used in the work of dramatists (and, by extension, in that of novelists and others) whenever they wish to reproduce the speech of an Irish character. Such a conventional language must, of course, bear *some* relationship to the speech of Irishmen, since it could hardly be invented out of nothing; its characteristic is that its features are repeated by a succession of writers without further reference to the real thing. It is likely, therefore, to become increasingly out of date : it will fail to reflect changes in Hiberno-English or (just as important) in Standard English. This last point can easily be overlooked : it is only *differences* between the two forms of language that would be worth recording, and these would vary according to changes in either.

§216. As far as we are concerned, "Stage Irish" is a written phenomenon. There might, of course, have been such a thing as spoken "Stage Irish" in the past as at the present day : actors playing the parts of Irishmen might well have embellished their performances with traditional pronunciations and turns of phrase. Nevertheless, even if such a spoken "Stage Irish" existed in the seventeenth century, this cannot be what is reproduced in our texts : it is impossible to conceive that each of a series of writers would independently take pains to reproduce in writing the conventional language used by the actors, and if the renderings were not independent, we should be dealing not with a spoken but with a written tradition. The evidence of Crowne (above, p. 174) suggests that in fact the actors made no special study of dialect, but relied on the dramatist to indicate to them what was required; and when, from about 1730 onwards, we find Irish actors regularly playing Irish parts on the London stage [Bartley (1954) 242–3], we also find fewer and fewer indications of pronunciation and usage in the printed plays. If we have to deal with "Stage Irish" at all, it must be as a written tradition, to which the actors gave spoken expression as best they could.

§217. It is easy to think of a number of reasons why an individual writer on a specific occasion might use "Stage Irish" : because he was lazy, or in a hurry, or because he distrusted his ability to reproduce what he had observed; because he believed that his audience preferred convention to realism; or because he wanted to pay homage to an earlier writer for whose work he had a special reverence. All these motives might be valid enough, and we shall see below (§221) that the last of them probably influenced two of our dramatists : but the fact remains that, however strong his incentive to use "Stage Irish" might be, no writer could do so unless a tradition of "Stage Irish" already existed, and it is far from easy to understand how such a tradition could have come into existence. We cannot claim that every writer was always lazy, or in a hurry, or distrustful of his own powers; an audience could not have preferred convention to realism unless a convention was already in existence. It seems that the only circumstance which could give rise to a tradition of "Stage Irish" would be a total lack of opportunity to observe the speech and habits of real Irishmen, so that writers would have had no choice but to imitate the usage of some unique predecessor who had exceptionally had the opportunities which were denied to them. As we have seen above (pp. 177–81), there were in fact plenty of Irishmen in England at least until the early years of the eighteenth century, so that opportunity to observe them was not lacking; it would be surprising if there were a tradition of "Stage Irish". However, speculation is not enough, and the presence of "Stage Irish" must be a matter of demonstration.

§218. If there had been a tradition of "Stage Irish" we should expect the representation of Hiberno-English by those who followed it to be both inaccurate and unrealistically stable. We have already seen in §§ 7–8 the reasons for inaccuracy : since, by definition, users of "Stage Irish" were unfamiliar with the speech of Irishmen, they could have had no rational expectations about the meaning of

313

the spellings used by their predecessors, and would certainly have misinterpreted them; in such circumstances they might, in their own imitations, have used the spellings wrongly. We have also seen in §215 the reasons for the unrealistic stability: the original representations of Irish speech, however accurate in the first place, could not have taken account of changes in Hiberno-English or in Standard English. These, then, are the features we must look for in our texts if we suspect the presence of "Stage Irish".

§219. It is difficult to test the accuracy of the representations of Hiberno-English in our texts, since we have nothing to compare them with; the best we can do is to see how easy it is to explain the features that we actually find. Judged by this criterion, the representations emerge with great credit. Of the features we can predict as historically and linguistically probable, the vast majority actually appear in our texts; most of the features we might not have predicted are readily explicable in terms of the historical phonology of English and Irish, so that the number of those which remain inexplicable is very small indeed; most of the outstanding problems are concerned with isolated forms, not with general tendencies. The only inexplicable general tendencies, found in no more than a few texts each, are the writing of *sh* for /s/ in all contexts (§90), the occasional writing of *s* for /ʃ/ (§96), the writing of *t* for /ð/ (§109), and the apparent voicing of /s/ to /z/ (§113). Individual forms which are difficult to explain are *skrivishner, skriviwnar* 'scrivener' (§11), *awn* 'own' (§56), *sonar* 'sooner' (§59), *starfing* 'starving', *Cofentry* 'Coventry', *deefil* 'devil' (§108), *Carick-vergus* 'Carick-fergus' (§112), *by dis chees* (§134), *spereen* (§135), and *gave* 'give!' (§186). This catalogue is respectably short.

§220. It is easy to show that, far from being unrealistically stable, the representation of Hiberno-English in our texts shows a steady chronological progression which can be plausibly linked with known sound-changes at a number of points; as far as vowels are concerned, it is the historical phonology of English which is important; as far as consonants are concerned, the historical phonology of Irish. Perhaps the most compelling piece of evidence is the replacement about 1680 of the spelling *ai/ay* by the spelling *aa* for ME $\bar{e}$ and $\bar{a}$ (§§ 42–6); this can be linked with the steady raising of the two ME vowels in Standard English in the course of the seventeenth century. The appearance of the spelling *aa* for ME *a* about 1680 can be linked with the final disappearance of the pronunciation /a/ for ME *a* in Standard English (§§ 32–3). About 1700 we can

314

observe the final disappearance of the spelling *ee* for ME ī (§40); presumably the pronunciation /iː/ had now finally been replaced by /əi/ even in Hiberno-English. Some changes in the representation of consonants which must be linked with developments in Irish are discussed in §§ 116–9. In the field of vocabulary there are some equally impressive chronological developments. The oaths attributed to Irishmen show a number of changes in the course of the period, and these are documented in §§ 127–32. In the earliest period the favourite oaths were *by my gossip's hand* and the like, *by God, by Christ, by my faith, i'faith,* and so on. Later we find *by my soul, faith,* and *the devil take me;* later still, *devil take me* and *upon my soul.* (Throughout the period we find *by St Patrick* and *a pox upon it.*) No doubt some of these oaths merely reflect fashions current in England, but this does not affect the point at issue : whatever the reason for the change, there is no continuous tradition of favourite oaths such as we might expect if we had to do with "Stage Irish". A similar progression is to be observed in the terms of endearment attributed to Irishmen (§§ 140–141) : *sweet face* occurs mainly in the earliest texts, but is found occasionally up to about 1690; from 1660 onwards *joy* becomes very popular, varied from about 1690 by *dear joy; honey* and *jewel* are later still. In this case it is not possible to invoke English fashion, since of these expressions only *honey* was used at all in England. As well as these chronological differences the regional differences discussed below (§§ 226–33) also tell against the use of "Stage Irish".

§221. However, in spite of all this evidence against the use of "Stage Irish", it would be a mistake to assume that there is no trace of it at all in our texts; it is in fact possible to observe two instances of it in points of detail, one virtually certain, the other highly probable. One of the inexplicable features listed above (§219) is the writing of *t* for /ð/ (§109). Apart from one or two special cases, such spellings occur in only two of our texts, *The Irish Masque* (VI) and *Hey for Honesty* (VIII); it cannot be a coincidence that the writers of these two pieces, Jonson and Randolph, were linked by "adoption" (above, p. 41), or that the younger man had a special veneration for the older, and therefore a special reason for imitating his usage, however eccentric it might seem. We are no nearer explaining Jonson's choice of this strange spelling (unless the omission of *h* after *t* had become wholly mechanical), but we need look no further for an explanation of Randolph's usage. Another inexplicable feature of Jonson's spelling is the writing of *sh* for /s/ in all contexts (§88); in this usage he is followed not only by Randolph as before, but also by Shadwell in *The Lancashire Witches* (XIV); and though Shadwell was not a contemporary of Jonson's, he was an avowed admirer of his (above, p. 49). In this case, however, many other later writers also follow the same usage, including Dunton (XVIII), Farquhar (XIX) and Michelburne (XX), writers who in other respects display acute observation and careful notation. It seems that, however mysterious it may be, there must be some phonetic basis for Jonson's usage; yet there is no reason to doubt that Randolph and Shadwell merely followed Jonson blindly.

§222. The instances cited in the last paragraph are the exceptions which prove the rule, and in general it seems that we are entitled to assume the reliability of the evidence presented in our texts. It does not follow, of course, that the evidence is complete, and indeed it seems certain that it is not. In the field of phonology there are many probable peculiarities of pronunciation which, if they existed, could not readily be indicated by the use of the Roman alphabet (above, §§ 7, 18, 33, 46, 93). Even in the fields of vocabulary and syntax, where there is no obvious impediment to accurate representation, it is likely enough that certain features were overlooked by some or most of our writers. The use of *my own self*, for instance, is a plausible calque on Ir. *mise féin*, and it can be paralleled in present-day Hiberno-English; yet it is recorded by only six of our twenty-seven texts (§179). We cannot expect a complete picture, but as far as it goes we can assume that the picture is accurate, and it remains to consider first, what general impression of Hiberno-English emerges, and second, what individual varieties of speech can be distinguished within the general pattern.

GENERAL CHARACTERISTICS OF HIBERNO-ENGLISH

§223. Early Modern Hiberno-English represents some variety of English acquired or re-acquired by bilingual speakers in the first half of the sixteenth century (§§ 66–8), and affected by strong and continuous influence from the Irish language. The influence of the Irish language needs no further exemplification, since hardly a paragraph in the foregoing analysis fails to advert to it. What does require further consideration is the nature of the English which was subjected to this influence. The concept of a standard spoken language first emerged in the sixteenth century, and Puttenham

316

gives us some useful information about it in his *Arte of English Poesy* (1589). According to Dobson's summary [(1955) 3], Puttenham tells us

> that the common people everywhere spoke dialect and the standard language was the possession only of the well-born and the well-educated; that in the Court and the Home Counties one might expect all well-born and well-educated people to use this standard language, but beyond those limits, though one might still find men who spoke pure standard English, the greater part of the gentry and scholars were influenced by the speech of the commonpeople (i.e. they spoke 'modified Standard'), and finally that in the far West and the North the standard did not apply at all.

The precise nature of the standard spoken language has been a matter of controversy. It seems clear that it was artificial, in the sense that it was cultivated; it has been claimed that it was artificial in another sense—that it was a purely theoretical standard, not in fact used by anyone. Holmberg, for instance [(1964) 19], says that "the feeling for a standard that did exist in the seventeenth century was largely theoretical, and hardly influenced the speech of the average educated speaker." This is an extreme view; it seems most probable that the standard was used in its purity by a small number of careful speakers, and that other educated speakers used a form of pronunciation which, while neither dialectal nor vulgar, still differed in various ways from the standard.

§224. There is no way of knowing the social and regional origins of the English administrators in Dublin from whom Irishmen presumably learned or re-learned their English; but there is no reason to suppose that they all came from London or the Home Counties, so that it is not surprising to find dialectal features in Hiberno-English, especially features belonging to the northern and western dialects. Such dialectal features do in fact occur, but they are not limited in their occurrence to particular groups of texts; presumably they were absorbed more or less at random from a variety of English-speakers. Scottish and northern English dialect features are particularly common, and include the following forms: *wees me* 'woe is me' (§49), *gued* 'good' (§50), *boosom* 'bosom' (§59), *ha* 'have' (§115), *whil* 'until' (§180). A number of western features are listed in §13; the use of *dis* 'these' (§174) is found in both the North and the West. The survival of the verbal prefix *y-* is a feature

317

of the south-western dialects of English, but since it occurs only in Fingallian (§185) it is more probably a survival from Mediæval Hiberno-English than a new introduction.

§225. As well as these specifically northern and western dialectalisms there are a number of features which are widespread in the dialects, and also a number of vulgarisms. It is difficult to distinguish between the two categories : a usage which is respectable when used by the speaker of a regional dialect may be a vulgarism when used by a speaker with some claims to education or social position. General dialect features which seem to have had no currency as vulgarisms are mentioned in §§ 13, 14, 29, 34, 36, 49, 59, 86, 109, 176 and 183. Dialect features which may also be vulgarisms occur almost exclusively in texts later than the 1680's : the lowering of ME *er* to *ar* (§31), the loss of postvocalic /r/ (§102), the use of /w/ for StE /ʍ/ (§112), and the use of the individual words *dem* 'those' (§174), *of* 'on', and *again* 'against' (§212). It seems probable that here we have to do with the effects of the Cromwellian plantations. According to a recent estimate [Corish (1976) 370–3], the confiscated lands had been distributed among some 1,000 adventurers (§166) and 12,000 soldiers; since the English upper classes had been predominantly Royalist, the adventurers were largely of the middle class, and most of the soldiers were of even humbler origin. Certainly it is a striking fact that a high proportion of the vulgarisms in our texts occur in pieces representing or purporting to represent the usage of the landowning classes, *Ballyally Castle* (IX), reflecting a plantation earlier than Cromwell's, and Swift's *Dialogue* (XXVI). As well as the vulgarisms already noticed, these texts include the following vulgarisms which seem never to have had much currency in the dialects : *wale(s)* 'walls', *drae* 'draw' (§54), *comishon, cumishon* 'commission' (§87), *without* 'unless' (§180).

REGIONAL VARIETIES OF HIBERNO-ENGLISH

Introductory

§226. In general terms, then, it can be said that Hiberno-English represents a variety of English which failed to conform in some respects to the contemporary standard, and which had been strongly and continuously influenced by the Irish language. There is no reason to suppose, however, that it was uniform all over the country, and in fact we have already met a number of differences which are almost certainly regional rather than chronological. Now is the time to bring these differences together and to delimit as far as possible the regional varieties which can be distinguished. In Irish there are two major dialect areas, the northern and the southern, divided by a line running roughly from Dublin to Galway [O'Rahilly (1932) 18]. In Hiberno-English, however, it seems that the primary division is between east and west, although (as we shall see below, §§ 229, 230) there is a relationship between the eastern variety of Hiberno-English and northern Irish, and between the western variety of Hiberno-English and southern Irish.

Fingallian

§227. The most easily recognizable variety of Hiberno-English is the dialect of Fingall. Not only have we three texts which explicitly claim to be Fingallian (XI, XIII, XVI), but we also have documentary evidence which enables us to specify certain features as characteristic of the dialect. All the historical sources from the sixteenth century onwards agree that there was a strong likeness between Fingallian and the dialect of the two Wexford baronies— even those sources which go on to observe that the two dialects were not in all respects identical (above, pp. 26–27). We are therefore entitled to assume that features shared with the dialect of Forth as recorded by Barnes (1867) are evidence in favour of a Fingallian origin. Stanihurst tells us (above, §16) that postponed stress in polysyllabic words was a characteristic of the dialect of Forth, and this observation is confirmed by Barnes; though Stanihurst's words leave some doubt whether he is attributing postponed stress to Fingall as well as to the Wexford baronies, its occurrence in our explicitly Fingallian texts makes it effectively certain that he intended to do so. Young tells us (above, p. 27) that the dialect of Fingall was distinguished from that of Forth by having a higher proportion of Irish words and phrases; it is perhaps possible that his phrase "more intermixed with irish in language, &c." refers to syntax as well as to vocabulary. Young's evidence is admittedly more than a generation later than the latest of our texts, but there is no reason to believe that the circumstances he describes were of recent origin. On the basis of historical evidence, then, we can list three characteristics of Fingallian : rare words found also in the dialect of Forth, postponed stress in polysyllabic words, and a high proportion of Irish words and phrases.

§228. All three of our explicitly Fingallian texts contain rare words found also in the dialect of Forth : *Good* 'God' (§37), *'ame*

COLLEGE LIBRARY
CARYSFORT PARK.
BLACKROC

'them' (§177), *ygo* 'gone' (§185). All three have postponed stress
(§19). *The Fingallian Dance* (XI) is very short, and *The Irish
Hudibras* (XVI) has been adapted to the English taste, but *Purgatorium Hibernicum* (XIII) has a high proportion of Irish words
and phrases. However, these are not the only three texts which
display one or more of the Fingallian criteria listed above. *Hic et
Ubique* (XII) agrees with the dialect of Forth in the use of *abow*
'above' (§82), *greyshy* 'ugly' and *guddy hang* 'gallows-bird' (§138);
though the word *donny* 'wretched' is not found in Forth it occurs
in *Purgatorium Hibernicum* as well as in *Hic et Ubique* (§159).
The same text has a number of instances of postponed stress (§19),
and a high proportion of Irish words and phrases (§159 etc.).
Captain Thomas Stukeley (I) has postponed stress (§19) and a high
proportion of Irish words and phrases (§§ 135, 137 etc.). *Ireland
Preserved* (XX) has a few instances of postponed stress (§19), but
none of the other criteria. As we saw in §21, we cannot be sure that
the criteria in question are necessarily limited to Fingallian : in
particular, we cannot exclude the possibility that the English of the
towns may have had something in common with Fingallian. Yet
the fact that the action of *Stukeley* and *Hic et Ubique* takes place
on the borders of Fingall, and the action of two of the scenes from
Ireland Preserved seems to take place actually in Fingall, seems to
make it probable that the crucial features were not very widely
distributed.

Eastern Hiberno-English

§229. The Fingallian dialect is included in a wider dialect area
which for convenience we may call "Eastern Hiberno-English"—
the type of Hiberno-English which shows signs of the influence of a
type of Irish found in parts of the east coast. The characteristics of
this type of Irish are themselves partly a matter of conjecture. The
fronting and raising of CG *á* to /ɛ:/ and the reduction of medial
/d'/ to /j/ are both documented for the Irish of north Leinster
and southern Ulster (§§ 46, 100); since these two features are found
more systematically in Manx Gaelic, it seems reasonable to assume
mutual influence of some kind (pp. 184–5), and to conjecture that
certain Manx developments of the verbal noun may also have taken
place on the eastern seaboard of Ireland (§193), with consequent
effects on the syntax of Hiberno-English (§198). The geographical
limits within which these developments took place remains uncertain. There is no evidence of their extension south of Dublin,

unless we count the use of the spelling *aa* in the dialect of Forth to represent both Ir. *á* (in such words as *coolaan* 'back of the head', Ir. *cúlán*, or *garraane* 'working horse', Ir. *gearrán*) and ME *ā* (in such words as *maake* 'make', *naame* 'name') [Barnes (1867) s.vv.]; it might be more accurate, though less convenient, to refer to "north-eastern Hiberno-English". We have three criteria for eastern Hiberno-English: spellings suggesting the value /ɛ:/ for ME *ā*, spellings suggesting the replacement of medial /dʒ/ by /j/, and a group of syntactic peculiarities; quite a large number of texts display one or more of these three criteria. Replacement of medial /dʒ/ by /j/ is found only in *The Irish Masque* (VI) (§100), though *Stukeley* (I) has /j/ for /d'/ in an Irish word (§161). The only texts which display both of the other two criteria are XII, XIII, XVI and XX, texts which we have already identified as representing Fingallian; it seems, therefore, that Fingallian is central to eastern Hiberno-English, and represents it in its purest form. The texts which display only the representation of ME *ā* by *ai/ay* or *aa* are VI, XIV, XVII, XVIII, XIX, XXIII and XXVII; the texts which display only syntactic and not phonological peculiarities are I, II, XXIV and XXV. Possibly these two groups of texts are distinguished only by the choice of features made by their respective writers for representation. Possibly, on the other hand, they represent two different varieties of eastern Hiberno-English; some clues which might help to localize them are discussed below (§231). Finally, we must add *Teigue and Dermot* (XXI), which displays none of the criteria of eastern Hiberno-English, but is firmly located in Dublin by the nature of its subject-matter.

Western Hiberno-English

§230. Only one other regional variety of Hiberno-English can be distinguished, and it will be convenient to call it "Western Hiberno-English", though it does not constitute so clear-cut a unity as eastern Hiberno-English. Its only positive criterion is the representation of ME *ā* by *au/aw*. In present-day Irish the realization of CG *á* varies according to the quality of neighbouring consonants, but also according to dialect: in general it is fair to say that Munster has [ɑ:], Connacht [a:], and Ulster a variety of sounds ranging from [a:] to [ɛ:]. If we could be sure that the spelling *au/aw* was intended to suggest [ɑ:] rather than [a:], it would suggest a southern origin for the texts in which it occurs; but it is difficult to see how else the sound [a:] could be represented, and the only sound which we can confidently feel is excluded is [ɛ:], the development found in parts of the east coast. To this positive criterion we can add the negative criterion of the absence of the distinctive peculiarities of eastern Hiberno-English. Negative criteria are always unsatisfactory, and especially so in this case, for a number of reasons. We have to allow for the possibility that a given writer would choose to reproduce one peculiarity of Hiberno-English speech and not another. As far as the representation of ME *ā* is concerned, it is important to remember that in eastern Hiberno-English its value was closer than the standard at the beginning of the seventeenth century and more open than the standard by the end of the century (§46); obviously there must have been a time at which it had the same value as the standard, so that no distinctive spelling would be called for. The absence of spellings suggesting /ɛ:/ may merely indicate that the writer himself used this realization of ME *ā*. The texts which use *au/aw* for ME *ā* are *The Honest Whore* (V), *Bog-Witticisms* (XV), *The Twin Rivals* (XIX) and *Ireland Preserved* (XX). The use of *aw* to represent Ir. *á* in loanwords in Swift's *Dialogue* (XXVI) proves nothing about the realization of ME *ā*; at so late a date the most probable value is /e:/. Two of the four texts listed above are listed also as representing eastern Hiberno-English. In *The Twin Rivals* (XIX) the spelling *au* is used in the single word 'take' (§47), beside *aa* in other words; confusion between *aa* and *au* is a possibility, especially in handwriting, but the spelling *tauk(e)* occurs more than once. In *Ireland Preserved* (XX) the position is different: in the first two of the scenes printed here the only spelling for ME *ā* is *aa*; in the third scene both *aa* and *au* occur. Possibly Michelburne was attempting (with some inconsistency) to represent two different varieties of Hiberno-English, the eastern variety in the first two scenes which seem to be set in Fingall, the western variety in the third scene set in Derry. Two more texts presumably also represent western Hiberno-English: Maurice Cuffe, the writer of *Ballyally Castle* (IX), was a native of Co. Clare; the action of *Páirlement Chloinne Tomáis* (X) takes place in Co. Kerry.

Northern features

§231. There remain three phonological features represented in some of our texts which seem properly to belong to Ulster: the survival of ME *ū* without diphthongization as the long vowel /u:/ (§51), the use of spellings suggesting the pronunciation /tʃ/ for initial /s/ (§92), and the lowering of ME *i* and *e* (§§ 29, 31). Lack of diphthongization of ME *ū* is a characteristic of Scottish dialects, and is found in Ulster in areas of Scottish settlement; /tʃ/ for initial palatal *s* is a characteristic of the Irish of south Ulster; lowering of ME *i* and *e* is found in the present-day dialects of Ulster. It is a curious fact that not one of our texts displays more than one of these three features : lack of diphthongization of ME *ū* is found in I, XIV and XIX, /tʃ/ for initial /s/ in XXIII and XXVII, lowering of ME *i* and *e* in XV, XVII, XX, XXI and XXV. In *Ireland Preserved* (XX) the lowering is to be found in the first and third scenes, though not in the second : that is, the lowering is attributed to the dialect of Fingall as well as to that of Derry. All but one of the ten texts showing northern features represent eastern Hiberno-English : two of them (I and XX) are Fingallian; five of them belong to the group of eastern texts which display phonological but not syntactic features (§229), and indeed constitute the major part of it (five out of seven texts); one of the texts (XXI) is located by its subject-matter in Dublin. Henry [(1958) 71, 156–7] cites instances of the lowering of ME *i* and *e* in late mediæval Dublin records, and documents the lowering of ME *e* in the present-day dialects of north Leinster as far south as Dublin. Unfortunately we are not much further towards being able to localize the eastern Hiberno-English texts other than the Fingallian ones; it is perhaps fair to say that the group showing phonological but not syntactic features may have a more northerly tinge than the others, but that is as far as it is safe to go.

Some doubtful cases

§232. There remain a number of texts for the localization of which we have no evidence at all. In *Henry V* (III) Shakespeare's portrait of MacMorrice is no more than a sketch, and it relies mainly on vocabulary and morphology, which give little clue to localization. Though *The Honest Whore* (V) can be identified as representing western Hiberno-English, neither *Old Fortunatus* (IV), which is also by Dekker, nor *The Welsh Embassador* (VII), which may be his work, can be localized at all. Dekker's non-standard spellings, which are rather few, are not very informative; the localization of *The Honest Whore* depends, not on spellings, but on a play on words (v 78–80); if there had been no play on words in *The Honest Whore* we should have been as ignorant of its localization as of that of the other two pieces. Dekker's authorship of

323

The Welsh Embassador cannot be proved, but seems very probable (above, p. 40). Certainly there is nothing in the representation of Hiberno-English to prove a difference of authorship, and there are a few points which suggest a common author : V and VII are the only texts to use the spelling *faat* 'faith' (§53), and the only ones to use the oath *yfaatla* (§131); IV and VII share the idiom *my footes and my toes* (iv 45), *my toes and my feete* (vii 21). It seems reasonable to assume that IV and VII represent the same kind of Hiberno-English as V, and to classify them as belonging to the western group. *Hey for Honesty* (VIII) gives us no clues at all to its localization. In *A Wife Well Managed* (XXII) Mrs Centlivre gives very little indication of pronunciation, relying mainly on a somewhat eccentric use of syntactic features (§§ 210, 214). It is perhaps unrealistic to look for a localization of these later texts, which may reproduce not the old but the new Hiberno-English introduced by the Cromwellian plantations.

Conclusions

§233. In conclusion it may be useful to list the classification of the texts suggested in the above paragraphs.

1. Eastern Hiberno-English.

    (a) Fingallian : *Captain Thomas Stukeley* (I), *The Fingallian Dance* (XI), *Hic et Ubique* (XII), *Purgatorium Hibernicum* (XIII), *The Irish Hudibras* (XVI), *Ireland Preserved*, first two scenes (XX).

    (b) First group, perhaps more northerly : *The Irish Masque* (VI), *The Lancashire Witches* (XIV), *The Irishmen's Prayers* (XVII), Dunton's *Sermon* (XVIII), *The Twin Rivals* (XIX), *The Play is the Plot* (XXIII), *The Brave Irishman* (XXVII).

    (c) Second group : *Sir John Oldcastle* (II), *The Pretender's Exercise* (XXIV), *Muiris O Gormáin* (XXV).

    (d) Dublin : *Teigue and Dermot* (XXI).

2. Western Hiberno-English.

    Old Fortunatus (IV), *The Honest Whore* (V), *The Welsh Embassador* (VII), *Ballyally Castle* (IX), *Páirlement Chloinne Tomáis* (X), *Bog-Witticisms* (XV), *Ireland Preserved*, third scene (XX), Swift's *Dialogue* (XXVI).

3. Unknown.

   Henry V (III), *Hey for Honesty* (VIII), *A Wife Well Managed* (XXII).

SOME FINAL CONSIDERATIONS

Mediæval Hiberno-English

§234. In common with other writers I have somewhat glibly referred (above, pp. 20–29) to the "survival" of Mediæval Hiberno-English in Fingall, in the baronies of Forth and Bargy, and possibly in the towns; it is perhaps worth while pointing out exactly how slender the evidence for any such survival is. It is true that in many of our texts ME (and MHE) *ī* survives undiphthongized as /i:/ (§40); but, since ME (and MHE) *ū* is represented by a diphthong in all but a handful of texts (§51), we cannot assume continuity of development; we have to postulate a re-acquisition of English in the first half of the sixteenth century (§68). Among the consonants, resemblances to developments in Mediæval Hiberno-English are due either to the influence of Irish articulation (§§ 82, 85) or to English dialectal peculiarities (§§ 96, 105, 112). The only phonological feature which suggests continuity (and that only indirectly) is the occurrence of postponed stress in the dialect of Fingall (§§ 16–21). There is no direct evidence of the occurrence of postponed stress in Mediæval Hiberno-English, except in so far as Middle English in general preserved the original stress of words borrowed from Norman French, but its occurrence in the dialect of the Wexford baronies is well documented; because of the wide geographical separation of Fingall and Wexford we are entitled to assume that any linguistic feature common to the two districts probably goes back to the Middle Ages. By the same argument, the words listed in §228 as common to Fingall and Forth may be presumed to have existed in Mediæval Hiberno-English, though the only one which is actually documented is MHE *ham* 'them', Fingallian *'ame*, Forth *aam*. Finally, the word *bodderd* 'deafened' can be assumed on phonological grounds to have survived from Mediæval Hiberno-English (§168); the same preservation of MIr. /ð/ occurs in the dialect of Forth in *butheraan* 'drum', Ir. *bodhrán* [Barnes (1867) 29]. This is not an impressive list of survivals : it conveys the impression, well enough supported by contemporary evidence, that by the end of the fifteenth century the English language was practically extinct in Ireland. In communities which had been bilingual a certain amount of simple English may have survived, as the survival of the pronoun 'them' suggests; it is likely enough, too, that certain colloquial or slang words like *guddy hang* (§138) might have entered the Irish of bilingual communities, only to re-emerge when English was revived or re-acquired; but apart from such minor exceptions it seems beyond a doubt that the Hiberno-English of the seventeenth century reflected an English that had been acquired or re-acquired after the end of the Mediæval period.

Dublin

§235. Despite its importance as the capital city and the gateway from England into Ireland, Dublin has been mentioned only rarely in this study. Only two of our texts are concerned with Dublin, *Hic et Ubique* (XII) and *The Dialogue of Teigue and Dermot* (XXI). In *Hic et Ubique* the Irish servant Patrick speaks a dialect which is plainly Fingallian (above, §229), and it is likely enough that many Dublin servants came from the adjacent rural district of Fingall. *The Dialogue of Teigue and Dermot* belongs to the eighteenth century, and many of its linguistic features are those which became prominent in later Hiberno-English, and reflect the new English introduced by Cromwell. Nevertheless, Dublin may have played an important part in the development of Hiberno-English. It was the centre of government, and an important mercantile centre; Irishmen from all parts of the country, both Irish-speaking and English-speaking, would have had occasion to visit it, and no doubt many of its inhabitants were not Dublin-born. For the early eighteenth century we have documentary evidence in the form of an Irish poem which lists the names of twenty-six Irish scholars with whom the author, Tadhg O Neachtain, had become acquainted in Dublin [O'Rahilly (1912–13)]: ten of them are described as natives of Leinster, six of Connacht, five of Munster, and one of Ulster. There is no reason to doubt the existence of a similarly multi-dialectal society in Dublin in the seventeenth century. The inter-reaction of different varieties of Irish and different varieties of English within a single city might have resulted in a form of language, or perhaps in several forms of language, whose characteristics it would be difficult to predict. Some of the features recorded in our texts which at present seem inexplicable (§219) may perhaps be due to just such a mixture of dialects; some of the texts, too, which cannot be very confidently localized (§232), may reflect the dialect of Dublin.

NOTES ON THE TEXTS

I. *Captain Thomas Stukeley*

The text is taken from the first edition, sig. D3[r]–[D3v]; the black letter of the original is here represented by roman type, the roman type of the original by italic. Lines 9–10, 13–17, 25, 28, 30, 34 and 37–40 were mistakenly printed as verse; the initial capitals of these spurious verse-lines have been silently adjusted, but otherwise the capitalization is that of the original. The British Library copy was reproduced in facsimile by J. S. Farmer, *Tudor Facsimile Texts* (1911); a modernized version of the text was printed by Richard Simpson, *The School of Shakspere* (1878) i 156–268.

11 Saint *Patrick* his cushin] This claim was apparently made by O'Neill when he was in London in 1562. According to Campion, "the courtiers, noting his hautines and barbaritie, devised his stile thus : Oneale the greate, cosyne to Saint Patricke, frend to the Queene of England, enemye to all the worlde besides" [Vossen (1963) 139].

24 *Mack Deawle*] The printer's use of roman type, here reproduced by italic, suggests that he took this phrase for a proper name.

47 the Fewes] Ir. *an Fiodh* 'the wood', the name of a district in south Co. Armagh. *Bealach Mór an Fheadha* was the name of the old main road from Dundalk to Armagh.

49] This line is quoted out of context in *Purgatorium Hibernicum* (p. 53) in the form *Slane lat, Rory Begg*.

II. *Sir John Oldcastle*

I have used the reprint by Simpson and Greg, *Malone Society Reprints* (1908). The scenes printed here correspond to lines 2311–35, 2336–49 and 2191–2209 of that text; because of a dislocation in the first quarto the scenes there appear in the wrong sequence, and the correct sequence has been restored here.

16 an Irish haire] See the note on vii 167–8.

III. *Henry V*

The text is taken from the First Folio, *Histories* p. 78 (second pagination).

IV. *Old Fortunatus*

I have used the admirable edition by Fredson Bowers, *The Dramatic Works of Thomas Dekker* i (Cambridge, 1953) 177–9; the scene printed here corresponds to Act IV, Scene ii in that edition.

8 apple Iohn] 'A kind of apple said to keep two years, and to be in perfection when shrivelled and withered' [*NED*]. Compare the Prince's joke at the expense of Falstaff in *Henry IV* Part II, II iv 4–8 : "the Prince once set a Dish of Apple-Iohns before him, and told him there were fiue more Sir *Iohns* : and, putting off his Hat, said, I will now take my leaue of these sixe drie, round, old-wither'd Knights."

81 Saint *Patrickes* Purgatorie] A punning reference to the famous place of pilgrimage at Lough Derg, which also provided the name *Purgatorium Hibernicum* (XII). Its discovery was described by Stanihurst [Holinshed (1577) f. 16r col. 1] :

> Finally by the especiall direction of God, he founde in the North edge of Vlster a desolate corner, hemmed in rounde, and in the middle thereof a pit, where he reared a Church . . . at the East end of the Churchyards a doore leadeth into a closet of stone lyke a long ouen, which they call S. Patricke hys purgatorye.

V. *The Honest Whore*, Part II

I have again used the edition by Fredson Bowers, *Dramatic Works* ii (Cambridge, 1955). The scenes printed here correspond to Act I, Scene i, Act III, Scene i and Act IV, Scene iii in that edition, pp. 137, 143, 168, 171–2, 179–80.

19 an Irishman cannot abide a fart] This very well-known characteristic of the Irish is also referred to in *The Welsh Embassador* (vii 129). For a very full list of references see Bartley (1954) 31.

35–6 runne at a towsand rings] A reference to the sport in which a rider tried to carry off on the point of his lance a ring suspended from a post.

VI. *The Irish Masque*

I have used the text of Herford and Simpson, *Ben Jonson* vii (Oxford, 1941) 399–403.

63 hish daughter] Lady Frances, daughter of Thomas Earl of Suffolk.

81 a sheamoynshter] An allusion to the sea-monsters which appeared in Jonson's *Masque of Blackness.*

83 a deuoish vit a clowd] Probably an allusion to a scenic device in a masque by Thomas Campion.

115 my little mayshter] Prince Charles, later Charles I.

116 te vfrow, ty daughter] Elizabeth, who earlier in the year 1613 had married the Elector Palatine, claimant to the throne of Bavaria. As the "Winter Queen" she acquired a legendary fame. It was through her that the Hanoverians traced their claim to the throne of England : George I was her grandson.

132 iustish Delounes hant] The justice has not been plausibly identified.

133 my Lo. deputish hant] The Lord Deputy was Sir Arthur Chichester.

145 te rugs] A reference to the hairy fringe at the collar of the Irish cloak; see the frontispiece to this book.

VII. *The Welsh Embassador*

I have used the diplomatic reproduction of the manuscript by Littledale and Greg, *Malone Society Reprints* (1920). The punctuation of the manuscript is scanty and unreliable, and I have therefore normalized the punctuation and capitalization; I have also systematized the scribe's incomplete attempt to use italics for proper names. The scenes printed here correspond to lines 1152–78, 1475–1552 and 2011–45 of the diplomatic text. The play is also printed in Fredson Bowers, *The Dramatic Works of Thomas Dekker* iv (Cambridge, 1961) 313–86; there are some marginal differences of transcription between the two editions.

83–6] Compare the passage from *The Honest Whore* Part II printed above, p. 177.

99–100, 104] These incomprehensible words are presumably intended to suggest the drunkenness of the revellers.

129 But not a fart] See the note on v 19.

167–8 so much haire ons head] English writers were invariably struck by the long hair of the Irish, known as *glibs*, and there are many descriptions of them. The fullest account is provided by Fynes Moryson [Falkiner (1904) 261]:

> The English-Irish for the most part have for many ages had the same attire and apparel with the mere Irish, namely the nourishing of long hair (vulgarly called glibs) which hangs down to the shoulders, hiding the face, so as a malefactor may easily escape with his face covered therewith, or by colouring his hair, and much more by cutting it off, may so alter his countenance as those of his acquaintance shall not know him.

178–9] The manuscript is defective at this point, and the ends of the lines are lost.

VIII. *Hey for Honesty*

The text is taken from the first edition, Act III, Scene i, pp. 21–2. Lines 59–61 are mistakenly printed as verse; the initial capitals of the spurious verse-lines have been silently adjusted. There is a reprint by W. Carew Hazlitt, *Poetical and Dramatic Works of Thomas Randolph* (1875) ii 431–4.

30–32] This kind of pedigree was plainly a standard joke, as a passage in *Sir John Oldcastle* shows [Simpson & Greg (1908) ll. 88–94]:

> *Davy.* Lord shudge, I wooll giue you pale, good suerty.
> 2. *Iudge.* What Bale? what suerties?
> *Davy.* Her coozin ap Ries, ap Euan, ap Morrice, ap Morgan, ap Lluellyn, ap Madoc, ap Meredith, ap Griffen, ap Dauy, ap Owen ap Shinken Shones.
> 2. *Iudge.* Two of the most, sufficient are ynow.
> *Sher[iff].* And't please your Lordship these are all but one.

60 *Brunduca*] Boadicea, queen of the Iceni. A similar corruption of the name is found in the title of Fletcher's play *Bonduca* (1619).

61 *Mall Cutpurse*] Mall or Moll Cutpurse was the nickname given to Mrs Mary Frith, a notorious female who flourished about 1600; she was the subject of Middleton and Dekker's play *The Roaring Girl* (1611). In Butler's *Hudibras* (1663) I ii 368 she is compared, as here, to Joan of Arc.

Long-meg of *Westminster*] The nickname of an earlier virago, about whom a pamphlet was published in 1582 [*NED* s.v. *Meg*[1]]; she too is referred to in *The Roaring Girl.*

79 blerawhee] Welsh *b'le'r ewch chwi?* 'where are you going?'

92 *Bridewell*] Originally the name of a house of correction in London, *Bridewell* became a generic name for a prison.

IX. *The Siege of Ballyally Castle*

I have used the text of Thomas Crofton Croker, *Narratives Illustrative of the Contests in Ireland in 1641 and 1690.* Camden Society O.S. 13 (1841) 16–19.

11 the Queene] Queen Henrietta Maria, at this time active in Ireland in the interest of her husband Charles I.

X. *Páirlement Chloinne Tomáis*

I have used the text of O. J. Bergin, "Páirlement Chloinne Tomáis", *Gadelica* i (Dublin, 1912–13) 148–9. The following is a translation of the passage printed :

It wasn't long before they saw a young Englishman approaching.

"Who's that Englishman who's coming?" said one of them.

"I know him," said another, "he's Robin the tobacco-man, and he usually has good tobacco."

"We'll buy some," said Bernard O Bruic, "but which of us will speak English to him?"

"My own self," said Tomás.

The young Englishman came up, and greeted them politely, and said "God bless you, Thomas, and all your company."

Tomás answered him urbanely, and this is what he said : "Pleshy for you, pleshy, good man Robin."

"By my mother's soul," said Bernard O Bruic, "you swallowed down a fine lot of English."

They all clustered round, wondering at Tomás's English.

"Ask the price of the tobacco," said Bernard.

Tomás spoke, and this is what he said : "What the bigg greate *órdlach* for the what so penny, for is the la yourselfe for me?"

Said Robin : "I know, Thomas, you aske how many enches

is worth the penny," and he raised two fingers as a sign, and said, "two penny an ench."

"By my gossip's hand, that's a good price," said Tomás.

"What's that?" said Diarmuid Dúr.

"An inch for two pennies," said Tomás.

"Make an agreement for us," said everyone.

"I will," said Tomás, and said : "Is ta for meselfe the mony for fart you all my brothers here."

Said Robin : "I thanke you, honest Thomas, you shall command all my tobacco."

"Begog, I thanke you," said Tomás.

At that word Tomás took the tobacco and gave it out to everyone.

XI. *The Fingallian Dance*

The text is taken from MS Sloane 900 in the British Library, f.53r. I have added punctuation and partly normalized the capitalization.

2 Bolring] Most towns and large villages had a bull-ring, used not only for bull-baiting but also for other sports, and (as here) for dancing; it is therefore impossible to localize the text more accurately from this reference.

XII. *Hic et Ubique*

The text is taken from the first edition, pp. 7, 18–19, 32, 46–7, 56–7, 57–8.

17 *Kilphatrick*] Ir. *Giolla Phádraig* 'servant of Patrick'. In earlier times it was considered improper to name a child after a saint. This is why Irish has variant forms of some names : *Seán* 'John', in contrast to *Eoin* '(St) John', *Máire* 'Mary', in contrast to *Muire* '(the Blessed Virgin) Mary'. In the list of names of Irish characters given in §143, *Patrick* is the only saint's name; in this play Patrick refers to himself as *Kilpatrick* not only here but also in lines 68 and 109.

56 your brogues] Apparently an ironic form of address. I have found no other instance of this or of any similar usage.

XIII. *Purgatorium Hibernicum*

The text is taken from MS 470 in the National Library of Ireland, pp. 88–93. This carelessly-written manuscript has required somewhat drastic treatment, as the number of textual footnotes shows. I have supplied punctuation and normalized the eccentric capitalization; I have silently normalized the use of *i/j* and *u/v*, which sometimes follows the mediæval pattern; and I have carried through the scribe's incomplete attempt to use italic script for words of Irish origin. In the textual footnotes colons : : represent illegible letters.

8] *Purgatorium Hibernicum* contains a great many proverbial expressions, some of which differ from the usual form. This variant of the well-known phrase *to cast a sheep's eye* was used also by John Heywood, "To cast a sheep's eye look out of a calf's head" [Farmer (1906) 185]; more to the point, it is used in Swift's *Polite Conversation* : "I have seen him often cast a Sheep's Eye out of a Calve's Head at you" [Davis (1957) 141].

15 *Ful Dea*] Ir. *fuil Dé!* 'God's blood!' The MS reads *Fut Dea*, and it is curious that the same error (*t* for *l*) occurs in the same expression in *Ireland Preserved* (p. 115), where *whit deah* is printed for *whil deah*.

33 vid her beares] I am unable to elucidate the reference to bears.

36] There is no gap in the MS, but it seems clear that something is missing. A proverbial saying in Swift's *Polite Conversation*, "I'll give you my Mother for a Maid" [Davis (1957) 164], suggests that the missing word might be *give*; but the meaning of the couplet remains obscure.

86] I have found no other instance of the proverb in quite this form. Swift's *Polite Conversation* has the more usual form, "an old Ape has an old Eye" [Davis (1957) 149].

104] *Marry, come up!* is a curious but common extension of the interjection *Marry!*, originally *Mary!*; the process is well documented. The oath *by Mary Gipcy!* 'by St Mary of Egypt' was contracted to *Marry gip!*; the element *gip* was associated, no doubt jocosely, with the cry *gip!* (i.e. *gee up!*) addressed to horses; and finally *gip!* was replaced by the synonymous *come up!*

The further extension *my dirty cousin* is even more curious but equally well attested. The complete expression is used by Swift in his *Polite Conversation* [Davis (1957) 180] and by Fielding in his *Tom Jones* [Battestin & Bowers (1974) i 205], and it is included by Ray (1678) and Kelly (1721) in their collections of proverbial sayings. According to Ray it is "spoken by way of taunt, to those who boast themselves of their birth, parentage, and the like";

333

according to Kelly it is "a reprimand to mean people, when they propose a thing that seems too saucy." The meaning most appropriate to the present context is the one given by *EDD*, which records the saying for Cheshire : "an expression used to those who are very fastidious or who assume a distinction to which they have no claim."

XIV. *The Lancashire Witches*

I have used the text of Montague Summers, *The Complete Works of Thomas Shadwell* (1927) iv 160–1. The scene is printed in italics in the original (above, p. 51), with proper names in roman.

47–8] A reminiscence of the proverbial saying *No penny, no Paternoster*, recorded by *NED* [s.v. *penny* 9.g] from 1546 to 1640; it occurs also in *Purgatorium Hibernicum* (p. 37) in the form "Noe penny, faith!, no *Paternoster*." The same idea is expressed in different words in Dunton's *Sermon* (xviii 134–8).

70] At this point Shadwell adds a marginal note "Vide Scott, *Discovery* &c." The reference is to Reginald Scott, *The Discoverie of Witchcraft* (1584) Book II, Chapter vi : "To procure the dissolving of bewitched and constrained love, the partie bewitched must make a jakes of the lovers shooe."

XV. *Bog-Witticisms*

The text is taken from the first edition, pp. 45–50 (second pagination). In the original each line of the Letter begins with an inverted comma.

32 *Tredagh*] An alternative anglicization of Ir. *Droichead Atha* 'Drogheda'. According to Fynes Moryson [Falkiner (1904) 218] Drogheda is "vulgarly called Tredagh."

50 Hole in de Vaal] Perhaps the name of an inn.

63–4] This witticism is versified in *The Irish Hudibras* (p. 95) : "This Fool his Letter Six-pence cost,/To save the charge of Penny-Post." The Penny Post referred to is not, of course, the service introduced by Rowland Hill in January 1840, but the more limited service introduced about 1680 and available only within ten miles of London.

XVI. *The Irish Hudibras*

The text is taken from the first edition, pp. 9–14, 18–20. In the original the speeches are in italics, without inverted commas. Mar-

334

ginal notes in the original, referred to by an asterisk or obelus before the word marked, are here replaced by footnotes, referred to by a superscript number after the word marked : in these footnotes the black-letter type used in the original for Irish words is replaced by small capitals.

4] The same blank occurs at the corresponding points in *Purgatorium Hibernicum* and *The Fingallian Travesty*. If the missing word is *arse* it is difficult to see why it should not have been printed, since it is printed in lines 10 and 74.

14 Wild-gees] An example of the kind of usage which later gave rise to the technical use of *Wild Geese* (above, p. 68).

24 vid finger in my mout] "To go *with your finger in your mouth* is to go on a fool's errand, to go without exactly knowing why you are going—without knowing particulars" [Joyce (1910) 189].

28 take a little] The reference is to snuff. It seems that there must have been an Irish fashion for a kind of Loyal Toast in snuff, since there are several other references in *The Irish Hudibras* in passages which, like this one, were added to the original text : "Take little sneezing for de King" (p. 65), "Joy, vilt dou take a little Snuff,/ For King and Queen? Joy, take enough" (p. 71).

39–44] For the technical terms in this passage see §166.

62 Spunk] "He had a tinder-box with which he stroke fire and lighted his sponke, which is the white film groweing on the lower part of the colts foot leafe, which they peel of, and drying, it becomes verie good tinder" [Dunton (1698) p. 6].

114 Evidaunsh-Place] "Bee Shaint *Patrick* Y vill buy an Evidanshes Plaush, dat may be a Livelyhood for de and Y" [*Bog-Witticisms*, p. 22 (second pagination)].

116 *Dermot o Con-noor*] Dermot O'Connor was a scion of the family of the O'Conor Don. During the wars of the last years of Elizabeth, while he was the leader of the Connacht forces in Munster, he was suborned by the English. Subsequently he supported the Irish cause again, but his authority was now gone. He was captured by an ally of the English and hanged in December 1600 [Falls (1950) 283].

XVII. *The Irishmen's Prayers*
I have used the reprint by H. E. Rollins, *The Pepys Ballads* (Cambridge, 1929–32) v 25–7.

335

Teede] This name seems not to correspond to any Irish name, and I have found no explanation for it.

24 unto de Bogs] Bogs were the traditional refuge of the Irishman when defeated in battle. As *Purgatorium Hibernicum* puts it (p. 3), "Therefore did Nature boggs bestow/To save him from pursueing foe." According to the *Brief Character* [(1692) 56–7], "the *Teigs* do only gaze about to see what Wood or Bog lies nearest, and can best shelter them in their Retreat."

28 de young Prince of *Wailesh*] James Stuart, later known to Jacobites as James III and to Hanoverians as the Old Pretender.

XVIII. *Report of a Sermon*

The text is taken from MS Rawlinson D.71 in the Bodleian Library, pp. 13–14. I have supplied punctuation and capitalization, and italicized the Latin quotations.

33–4 *quod semen mulieris frangeret caput serpentis*] A reminiscence (it can hardly be called a quotation) of *Genesis* iii 15 : "Inimicitias ponam inter te et mulierem, et semen tuum et semen illius : ipsa conteret caput tuum, et tu insidiaberis calcaneo eius."

104–5 prepar'd *pro Satana et eius angelis*] A misquotation of *Matthew* xxv 41 : "qui paratus est diabolo, et angelis eius."

107–9] A somewhat inaccurate quotation of Virgil, *Æneid* vi 126–9 :

> facilis descensus Averno :
> noctes atque dies patet atri ianua Ditis;
> sed revocare gradum superasque evadere ad auras,
> hoc opus, hic labor est.

The same lines are freely translated in *The Irish Hudibras* (p. 22) :

> To go's, as plain as A, B, C;
> But Back's all the Concavity.
> The Way thou easily may'st find,
> But thou'lt return when th' Devil's blind.

115–32] The parable is told in *Luke* xvi 19–31. In the Middle Ages Latin *dives* 'rich (man)' was regularly taken as a proper name *Dives*.

136 pray you out of Purgatory] See the note on xiv 47–8.

139 *teget multitudinem peccatorum*] A misquotation of *I Peter*

iv 8, "charitas operit multitudinem peccatorum"; cf. also *James* v 20, "operiet multitudinem peccatorum."

150–2] The words in square brackets are written so small in the MS that they are illegible; they have been supplied from the Vulgate version.

XIX. *The Twin Rivals*

The text is taken from the first edition, pp. 33–4, 35–6, 48, 51–2.

71 St. *Patrick* and the Wolf-Dogs] The word *Wolf-Dog* presumably reproduces Ir. *faol-chú* 'wolf', in which the second element *cú* means 'dog'. I have been unable to trace the story referred to, but many similar stories are told in some of the lives of St Patrick and recur in folklore.

156 *Bashtile*] The earliest instance cited by *NED* [s.v. *Bastille* 4] of the general meaning 'prison' is dated 1790.

XX. *Ireland Preserved*

The text is taken from the first edition, pp. 15–16, 18–19, 87–8 (second pagination).

79 dy Fadder is a Priest] "The Priests themselves are very poor, and mind nothing but gathering of Goods, and getting of Children. . . . They commonly have their Children succeed them in their Churches, for whose Illegitimation they are dispensed withal" [Eachard (1691) 21].

110 my Teet water] A variant of the familiar phrase *my mouth waters*; *NED* [s.v. *tooth* 8.g] cites instances from 1600 to 1724.

122–5] Plainly a widespread belief, since it is reflected also in the quotation from George Story printed in §145 above.

XXI. *A Dialogue between Teigue and Dermot*

The only known copy of this broadsheet is in the Thorpe Collection in the National Library of Ireland, Volume xii, page 88. It was reproduced in facsimile by the Public Record Office of Northern Ireland, Education Facsimile No. 237.

42–3] Flight was the traditional recourse of the Irishman in time of trouble. In *Purgatorium Hibernicum* (p. 2) the hero Nees is described as

Proud and rebellious, feinte and mighty,
And valiant as e're run from fight he;
For Nees his wings did not apply
To fight or sally, but to fly.

According to the *Brief Character* [(1692) 34] "It is an Irish observation . . . that whenever two Armies meet in *Battle*, the one must
run, for both cannot *conquer*, and since one must give *way*, why
not at the *beginning* before much Bloodshed, rather than after too
many lives are *lost*; and since one of them must, or generally does
run, who fitter to *run* than they whom Nature has provided with
better *Legs* to run, than *Hands* or *Hearts* to *fight*; therefore they
commonly do *run*, and *run* betimes."

48 his Grace] The Duke of Shrewsbury, Lord Lieutenant of Ireland.

XXII. *A Wife Well Managed*

The text is taken from the edition of 1737, pp. 5–8; I have not
been able to see the first edition of 1715.

XXIII. *The Play is the Plot*

The text is taken from the first edition, pp. 38–9, 44–6.

8 *the Fight of* Dumblain] The battle of Sheriffmuir, 13th November
1715.

70–74] This passage is based on an anecdote in *Bog-Witticisms*
(p. 59, second pagination):

> An English Gentleman Travelling from *Corke* to *Waterford*,
> met a Native, of whom he enquired, How many Miles it was
> from *Corke* to *Waterford*? The other considering of it a while,
> at length returned: *Bee Creesht*, Dear Joy, *Y cannot tall dee
> hoow mauny milesh it ish from* Corke *to* Waterford; *bot it ish
> aboot ayteen Milesh from* Wauterford *to* Corke.

XXIV. *The Pretender's Exercise*

The only known copy of this piece is in the Library of Trinity
College, Dublin, Pressmark A. 7. 4, f.120. Near the top of the
second column of the verso (line 41 of the present text) the roman
type is replaced by italic, apart from a few words in roman; here
the italic is replaced by roman, and the words in roman are printed
in italic.

2 *Byrn*] The name *Byrne* is very common in Co. Wicklow.

XXV. *Muiris O Gormáin*

The text is taken from the oldest manuscript, MS Additional 18749 in the British Library, f.94*r* – f.95*r*. I have edited it conservatively, so that many linguistic features of the Irish text remain : accents have been added without notice, but all other alterations are recorded in the textual footnotes. Irish script is here represented by italic type, English script by roman type. The poem has been printed a number of times : David Comyn, "Unpublished Poems of Peadar Ua Doirnín II", *Gaelic Journal* vi (Dublin, 1895–6) 120–3; L. P. Murray, "Poets and Poetry of the Parish of Kilkerley, Haggardstown", *County Louth Archæological Journal* iii (Dundalk, 1912–15) 369–84; Seán de Rís, *Peadar O Doirnín, a Bheatha agus a Shaothar* (Dublin, 1969) 28–9; Breandán O Buachalla, *Peadar O Doirnín: Amhráin* (Dublin, 1969) 51–2. The following is a translation of the poem :

On Tuesday morning as I was going to Drogheda I met the lady on the Turnpike Road; she is the nicest woman I ever met from the day I was born till I saw that jewel; I took her hand as if to say, "Shal Travel vith *bláth na finne*, sweet Joy!" "Yes, *dar* be me oan trath," said she in answer, "Far vill se kal, or feadar shal go?"

Then I answered the lily with the white hands, twice as bright as apple-blossom, and when I realized that the ringleted maiden was a foreign English child I raised my voice : "Me is go to *Draeidheacht Aath*, shal give you a *cárta*, and heartily *fáilte*, Madam, vith *póg!*" She considered my offer and smiled : "Shad is the kas, me Money has None !"

Then I saw a wink coming from the eye like the sun on a cloudless morning, and sooner than the wealth of Marcus and Cæsar I would like her and me to be drinking in company together; I flamed forth in English and said to her, "If him had apron file of the *ór*, the Devil a halfpenny me Let you pay—shal Drink the good ale Whil feather-Cock crow !"

My elegant English pleased the maiden with eyes very like bright stars, and she spoke in a soft voice sweeter than string music : "Fath was you Name, or town was you home?" I answered that perfection of beauty : "Me is Cristan Moresious Goraman *cóir*, I is Very school-Measther; *dar* bi my soulvation shal Carry good favour for you *go deóigh.*"

When we got to the tavern we sat at the table like Paris from Troy and Helen from Greece; I was kissing her and she,

339

like a gleam of light without sorrow, was praising my erudition:
"You is Very fine Cloaths, you is pretty bright proges, you is
Latin vell spoke, and fath me can't Name." But we were
drinking till I fell into a stupor, and divil a bit of use did
Maurice get out of her.

When I came out of my stupor I looked all round the room
where the fair lady was while I was under the table, but I saw
no one who could give me any information but a witless boy
who could not understand my speech. "Did you see fair, fine,
hansome white Lady, that was me Comrady Night Last *aig ól?*"
"She make run away Vith a shantleman brave—Back horse
with race, and Up the *ród mór!*"

The metre of the poem depends on assonance. In each line there
are two assonating words, one in the middle and one at the end;
in each couplet the first three assonating words assonate together;
in each stanza the four couplets have the same assonances. In the
first two stanzas the pattern is *á á á ó*; in the third, fourth and
sixth, *é é é ó*; in the fifth, *ó ó ó é*.

47 a shantleman brave] Apparently O Doirnín himself.

XXVI. *A Dialogue in Hybernian Stile*

The text is taken from my own edition : *A Dialogue in Hybernian
Stile . . . and Irish Eloquence by Jonathan Swift* (Dublin, 1977)
74–5.

41 puckawn] There is ample evidence in Irish folklore that it is
lucky to let a he-goat run with the cows [Bliss (1977) 84–5], but I
have found no precise parallel to the belief implied here that a goat
will improve the yield of milk.

XXVII. *The Brave Irishman*

The text is taken from the first edition, pp. 3–7.

143–55] This passage is based on an anecdote in *Bog-Witticisms*
(p. 36, second pagination) :

A Lady in Covent-Garden demanded of *Donnel* her Footman, which way the Wind sate? He reply'd *Bee Creesht,
Madam, Y cannot tell vhich vay it shits, for it hath chainged
foure or five timesh dish day: Vhen Y vent to* White-hall *in de
morning it vash in mee Faash, and vhen Y came home it vas
in mee Baak; and vhen Y vent to de* Pall-mall, *it vash in mee
Faash; and vhen Y vent to* Lincolnesh-Inn-Fieldsh, *it vash in
mee Baak again: Dee'l tauke mee, Y tinke it shits every vay.*

340

BIBLIOGRAPHY

The Bibliography gives details of all the books cited in this study, and also of a few which I have used but have not found it necessary to cite. Editions later than the first are only included if they contain substantial revisions or additions. The place of publication is London unless otherwise specified.

Adams, G. B., "An Introduction to the Study of Ulster Dialects", *Proceedings of the Royal Irish Academy* lii (Dublin, 1948) 1–26.

Adams, J. Q., "Captain Thomas Stukeley", *Journal of English and Germanic Philology* xv (Illinois, 1916) 107–29.

———— "Hill's List of Early Plays in Manuscript", *The Library* Fourth Series xx (Oxford, 1939) 71–99.

Arber, Edward, *A Transcript of the Register of the Company of Stationers, 1554–1640* (1875–94).

———— *The Term Catalogues* (1903–6).

Baker, D. E., *Biographia Dramatica* (Dublin, 1782).

Ball, F. E., *Howth and its Owners* (Dublin, 1917).

Barnes, William, *A Glossary . . . of the Old Dialect of . . . Forth and Bargy* (1867).

Bartley, J. O., "Bulls and Bog Witticisms", *The Irish Book Lover* (Dublin, November 1947) 59–62.

———— "Dundalk on the Elizabethan Stage", *Tempest's Annual* (Dundalk, 1951).

———— *Teague, Shenkin and Sawney* (Cork, 1954).

Battestin, M. C. and Bowers, Fredson, *The History of Tom Jones, by Henry Fielding* (Oxford, 1974).

Beckett, J. C., *The Making of Modern Ireland, 1603–1923* (1966).

Bentley, G. E., *The Jacobean and Caroline Stage* (Oxford, 1941–68).

Bergin, O. J., "Páirlement Chloinne Tomáis", *Gadelica* i (Dublin, 1912–13) 35–50, 127–31, 137–50, 220–36.

Bliss, A. J., "Languages in Contact: Some Problems of Hiberno-English", *Proceedings of the Royal Irish Academy* lxxii (Dublin, 1972), 63–82.

———— *A Dialogue in Hybernian Stile . . . and Irish Eloquence by Jonathan Swift* (Dublin, 1977).

341

Bowers, Fredson, *The Dramatic Works of Thomas Dekker* (Cambridge, 1953–61).

———— et al., *The Dramatic Works in the Beaumont and Fletcher Canon* (Cambridge, 1966).

A Brief Character of Ireland, With some Observations of the CVSTOMS, &c. of the Meaner Sort of the Natural Inhabitants of that Kingdom (1692).

Burchfield, R. W., *A Supplement to the Oxford English Dictionary, Vol. I A – G* (Oxford, 1972).

Burnet, Gilbert, *History of his Own Time* (1723–34).

Camden, William, *Britannia*. Translated by Philemon Holland (1610).

Chambers, E. K., *The Elizabethan Stage* (Oxford, 1923).

Clarke, Aidan, *The Old English in Ireland 1625–42* (1969).

Comyn, David, "Unpublished Poems of Peadar Ua Doirnín II", *Gaelic Journal* vi (Dublin, 1895–6) 120–3.

Contributions = *Contributions to a Dictionary of the Irish Language*. The Royal Irish Academy (Dublin, 1913–75).

Corish, P. J., "The Cromwellian Regime, 1650–60", in *A New History of Ireland* iii (Oxford, 1976) 353–86.

Croker, T. C., *Narratives Illustrative of the Contests in Ireland in 1641 and 1690*. Camden Society (1841).

Crowne, John, *The Dramatic Works* (Edinburgh, 1874).

Crump, G. M., *Poems on Affairs of State 1685–1688* (New Haven, 1968).

Curtis, Edmond, "The Spoken Languages of Medieval Ireland", *Studies* viii (Dublin, 1919), 234–54.

———— and McDowell, R. B., *Irish Historical Documents 1172–1922* (1943).

Davis, Herbert, *Prose Works of Jonathan Swift* iv (Oxford, 1957).

de Bhaldraithe, Tomás, "Nua-Iasachtaí i nGaeilge Chois Fhairrge", *Eigse* vii (Dublin, 1953–5) 1–34.

———— *The Irish of Cois Fhairrge, Co. Galway*. Revised Edition (Dublin, 1966).

———— Review of Mhac an Fhailigh, *The Irish of Erris*, in *Studia Celtica* v (Cardiff, 1970) 163–5.

de Búrca, Seán, *The Irish of Tourmakeady, Co. Mayo* (Dublin, 1958).

de Rís, Seán, *Peadar O Doirnín, a Bheatha agus a Shaothar* (Dublin, 1969).

Dinneen = Dinneen, P. S., *An Irish-English Dictionary*. Second

Edition (Dublin, 1927).

Dobson, E. J., "Early Modern Standard English", *Transactions of the Philological Society* (Oxford, 1955) 25–54.

——— *English Pronunciation 1500–1700*. Second Edition (Oxford, 1968).

Dolan, T. P. and O Muirithe, Diarmaid, *A Glossary . . . of the Old Dialect of . . . Forth and Bargy* (Wexford, 1979).

Duggan, G. C., *The Stage Irishman* (Dublin, 1937).

Dunton, John, *Letters from Ireland* (1698). Bodleian Library, MS Rawlinson D. 71.

Eachard, Laurence, *An Exact Description of Ireland* (1691).

EDD = The English Dialect Dictionary, edited by Joseph Wright (Oxford, 1896–1905).

Elliott, R. W. V., "Isaac Newton as Phonetician", *Modern Language Review* li (Cambridge, 1954) 5–12.

Falkiner, C. L., *Illustrations of Irish History and Topography* (1904).

Falls, Cyril, *Elizabeth's Irish Wars* (1950).

Farmer, J. S., *The Proverbs, Epigrams, and Miscellanies of John Heywood* (1906).

——— *Captain Thomas Stukeley* (1911).

Flower, Robin, *Catalogue of Irish Manuscripts in the British Museum* ii (1926).

Furnivall, F. J., *Andrew Boorde's Introduction of Knowledge, 1547.* Early English Text Society E.S. v (1870).

G[ainsford], T[homas], *The Glory of England* (1618).

Gilbert, J. T., *A Contemporary History of Affairs in Ireland from 1641 to 1652* (Dublin, 1870).

Greene, David, *The Irish Language* (Dublin, 1966).

——— "The Growth of Palatalization in Irish", *Transactions of the Philological Society* 1973 (Oxford, 1974) 127–36.

Greg, W. W., *Henslowe's Diary* (1904–8).

——— *Dramatic Documents from the Elizabethan Playhouses* (Oxford, 1931).

Gregg, R. J., "Scotch-Irish Urban Speech in Ulster", in *Ulster Dialects: an Introductory Symposium* (Belfast, 1964) 163–92.

Hamilton, H. C., *Calendar of the State Papers Relating to Ireland . . . 1574–1585* (1867).

Hardiman, James, *A Chorographical Description of West or h-Iar Connaught, by Roderic O'Flaherty* (Dublin, 1846).

Hazlitt, W. C., *Poetical and Dramatic Works of Thomas Randolph*

343

(1875).

Henry, P. L., *An Anglo-Irish Dialect of North Roscommon* (Dublin, 1957).

———— "A Linguistic Survey of Ireland : Preliminary Report", *Lochlann* i (Oslo, 1958) 49–208.

Herford, C. H. and Simpson, Percy and Evelyn, *Ben Jonson* (Oxford, 1925–52).

Heuser, W., *Die Kildare-Gedichte* (Bonn, 1904).

Historical Manuscripts Commission, Tenth Report. Appendix, Part V (1885).

Hogan, J. J., *The English Language in Ireland* (Dublin, 1927).

Holinshed, Raphaell, *The Firste Volume of the Chronicles of England, Scotlande, and Irelande* (1577).

Holmberg, Börje, *On the Concept of Standard English and the History of Modern English Pronunciation* (Lund, 1964).

Holthausen, F., *Vices and Virtues*. Early English Text Society O.S. 89 (1888).

Hore, H. F., "Particulars Relative to Wexford and the Barony of Forth : by Colonel Solomon Richards, 1682", *Journal of the Royal Society of Antiquaries* iv (Dublin, 1862–3) 84–92.

Hughes, Charles, *Shakespeare's Europe: Unpublished Chapters of Fynes Moryson's Itinerary* (1903).

Hyde, Douglas, *A Literary History of Ireland* (1899).

Jackson, Kenneth, " 'Common Gaelic' : the Evolution of the Goedelic Languages", *Proceedings of the British Academy* (1951) 71–97.

———— *Contributions to the Study of Manx Phonology* (Edinburgh, 1955).

———— "The Celtic Languages during the Viking Period", *Proceedings of the International Congress of Celtic Studies, 1959* (Dublin, 1962) 3–11.

Jacobs, Joseph, *The Familiar Letters of James Howell* (1892).

Jarrell, M. L., "The Proverbs in Swift's *Polite Conversation*", *Huntington Library Quarterly* xx (San Marino, 1956) 15–38.

Jordan, Richard, *Handbuch der Mittelenglischen Grammatik* (Heidelberg, 1934).

Joyce, P. W., *English as we Speak it in Ireland* (1910).

Judges, A. V., *The Elizabethan Underworld* (1930).

Kavanagh, Peter, *The Irish Theatre* (Tralee, 1946).

Kinsman, R. S., *John Skelton: Poems* (Oxford, 1969).

Kinvig, R. H., *A History of the Isle of Man* (Liverpool, 1950).

344

Kneen, J. J., *A Grammar of the Manx Language* (Oxford, 1931).
Laoide, Seosamh (= Lloyd, J. H.) *Sgéalaidhe Oirghiall* (Dublin, 1905).
————— *Duanaire na Midhe* (Dublin, 1914).
Lawlor, H. J., *The Diary of Archbishop King* (Dublin, 1903).
Lawrence, W. J., *Speeding up Shakespeare* (1937).
Littledale, H., and Greg., W. W., *The Welsh Embassador* (1920).
Lloyd, Bertram, "*The Noble Soldier* and *The Welsh Embassador*", *Review of English Studies* iii (1927) 304–7.
————— "The Authorship of *The Welsh Embassador*", *Review of English Studies* xxi (Oxford, 1945) 192–201.
Lloyd, J. H. (= Laoide, Seosamh), "Mid-Sixteenth-Century Numbers and Phrases", *Eriu* vii (Dublin, 1914) 18–25.
Lowndes, W. T., *The Bibliographer's Manual of English Literature*. Revised by H. G. Bohn (1871).
Luick, Karl, *Untersuchungen zur Englischen Lauteschichte* (Strassburg, 1896).
————— *Historische Grammatik der Englischen Sprache* (Leipzig, 1914–40).
Mac Eoin, Gearóid, "Genitive Forms as Nominatives in Irish", *Zeitschrift für Celtische Philologie* xxxiii (Tübingen, 1974) 58–65.
MacErlean, J. C., *Duanaire Dháibhidh Uí Bhruadair: The Poems of David O Bruadair* (Dublin, 1910–17).
McIntosh, Angus and Samuels, M. S., "Prolegomena to a Study of Mediæval Anglo-Irish", *Medium Ævum* xxxvii (Oxford, 1968) 1–11.
MacLysaght, Edward, *Irish Life in the Seventeenth Century*. Second Edition (Cork, 1950).
Malone, Kemp, "Bonnyclabber", *Celtica* v (Dublin, 1960) 142.
Matheson, Angus, "Some Words from Gaelic Folktales", *Eigse* viii (Dublin, 1956–7) 247–58.
Mayhew, George, *Rage or Raillery: the Swift Manuscripts at the Huntington Library* (San Marino, 1967).
MED = Middle English Dictionary, edited by Hans Kurath, Sherman Kuhn and others (Ann Arbor, 1952—).
Mhac an Fhailigh, Eamonn, *The Irish of Erris, Co. Mayo* (Dublin, 1968).
Miller, Liam and Power, Eileen, *Holinshed's Irish Chronicle* (Dublin, 1979).
M[offet], W[illiam], *Hesperi-neso-graphia: or, a Description of the Western Isle* (1716).

345

Moryson, Fynes, *An Itinerary* (1617).

Mullenaux, Samuel, *A Journal of the Three Months Campaign of His Majesty in Ireland* (1690).

Murphy, Gerard, "Callen o custure me", *Eigse* i (Dublin, 1939–40) 125–9.

———— "English 'Brogue' Meaning 'Irish Accent' ", *Eigse* iii (Dublin, 1941–2) 231–6.

———— "A Folksong Traceable to Elizabethan Times", *Eigse* vii (Dublin, 1953–5) 117–20.

Murray, L. P., "Poets and Poetry of the Parish of Kilkerley, Haggardstown", *County Louth Archæological Journal* iii (Dundalk, 1912–15) 369–84.

NED = *A New English Dictionary on Historical Principles*, edited by Sir James Murray and others (Oxford, 1884–1928). Re-issued in 1933 as *The Oxford English Dictionary*.

O Buachalla, Breandán, *Peadar O Doirnín: Amhráin* (Dublin, 1969).

O Cuív, Brian, *The Irish of West Muskerry, Co. Cork* (Dublin, 1944).

O'Rahilly, T. F., "Irish Scholars in Dublin in the Early Eighteenth Century", *Gadelica* i (Dublin, 1912–13) 156–62.

———— "The Vocative in Modern Irish", *Eriu* ix (Dublin, 1921–3) 85–91.

———— "Notes on Middle-Irish Pronunciation", *Hermathena* xx (Dublin, 1930) 152–95.

———— *Irish Dialects Past and Present* (Dublin, 1932).

O Siadhail, Mícheál and Wigger, Arndt, *Córas Fuaimeanna na Gaeilge* (Dublin, 1975).

Palmer, R. E., *Thomas Whythorne's Speech* (Copenhagen, 1969).

Pender, Séamus, *A Census of Ireland, circa 1659* (Dublin, 1939).

Petty, Sir William, *The Political Anatomy of Ireland* (1691).

Piatt, Donn, *Dialect in East and Mid-Leinster Gaelic Survivals* (Dublin, 1933).

Prendergast, J. P., "The Ulster Creaghts", *Journal of the Royal Society of Antiquaries* iii (Dublin, 1854–5) 420–30.

———— *The Cromwellian Settlement of Ireland* (1865).

Quinn, D. B., " 'A Discourse of Ireland' (circa 1599)", *Proceedings of the Royal Academy* xlvii (Dublin, 1941–2) 151–66.

———— *The Elizabethans and the Irish* (Ithaca, 1966).

Renwick, W. L., *Edmund Spenser, A View of the Present State of Ireland* (1934).

Rhys, Sir John, *The Outlines of the Phonology of Manx Gaelic* (Douglas, 1894).

Risk, Henry, "French Loan-Words in Irish", *Etudes Celtiques* xii (Paris, 1968–71) 585–655, xiv (1974–5) 67–98.

Rollins, H. E., *The Pepys Ballads* (Cambridge, 1929–32).

Sheldon, E. K., *Thomas Sheridan of Smock-Alley* (Princeton, 1967).

Shirley, E. P., "Extracts from the Journal of Thomas Dineley, Esquire", *Journal of the Kilkenny Archæological Society* iv (Dublin, 1856–7) 143–6, 170–88.

Simms, J. F., *Jacobite Ireland 1685–91* (1969).

Simpson, Percy and Greg, W. W., *Sir John Oldcastle* (1908).

Simpson, Richard, *The School of Shakspere* (1878).

SND = The Scottish National Dictionary, edited by William Grant (Edinburgh, 1931–76).

Sommerfelt, Alf, "The Norse Influence on Irish and Scottish Gaelic", *Proceedings of the International Congress of Celtic Studies, 1959* (Dublin, 1962) 73–7.

State Papers: Henry VIII, Vols. II and III (1834).

Stockman, Gerard and Wagner, Heinrich, "Contributions to a Study of Tyrone Irish", *Lochlann* iii (Oslo, 1965) 43–236.

Story, G. W., *A True and Impartial History of the Most Material Occurrences in the Kingdom of Ireland during the Two Last Years* (1691).

Sullivan, J. P., *The Genesis of Hiberno-English: a Socio-historical Account*. Doctoral dissertation, Yeshiva University (New York, 1976).

Summers, Montague, *The Complete Works of Thomas Shadwell* (1927).

Thomson, R. L., "The Syntax of the Verb in Manx Gaelic", *Etudes Celtiques* v (Paris, 1950–51) 260–89.

———— "Svarabhakti and some Associated Changes in Manx", *Celtica* v (Dublin, 1960) 116–26.

———— "The Stressed Vowel Phonemes of a Manx Idiolect", *Celtica* xi (Dublin, 1976) 255–63.

Vossen, A. F., *Two Bokes of the Histories of Ireland, Compiled by Edmunde Campion* (Assen, 1963).

Wagner, Heinrich, "A Linguistic Atlas and Survey of Irish Dialects", *Lochlann* i (Oslo, 1958) 9–48.

———— *Linguistic Atlas and Survey of Irish Dialects* (Dublin, 1958–69).

Weinreich, Uriel, *Languages in Contact: Findings and Problems*

347

(The Hague, 1963).

Wing, Donald, *Short-Title Catalogue 1641–1700* (New York, 1945–51). Second Edition, Vol. I (New York, 1972).

Wood, Anthony à, *Athenæ Oxonienses* (Oxford, 1721).

Wright, Joseph, *The English Dialect Grammar* (Oxford, 1905).

Wyld, H. C., *A History of Modern Colloquial English* (Oxford, 1936).

Young Arthur, *A Tour in Ireland . . . in the Years 1776, 1777, 1778* (1780).

Zettersten, Arne, *The Virtues of Herbs in the Loscombe Manuscript* (Lund, 1967).

GLOSSARIAL INDEX

The Glossarial Index is designed to serve two purposes : on the one hand to list all the non-standard spellings found in the texts; on the other hand to give the meaning of every word or form which might cause difficulty to the reader. To facilitate the first aim, all the non-standard spellings of each word are listed under a single heading; so as not to prejudice the second aim, every form is provided with a cross-reference in its alphabetical place. The entries follow two different patterns corresponding to the two different aims : if a form is merely a spelling-variant of a standard English word (that is, if its abnormality is phonological) it is followed by the sign = and the standard English spelling; if a form represents a non-standard word, or a standard word in an unfamiliar meaning (that is, if its abnormality is morphological or semantic) the meaning is given between quotation marks. Sometimes, of course, there is more than one abnormality in a single form, and in such cases both devices may be used. Occasionally I have found it convenient to use a hypothetical headword, easily recognizable as such from the absence of any line-reference. A few words not forming part of the speech of Irishmen have been included if they might cause difficulty; in such cases the headword is enclosed in square brackets.

The spelling of each form is that of the texts, except that capitalization and the use of *i/j*, *u/v* have been normalized; word-division, which may be significant, is left unchanged, and no attention is paid to it in the alphabeticization. The meaning is normally enclosed between single quotation marks; however, in *The Irish Hudibras* (XVI) some of the words are glossed in the text, and when the meaning given is one of these glosses it is enclosed between double quotation marks. Each form is provided with no more than one line-reference for each text in which it occurs, but if the same form occurs more than once in a text the line-reference is followed by *&c.* : thus the absence of *&c.* shows that the form is isolated and (if it is very unusual) may be due to an error; the presence of *&c.* means that other instances can readily be found if they are needed. If any form is the result of an emendation the line-reference is followed by an asterisk. If a word is of Irish origin the etymon is

349

cited, unless the spelling of the Irish etymon is the same as that of the headword, in which case the word "Irish" is sufficient; if the word is not of Irish origin but may have been influenced in form or meaning by an Irish word, the citation of the Irish word is preceded by *cf.* The numbers between square brackets refer to the paragraphs of the linguistic analysis (pp. 186–326) in which the headword or one of its variant forms is discussed.

a 'of' v 32, vi 87, vii 23. [15]
a 'on' v 16, vi 27, vii 32. [15]
aal, see *aul.*
abateing 'deducting, subtracting' xi 6.
abell = able ix 18 &c. [61]
aboo! boo!, see *ub, ub, ub, boo.*
aboote = about i 36. [51]
abow = above xii 40. [82]
abrode = abroad xix 140. [49]
absolushon = absolution xx 124. [87]
a callagh 'O hag' xiii 97*. Ir. *a chailleach.* [137]
accation = occasion ix 84. [62, 110]
a-ceers = acres xvi 47. [19, 20]
a cree 'my dear' ii 60; *achree* xii 8 &c. Ir. *a chroidhe.* [139]
advansh = advance xxiv 24*, 28; *advanch* xxiv 30. [88, 92]
advies = advice ix 88. [113]
affuction = affection xv 59. [81]
aftar = after ix 10. [61]
after-clapps 'unexpected results' xiii 29.
again 'back' xx 88; 'in return' xxiv 7; 'against' xxvi 2. [183, 212]
a gra 'darling' v 61; *agra* xii 35, xix 142. Ir. *a ghrá(i)dh.* [139]
ahone, see *o hone.*

aig ól 'drinking' xxv 46. Irish. [162]
alarbor 'to larboard' xiii 5. [114]
aldough = although xviii 27 &c. [84]
ale = ail xii 10. [52]
all-dewoureing = all-devouring xviii 62. [82]
allway, see *alwash.*
altard = altered ix 14. [61]
alwash = always xv 60; *allway* xx 93. [52, 94, 182]
a mawhisdeer 'O master' v 61*. Ir. *a mháighistir.* [57, 139] See also *moister.*
'ame 'them' xi 7 &c. [177]
an, see *aund.*
and be = and't be 'if it be, indeed' xii 21, xiii 23 &c., xiv 72; *and bee* vi 143, xiii 85, xiv 65; *an't be* vi 2; *ant be* vi 61; *andt be* vi 72; *ant bee* vi 146. Cf. Ir. *má 'seadh, muise.* [133]
ane, see *aund.*
anodder = another xv 28; *anoder* xviii 29, xx 42; *anoter* vi 148. [84, 109]
anshwerd, see *aunswer.*
ant, see *aund.*
ant be(e), see *and be.*
apple John 'a kind of apple said

350

to keep two years, and to be in perfection when shrivelled and withered' [*NED* s.v.] iv 8.

arra 'indeed' xii 18 &c., xiii 29 &c., xvii 2, xxii 12 &c., xxvii 68 &c.; *arrah* xx 37, xxiii 77 &c., xxvii 33; *arah* xix 38; *arrow* xii 107. Ir. *ara.* [125]

arraball 'soon' xii 23. Ir. *ar ball.* [159]

arrah, see *arra.*

arrands = errands xxii 61. [31]

arrow, see *arra.*

ash = as vi 65 &c., xxiv 23 &c. [94]

ashame 'ashamed' xi 14, xxiv 69. [188]

athorety = authority ix 27. [54, 62]

aufternoons 'afternoon' xv 49. [35, 182]

aul = all xv 12 &c.; *aal* xv 20 &c. [32, 54]

auld = old xix 164. [49]

aund = and xv 12 &c.; *an* xix 109, xxii 12; *ane* i 36; *ant* vi 8 &c.; 'if' vi 3 &c. [34, 107, 114]

aunswer = answer xv 47; *anshwerd* ix 28. [55, 89]

auny = any xv 33. [13, 47]

aut = at xv 50. [34]

avay = away xiii 24. [80]

awn, see *one.*

axell = axle ix 53. [61]

axshept = except xx 98. [63]

baane, see *garron.*

bacoan = bacon xx 8 &c. [19, 20]

bad = bed xx 24. [31]

bagge 'dismissal' xiii 68. [168]

ball 'shouting, uproar' xxi 18. [170]

bandy-shoulder'd xxvii 126. [167]

banesh = banish ix 29. [61]

banniclabber, see *bonny clabber.*

bannoke 'enclosed field' vi 111. Ir. *bánóg.* [161]

bate = beat xx 8. [45]

be = by ii 5, iii 47, vi 8 &c., xi 5, xii 21, xiii 21 &c., xv 8 &c., xix 4 &c., xxiii 61 &c., xxv 7; 'for, on behalf of' vi 58; *bee* i 32, vi 5, vii 22, xiii 25. [15, 40, 212]

be 'are' vi 51, xx 34 &c., xxiii 62; 'who are' xxiv 38; 'is' xx 36 &c.; 'I am' ii 8. [185, 186, 195]

bear = beer xxvi 13. [14]

bear 'coarse barley' xxiv 15.

becash = because vi 91. [36, 54, 94]

bee, see *be.*

beg 'little' i 49. Ir. *beag.* [158]

began 'begun' ix 40. [187]

begog 'by God' x 38. [129]

belching 'expectorating' xiii 91. [168]

belived = believed xiii 53 [59]

beseech'd = besieged iii 46. [98]

beshides = besides xviii 28. [88]

besht = best vi 38*, 71, viii 19 &c. [89]

bettar = better ix 86; *betters and betters* xxiii 65. [61, 182]

beyand = beyond ix 92. [36]

bid 'bade' vii 42. [187]

biggesht = biggest vi 98. [89]

bin = been ix 70, xx 70. [58, 59]

bishness = business xix 144. [94]

351

blaake = black xx 11. [32]
blankead = blanket i 14. [19, 20]
bláth na finne 'flower of beauty' xxv 6. Irish. [162]
blesh = bless i 22 &c., vi 18 &c.; *pleshy* = bless ye x 14. [88, 103, 107]
blowed 'blown' iii 28. [187]
boddah, see *bodeaugh breene*.
bodderd 'deafened' xxvi 3. Cf. Ir. *bodhar* 'deaf'. [168]
bodeaugh 'lout' i 18; *buddogh* xxvi 25. Ir. *bodach*. [137]
bodeaugh breene 'rotten lout' i 9; *boddah breen* v 46; *vodee brane* xxiv 53. Ir. *bodach bréan, (a) bhodaigh bhréin.* [137]
bonny clabber 'thick milk'; *bonny clabbe* vi 92; *bonny clabbo* vii 126; *bony clabber* xii 110, xv 40; *banniclabber* xvi 53. Ir. *bainne clabair.* [151]
boosom = bosom xviii 133. [59]
booygh 'tiny' i 15. Ir. *buidheach.* [100, 161]
borning 'being born' xviii 79. [187]
bot = both xvii 9 &c., xxiii 101; *bote* xix 152 &c. [83]
bot '?' xx 105. [170]
bourying = burying xviii 6. [13]
braave = brave 'fine' xiv 15 &c., xx 143; *brave* xxv 47; *bravest* xix 9. [46]
brane, see *bodeaugh breene*.
brauler a skeal "pox on thy tail" xvi 81 fn. Ir. *breall ar an scéal.* [132, 160]
brave(st), see *braave*.
break 'broken' xii 44. [188]

breen(e), see *bodeaugh breene*.
breesh = breech xiii 84*. [97]
bremston = brimstone xviii 95; *bremstone* xviii 102. [29]
breng = bring xv 63. [29]
bridle 'bridled' xx 112. [188]
bring 'brings' vi 70; *brings* 'bring' ix 22. [186]
broder 'brother' vii 12, xvii 1 &c., xx 67. [84]
brogue 'shoe' xiii 90, xxvii 63; *broge* xxiv 50; *brogue* 'shoes' xx 12 &c.; *broge* xxiv 47; *brogues* xvi 12; *proges* xxv 37*. Ir. *bróg.* [107, 147]
[*brogue*] 'Irish way of speaking' xix 16, xxiii 12 &c., xxvii 62; [*brogue upon your tongue*] xxiii 128. Ir. *bróg* 'shoe'. [148]
buddogh, see *bodeaugh*.
bult = built ix 55 &c. [13]
burne-breech '?' xiii 72. [169]
burrough 'warren' xxvii 21. [167]
buse = abuse xii 30. [63]
but 'than' iv 43. [180]
buttar = butter xv 40. [63]
buttons 'lumps of excrement' xvi 2. [168]
by and preshently 'by-and-by' xii 17. [214]

Caatholick = Catholic xiv 14 &c.; *Cathelick* ix 17; *Catalick* xxiv 12; *Caatholicks* xiv 36 &c.; *Catolicks* xviii 5. [46, 63, 83]
cadaver 'corpse' xviii 7.
caddow 'rough cloak' xxvi 34. Ir. *cadódh.* [157]
call 'calls' iii 47; 'called' xxi 34. [186, 188]

callagh, see *a callagh*.

cangrane 'ugly head' xxvii 32;
  kingrann xxvii 94. Ir. *ceann*
  gránna. [125]

cárta 'quart' xxv 13. Irish. [162]

cashe = case xix 115; *kas* xxv
  16. [48, 88]

casht = cast vi 76. [89]

cashtell = castle vi 78. [63, 89]

cashter-monger = costermonger
  vi 5; [*costermonger*] viii 21.
  [36, 89]

Catalick, see *Caatholick*.

catches 'catch' xxvii 6. [186]

Catolicks, see *Caatholick*.

cauf = calf xv 41. [54]

chaffing 'raging' xiii 61.

chaunce, see *shance*.

cheeld, see *shild*.

chees: by dis chees '?' xiii 70.
  [134]

cheester, see *shister*.

chergeant = sergeant xxvii 2 &c.
  [92]

chister's, see *shister*.

Chreesh, Chrish, Christis, see
  Creesh.

chureeh crave ruagh 'Red
  Branch knight' xii 48*. Ir. (*a*)
  churaidh craobhruaidhe. [159]

clam-peer 'noise' xvi 74; *court
  of clamper* "court of claims"
  xvi 40. Ir. *clampar*. [19, 160,
  166] See also *esta clamper*.

clap 'clapped' xii 45. [188]

clarke = clerk vi 8; *cleark* xii
  91. [31]

cleave 'basket' xxi 17. Ir. *cliabh*.
  [157]

cleere = clear ix 75. [14]

clootough 'deceitful' xxiv 53. Ir.

cliútach. [137]

clot = cloth xx 104. [83]

cloutes 'cloths' v 93.

cloysh = clothes vi 76 &c.;
  cloyshs vi 143. [38, 49, 94,
  115]

coasht = coach xviii 130. Cf.
  Ir. *cóiste*. [97]

coggin = cogging 'deceitful' vii
  137. [105]

cóir 'true, truly' xxv 30. Irish.
  [162]

comandars = commanders ix
  42. [61]

come 'came' vi 65, vii 13. [187]

comishon = commission ix 15;
  cumishon ix 33. [62, 87]

comrady 'comrade' xxv 46; *comrague* 'fellow-rogue' vii 162.
  Cf. Ir. *comrádaidhe*. [48, 163]

conferrmant 'preferment' xv 38.
  [102, 167]

connaugh: in connaugh 'for sale'
  xxvi 28. Ir. *ar ceannach*. [161]

consharning = concerning xv 18
  &c. [31, 88]

conshence = conscience vi 3.
  [87]

conshider = consider xviii 115.
  [88]

consideraation = consideration
  xiv 6. [46]

contradik 'contradiction' xxiv
  44.

conversation 'company' xxvii 71.
  [167]

cooncel = council xiv 51 &c.
  [51]

coow = cow xv 35 &c.; *cowesh*
  vi 119. [51, 94]

cople = couple xv 27. [11]

cornersh = corners vi 102. [94]

corp 'body' xviii 7. Cf. Ir. *corp*. [163]

coshers 'lodges' xxvi 25. Ir. *cóisir* 'banquet'. [157] See also *ycoshere*.

cosht = cost vi 76. [89]

countys 'county' xxiv 5. [182]

cowar = cover; *cowars* xviii 139; *covard* ix 71. [61, 82]

cowesh, see *coow*.

crame = cream xv 40. [42]

cram-ma-cree, see *gra-ma-cree*.

crangore '?' xiii 49. [169]

crates 'houses' xvi 13. Ir. *creat(a)*. [150]

creation 'recreation' xxvii 7. [167]

cree, see *a cree*.

creecrator 'vexation to you!' xxiv 52. Ir. *croidhe cráidhte ort*. [135]

Creesh = Christ vi 20; *Cresh* i 22, vi 22; *Crees* v 2 &c.; *Chreesh* vi 40 &c.; *Chrish* iii 25 &c.; *Creez* iv 39 &c.; *Creeze* iv 21; *Chreeshes* = Christ's vi 1; *Christis* xii 67. [40, 89, 113, 114]

creshes = cresses vi 48. [88]

cristan 'christened' xxv 30. [188]

cro-naan 'song' xvi 78. Ir. *crónán*. [46, 155]

croon = crown xix 116. [51]

cry 'who cry' xxiv 35; *crys* 'who cries' xxiv 34. [195]

cuff 'fisticuffs' xii 74.

culleens 'yokels' xvi 14. Ir. *coilín*. [146]

cumishon, see *comishon*.

cunt—stable = constable xii 47. [114]

curshed = cursed xvii 30 &c. [89]

cushin = cousin i 11; *cushen* xxiii 67. [94]

cut 'cuts' iv 40. [186]

daamask = damask xx 104. [32]

daan, see *den*.

daingeroes = dangerous ix 3. [13, 61]

dan = than xiv 24, xv 25; *den* iv 7, v 59, vii 155, xviii 136 &c.; *ten* vi 34 &c. [14, 84, 109] See also *den*.

dar 'by' xxv 7 &c. Irish. [162]

dare, see *dere*.

dart 'light spear' vii 29 &c. [149]

dat = that iv 18 &c., vii 23 &c., xii 87 &c., xiii 38 &c., xiv 35 &c., xvi 7 &c., xvii 7 &c., xviii 5 &c., xix 74 &c., xx 62 &c., xxi 4 &c., xxii 35, xxiv 10; *daat* xiv 38, xv 15 &c.; *datt* vii 137; *tat* i 22, vi 17 &c.; *dats* = that's xvii 12; *dat's* xxiv 30. [32, 84, 109]

daunceirs = dancers xi 3. [19, 20]

daunsh = dance vi 72 &c.; *daunch* vi 85 &c. [55, 88, 92]

daury = dairy xv 36. [14, 47]

day 'days' xx 112. [182]

de = the i 42, ii 36, iv 7 &c., v 8 &c., vi 38, vii 7 &c., xii 1 &c., xiii 19 &c., xiv 16 &c., xv 9 &c., xvi 15 &c., xvii 3 &c., xviii 5 &c., xix 88, xx 1 &c., xxi 5 &c., xxiii 111, xxiv 5 &c.; *dee* xii 36, xiii 40; *te* vi 1 &c., viii 18 &c. [84, 109, 213] See also *dee*, *dey*.

dear joy 'my friend' xv 46 &c., xvi 5 &c., xix 9 &c., xx 40; *deer joy* xx 23; *dear joy* 'Irishman' xv 61; *dear-joys* xvi 1, xvii 5 &c. [14, 141] See also *joy.*

deat = death xviii 8 &c.; *deat's* xviii 62. [83]

deawle, see *mack deawle.*

debenturers 'holders of debentures' xvi 43. [166]

dee = die xvi 101; *tie* ii 30; *dees* i 28. [40, 107]

dee = thee v 10 &c., vii 10 &c., xii 27 &c., xiii 16 &c., xiv 8 &c., xv 15 &c., xvi 30 &c., xx 53 &c.; 'thou' xv 48, xx 106; *de* v 45 &c., xii 117, xx 77 &c.; *tee* vi 24 &c., viii 62. [15, 84, 109, 175] See also *de, dy.*

deefil, see *divel.*

deel, see *deole.*

deer joy, see *dear joy.*

deevil, see *divel.*

deir = their xviii 20 &c., xx 98 &c., xxi 40; *dere* xiv 45; *der* xvii 7 &c.; *teyr* vi 78 &c.; *ter* vi 12 &c. [84, 109] See also *dere.*

del, see *teale.*

dem = them xiv 45 &c., xviii 49 &c., xix 117, xx 52 &c., xxiv 17 &c.; *tem* vi 100 &c.; *t'em* vi 145; *dem* 'those' xxiv 25 &c.; *them* xxvi 1. [84, 109, 174]

demshelves = themselves xx 63. [84, 88]

den = then iv 40, xiii 67, xiv 33, xvii 5 &c., xviii 68 &c., xx 2

&c.; *dan* xv 43; *daan* xv 18; *ten* vi 45 &c.; *thin* xxi 34 &c. [14, 30, 32, 84, 109] See also *dan.*

deóigh, see *go deóigh.*

deole = devil xii 10; *deel* xix 18 &c. [30, 115] See also *divel.*

deputish = deputy's vi 133. [94]

der, see *deir.*

dere = there v 93, xii 27 &c., xiv 17, xvi 111, xviii 74 &c., xix 11 &c., xx 97 &c., xxiv 1 &c.; *der* i 32, vii 151; *dare* xv 28, xx 20 &c.; *deir* xviii 63; *tere* vi 59 &c., viii 88. [42, 45, 84, 109] See also *deir.*

dereby = thereby xviii 22. [84]

derefore = therefore viii 40. [84]

dese = these xiii 26, xvi 11, xviii 148, xxi 18 &c.; *dis* iv 31, xx 48 &c.; *des* xx 46 &c. [59, 84, 174]

desheas 'deceased' xviii 70. [88, 188]

deshensus = Lat. *descensus* xviii 107*. [88]

deshent = decent xviii 9. [88]

deshire = desire xiv 44. [94]

desiroes = desirous ix 38. [61]

deulmore "great desire" xvi 103 fn. Ir. *dúil mhór.* [160]

deveat = defeat xvii 29. [112]

devoish = device vi 83. [41, 88]

devoure 'devoured' xviii 8. [188]

dewotions = devotions xviii 65. [82]

dey = they xiv 28 &c., xvii 16, xviii 22 &c., xx 128 &c., xxi 12 &c.; *deye* xxi 10; *day* xx 49 &c.; *de* xi 9; *tey* vi 13 &c.;

355

dey'd = they'd xxi 19; *dey'll*
= they'll xvii 37 &c., xx 140;
dey'l xvii 8. [15, 84, 109]
di, see *dy*.
didder = thither iv 46. [84]
didsh = didst vi 26. [88, 114]
die, see *dy*.
dimetrie = diameter ix 85. [11]
dine = thine v 12, vii 18 &c., xii
108, xv 61; *dyne* v 60, xv 25
&c.; *tine* vi 104 &c. [84, 109]
dis = this iv 30 &c., v 31 &c.,
vii 42*, 132, xiii 12 &c., xvi
86 &c., xvii 33, xviii 6 &c., xx
22 &c.; *dish* xv 58, xvii 63,
xix 107 &c.; *tish* vi 3 &c., viii
25; *thish* xix 74. [84, 88, 92]
See also *dese*.
dishtansh = distance xv 56. [88,
89]
dissuade 'persuade' xxvii 154.
[167]
divars = divers ix 89. [61]
divel = devil xviii 94 &c.; *divell*
vi 46; *divill* vii 25; *divil* xxi
19 &c.; *de-vil* xii 21; *deevil*
xv 14 &c.; *deefil* xxiii 103;
tevil xii 91; *tivel* xvii 56; *tivil*
xxiv 5 &c.; *divell's* xviii 137.
[30, 59, 107, 108] See also
deole.
do 'does' xx 33 &c.; 'dost' xx
106. [186]
do', see *dough*.
donny 'wretched, miserable' xii
30, xiii 26. Ir. *donaidhe*. [159]
dose = those xvii 56, xviii 44
&c., xx 62 &c.; *doos* iv 18.
[49, 84]
doshen = dozen vi 71. [94]
dosht = dost xiv 22 &c. [89]

dot = doth xviii 53. [83]
dou = thou xii 91, xiii 15 &c.,
xiv 6 &c., xv 47, xvi 5 &c., xx
3 &c.; *dow* iv 76, v 18 &c.,
vii 83 &c.; *tou* vi 3 &c.; *tow*
v 13 &c., vi 37 &c., vii 73 &c.,
xii 107; *doul't* = thou'lt xvi
26. [54, 84, 109]
dough = though xviii 91; *do'*
xiii 101. [56, 84] See also
garron.
dow '?' ii 8. [170] See also *dou*.
dowres = doors ix 60. [50]
drae = draw ix 1 &c. [54]
dree = dry i 26 &c. [40]
drenk = drink xv 6. [29]
dubell = double ix 67. [61]
dus = thus xvii 61. [84]
dy = thy ii 7, vii 130 &c., xii
2 &c., xiv 12 &c., xv 23 &c.,
xvi 13 &c., xx 4 &c.; *di* iv 40
&c., v 10 &c.; *die* vii 32; *dee*
ii 6 &c., xi 18, xiii 66 &c., xvi
6 &c.; *ty* vi 6 &c., viii 17 &c.;
ti vi 4 &c. [40, 84, 109]
dye 'died' xviii 132. [188]
dyne, see *dine*.
dyselfe = thyself xvi 78. [84,
88, 179]

eart = earth xviii 47 &c. [83]
eder oder 'either' vi 36; *edder
odder* viii 19. [84]
Eerish = Irish xiv 29; *Ierish*
xvii 8 &c. [40]
efry = every xii 122. [108]
egg 'eggs' xx 7 &c. [182]
eight = eighth xviii 149. [83]
eleavent = eleventh xviii 150.
[11, 83]
elementsh = elements vi 101.

356

[88]

[*enches*] = wenches vii 122.

[115]

Englishes 'English' xxiv 20. [182]

entrayt = entreat vi 28. [42]

enuff = enough xviii 23 &c. [11]

esta clamper 'hush your noise' i 17. Ir. *éist do chlampar.* [135] See also *clam-peer.*

estaats = estates xviii 134. [46]

evidaunsh-place 'employment as a professional witness' xvi 114. [88, 146]

evidensh = evidence 'witness' xix 108, xxiii 123. [88, 146]

excamenation = examination ix 31. [11]

exsamen = examine ix 32. [11]

exshepting = excepting xix 10. [88]

eye, see *great eye.*

faace, see *fash.*

faader, see *fader.*

faarme, see *varm.*

faash, see *fash.*

faat, see *fat, fait.*

fader = father xvii 20; *fadder* xx 79 &c.; *faader* xviii 11 &c.; *fa-deer* xvi 94 &c.; *fader's* = father's xii 128, xiii 22; *faders* xii 16 &c.; *fadders* xx 6 &c.; *fadersh* xv 13; *faters* vi 95; *faather's* xiv 14; *faders* = fathers xviii 75; *fadders* xx 84; *fa-deers* xvi 48. [13, 19, 20, 46, 84, 94, 109]

fading, some dance vi 72 &c. [156]

fadow, some dance vi 87. Ir. *fadó* 'long ago'. [156]

fafteen = fifteen xx 7 &c. [29]

fáilte 'welcome' xxv 14. Irish. [162]

faish, see *fash.*

fait = faith xiv 48, xv 21 &c., xvi 51 &c., xx 5 &c., xxiii 61 &c., xxvii 100; *fayt* iv 12 &c., vi 25 &c.; *fat* iv 7 &c.; *faat* v 7*, 10*, 55 &c.; *fate* xiii 88, xvi 36 &c.; *feat* i 11, xii 51 &c.; *feate* i 5; *fet* xix 9 &c.; *fete* xxi 45. [53, 83]

famise = famish ii 30. [96]

fan, see *fen.*

far, see *fere.*

farced, see *forsht.*

farie, see *fery.*

fart '?' x 34. [170]

fash = face iv 30 &c., viii 19, xvi 69, xxiv 63 &c.; *faash* xxvii 70 &c.; *faish* vi 2 &c.; *faysh* vi 121; *faush* xv 23 &c.; *faace* xix 160. [46, 47, 59, 88]

fashilis = Lat. *facilis* xviii 107. [88]

fasht = fast xxi 43. [89]

fat = what xi 8, xiii 17 &c., xvi 63 &c., xix 30 &c., xx 132, xxi 25 &c., xxiii 52 &c., xxiv 1 &c.; *fate* i 3 &c.; *faat* v 28 &c.; *fatt* xxi 1 &c.; *fath* xxv 28 &c.; *fuat* xii 65 &c.; *fuate* xii 10 &c.; *fwat* xviii 29 &c.; *phat* vi 20 &c., xxvii 12 &c.; *phaat* xiv 6 &c.; *vat* ii 49 &c., vi 19, viii 20, xvii 2 &c., xx 128; *vaat* xv 19 &c.; *wat* iv 22; *fwat's* = what's xviii 69. [32, 33, 79, 85, 112, 117] See also *fait.*

fate, see *fat, fait.*

357

faush, see *fash*.
favour 'love-token' xxv 32.
faysh, see *fash*.
fayt, see *fait*.
feadar, see *fether*.
feagh 'look!' i 18. Ir. *féach*.
[135]
feat(e), see *fait, feete*.
feather-cock = weather-cock xxv
24. [108]
feaver = fever xviii 81. [11]
fee, see *ve*.
feend = find xv 20. [40]
feene = fine iv 1 &c. [40]
feete = white i 13 &c.; *feat* i
20; *phoit* vi 11; *phoyt* vi 67.
[40, 41, 79]
feete-liverd = white-livered i 25.
[40, 79]
feeve = five iv 21 &c. [40]
feir, see *fere*.
feisting 'farting' xx 10. [168]
fell, see *vell*.
fen = when xiii 67 &c., xix 81
&c., xx 16 &c., xxiii 50; *fan* i
15 &c.; *fwen* xviii 18 &c.;
ven xvii 19; *vhen* xvii 41; *van*
xv 26; *whin* xxi 22 &c.; *phin*
xxvii 136. [14, 30, 79, 112]
fere = where xix 43, xxi 46,
xxiv 8 &c.; *fer* xxiv 3; *feir* xii
89; *far* xxv 8; *fwere* xviii 50
&c.; *phair* vi 1 &c.; *phare* xiv
17 &c. [42, 79]
fery = very xix 47, xx 28 &c.;
ferry xx 63; *farie* iv 12. [31,
108]
fese = fees xv 52. [11]
fesh = fetch vi 83. [97]
fet, see *fait*.
fether = whither viii 80 &c.;

feadar xxv 8. [29, 79, 84]
fid, see *vid*.
fie, see *fwy*.
fight 'fought' viii 23. [188]
file = fill '-full' xxv 22.
fill, see *vill*.
fineshed = finished ix 87. [61]
firres = fires ix 89. [58]
firsht = first xxiv 19 &c. [89]
fither, see *whedder*.
fo = who i 22; *fwo* xviii 35 &c.;
foo xix 141; *fwom* = whom
xviii 8 &c. [49, 79]
foh!, ejaculation xxi 28. [126]
foile 'frustration' xiii 70*. [168]
fole = whole xix 73, xxiv 52*.
[79]
foo, see *fo*.
footes 'feet' iv 45; *foots* xx 12.
[181]
for 'of' xx 135. [211]
foreces = forces ix 17. [14]
foremarly = formerly ix 37.
[14, 61]
forgeats = forgets i 34. [11]
fornicaation = fornication xiv
62. [46]
forsht = forced xvii 29 &c.;
farced ix 46. [36, 89]
fortiet, see *won-and-fortiet*.
for to 'to' xvi 22 &c. [212]
Franch-man = Frenchmen xx
143. [31, 192]
frawhawns 'bilberries' xxvi 22.
Ir. *fraochán*. [47, 153]
fuat(e), see *fat*.
fuckation 'sexual intercourse' xii
35. [206]
fuillilaloo 'alas!' xii 28; *who-la-
loo* xx 12 &c.; *pulilillew* xxi
57. Ir. **fuililiú, puililiú*. [117,

125]
ful Dea 'God's blood' xiii 15*.
   Ir. fuil Dé. [125]
furthar = further ix 31. [61]
fuy, see fwy.
fwat, see fat.
fwen, see fen.
fwere, see fere.
fwich = which xviii 20 &c.;
   phich vi 1 &c.
fwo(m), see fo.
fwores = whores xviii 124. [79]
fwose = whose xviii 11 &c. [79]
fwy = why xviii 44 &c.; fuy xii
   35; fy xx 22 &c.; fie xxi 42;
   phy xiv 40. [79, 117]

gaallant = gallant xiv 16. [32]
gallinglasse 'heavily armed foot-
   soldier' i 44. Ir. gallóglach.
   [144]
garden, see potatoe-garden.
garron 'horse' vii 127; garran
   xx 111; garranes vi 77*; garrawns xxvi 30; garraane baane
   'white horse' xii 122; garrane
   dough 'black horse' xii 112;
   garon-reagh 'roan horse' xxiii
   93 &c. Ir. gearrán (bán, dubh,
   riabhach). [46, 47, 149]
gar-soon 'boy' xvi 92. Ir. garsún.
   [19, 20, 160]
gave 'give' xiii 80. [186]
gedering = gathering xxi 12.
   [14, 84]
geeven = given xv 63; give iii
   26 &c. [29, 188]
gillore 'in plenty' xvii 52. Ir.
   go leor. [157]
gitt = get xxi 52. [30]
give, see geeven.

gives 'gave' ix 88. [188]
glash = glass xix 161. [88]
glun ta mee 'listen to me' xii
   xii 36*. Ir. (an) gcluin tú
   mé? [159]
go deóigh 'for ever' xxv 32. [162]
Good, see Got.
goon = gun ix 83, xxvii 3 &c.
   [39]
gooses 'geese' xxiv 63. [181]
goot = good vi 106 &c.; gued
   xx 96. [50, 107]
gossip 'friend' xx 1 &c.; gossops
   = gossip's 'godfather's' xii 16,
   xvi 55; goships vi 44. [63,
   88]
Got = God vi 2 &c., xii 78;
   Good xiii 99, xvi 95; Gud xxi
   26; Gotsh = God's vi 27. [37,
   94, 107]
gow = go i 43. [49]
graases, graash(es), see grash.
graat, see grate.
graish, see grash.
gra-ma-cree 'darling' xiii 82;
   cram-ma-cree xvi 29. Ir. grádh
   mo chroidhe 'love of my
   heart'. [139]
granach, see strepoh granach.
granados 'hand-grenades' xvi 54.
granagh 'loathsome' xxiv 53*.
   Ir. gráineach. [137] See also
   strepoh granach.
granfader = grandfather xix 69.
   [84, 114]
grash = grace viii 17 &c., xix
   165; graish vi 25 &c.; graash
   xx 14 &c.; graashes = grace's
   xx 59; graases = graces xxiii
   105; grash a 'thanks to' viii
   42; vith a grash 'please' xxiv

359

31. [46, 59, 88, 214]
grate = great xv 53; *graat* xxiii
59 &c. [42, 45]
great eye "great desire" xvi 103.
Cf. Ir. *súil mhór*. [160]
greyshy = greasy 'ugly' xii 33
&c.; *greisie* xii 120. [42, 94,
138]
grieve 'grieved' xviii 26. [188]
grist 'flattery' xiii 92. [164]
Gud, see *Got*.
guddy hang 'gallows-bird' xii 33
&c. [138]
gued, see *goot*.
[*guesse*] = guests ii 32.

ha, see *hauve*.
haast = haste xx 60. [46]
hacknes '?' xiii 72. [169]
hadgard = haggard 'stack-yard'
ix 92. [11, 165]
haggat, see *slane haggat*.
ham = hem xv 12. [31]
hang 'hung' i 14, xxiv 54. [188]
hang 'hanging' xvi 18. [206]
hant = hand vi 132 &c.; *hawnd*
vii 22 &c. [34, 106]
har = her ix 12 &c. [31]
hash = has viii 41, xvii 41;
hasht = hast vi 107 &c., xx
65. [89, 94]
hate = hath xviii 8 &c. [15, 83]
hauve = have xv 43 &c.; *ha* ii
52; *ha'* vi 138. [15, 47, 115]
hawnd, see *hant*.
hay 'reel' vii 57. [155]
hearts 'heart' xxiv 67. [182]
heelsh = heels vi 118. [94]
heere = hear ix 19. [14]
hees = he's 'he has' i 27.
heet = heed vi 19 &c. [107]

her 'me' ii 30; 'his' viii 24; 'their'
xvii 27. [176]
here'sh = here's vi 35. [94]
hest = hist i 7. [29]
hidder = hither iv 45, vii 21;
heter vi 101. [29, 84, 109]
him 'it' xix 6, xxiv 5; 'you' xxv
22. [176]
himshelf = himself xii 49, xxiv
66. [88]
hindar = hinder ix 58. [61]
hish = his vi 9 &c., viii 43, xx
14; *ish* xxiv 55 &c. [94, 115]
hobby 'pony' v 20. [149]
hobby-horse 'pony' v 20; 'buffoon' v 94. [149]
Hollen = Holland (linen) v 84.
[114]
holly = holy xviii 20 &c. [59]
hollyness = holiness xviii 61. [59]
hon(e), see *o hone*.
honesht = honest vi 105 &c.;
honesh vi 122. [89, 114]
honny 'darling' xxii 78. [141]
hoondrad, see *hundret*.
hoose = house i 29*, xix 159.
[51]
horsh = horse xxiv 35 &c. [89]
housh-kepin = house-keeping xv
44. [88, 105]
hub (*hub*), *hub-bub-boo*, see *ub*,
ub, ub, boo.
huckes = hooks ix 61. [58]
huckle-backs 'humps' xxvii 127.
[167]
[*hum*] 'double ale' vii 100.
humbuggs 'hoaxes' xxvii 137.
[168]
hundret = hundred vi 129;
hoondrad xv 57. [39, 63, 107]

360

Ierish, see *Eerish*.
ifaatla, see *yfaat*.
ilse = else xxi 56. [30]
imbasheters = ambassadors vi
  10 &c. [63, 88, 107]
imploys 'occupations, trades' xvii
  8.
inclinaation = inclination xx
  117. [46]
Ingaland = England xvii 53;
  Ingalands = England's xvii
  38 &c. [64]
Ingalish = English xvii 3 &c.
  [64]
Irisman = Irishman ii 11 &c.
  [96]
ish = is i 22, iii 25 &c., vi 1 &c.,
  xix 11 &c., xxiv 9 &c.; 'it is'
  iii 61, vi 29; 'are' xxiv 29;
  ishe '(who) is' i 22; *is* 'I am' ii
  11 &c.; 'am' xxv 31; 'are' iii
  50, xxiv 25, xxvi 1; 'have' xxv
  37 &c.; *ishn't* = isn't xxvii 12
  &c.; *isht* = is't vi 147. [94,
  186, 195, 196] See also *hish*.
it 'her' xiii 30; 'me' xvi 98 &c.
  [176]
it shelf = itself xix 74. [88]

jaakes = jakes 'privy' xiv 71.
  [46]
jeast = jest xiii 77. [11]
Jesuite 'Jesuits' xx 135. [182]
joy 'my friend' xii 65 &c., xiv 6
  &c., xvi 29, xx v &c., xxiii 54
  &c., xxv 6, xxvii 115. [141]
  See also *dear joy*.
justish = justice vi 132. [88]

kal = call xxv 8. [48]
kana 'whelp' i 25. Ir. *cana*. [137]

kanave, see *knave*.
kara ma gus 'I place my foot'
  vii 109*. Ir. *cuirim mo chos*.
  [156]
kas, see *cashe*.
kepin, see *housh-kepin*.
kerne '(company of) lightly-
  armed foot-soldiers' i 44. Ir.
  ceithearn. [144]
kill 'killing' xii 65; *kil* xii 69.
  [206]
kind 'mode of action' xii 19.
kindnesh = kindness xix 164.
  [88]
kingrann, see *cangrane*.
kish = kiss xv 22 &c., xix 94;
  kishes xv 57. [89]
knave: kanave = knave ii 9;
  knavesh vi 123. [94, 104]
kno = know i 5; *no* xxiv 26 &c.;
  know 'knowest' xiii 87; *know'd*
  'knew' xix 46. [56, 104, 186,
  187]
knoke 'knocked' vi 65. [188]
know('d), see *kno*.
knuckle-bones 'huckle-bones, hip-
  bones' xx 55. [167]

la, ejaculation iv 22 &c., v 7 &c.,
  vii 10 &c.; *law* iii 25 &c. [130,
  131] See also *yfaat*.
laat, see *slane lets*.
lamb 'lambs' xx 75. [182]
laubour = labour xx 98. [47]
law, see *la*.
lee = lie n. xix 85 &c. [40]
lee = lie v. i 29, xix 122; *lyesht*
  = liest vi 37 &c. [40, 89]
leef = life xi 18, xvi 8. [40]
leek(e), see *lick*.
leetell, see *lettle*.

361

lesar = lesser ix 75. [61]
lest = least ix 7. [58]
lethar = leather ix 86. [61]
letheren = leathern ix 22. [64]
lets, see *slane lets*.
lett 'emitted' vii 130. Cf. Ir.
leigim. [164]
lettle = little i 15; *leetell* ix 86.
[29]
leufter '? vagrant' ii 12. [170]
leursuh 'by this book' xxi 40.
Ir. (*dar an*) *leabhar so*. [127]
levars = levers ix 56. [61]
lick = like ix 65 &c.; *leeke* vi
74; *leek* xii 43. [40, 58]
lickwaies = likewise ix 44 &c.
[58]
lift = left *n.* xxiv 22*, 26 &c.
[30]
lift = left *v.* xxi 37. [30]
like 'likest' vi 142. [186]
lish = lice viii 40 &c. [88]
livein = living xv 44. [105]
loate = loth vii 18. [83]
lofe = love xv 14. [108]
lond = land viii 63. [34]
long = along (with) xxiv 57.
[63]
looky = look ye xii 49. [103]
loough, see *lough*.
lort = lord ii 55. [107]
losh = loss xvii 28. [88]
love 'loves' iv 41. [186]
lough 'lake' xviii 95; *loough*
xxvi 18. Ir. *loch*. [157]
lowar = lower ix 60 &c. [61]
luck = look ix 13. [58]
ludging = lodging ii 29. [37]
lyesht, see *lee*.

maade, see *mad*.

maak = make xiv 8 &c.; *maake*
xix 110, xx 2 &c.; *mauke* xv
7 &c.; *make* 'made' xiii 30,
xxiv 39 &c.; *maaking* =
making xx 83; *mauking* xv 23
&c. [46, 47, 188]
maatre, see *matre*.
mack deawle 'son of a devil' i
24. Ir. *mac diabhail*. [137]
mad = made ix 52 &c.; *maade*
xxiii 72; *made* 'that made'
xviii 51. [46, 58, 195]
maddor 'wooden cup' xxvi 33.
Ir. *meadar*. [154]
made, see *mad*.
magnifies 'signifies' xxvii 13 &c.
[167]
maishter, see *mester*.
make, see *maak*.
mak-keer = maker xvi 16. [19,
20]
manam a dioule 'my soul to the
Devil' xii 120; *monomundioul*
xxvii 5 &c. Ir. *m'anam do'n
Diabhal*. [125]
mans 'man' xxiv 66; 'men' xx
69 &c.; *mens* 'men' xxiv 54
&c. [181, 182]
marafastot 'a curse on you' i 24;
marragh frofat v 46. Ir.
marbhthásc ort. [135]
Mash = Mass xx 93 &c. [88]
matre = matter xv 19; *maatre*
xv 19. [32, 63]
maure = mare xv 42. [47]
mauke, mauking, see *maak*.
mawhisdeer, see *a mawhisdeer*.
mawrry'd = married xv 51;
mawrried xv 54. [13, 47]
mayesty = majesty vi 56 &c.;
mayesties vi 4 &c. [98, 100]

mayshter(s), see mester.
me = my ii 20 &c., vi 4 &c., xi
5, xii 21, xiii 37 &c., xv 8 &c.,
xix 4 &c., xxiii 61 &c., xxv 7;
mee vi 5, xiii 28 &c., xvi 8 &c.
[15, 40]
me 'I' xii 115, xxv 16 &c.; mees
= me is 'I am' ii 22; me is
xxv 13 &c. [175]
measther, see school-measther.
meddoag 'dagger' xviii 83. Ir.
meadóg. [149]
meditaation = meditation xiv
6. [46]
mee(s), see me.
meeself = myself xvi 103; my
shelf 'I' xii 22 &c., xx 3 &c.,
xxiv 24 &c.; 'me' xii 9 &c.,
xxiv 30 &c.; my self 'I' xx 25.
[40, 88, 179]
mens, see mans.
meshage = message vi 12. [88]
mester = master ii 5 &c., iv 19;
maistre xxii 36 &c.; mayshter
vi 115; maishter xix 4 &c.;
maishter's xix 143; maishters
xix 138; mayshters vi 71 &c.
[13, 52, 89]
[metheglin] 'spiced mead' vii 93
&c. Welsh meddyglyn 'medi-
cinal liquor'.
meyning = meaning xii 87. [42,
43]
michear = micher 'thief' xii 39;
micheer xii 121; micharr xx
v. [19, 20, 63, 102]
min = men xxi 23. [30]
mine 'my' xv 13.
minstar = minister ix 47; minishteers = minister's xx 129.
Cf. Ir. ministir, ministéar. [19,

20, 61, 62, 89]
mi-ra-cles = miracles xvi 71.
mistresh = mistress vi 23 &c.
[88]
moccage 'mockery' xvi 76.
moddar = mother xv 25; mothar ix 12; mooder xviii 16
&c.; moddarsh = mother's xv
12 &c.; moders vii 161. [39,
59, 84]
moidore 'piece of gold' xxii 12
&c.
moister 'master' xii 30 &c.; moistere xii 1; moistare xii 8 &c.;
moyster xii 68 &c. Ir. máighistir. [19, 20, 57, 159] See also
a mawhisdeer.
Monaghan 'clown' xxvi 32;
Monaghans xvi 60. [138]
monomundioul, see manam a
dioule.
mont = month 'months' xx 126.
[83, 182]
mooder, see moddar.
moor 'great' xxiii 64. Ir. mór.
[158] See also deulmore, ród
mór.
mothar, see moddar.
mout = mouth vi 47, xvi 24
&c., xviii 63; moute xviii 99;
mouthsh vi 12. [83, 94]
moutfull = mouthful xviii 126.
[83]
mouthsh, see mout.
moynshter, see sheamoynshter.
moyster, see moister.
muck 'pigs' xx 31; mucke xx 46.
Ir. muc, pl. muca. [161]
mulaghane 'buttermilk cheese'
xii 111. Ir. mulchán. [152]
[mum] 'German beer' vii 100.

363

mush = much vi 67 &c., xii 17, xx 104. [97]

musht = must vi 85, xv 28. [89]

my shelf, myself, see meeself.

naam = name xix 30 &c. [46]

nailesh = nails xvii 27. [94]

narsum 'arse' xii 45. [178]

nashion = nation xxiv 52. [87]

neare, see neere.

neder noder 'neither' vi 35; nedder nodder viii 17. [59, 84]

neere = near ix 83; neare 'nearer' xiii 87. [13]

ner = never vi 80. [115]

never 'ever' xxvii 135. [184]

newesh = news vi 60. [94]

niff 'an if' xxi 7.

no 'not' xii 115, xiii 18; 'any' xxii 60, xxvii 104. [184]

noggans 'quarter-pints' xxiii 54. Cf. Ir. naigín, noigín, ScG. noigean.

none 'no' viii 23, xv 55; 'any' xviii 25. [184] See also nown.

noow = now xv 26 &c.; noo xix 89. [51]

nor 'than' xviii 48. [180]

Nort = North xx 97. [83]

nosh = nose viii 21. [94]

noting = nothing xii 108, xviii 69, xix 65 &c.; notinge vii 96. [83]

nott = note 'tune' ix 13. [58]

now 'indeed' xxii 13 &c. Cf. Ir. anois. [164]

nown 'own': my nown xix 10; di none iv 32 &c.; his nown xxiii 103; him nown self 'he' xix 46. [178, 179]

nyes: dy nyes = thine eyes vii 132. [178]

o' = on vi 65. [15]

oan, see one.

occupaation = occupation xviii 13. [46]

ochone, see o hone.

oder = other vii 7, xviii 76; odder viii 62; oders xx 66. [59, 84] See also eder oder.

of 'on' xxii 60. [212]

o hone 'alas!' xvi 97; ohone xviii 63; oh hone xxvii 92 &c.; oh, oh, hon xix 60; oh! oh! hone xxi 3 &c.; ochone xviii 35; ahone ii 60 &c. Ir. ochón. [125]

ól, see aig ól.

on 'of' vi 90, xvi 84, xxiv 69; on's 'of his' xiii 11; on't 'of it' xxvii 22. [212] See also von.

one = own vi 55, xviii 13 &c.; awn xv 19; oan xxv 7*. [56]

one = on ix 54 &c. [11]

oord, see vord.

oore = our i 44. [51]

oot = out i 4; oote i 14 &c. [51]

ór 'gold' xxv 22. Irish. [162]

órdlach 'inch' x 22. Irish. [162]

outtar = outer ix 48. [61]

ovare = over i 10; ovar ix 71. [19, 20, 61]

owe, ejaculation i 2. [126]

owercome = overcome xviii 66. [82]

owns 'own' xx 2. [182]

o yea 'indeed' xii 8 &c.; o yei xxi 26. Ir. ó dhe. [125]

oyster 'gob of phlegm' xiii 91. [168]

364

paage = page xxiii 50. [46]

pace, see *peash.*

Padeen 'Patrick' xvi 27. Ir. *Páidín.*

pail = pale xiii 10. [46]

paishtry-cooks = pastry-cook's xix 13. [46, 88]

par-doon = pardon xvi 91. [19, 20]

parentsh = parents xv 53. [88]

parson = person xxiii 132*. [31]

pashes 'fragments' viii 27. [168]

pauper = paper xv 58. [47]

Payle = Pale vi 55. [46]

payt = pate vi 65. [46]

pearsh = pears vi 48. [94]

peash = peace vi 14 &c., xxiii 132; *pace* xxi 7. [45, 88]

peece 'gun' ix 22 &c.

peek-man = pikeman xii 33. [40]

peep = pipe i 45; *peepe* vi 136. [40]

peepin = pippin iv 23; *peepins* iv 2 &c. [29]

peeps 'pippins' iv 2 &c.; *peep'sh* vi 6; *peepsh* vi 48. [29]

pelly = belly v 3. [107]

penny-posht = penny-post xv 64. [84]

peoples 'people' xviii 62, xx 135. [181]

performsh 'performance' xvi 104. [95]

pet 'favourite' xxvi 7. Cf. Ir. *peata.* [164]

peternell = petronel ix 99. [64]

pewritan = puritan ix 5. [11]

phaat, see *fat.*

phair, phare, see *fere.*

phat, see *fat.*

phich, see *fwich.*

phin, see *fen.*

phip a Dunboyne = whip of Dunboyne vi 87. [79, 155]

phipping = whipping xxvii 13. [79]

phipt = whipped xxvii 8. [79]

phit, see *vid.*

phoit, see *feete.*

phoo, see *phugh.*

phoyle, see *whil.*

phoyt, see *feete.*

phugh, ejaculation xxvii 132; *pugh* xxvii 150; *phoo* xxvii 162. [126]

phy, see *fwy.*

pic-ture = picture xvi 68. [19, 20]

pieceish = pieces xix 116. [94]

pishfork = pitchfork xii 37 &c. [97]

pishtol = pistol xii 80. [89]

plaace, see *plash.*

plaagues = plagues xx 70. [46]

plaas(e), plaash(e), see *plash.*

plaat = plate xx 107. [46]

plack 'farthing' xvi 19. Cf. Ir. *plaic.*

plack-keet = placket xi 9*. [19, 20]

plash = place viii 18, xvii 13, xxiv 22; *plashe* xxiv 9; *plaash* xx 66 &c., xxvii 2; *plaashe* xiv 45; *plaas* xxiii 74; *plaase* xix 9; *plaace* xviii 6 &c., *plauce* xv 38. [32, 34, 59, 88]

plawgy = plaguy xx 109. [47]

pleash = please vi 49 &c., viii 17. [94]

pleshy, see *blesh.*

ploud = blood viii 22. [50, 107]

podyes = bodies 'body' xii 122.

365

[107, 182]
poge 'kiss' xiii 80; *póg* xxv 14.
Ir. *póg*. [161, 162]
poiet = poet xviii 109. [11]
pole bushell '?' xiii 102. [169]
pome water 'large juicy apple'
iv 8, vii 29; *pomwater'sh* vi 6.
[94]
pon = upon xii 122, xxiv 21 &c.,
23*; '*pon* xxii 28 &c. [63]
See also *upon*.
ponds = bonds xii 89. [107]
porks 'pigs' xiii 57.
porsh = porch vi 135. [97]
port-mantel 'portmanteau' xix 4
&c.
posh = pox viii 41. [88, 115]
postpond 'kept waiting' xvi 42.
[166]
potatoe-garden 'potato field'
xxvii 18. [165]
pottados = potatoes xvi 53. [111]
poul = poll xxi 2. [56]
powthar = powder ix 104. [61,
86]
praie dee, see *predee*.
pray-ere = prayer xvi 6. [19, 20]
preashing = preaching xxiii 95.
[97]
predee = prithee v 78, xiv 33
&c.; *pre dee* vi 31 &c.; *pred-
dee* v 84; *predy* v 57; *preddy*
v 72; *priddy* vii 32 &c.; *praie
dee* xiii 79*; *pretee* vi 120 &c.;
pre tee vi 23 &c., 72*; *pray
tee* vi 126. [52, 84, 109]
preed = breed viii 43. [107]
preeson, see *prishon*.
preez, see *prishe*.
prefarment = preferment xxiii
87. [31]

preshance = presence xx 59. [94]
preshently = presently xii 17.
[94]
preserve = preserve vi 101. [94]
presht = priest xv 29. [89]
pretee, pre tee, priddy, see
predee.
priest 'priest's' xx 35. [182]
prishe = price vi 78; *preez* iv 24.
[40, 88, 113]
prishon = prison xii 129, xix
154; *preeson* xxiii 130. Cf. Ir.
príosún. [29, 94]
prishoner = prisoner xix 139;
prishoners i 41. [94]
prittle and prattle 'idle chatter'
viii 22.
proges, see *brogue*.
prood = proud i 26. [51]
puckawn 'he-goat' xxvi 41. Ir.
pocán. [47, 161]
pugh, see *phugh*.
pulilillew, see *fuillilaloo*.
purchas 'robbery' xx 101.
purposh = purpose viii 23. [88]
[*purr*] 'water cider' vii 99.

[*Q:*] 'cue' vii 89.
Quaakers = Quakers xx 132 &c.
[46]
quar-teer = quarter xvi 32. [19,
20]
quarters 'hind-quarters' xviii 132.

rac-keet = racket xi 12. [19, 20]
raison = reason xx 54. [42]
rapparees 'guerrillas' xx 95. Ir.
rapairí pl. [145]
rascalls 'rascal' vii 137. [182]
rauvish = ravish n. xx 100. [13,
47]

366

reader = reader ix 19. [61]
ready "mony" xvi 19. [168]
reagh, see garron.
rebelsh = rebels vi 123. [94]
recovar = recover ix 102; recovard ix 48. [61]
recreaations = recreations xviii
23. [46]
reet = right 'true' iv 9. [40]
relashon 'relations' xx 65 &c.;
relashons xxiii 66 &c. [87, 182]
relishion = religion xxiv 11. [98]
reprisal 'compensation' xvi 39.
[166]
reshted = wrested xviii 62. [89]
restord 'reinstated' xvi 39. [166]
revell = reveal ix 43. [58]
rhoo 'indeed' xii 10. Ir. arú. [125]
rid 'rode' xx 111. [187]
rish = rich vi 127. [97]
ro 'sweetheart' xiii 15. Ir. rogha
'choice'. [139, 141]
rob 'robbed' ii 21. [188]
ród mór 'highroad' xxv 48. Irish.
[162]
rogges = rogues ix 5. [58]
roon 'darling' xvii 1. Ir. (a)
rú(i)n. [139]
rosted '? arrested' xiii 100. [168]
ruffe = roof ix 60. [58]
rumbel 'ramble, make one's way'
ix 34.
runne 'ran' vii 6; run ix 54,
xxvii 91. [187]
ruscaan 'bark vessel' xx 4. Ir.
rúscán. [46, 153]

sa, sa', see shave.
saam, see shame.
sacrifize = sacrifice xx 119. [113]
sadle 'saddled' xx 112. [188]

sall = shall i 9 &c., viii 40 &c.,
xx 75; shaul xv 55; shal
'I shall' xxv 6, 'you shall' xxv
24; salt = shalt xx 40; shaut
xv 47. [15, 54, 96, 101]
salvation, see shalwashion.
say 'says' iv 12. [186]
sayk, see shake.
says I 'I said' xxvii 140. [186]
scape = escape xviii 96. [63]
school-measther = schoolmaster
xxv 31. [13, 52, 85]
scrashtee 'sluggard' xxiv 52. Ir.
(a) scraiste. [137]
scriboner = scrivener xii 86;
scribner xii 86; skrivishner xv
7; skriviwnar xv 48. [11, 82]
se '?' xxv 8. [170]
seed = side i 8 &c.; sid ix 98.
[40, 58]
seep = sheep xx 31 &c.; seeps
xviii 121. [96, 181]
sendes 'send' ix 23. [186]
sent, see shaint.
serve 'served' vii 6. [188]
shaad 'louse' xx 10. Ir. sead.
[33, 137]
shaak, see shake.
shad = sad xviii 24 &c., xxv 16.
[88]
shaddle = saddle xii 16. [88]
shadness = sadness xviii 31. [88]
shaine = chain ii 7. [97]
shaint = saint xv 32, xvii 21
&c.; sent ii 52. [52, 88]
shake = sake xii 67; shaak xiv
66; sayk vi 1; shakes v 71.
[46, 88]
shal, see sall.
shalwashion = salvation xv 21
&c.; soulvation xxv 31; soul-

wation xii 121; *shoulvation* xxii 35; *shoulvaation* xiv 56. [46, 48, 82, 87, 88, 91]

shamber = chamber xx 20 &c. [97]

shame = same xviii 72; *saam* xix 38, xxiii 100. [46, 88]

shampion = champion xviii 53. [97]

shamrokes = shamrocks vi 47. Ir. *seamróg.* [157]

shance = chance xiii 65; *chaunce* xvi 83. [55, 97]

shantleman, see *shentleman.*

shapter = chapter xviii 1 &c. [97]

sharge = charge xii 46 &c., xx 133. [97]

sharity = charity xviii 139. [97]

sharvish, see *shervish.*

sha, sha 'yes, yes' xii 25. Ir. *'seadh, 'seadh.* [159]

shat = shot xxi 36. [36]

shaul, shaut, see *sall.*

shave = save vi 40 &c., xv 64; *sa* v 2, vii 25 &c.; *sa'* iii 48 &c., vi 138; *shaved* xx 73. [88, 115]

shaw, see *shee.*

shay = say vi 20 &c., xiv 26 &c., xvii 17 &c.; *shaysht* = sayest vi 19; *shaying* = saying xvii 32. [88, 89]

sheamoynshter = sea-monster vi 81. [38, 49, 88, 89]

sheas = seas vi 75. [88]

sheat = cheat xii 98 &c., xvii 30, xviii 81; *sheate* xviii 67; *sheats* xviii 125. [97]

shecretary = secretary i 5. [88]

shee = see vi 24 &c., xiv 43,

xviii 5 &c., xix 159, 160*; *shaw* = saw xviii 28; *sheeing* = seeing xviii 31 &c.; *sheen* = seen xiv 41, xix 9. [88]

sheed = seed xviii 32. [88]

sheeing, see *shee.*

sheek = seek xvii 20. [88]

sheeks = cheeks xii 127. [97]

sheen, see *shee.*

sheet, see *shit.*

sheif = chief xvii 43. [97]

sheild, see *shild.*

shelf = self xii 2 &c., xix 51 &c., xx 3 &c., xxiv 24 &c. *shelfe* vi 31 &c., xv 18 &c., xx 45; *shelves* = selves vi 128, xv 38, xviii 26. [88]

shell = sell xv 38. [88]

sheltar = shelter ix 94; *sheltars* ix 93. [61]

shelves, see *shelf.*

shempiterna = Lat. *sempiterna* xviii 37. [88]

shend = send xv 9 &c., xviii 19; *shent* = sent xix 140. [88]

shentleman = gentleman xix 35 &c., xx 78, xxvii 38 &c.; *shantleman* xxv 47; *shentleman's* xxvii 7; *shentlemens* xxiv 19 &c. [31, 88, 181]

shentry = gentry xvii 35. [98]

sherimony = ceremony xv 29. [88]

sherpent's = serpent's xviii 33. [88]

shervants = servants xviii 122 &c., xix 138. [88]

sherve = serve vi 4, xviii 71 &c.; *sherv'd* xx 61. [88]

shervish = service vi 41, xix 29; *sharvish* xv 58. [31, 88]

368

Shesuits = Jesuits xvii 51. [98]
shet = set xv 44. [88]
shick = sick xvii 25. [88]
shickness = sickness xviii 82. [88]
shild = child xii 19 &c.; *sheild* xviii 11; *cheeld* xvi 6 &c.; *shildrens* xx 119. [40, 97, 181]
shillela 'oaken cudgel' xxvii 48. Ir. *Síol Ealaigh*, place-name. [149]
shilly = silly xviii 21. [88]
shilver = silver xviii 129. [88]
shine = sign xviii 142. [88]
shing = sing xv 39. [88]
shinkeing = sinking xviii 42. [88]
shinners = sinners xviii 101. [88]
shins = sins xviii 140 &c. [88]
shister = sister xviii 84; *cheester* xxiii 106; *chister's* xxvii 122. [29, 88, 92]
shir = sir xxvii 53 &c. [88]
shit = sit vi 135 &c., xx 55, xxiv 14; *sheet* v 7 &c.; *shit* 'sat' vi 146. [29, 88, 188] See also *shweet*.
shitty = city xix 11; *shity* xxiii 70. [88]
shivil = civil xix 148, xxvii 41 &c. [88]
shixe = six vi 29; *shix* xix 13. [88]
shixpensh = sixpence xv 63. [88]
shmell = smell xix 12. [89]
sho = so vi 70, xiv 71, xv 14 &c. [88]
shoakeing = choking xviii 104. [97]

shoak't = choked xviii 99; *shoaked* xviii 101. [97]
shoh 'take turn and turn' xxvi 27. Ir. *seach*. [157]
shole, see *shoul*.
sholl de crow 'get hanged!' vii 179; *shulecrogh* viii 80; *shoole a crogh* xii 120. Ir. *siubhail go croich!* [135]
shome = some vi 41, xiv 22 &c., xviii 145; *shom* 'some' xv 7. [88]
shommers = summer's xiv 24. [88]
shons = sons xxvii 44. [88]
shoole a crogh, see *sholl de crow*.
shore = sore xxvii 76. [88]
shorrow = sorrow xvii 54. [88]
short = sort xxvii 41. Cf. Ir. *seort*. [88]
shoul = soul xv 9 &c., xvi 95, xix 35 &c., xx 73, xxi 1 &c., xxii 13 &c., xxiv 15, xxvii 1 &c.; *shoule* xiv 23 &c., xix 4 &c.; *shole* xi 5; *sole* xiii 22; *shouls* xviii 113; *shoules* xiv 41. [56, 88, 91]
shoul-deer = shoulder xvi 98; *shouldar* xx 11. [19, 20, 63]
shoule, see *shoul*.
shoulvaation, see *shalwashion*.
shpeake = speak vi 13 &c.; *speake* 'spoke' vii 11; *spaake* xx 63; *spoke* 'spoken' xxv 38. [46, 89, 187]
shpend = spend vi 119. [89]
shquires = squires vi 68. [89]
shtay = stay vi 136. [89]
shubshects, see *supjack*.
shucking = sucking xx 31. [88]
shud = should xxi 40 &c. [11]

shuffer = suffer xix 139. [88]

shulecrogh, see *sholl de crow.*

shuperasque = Lat. *superasque* xviii 108. [87]

shure = sure xviii 23; *shurely* xxi 11. [87]

shurt = shirt i 13. [13]

shuttene = shutting i 37. [105]

shweet = sweet vi 2 &c., xv 11 &c., xix 137, xx 58*; *shit* viii 17 &c.; *suit* xiii 37*. [59, 89]

shwering = swearing ix 2. [58, 89]

sid, see *seed.*

siegne = sign i 3 &c.; *sieegne* i 30. [40]

sirreverence 'lump of excrement' xiv 72. [168]

skeal 'story, news' xvi 24. Ir. *scéal.* [160] See also *brauler a skeal.*

skeene 'knife' vii 133; *skean* xii 74; [*skein*] xx 118; *skenes* ix 2. Ir. *scian.* [149]

skrivishner, skriviwnar, see *scriboner.*

slane haggat 'farewell!' i 48*. Ir. *slán agat.* [135]

slane lets 'farewell!' i 49*; *slawne laat* v 45*. Ir. *slán leat(sa).* [33, 47, 135]

slats = slates xvii 55. [59]

[*smoke*] 'take note of' xxvii 36. [168]

smuddering = smothering xviii 104. [84]

snuffe 'fit of passion' xiii 63. [168]

soldering, see *soujer.*

sole, see *shoul.*

solidity 'good judgment' xiv 37.

sonar = sooner ix 40. [59, 61]

sougare, see *soujer.*

sougawn, see *suggain.*

soujer = soldier xii 22; *sougare* xii 32; *souldars* ix 7; *soldering* xvi 113. [19, 20, 56, 63, 101]

sould = sold xxiii 97. [49]

souldars, see *soujer.*

soulvation, soulwation, see *shalwashion.*

sound 'sounds' iii 26. [186]

sow 'siege engine' ix 49 &c.; *sowes* ix 21 &c.

sowins 'flummery' xxvi 21. Ir. *súghán.* [153]

spaake 'speech' xx 14 &c.; *spake* xxi 29. [45, 165] See also *shpeake.*

spalpeen 'itinerant labourer' xxvii 6; *spawlpeen* xxvi 32; *spalpeens* xxvii 16 &c. Ir. *spailpín.* [146]

speake, see *shpeake.*

spee = spy xi 5. [40]

spereen "despair" xvi 83. [135]

spice 'slight touch' xiii 56.

spleece = splice 'split' xiii 98. [40, 132, 168]

spoke, see *shpeake.*

spunk 'tinder' xvi 62. Cf. Ir. *sponnc.*

starfing = starving xii 127. [108]

stawnd = stand 'stood' vii 21. [34, 188]

stirabout 'porridge' xxvi 21. [153]

stockins = stockings xx 57. [105]

stout 'haughty' xiii 108.

strangullion 'urinary infection' xiii 56*.

strapp 'whore' xiii 3. [137]

streepo 'whore' i 33. Ir. *strío-pach*. [137] See also *strepoh granach*.

strengt = strength xviii 54; *strent* xviii 61. [83, 105]

strepoh granach 'loathsome whore' xii 127. Ir. *stríopach ghráineach*. [137]

stroke '?' ix 68. [170]

sturdy 'intractable' xiii 108.

suggain 'straw-rope' xiii 14*; *sougawn* 'straw saddle' xxvi 31. Ir. *súgán*. [46, 47, 157]

suit-heart = sweetheart xiii 37*. [59, 89, 140]

sumen = summon ix 25. [61]

supjack = subject xii 9; *shub-shects* vi 52 &c. [31, 88, 98, 107, 114]

sush = such vi 129. [97]

swoop, swoop, ejaculation xiii 97. [126]

ta 'it is' xii 25. Ir. *tá*. [159]

ta '?' x 33. [170]

taak = take xiv 16 &c., xviii 114; *taake* xx 7 &c.; *tayk* vi 20 : *tayke* vi 46; *tauke* xv 5 &c., xix 18 &c.; *taaken* xx 116. [46, 47]

taalk = talk xiv 22; *taaking* xix 117. [47, 54]

tail, see *tayle.*

tall = tell xv 22, xxi 8. [31]

tanke = thank vi 30. [83]

tat, see *dat.*

tauble = table xx 104. [47]

taught(s), see *tink, tought.*

tauke, tayk(e), see *taak.*

tayle = tale vi 30; *tail* xvi 81; *tayles* vi 124. [46]

te, see *de.*

Teague 'Irishman' xxiii 30. Ir. *Tadhg.* [143]

teale = deal iv 28, vii 159; *del* xv 25. [59, 107]

tee, see *dee.*

teef(e), see *tief.*

teem = time xvi 32. [40]

teere = dear iv 13. [14, 107]

teet = teeth vii 130, xx 110. [83]

tell = till ix 62. [29]

tell 'told' vii 13. [188]

tells 'tell' xxvii 2. [186]

tem, t'em, see *dem.*

ten, see *dan, den.*

ter, see *deir.*

tere, see *dere.*

tevil, see *divel.*

tey, see *dey.*

teyr, see *deir.*

them, see *dem.*

thin, see *den.*

thirteen 'thirteenth' xx 110. [183]

thish, see *dis.*

thoo, see *dou.*

thorrow 'through' xxvii 8.

thraash = thresh xx 27. [14, 32]

ti, see *dy.*

tie, see *dee.*

tief = thief xxiii 55, xxiv 7 &c.; *teefe* vii 179; *teef* xvi 7; *tiefs* xxiv 63 &c. [83, 137, 181]

tiff 'cheap liquor' xv 41. [168]

till 'so that' xxvi 37. [180]

timbar = timber ix 53 &c. [61]

tinck, see *tink.*

tine, see *dine.*

ting = thing xv 33, xvi 72, xviii 68 &c., xix 38, xx 33 &c.; *tyng* v 3; *tings* viii 42, xii 108,

xviii 51 &c., xxiv 25 &c. [83]
tink = think xiii 64, xv 18, xvii
28, xx 93, xxiii 54; *tinke* vi
68 &c., xviii 35 &c.; *tinck*
vii 143; *tinksh* vi 69; *tinking*
xxi 31; *tought* = thought xix
146, xx 138; *taught* xxi 10 &c.
[56, 83, 88]
tish = 'tis i 25, iii 25 &c., xix
82 &c.; *'tish* xix 18. [94] See
also *dis.*
tivel, tivil, see *divel.*
toback 'tobacco' xvi 20. Cf. Ir.
tobac. [163]
toder = tother v 9, xx 25. [84]
togedder = together xv 28;
togeder xx 32, xxi 18; *togadder* xv 45. [31, 84]
too, see *dou.*
toone = town i 10 &c. [51]
tory 'guerrilla' vii 88*, xiii 75;
tories 'members of the Tory
party' xxi 13. Ir. *tóraidhe.*
[145]
tou, tow, see *dou.*
touch 'short period' xiii 31.
touch 'touched' v 38. [188]
tought = thought xiii 27, xvi
84; *toughts* xviii 138; *taughts*
xxi 5. [56, 83] See also *tink.*
Toulsill = Tholsel xxi 30. [56,
63]
tousand = thousand vi 129,
viii 89, xviii 80; *towsand* v 36,
vi 77, vii 14. [83]
trat, see *trote.*
tree = three i 40 &c., iv 23, v
65, vi 58, xv 34, xviii 22, xx
126 &c., xxiii 54. [83]
trew, see *t'rough, trow.*
tro = trow xvi 81. [56] See

also *trote, t'rough.*
troate = throat i 30; *trote* ii 6;
troat xix 132; *troats* xxi 40.
[83] See also *trote.*
troo, see *t'rough.*
trooparr = trooper xx 6 &c. [63,
102]
troops 'troop' xxiv 15. [182]
trooses, see *trouzes.*
trote = troth vi 5 &c., xiii 101;
trot xiv 42 &c.; *troate* xx 71;
tro ii 28; *trat* iv 9 &c.; *trath*
xxv 7. [38, 83, 115] See also
troate.
t'rough = through vi 110; *troo*
xix 161; *tro* xx 85; *trew* xxi
36. [11, 83]
trouzes 'close-fitting trousers' i
13; *trouses* xvi 12; *trooses* vii
32 &c. Ir. *triús.* [51, 147]
trow = throw xx 9; *trew* =
threw xxi 33; *trown* = thrown
xviii 94. [83]
trush = trust vi 7. [88, 114]
trust = thrust vii 132, xviii 26
&c. [83]
trut = truth xx 141. [83]
tuck = took ix 97. [58]
tuggemi 'I understand it' xii 25.
Ir. *tuigim é.* [159]
tunder = thunder xvii 47. [83]
turd = third i 42, xviii 1 &c.
[14, 83]
turne 'return' iv 71. [167]
[*twig*] 'look at' xxvii 35. [168]
ty, see *dy.*
tyng, see *ting.*

ub = up xxiv 14. [111]
ub, ub, ub, boo 'alas!' xii 107;
ubbo bo-boo xxiii 116; *aboo!*

372

boo! xiv 69; *hub-bub-boo* xx
12 &c.; *who-bub-boo* xx 83;
hub, bub, bub, bu xxii 11; *hub!*
hub! hub! hub! xxiv 33; *hub*
hub xxiv 34; *hub* xxiv 35 &c.
Ir. *obó.* [125]
[*udcocks*] = woodcocks vii 121.
[115]
uf, uf, ejaculation xix 11. [126]
undoo 'undone' ii 22. [188]
unhapely = unhappily ix 36.
[62]
untel = until xv 41. [29]
[*untrusse*] 'undress' ii 17.
unvordy = unworthy xiii 74.
[80, 84]
unwell 'sick' xxvi 6. [165]
upjack = object xii 9. [31, 107,
114]
upon 'in' xii 80; 'to' xv 9; 'for'
xii 108; *pon* xxiv 51. [211]
urship's, see *vorship.*
ush = us vi 65 &c., xvii 30, xxi
56. [88]
usquebagh 'whiskey' vi 93;
usque bah vii 96; *usquebah*
xv 13, xvi 64; *usquebaugh*
xxiii 54 &c.; [*usqua*] vii 97.
Ir. *uisce beathadh.* [154]

vaaking = waking xv 16. [46,
80]
vaal, see *vall.*
vaat, see *fat.*
vaaterman = waterman xv 63;
waaterman xv 10. [13, 32, 80]
vagge = wag xiii 67*. [80]
vaiter, see *vater.*
vall = wall i 18, xxiv 17; *vaal*
xv 50; *val* xxiv 68; *wale* ix 62;
valls sg. xxiv 23*, 27; *vals* xxiv

60; *valles* pl. i 10 &c.; *vales*
xiii 69; *valls* xx 140; *wales* ix
66. [32, 54, 80, 182]
van, see *fen, von.*
vare = ware 'wares' vi 28. [80,
182]
varm = warm xiii 64; *faarme*
xx 28 &c. [35, 80, 108]
varrant = warrant vi 31 &c. [80]
vars = wars xix 71. [80]
vas = was xiii 17 &c., xvi 82,
xviii 21 &c., xxi 35 &c.; 'is'
xxiv 19 &c.; *vash* vi 55 &c.,
xv 13; 'were' xxiv 3; *was*
'were' ix 54, xxi 51; 'is' xxv
28. [80, 94, 186, 188]
vat, see *fat.*
vatch = watch xiii 69. [80]
vater = water i 7 &c., vi 110;
vayter vi 48 &c.; *vaiter* xii 89
&c.; *va-teer* xvi 93 &c.; *wattar* ix 95; *watar* ix 102; *vaters*
sg. xxiv 18 &c. [13, 19, 20,
46, 61, 80, 182]
vay = way vi 24, xvii 57, xxiv
64; *vays* sg. xxiv 64. [80, 102]
vayter, see *vater.*
ve = we vi 69, xiii 38 &c., xvii
2 &c., xxi 20; *vee* xv 35 &c.,
xxi 32 &c.; *fee* xx 2. [80, 108]
veare = wear; *vweare* xviii 129;
veares vi 98. [80]
vearse = verse xviii 2 &c. [31]
veary = weary vi 148. [80]
vedding = wedding vi 73, xv
13 &c. [80]
vee, see *ve.*
vel, see *vell.*
velcome = welcome vi 126. [80]
vell = well xiii 85, xvi 82 &c.,
xvii 36, xxiv 13 &c., xxv 38;

vel xiii 84; *vwell* xviii 86; *vwel* xviii 126; *fell* xx 41 &c. [80, 108]

ven, see *fen*.

vench = wench xiii 12 &c. [80]

vent = went xiii 24*, xix 87, xxi 12 &c.; *vwent* xviii 130; *wint* xxi 30. [30, 80]

vere = were vi 74, xxiv 24 &c.; *weare* vii 160. [11, 80]

very 'true, genuine' xxv 31.

Vfrow = Frau vi 116. [112]

vhen, see *fen*.

vhile, see *whil*.

vid = with xii 91, xiii 33, xv 6 &c., xvi 24 &c., xxi 29 &c., xxiv 67; *vit* vi 13 &c.; *vith* xix 87, xxiv 31, xxv 6 &c.; *wid* v 8, xii 37 &c., xvii 10, xviii 34 &c., xx 23 &c.; *wit* xii 20, xix 166; *wyd* i 33; *fid* xx 3; *phit* vi 11 &c. [80, 84, 108, 109, 211]

viddout, see *vidout*.

vidin = within 'in' xvi 96. [80, 84, 212]

vidout = without xv 32, xvi 23 &c.; *viddout* xv 51; *widout* xx 122 &c. [80, 84]

vil, see *vill*, *vilt*.

vild = wild vi 75, viii 20, xxiv 63. [80]

vile, see *whil*.

vill = will *n.* xiii 24. [80]

vill = will *v.* vi 41 &c., viii 42, xiii 40 &c., xiv 8 &c., xv 21 &c., xvi 17 &c., xvii 4 &c., xx 126 &c., xxi 52 &c., xxiv 53 &c., xxv 8; *vil* vi 110 &c., xii 122*, xix 43, xxiv 55; *vwill* xviii 93 &c.; *fill* xx 2 &c.; *fell*

xx 71 &c.; *vill* 'shall' xiv 23 &c.; *vil* xiv 27. [29, 80, 108, 186]

vilt = wilt vi 7, viii 80 &c., xiv 52 &c., xv 48; *vil* xvi 5; *vill* xvi 28, xx 128; *will* xvi 10; *wut* v 13 &c., 21*. [14, 80, 101, 186]

vin = win xxi 11. [80]

vind = wind xvi 77; *vindsh* vi 100. [80, 94]

virmine = vermin vii 148. [30]

viry 'Mary!' xxiv 52. Ir. (*a*) *Mhuire*. [125]

vit, see *vid*.

vodee, see *bodeaugh breene*.

voman = woman xiii 76, xv 27, xviii 19 &c.; *womands* = woman's xiv 70; *womans* 'women' xx 101 &c. [80, 114, 181]

von = one xvii 11, xxiv 10 &c.; *van* xxi 23 &c.; *won* xviii 64 &c.; *on* xv 28. [36, 59, 80]

vonder = wonder xiii 101. [80]

vonse = once xxvii 108. [80]

vont = wont xvi 82. [80]

vord = word xx 138; *oord* xiv 57; *wort* vi 9; *vords* sg. xxiv 20. [80, 107, 115, 182]

vork = work xx 140. [80]

vorld = world xviii 19 &c. [80]

vorship = worship xviii 40; *urship's* xxiii 104. [80, 115]

vorsht = worst vi 40. [80, 89]

vort = worth xiii 102; *woort* xviii 21; *wort* xx 36. [80, 83, 214]

vould = would xiv 44, xviii 25 &c.; *voud* xvi 84, xvii 56, xviii 30 &c., xxi 11; *vou'd* xxi

374

17; *vud* xvii 22. [80]
vrite = write xv 7. [80]
vud, see *vould*.
vulgus 'common people' xviii 10.
vweare, see *veare*.
vwell, see *vell*.
vwent, see *vent*.
vwicked = wicked xviii 92. [80]
vwill, see *vill*.
vysher, see *weeze*.

waacancy = vacancy xx 72 &c. [46, 82]
waaterman, see *vaaterman*.
wal(e), see *vall*.
wardars = warders 'men on duty' ix 32. [61]
warding 'keeping guard' ix 26.
ware 'take care' xx 89.
warrant 'authority by inheritance' xxvi 19. [164]
was, see *vas*.
wat, see *fat*.
wattar, see *vater*.
weare, see *vere*.
weef = wife xi 15, xii 36 &c. [40]
wees me ? = woe is me ii 20. [49]
weeze = wise i 12; *vysher* = wiser xv 55. [40, 80, 94, 110]
what for 'what kind of' xxii 6. [214]
whedder = whether vii 140; *fither* xix 149. [30, 79, 84]
whil = while 'until' xxv 24; *vile* 'while' xv 6; *vhile* xvii 21 &c.; *phoyle* vi 146. [41, 79, 112, 180]
who-bub-boo, see *ub, ub, ub, boo*.

who-la-loo, see *fuillilaloo*.
whome 'who' ix 42 &c. [174]
wia = Lat. *via* xviii 78. [82]
wickes = weeks ix 35. [58]
wid, see *vid*.
widdraw = withdraw xviii 143. [84]
widout, see *vidout*.
will, see *vilt*.
wit, see *vid*.
witæ = Lat. *vitæ* xviii 78. [82]
without 'unless' xxvi 36. [180]
witnesh = witness xv 30. [88]
woman(d)s, see *voman*.
won-and-fortiet = one-and-fortieth xviii 1. [59, 83]
woordy = worthy 'worthily' xviii 14. [39, 59, 84, 183]
woort, see *vort*.
wort, see *vord*.
wut, see *vilt*.
wyd, see *vid*.

ycome 'come' xvi 23. [185]
ycoshere 'lodge' xvi 31. Ir. *cóisir* 'banquet'. [157, 185] See also *coshers*.
y-cree 'cry' xi 11. [40, 185]
yea 'yes' xii 54. See also *o yea*.
year 'years' xx 88. [182]
yei, see *o yea*.
yerrou 'oh!' xxi 4. Ir. *dhera*. [125]
yesh = yes vi 30, xix 33, xxvii 44. [88]
yfaat = i' faith v 36, vii 18 &c.; *yfaat la* v 29 &c.; *yfaatla* vii 10 &c.; *ifaatla* vii 95. [33, 130, 131]
yfeel 'feel' xvi 100. [185]
ygo 'gone' xvi 23. [185]

375

yknows '(who) knows' xvi 34. [185, 195]

y-make 'make' xi 12. [185]

yoalk 'centre, heart' xiii 57.

yong = young xv 27. [11]

you 'your' xxv 28. [175]

your shelf = yourself xix 51; *your shelfe* 'you' xx 45; *your-*
shelves 'you' xviii 26 &c. [88, 179]

y-rore 'roar' xi 11. [185]

y-yore 'old times' xi 10. [185]

zee 'I' i 32 &c.; *zeele* 'I'll' i 30. [177]

NAMES OF PERSONS

The list is selective : familiar names and the names of characters in the texts are included only if the form is of phonological interest.

Alexander de Greete xviii 47 : Alexander the Great, King of Macedon, who defeated Daryus, King of Persia.

Batty, Shone xii 116; St John the Baptist. Ir. *Seán (Seon) Baiste.* [129]

Bellarmine xviii 53 : Roberto Francesco Romolo, Cardinal Bellarmine (1542–1621).

Brunduca viii 60 : Boadicea, Queen of the Iceni.

Chapling, Andrew ix 47.

Coalpes, Mr ix 40.

Crœsus xviii 57 : Crœsus, King of Lydia, reputedly the richest man in the world.

[*Cutpurse, Mall*] viii 61 : Mrs Mary Frith.

Dœardœry vii 11 &c. : said to have been the queen of Murchadh Mac Briain. Ir. *Déirdre.*

Darenus xviii 47 : Daryus, King of Persia, defeated by Alexander the Great.

[*Debora*] viii 59 : Deborah, the prophetess who ruled the Jews in *Judges* iv–v.

Deedy, see *Dydy.*

Deloune, Justish vi 132 : perhaps Sir Lucas Dillon, Chief Baron of the Exchequer in 1572 [Herford & Simpson (1925–52) x 544]; but the identification seems quite uncertain.

Dennish vi 4 &c. : Dennis. [88]

Dives xviii 116 &c. : the "rich man" of *Luke* xvi 19–31.

Dydy xiii 2 &c.; *Deedy* xiii 36 : Dido, Queen of Carthage. [40]

Ecclesiasticus xviii 41 : the supposed eponymous author of *Ecclesiasticus,* one of the apocryphal books of the Old Testament.

Flaherty, Captain xxvii 138 : Ir. *Flaithbheartaigh.*

Gilarnoo xiii 21* : Giollarnaomh Mac Cuinn na mBocht 'St Giollar, son of Conn of the poor.'

Glasmogonogh, Miss Owney xxvii 139 : perhaps Ir. *Uaine Glas Mhac Dhonnchadha*; if so, *Glas* 'green' must be a nickname, since *Uaine* also means 'green'.

Gradey, see *O'Gradey, Henry.*

Jamish, see *Yamish.*

Juane, see *Shuane.*

Kilphatrick xii 17; *Kilpatrick*

377

xii 68; *Kilpathrick* xii 109 : Ir. *Giolla Phádraig* 'servant of Patrick'. [78, 85]

Lave-yarach, Dermott vii 12 : Ir. *Diarmuid Láimh-Dhearg* 'Dermot of the Red Hand'; no such name is known in Irish history, and it is perhaps based on the name *Cathal Crobh-Dearg.*

Lazarus xviii 126 &c. : the beggar of *Luke* xvi 19–31.

Lee, S. Rishard ii 5.

[*Long-meg of Westminster*] viii 61 : a notorious Elizabethan female criminal.

Mac Breean, Morrogh vii 6 : Murchadh Mac Briain, son of Brian Boru and hero of the Battle of Clontarf.

Mac Breean, Teage vii 16 : Ir. *Tadhg Mac Briain*, the name of another son of Brian Boru, and the name chosen by Edmond for his Irish masquerade.

Mac Cool, Fan xviii 56 : Fionn Mac Cumhaill, leader of the Fianna who defended Ireland in the reign of Cormac Mac Airt. The form *Fan* is unique and inexplicable.

Macfadin xix 86 : Ir. *Mac Pháidín.*

Mackener, Neale i 6; *Mackener* i 24 &c. : Ir. *Niall Mac an Fhir.*

Macmohon, Manus xx 68 : Ir. *Maghnus Mac Mathghamhna.*

Mack Phelemy, Brian i 33; *Brian Mack Phelem* i 3; *Bryan*

Mac Phelemy i 48 : Ir. *Brian Mac Feidhlimidh.*

Macshaan xxiii 67 : Ir. *Mac Seáin.*

Magennis i 38 : Ir. *Mac Aonghusa*, the name of one of the most powerful chieftains of east Ulster.

Maghloghan Moor xxiii 64; *Maghloghans* xxiii 66 : probably Ir. *Mac Lochlainn Mór*; the name *Mac Leocháin*, though closer to the anglicized form, is very rare. [158]

Mulfinin, Miss xxvii 138 : Ir. *Maolfhionnáin.*

Nees xiii 5 &c., xvi 3 &c. : Æneas.

Nosheen xviii 56 : Oisín, son of Fionn Mac Cumhaill : the initial *n* is unique and inexplicable.

O'Brien, Sir Danell ix 88 : Sir Daniel O'Brien, brother of the fourth earl of Thomond and uncle of Sir Barnabas, the sixth earl.

Ocane i 38 : Ir. *O Catháin.*

O Con-noor, Dermot xvi 116 : Ir. *Diarmaid O Conchubhair.*

O'Gradey, Henry ix 24; *Gradey* ix 45 : Ir. *(O) Grádaigh.*

O Hanlon i 39 &c.; Rory O'Hanlon (Ir. *Ruaidhrí O hAnluain*), a well-known comrade-in-arms of Shane O'Neill.

Oliver xii 22 : Oliver Cromwell.

Oneale i 7 &c., viii 23; *O'Neils* xx 79 : Ir. *O Néill.*

O'Neale, Sir Philem ix 6 : Sir Phelim O'Neill, a leader of the rising of 1641.

Oneal, Shan i 20 : Ir. Seán O Néill.

O'Neil, Shan-Duffe- xx 67 : Ir. Seán Dubh O Néill.

O'Neils, see Oneale.

Oscar xviii 56 : son of Oisín and grandson of Fionn Mac Cumhaill.

O Shahanassah vii 12* : Ir. O Seachnasaigh.

Pathrick xii 116; Phaatrick xiv 27; Pautrick xv 32; Phatrick vi 37 &c.: Patrick, Ir. Pádraig. [34, 78, 85]

Petre, Fader xvii 20 : Father Edward Petre (1631–99), James II's Jesuit confessor.

Pha(a)trick, see Pathrick.

Rishard ii v : Richard. [97]

Robyne vi 62 : Robert Carr, Earl of Somerset.

Rorie beg i 48 : Ir. Ruaidhrí Beag (O hAnluain) 'Little Rory (O'Hanlon)'. [158]

Sampson xviii 54 : Samson.

Scanderbeg viii 4 : the Turkish name of George Castriot (1403–67), prince of Albania and hero of the fight against the Turks.

Scomberg xvii 4 &c.: Frederick Herman, Duke of Schomberg (1615–90), William III's chief commander in Ireland.

Shagnassy, Scheela xxvii 133 : Ir. Sighle (Ní) Sheachnasaigh.

Shuane xii 52; Juane xii 109 : Ir. Siobhán 'Joan'. [158]

Sichy xiii 95 : Sychæus.

Sonday, St. xii 19 : St. Dominic. [129]

Taffie, see Tavy.

Tamberlane viii 5: Timurlane, a descendant of Genghiz Khan, well known as the hero of Marlowe's play Tamburlaine (1590).

[Tavy, St.] vii 106; [St. Taffie] viii 36 : St David.

Tirconnel, see Tyrconel.

Toumaish vi 63 &c. : Thomas, earl of Suffolk. [63, 88]

Tyrconel xvii 25; Tirconnel xx 49, &c.: Richard Talbot, earl and later duke of Tyrconnel, James II's chief commander in Ireland. Tír Chonaill is the Irish name of Donegal; it had previously been the lordship of the O'Donnells.

[Utter Pendragon] viii 54: Uther Pendragon, father of King Arthur.

Willam xvii 62 : William III. [101]

Yamish vi 4 &c.; Yeamus xvii 18 &c.; Jamish xix 87 : James (James I or James II). [64, 94, 98, 99]

NAMES OF PLACES

The list is selective : familiar names are included only if the form is of phonological interest.

Balecare ix 39 : Ballycar, Co. Clare. Ir. *Baile Uí Charthaigh.*

Ballrootherie i 45* : Balrothery, Co. Dublin. Ir. *Baile Ruaidhrí.* [155]

Ballyshamus Duff xxvii 23* : Ballyjamesduff, Co. Cavan. Ir. *Baile Shéamais Dhuibh.*

Bashtile xix 156 : the Bastille; hence, a prison. [89]

Bolring xi 2 : Bull-ring.

Boyn xxi 45 : the river Boyne. Ir. *Bóinn.* [57]

Carick-Vergus xix 11 : Carrickfergus, Co. Antrim. Ir. *Carraig Fhearguis.* [112]

Carlingford i 38 : Carlingford, Co. Louth.

Cnockany ix 24 : Knockanee, Co. Limerick. Ir. *Cnoc an Fhiaidh.*

Cofentry xxiii 90 : Coventry. [108]

Connough vi 54 : the province of Connacht.

Corke xvii 9 : Cork. Ir. *Corcaigh.*

Derry xx 113 &c.; *Darry* xx 108; *Londonderry* xvii 12 : in 1610 the City Companies of London entered into an agreement with the Crown to rebuild and fortify the City of Derry (Ir. *Doire*), which was therefore re-named *Londonderry.* [31]

Dumblain xxiii 8 : Dunblane, Pertshire.

Dunboyne vi 87: Dunboyne, Co. Meath. Ir. *Dún Búinne.* [155]

Dundalke i 10 &c.; *Dundalk* i 31 : Dundalk, Co. Louth. Ir. *Dún Dealgan.*

Fewes i 47 : the Fews, a district in south Co. Armagh. Ir. *An Fiodh.*

Fingall xx s.d. : Fingall, north Co. Dublin. Ir. *Fine Gall.*

Galloway xvii 10 : Galway. Ir. *Gaillimh.*

Glanmalora xxiv 9: Glenmalure, Co. Wicklow. Ir. *Gleann Maolúra.*

Hoath xxvii 85 : Howth, Co. Dublin. ON *höfuð* 'head'.

Inish ix 70 : Ennis, Co. Clare. Ir. *Inis.*

Killamountains xxiv 4 : Co. Wicklow, in Irish *Cill Mhanntáin.* [182]

Kingshail xvii 9 : Kinsale, Co.

Cork. Ir. *Cionn tSáile.* [88]
Leinster vii 7; *Leynster* vi 54* :
the province of Leinster.
Formed from Ir. *Laighin*
'Leinster' and *tír* 'region'.
Limrick ix 24; *Limbrick* xvii
10 : Limerick. Ir. *Luimneach.*
London-Derry, see *Derry.*
Lusk xiii 5; *Luske* xiii 57 : Lusk,
Co. Dublin. Ir. *Lusca.*
Mabline xiii 48 : apparently the
rocky islet off the coast of
Fingall now known as Rocka-
bill. The name occurs only in
Purgatorium Hibernicum.
Munster vi 54 : the province of
Munster. Formed from Ir.
Mumhain 'Munster' and *tír*
'region'.
[*Oleance*] viii 60 : Orleans.
Pool-pheg xxvii 81 : Poolbeg,
part of Dublin Harbour. Ir.
Poll Beag 'little inlet'.
Rings-end xxvii 80 : Ringsend,
a district in Dublin close to
Poolbeg.
Shuffolke vi 64 : Suffolk. [88]
Swords xvi 58 : Swords, Co.

Dublin.
Tamasco iv 1 &c. : Damascus.
[107]
Thomond ix 7 : north Munster,
corresponding approximately
to the present Co. Clare. Ir.
Tuath-Mhumhain.
Tiperary xxiii 78 : Tipperary.
Ir. *Tiobraid Arann.*
Tredagh xv 34 : Drogheda, Co.
Louth. An alternative anglici-
zation of the Irish *Droichead
Atha.*
Tuchland vi 116 : Germany.
[107]
Ulster vi 54 : the province of
Ulster. Formed from Ir.
Ulaidh 'Ulster' and *tír* 'region'.
Wailesh xvii 28 : Wales. [46, 94]
Wicklows xxiv 6 : Wicklow. The
first element is ON *víkinga*
'Vikings' ', the second element
is obscure. [182]
Wirginny xxvii 105 : Virginia.
[63, 82]
Youghail xvii 10 : Youghal, Co.
Cork. Ir. *Eochaill.*

381